Reelin'
In the
Years

Boxing and More

ISBN: 1-4392-0541-8
ISBN-13: 9781439205419

Visit www.booksurge.com to order additional copies.

For Allison and Matthew

Every man's memory is his private literature.
—Aldous Huxley

Other Books by Theodore R. Sares

Boxing is my Sanctuary

CONTENTS

REELIN' IN THE YEARS

The test of a good book's appeal is how many times you go back to it. With *Reelin' In the Years, Boxing and More*, Ted (The Bull) Sares has produced another engrossing tome of fascinating stories about our favourite fighters from the ages, to which the reader is compelled to constantly return.

When describing the decades, Ted teases the memory bank using a fast moving, unique narrative style.

With his trademark passion for the grand old game, Ted reminds us of great fighters, good fighters, and average fighters, each linked by their ability to leave us with golden memories. Here you will find champions, barnstormers, globetrotters, journeymen, nearly men, and forever men who seemed to ply their trade for an eternity.

This time around, he gives many fighters from the UK and other global locales their due. In many instances, he lets the numbers tell the story rather than embellishing them with the false claims of someone who was not there. As just one of many examples, he does this when he writes about journeyman Anthony "Poison" Ivory.

The fighters answer the bell once more against the lush backdrops of their respective eras as Mr Sares paints each canvas with the delicious whiffs of cigar smoke, beer, and bourbon. There is a wonderfully evocative study of the fabulous fifties, where we can almost smell the gas from the classic automobiles, the perfume of glorious gals, and the sweat of such ring mechanics as Joey Giardello, Billy Graham, Sandy Saddler, and Carmen Basilio.

The market is awash with twelve-round boxing books, but why have a burger when you can have a steak? This is a fifteen-round treat, so touch gloves with The Bull and enjoy the ride!

Note: *Mike Casey is a boxing journalist and historian. He is a member of the International Boxing Research Organization (IBRO), an auxiliary member of the Boxing Writers Association of America, and founder and editor of the Grand Slam Premium Boxing Service for historians and fans.*

PREFACE

Many people have been fortunate to live long enough to see multiple generations of fighters, and I'm one of them. Being seventy-one gives me some advantages, particularly since over the years I have seen literally thousands of fights, have been blessed with a sharp memory, and have at least a reasonable ability to translate my memories to the written word. Unlike others who talk as if they were at ringside, I was splattered by the sweat and stained by the blood. Hell, I was there and don't need a video clip to tell me what happened.

I still ride the pendulum that switches from love to hate. In my book *Boxing is my Sanctuary,* I wrote a line denouncing boxing in the chapter on Jerry Quarry, as follows: "I wonder why Saoul Mamby was allowed to fight at age 53." Mamby fought again on March 8, 2008, in the Cayman Islands. He was sixty years old. It remains what it is. But then, on the other side of the ledger, Wladimir Klitschko donates $500,000 to The Laureus Sport for Good Foundation. And once again, the pendulum swings from bad to good.

Yes, I detail the poor records of fighters who lose far more often than they win, but I know of no other way to distinguish between the potential for terrible mismatches and fights that are matched to last the distance without undue harm to the loser. No disrespect is intended for any boxers who enter the ring, because when they do, they are noble and courageous. Let there be no doubt of that.

That said, the following essays are boxing-related memories that have stayed with me and now deserve their due. With boxing as the linchpin, they are dovetailed into the different decades. In order to achieve a balanced appeal, I have attempted to blend names from the past with fighters that are more recent. I deal with the likes of Joey LaMotta, Randy Sandy, and Dave Boy Green. Boxers from the past, the not-so-distant-past, and the present;–Tiger Jack Fox, Sugar Ray Leonard, Ricardo Mayorga, and Andrew Golata. Still, the many fighters named in this book are representative of all fighters; if I could, I would list each and every one.

Come with me now and let's intertwine the decades with the fights and see what we come up with.

I

REELIN' IN THE YEARS: PART ONE

Over the years, the sport of boxing has reflected the nuances and idiosyncrasies of each decade with a remarkable degree of accuracy. The defiance of Ali, for example, was in perfect sync with the volatility of the '60's, just as the sinister persona of Liston matched the gangster-noir of the late '50's and early '60's. Let's looks back now and see how this plays out with boxing as the centerpiece of each decade.

The '50's

**Ex-boxers Tony Galanto and Tami Mauriello
in *On the Waterfront.*
(Photo from Public Domain)**

The fifties: Men wear dress hats to work and Stepford-type wives wait for them to come home as they discover Valium. It is all about noir without anyone realizing it is all about noir. It is "back in the day" and returning servicemen. It is happy times. The baby boom is underway-Levittown.-people can afford single-family dwellings and suburbia is born. College is a rare privilege; not an entitlement. The smell of burning leaves on a crisp fall day. Schwinn bikes, drive-in movies, and thick malts. "I like Ike" memories and at the hop.

Red Prysock and Bill Doggett slam out the beat while Ray Charles sings "Mess Around" before anyone ever heard of him. He "lets "the good times roll." So do Count Basie and Duke Ellington. Dave Brubeck and Paul Desmond visit colleges.

Dysfunctional families, attention deficit, and bipolar disorders are unknown concepts. Those who suffer from them do so in silence without awareness, recourse or remedy. No one uses words like "dysfunctional" or "depression." Many are consumed by emotions that are kept closeted and cannot be articulated. They suffer silently.

There are no graffitied tenements, sinking potholed streets, or garbage-strewn parks, but the smell of winos and urine in the subways exists and there are plenty of slums to go around.

Chopped and channeled Mercury coupes and rumbling dual pipes. Drag races on city streets and old airport runways. Outlaw biker gangs. One per-centers. Rebels without causes. Leather jackets, engineer boots, and skin-tight Levi's or khaki's and loafers. Blue suede loafers. Greasers and mods. "Hollywood" and "Detroit" hair-styles or flat tops or crew cuts–split the difference with a "Duck's Ass."

No political correctness here. You eat what you want to eat and smoke where you want to smoke. No seat belt laws because there are no seat belts. People eat lardy chili and greasy bacon and eggs in diners late at night with no guilt. Apple pie with a slice of American cheese is yummy. The Kinsey Report findings shock, but maybe only the naïve. Sexual awareness comes flying out of the closet.

In the early '50s, city kids go to "Geek" shows that are featured in some of the traveling carnivals that come to the outskirts of urban centers. These geeks, however, are not like today's hi-tech ones. Stag films are precursors to porn. Juke joints, gambling, even moonshine are all part of the scene.

The Wild One, "What are you rebelling against, Johnny?" "Whadda ya got?" Brando and Dean, and Sidney Poitier calls Glenn Ford "Mr. Daddio" in Blackboard Jungle. The heros are Joe Louis, Marciano, Joe DiMaggio, Willie Mays, Sugar Ray, and Ted Williams. Marilyn Monroe, Gable, Bogart. Bad Day at Black Rock, with Spencer Tracy, Robert

Ryan, Ernest Borgnine, Lee Marvin, Anne Francis, and Walter Brennan all in one movie. The pure noir of *The Killing* and *The Sweet Smell of Success*; they thrill. Henry Fonda, Lee J. Cobb, Martin Balsam, Ed Begley, Jack Klugman, E.G. Marshall, Jack Warden and Robert Webber are among *12 Angry Men,* all in the same room. *On the Waterfront*—it's about union corruption and violence. *A Streetcar Named Desire* and *Death of a Salesman.* It's heady stuff.

The Organization Man, Ayn Rand, *The Affluent Society, The Man in the Gray Flannel Suit, The Martian Chronicles, The Catcher in the Rye,* Jack Kerouac. *The Lonely Crowd.* Things are starting to happen. Beats and Beatniks are coming out wearing berets.

Sports in the '50s are Willie Mays and Bob Cousy; Jackie Robinson and Jim Brown. Ted Williams, the "Mick," and Dolph. Television in the '50s makes pro football more popular than college football.

· · ·

Boxing, thanks to television, is big in the '50s. Names like Stillman's Gym. Whitey Bimstein, Fred Abatello, Arthur Mercante, Artie (counting at the bell) Aidala, Johnny Addie, Don Dunphy, Jimmy Powers, and Ruby Goldstein are hip. Unlike today's motor mouths, Dunphy understands that his primary purpose is to describe the ring action and to do it with minimal intrusion on the real attractions, the fighters. Johnny Addis's smooth tenor holds court at New York's Madison Square Garden. When he surveys the crowd and declares, "everybody is here tonight," shivers of anticipation go down spines. It never gets any better.

Everyone watches boxing "with his dad" on the Friday Night Fights and the *Gillette Cavalcade of Sports.* It's macho before macho. Standing outside a department store window where a nine-inch Admiral TV set allows us to watch Teddy "Red Top" Davis fight Paddy DeMarco is a real treat even during ten degree Chicago weather. We drink hot coffee mixed with something stronger and boys and men bond without knowing they are bonding. The Friday Night Fights often feature Gaspar Ortega vs. Isaac Logart. Yama Bahama, from Bimini, is another favorite. Other regulars include Kid Gavilan, Joey Giardello, the rugged Fullmer brothers, Carmen Basilio, and middleweight Joey Giambra.

This is a golden age of boxing if ever there was one. Guys like Davis fight over 100 times. Names like Billy Graham, Sandy Saddler, Carl "Bobo" Olson, Orlando Zulueta, Tony DeMarco,

Ralph Dupas, Wallace "Bud" Smith, Johnny Saxon, and Johnny Bratton become commonplace. They appear in the early days of televised boxing, on Monday nights from St. Nicholas Arena or the Sunnyside Gardens. LaMotta, Castellani, Basilio, Marciano, LaStarza, Janiro, Durando, Fusari, Giardello and others add Italian spice to the multi-ethnic mix. Sugar Ray dazzles. Many engage in over 100 fights; they are sportsmen who respect one another and don't talk trash. These are ring-tested warriors who meet one top ten contender after another to earn a championship opportunity. Fighting fifteen times a year is not uncommon.

LaMotta, far behind, KO's Laurent Dauthuille with just thirteen seconds remaining in the fifteenth round in Detroit to retain the middleweight title. Joey Maxim retains the light heavyweight title when middleweight champion Ray Robinson collapses from heat exhaustion and dehydration and is unable to come out for round fourteen in New York. The defeat will be the only time in the twenty-six year career of Robinson that he is unable to finish a fight. In a classic between two great champions, Rocky Marciano gets off the deck in the second round and floors light heavyweight champion Archie Moore multiple times, knocking him out in the ninth round. It's Marciano's forty ninth consecutive victory and his last. In the greatest fight of his career, Archie Moore, down three times in the first round and once in the fifth, comes back to floor Yvonne Durelle three times before taking him out in eleven rounds in Montreal to retain the light heavyweight title. It may be the greatest fight of all time.

Eugene "Silent" Hairston appears regularly and is a great fan favorite. Good God, he is legally deaf and needs lights to flash from the ring corners to signal the end of a round. The '50s are not without tragedies too. Nine fighters lose their lives in 1950 alone.

Patterson and Johansson start what will be a memorable piece of boxing history. They finish it in the next decade. Meanwhile, Sonny Liston destroys his opposition, and Harold Johnson, Joe Brown, and Jose Becerra show their stuff. This is the '50S. Chico Vejar is pure '50s.

• • •

The H-Bomb and a fragile peace co-exist. Not everything is Pollyannaish. Some things seem to have a gangster-ridden, edgy quality that is palpable. Modern jazz is cool, man. The giants are Bird, Miles, Dizzy, Kenton and Chet. Chicago blues are performed by blacks who travel north from the Delta on the Illinois Central Railroad. The decade features Little Walter, Howlin' Wolf, Jackie Wilson, Jimmy Reed, Fats, Chuck Berry, Little Richard, The Big Bopper, and Doo-wop. Honky tonk is cool. The sound of the harp is in. Hard bop, rebop, West Coast jazz and Delta blues are the '50s. Here comes Elvis, Jerry Lee and rock and roll. The first hit is from Bill Haley and his Comets. Grooving at the 708 Club on Chicago's South Side where Muddy Waters and Bo Diddley reign supreme. "Hoochie Coochie Man," "I'm Ready," and "I Just Want to Make Love to You" resonate as boys become Mannish Boys and then become men many of whom soon fight in a faraway place called Korea.

The Korean War–June 1950 to July 1953– becomes the "Forgotten War," but there are at least 36, 576 reasons never to forget it. It is later recalled by M*A*S*H on television, but it becomes a footnote in our history. Veterans of that intense and deadly conflict wear jackets from Rhein-Main, Quantico, Parris Island, Great Lakes, Fort Leonard Wood, and Cherry Point. Men who did their duty return without complaint. Many paid dearly.

It's a time of extreme anti-communist suspicion. McCarthyism becomes synonymous with demagogic, reckless, and unsubstantiated accusations. Black lists. It's the '50s version of the Patriot Act. Decency finally wins out. Senator Joe, a gifted demagogue, is censured into obscurity by a vote of sixty seven to twenty two, and an attorney named Joseph Nye Welch goes after him in the Army-McCarthy hearings. Roy Cohen lurks.

Racism undergoes subtle changes for the better. Still, it rears its ugly head far too often. Callous cruelty and unfairness are commonplace until the '60s. Being called a "kike," "mick," "wop," "Polack" or "spic" is an everyday experience. Many first generation Americans suffer quietly. There are scary white sheets and burning crosses. The Ku Klux Klan is nasty. Then 1964, civil rights and hope. Martin Luther King. Malcolm, Rosa Parks, and The Little Rock Nine all mean hope.

The '50s are a time of laid-back innocence, but a time mixed with portions of fear and loathing as well. Of course, looking in the rear view mirror through the prism of nostalgia makes everything look better. The innocence is soon replaced with a grim reality, turbulence and cynicism that manifests itself through the next decade. A Cuban missile crisis, Vietnam, the draft, multiple assassinations, hippies, drugs, protests, riots and racial unrest that explodes. The '60s vibe big trouble–very big.

...colleges being nothing but grooming schools for the mid-dleclass non-identity which usually finds its perfect expression on the outskirts of the campus in rows of well-to-do houses with lawns and television sets is each living room with every-body looking at the same thing and thinking the same thing at the same time while the Japhies of the world go prowling in the wilderness...
- Jack Kerouac

I can think of nothing more boring for the American people than to have to sit in their living rooms for a whole half hour looking at my face on their television screens.
-Dwight D. Eisenhower

The '60s

(Photo from Public domain)

The conduit from the '50s carries cheerful optimism. John Fitzgerald Kennedy asks not what your country can do for you- he asks what you can do for your country. It's inspiring. Jackie sets the example in class. Fear of nuclear war comes to a head with the Cuban Missile Crisis in 1962. Soviets back down. *"Ich bin ein Berliner."* JFK at the helm equals comfort and security. Everyone is proud to be an American.

Dallas makes it all a bad joke. Dallas destroys Camelot and justifies cynicism. No more peering through rose-colored glasses. Was it Oswald or a conspiracy? Jack Ruby. Dealey Plaza, the Depository, Stemmons Freeway bring back memories that chill.

The '60s after 63–full-tilt boogie, balls to the walls. Flashpoints going off like photographers' light bulbs. There are too many to track. Riots begin on August 11, 1965 in Watts after which blacks are no longer taken for granted. Then, amid coups and assassinations, Vietnam breaks out in earnest. More justified cynicism. Body bags and Jane Fonda. People hate Jane; they still do. Vo Nguyen Giap and Westmoreland.

James Meredith becomes the first black student at Ole Miss. Violence but also hope abounds. Then Medgar Evers is killed by an assassin's bullet amid voter registration in the South. It's "Bloody Sunday" in Selma with dogs and hoses. More unrest and more killings occur. Malcolm being gunned down punctuates the morass. It's bad juju.

"I Have a Dream" renews hope. The 1964 Civil Rights Act. MLK is awarded the Nobel Peace Prize. The Stonewall Riots in New York are a turning point in the struggle for homosexual equality. Gays stand up and say "We will not take it any more"

Nation of Islam and Black Panthers, Weather Underground Organization, SDS, "Black Power," Berkley,the sexual revolution, feminism and gay rights. The flash bulbs are going off constantly.

To Kill a Mockingbird, Norman Bates and *Psycho, The Apartment, On the Beach, Lolita,* James Bond, *The Group, In Cold Blood, The Peter Principle, Profiles in Courage, Elmer Gantry, Who's Afraid of Virginia Woolf?, In the Heat of the Night, The Green Berets, Midnight Cowboy, Butterfield 8, One Flew Over the Cuckoo's Nest, Easy Rider.* Motown. Smoky Robinson is suprme. Boston Celtics, Green Bay Packers. Andy Warhol, surfing. The Beatles hit the big time. Elvis's star rises and fades over the decade. The Pill arrives and so does the miniskirt. The Space Race permeates.

Charlie Manson's family does its horrific thing. The Boston Strangler snuffs out the dreams of thirteen women.

In sports, Bill Russell's battles against Wilt Chamberlain are the stuff of legends. In 1961, Sandy Koufax amazes batters with his fast stuff. The first Super Bowl game is played in 1967.

1968 is the seminal year; it's about politics, culture, innovation, and mostly unrest.

The nation staggers through twelve months of turbulent and cataclysmic events that will remain with us forever. The year 1968 is all about countercultural freedom.

Robert F. Kennedy declares his candidacy for president. President Lyndon B. Johnson announces that he will not seek reelection. Walter Cronkite doubts the potential for American victory in Vietnam.

Abbie Hoffman says, "People coming to Chicago should begin preparations for five days of energy-exchange." The Yippies are coming, but Chicago police are energized and waiting. Young people seem to reject all forms of authority. Speak out, protest, and march. Rebels with causes. Every injustice or perceived inequality suddenly becomes fair game for examination and protest. Chicago, Daley, and Nixon are all part of the mix.

And then, "I'm happy tonight. I'm not worried about anything. I'm not fearing any man. My eyes have seen the glory of the coming of the Lord!" But Memphis shatters the Dream as Reverend King is murdered and bloody riots break out in the cities. Newark and Detroit feel the heat big-time. Robert Kennedy delivers a stirring eulogy. The unflinching dignity of the civil rights marchers wears down the oppressors. The Dream prevails.

The Tet Offensive turbo-charges the war. Bobby Kennedy declares his candidacy, and then says, "I have traveled and I have listened to the young people of our nation and felt their anger about the war that they are sent to fight and about the world they are about to inherit." Later, he says, "There are those who look at things the way they are, and ask why...I dream of things that never were, and ask why not? More hope.

Sirhan Sirhan snuffs out that dream as well as Bobby is assasinated within minutes of giving a victory speech at the California primary. The country mourns—again. The direction of the country once again is irretrievably changed.

Amid mass rioting and chaos, Nixon wins over Humphrey on a "law and order" platform while Chicago police incongruously sap anti-war protesters in Lincoln Park. Nixon is the ONE.

"I Am a Woman-Not a Toy, a Pet, a mascot" states a sign at a Miss America Beauty Pageant Protest. Sisterhood is powerful. Shirley Chisholm is the first black woman elected to Congress.

Meanwhile, Jimi, Timothy Leary and the guru Maharaji-ji have the beat. Hippies, bell-bottoms, Woodstock, acid, LSD are all part of this mix. Psychedelic times enjoyed at Haight-Ashbury. "Turn on, tune in, and drop out." Jimi says, "Excuse me while I kiss the sky." Steppenwolf sings "Born to Be Wild." Like wow.

James Brown says, "Say It Loud-I'm Black and I'm Proud." John Carlos and Tommie Smith listen and raise their fists for black power and human rights at the Olympics in Mexico City. Cesar Chavez leads a farm workers' movement in the rural sector.

The Apollo program's race to space is big stuff. The U.S. the UK and the Soviet Union sign the Nuclear Non-proliferation Treaty. This is big stuff, too. The year seems to end on a peaceful and hopeful note.

. . .

In boxing, Cassius Clay knocks out Sonny Liston. Later he becomes Muhammad Ali, the right man for the right time. He "floats like a butterfly and stings like a bee." With television not being as important for boxing in the '60s, he uses his mouth and his brashness to attract attention and soon reigns supreme. He calls opponents bums and chumps and it starts something different from the prior decade; trash talk. A new bravado begins. His sociopolitical defiance is in sync with the times. He transcends boxing.

On national TV, Griffith knocks out Benny Kid Paret with seventeen unanswered power shots. The Kid dies shortly after. There is the usual knee-jerk response to ban boxing. It fails.

Television supercharges boxing toward the end of the decade, and people enjoy it in their own homes or favorite pubs as big screen sets become the norm. Somebody named Joe Frazier debuts in 1965, Ken Norton debuts in 1967 and George Foreman in 1969. People watch great fights like Emile Griffith vs. Nino Benvenuti in 1967.

Fewer ethnic fighters toil in the ring and the blacks and Hispanics rule the sport. Boxers from the old school give way to a new and more turbulent wave of fighters who are young, enthusiastic, and who seek bigger paydays.

. . .

The Woodstock Music Festival at Max Yasgur's farm in August 1969. Jimi does his thing with Manic Depression and Purple Haze. Joan Baez and Santana rule. Janis is no Foxy Lady but she sings like one. Sly takes us higher. People gather together in the spirit of caring and sharing, Unique and legendary stuff. It's a new beginning, as men walk on the moon in 1969.

The Altamont Music Festival is held later in 1969. The Dead, Jefferson Airplane, Crosby, Stills, Nash & Young, and the Stones headline the event. Bikers serve as the security force. The real music becomes "Sympathy for the Devil." It's a unique and chilling counterpoint to Woodstock. Fans are held "Under My Thumb." Someone stabs a man holding a gun in front of the stage. It's a downer at the end. Cosmic flower children wander across the hills toward home and an uncertain future with spooky windmills in the background.

A bad way to end the '60s, but it's about a generation that realizes it can make a difference just by standing up and being heard-and it does just that.

> *I like ideas about the breaking away or overthrowing of established order. I am interested in anything about revolt, disorder, chaos, especially activity that seems to have no meaning. It seems to me to be the road towards freedo-external freedom is a way to bring about internal freedom.*
> -Jim Morrison of The Doors
>
> *[In the'60s] there was madness in any direction, at any hour,... You could strike sparks anywhere. There was a fantastic universal sense that whatever we were doing was `right', that we were winning...*
> -Hunter S. Thompson, Fear and Loathing in Las Vegas

The '70s

The radical ideas of the '60s gain acceptance and are eventually mainstreamed and assimilated into American life and culture. The '70s prove to be a sharply different, though more tranquil decade.

As the Vietnam War ends, we lose a vice president and president to resignations. Watergate, impeachment hearings and Deep Throat, but not Linda Lovelace's kind. "I'm no crook." Gerry Ford is the right man for the right time and has a cohesive impact. The peanut farmer promises hope but ends up creating a crisis of confidence which leads to his being a one-term disappointment. Nixon (1969-1974), Ford (1974-1977), and Carter (1977-1981). Make way for the "Great Communicator."

The Vietnam War continues to divide us. Republican Governor James Rhodes of Ohio sends national guardsmen onto the Kent State University campus in 1970 resulting in the shooting deaths of four students who are protesting the war. Two days after the

Kent State shootings, Rhodes loses the Republican primary election to the U.S. Senate. Enough is enough. The war finally ends, as people flee Saigon in helicopters. The war's aftermath influences the themes of several movies, including *The Deer Hunter*, *Coming Home*, and *Apocalypse Now*. Oliver Stone documents things for future telling.

Later, the Iran Hostage Crisis humiliates America and destroys Carter's hopes for a second term. Hey, sixty-six Americans are held hostage for 444 days in what is our first encounter with Radical Islam. Of the approximately ninety people inside the embassy, fifty-two remain in captivity until the end of the crisis. Days of rage for frustrated Americans as an attempted rescue mission fails.

The United States experiences an economic recession. As if to further humiliate, the economy of Japan prospers. Say what?

The Iran Crisis leads to a gas shortage as lines stretch for miles and people argue at the pumps. Everyone rushes to "top off" even if the tank doesn't need it. It isn't that people cannot afford gas; hell, there is no gas to sell. Attendants fill tanks while wearing guns. It's bad karma.

Updike, Vonnegut and Oates write books, and Simon, Shepard, and Mamet write plays. The books are about man's alienation from his spiritual roots. Toni Morrison emerges as a strong literary voice who writes about the Black American experience in a new and compelling way. Other influential books are *The Outsiders* by S.E. Hinton, *Jonathan Livingston Seagull* by Richard Bach, *The Happy Hooker* by Xaviera Hollander, and *Fear of Flying* by Erica Jong.

Movies range from *The Godfather* to *Dog Day Afternoon*, with *Jaws*, *Taxi Driver*, *The Exorcist*, *Grease*, *Rocky*, *A Clockwork Orange*, *One Flew Over the Cuckoo's Nest*, *The Rocky Horror Picture Show*, *Chinatown*, and *Annie Hall* in between. Jack Nicholson makes his considerable mark.

Killer Clown, John Gacy, is a real horror show. So is the Zodiac, the Son of Sam, and the Atlanta Child murderer. Handsome and articulate Ted Bundy punctuates this as a decade marked by serial killers extraordinaire.

Unlike the sixties, the seventies are the "Me Decade." Activism switches to activities for one's own pleasure. Cocaine-fuelled, hedonistic parties are cool.

Environmentalism as a movement is an exception and takes root. Religion, family values, and faith and trust in the government lose ground. Pre-marital sex is an integral part of the sexual revolution, which in turn is fueled by the impact of the Pill.

Idiots streak nude through public places, while mellowed-down families vacation in station wagons. Everyone wants an RV. Pet rocks, mood rings, and wild fashions are in stark contrast to serious issues like the gasoline shortage and the hostage crisis.

On the bright side, many medical breakthroughs in cancer research and heart surgery are happening, and that is great news.

Affirmative action becomes a controversial policy. Minorities and women assert their rights to jobs and quality education. Right On! Native Americans demand attention to their plight as well; casino ownership is yet to come. Women, minorities, and gays increasingly demand legal equality and privileges in society. Gay Pride parades shock at first and then become boring. Hippies peak and begin a subtle morph to yuppie.

"I am woman, hear me roar." By the end of the decade, the feminist movement helps change women's working conditions. The proportion of women in state legislatures increases dramatically. Women surpass men in college enrollment by 1979.

Cities such as Los Angeles, Detroit, and Atlanta elect their first African-American mayors. U.S. Representative Barbara Jordan gains prominence with her eloquence during the Watergate investigation and hearings.

Meanwhile, while American culture flourishes, disco ducks quack. Far Out, Man!

The influence of sixties hippies is mainstreamed in the seventies, as men sport shoulder-length hair and long sideburns. Non-traditional clothing becomes the rage, including bell-bottom pants, hot pants, platform shoes, clogs, hip-huggers, earth shoes, and gypsy dresses. Knits and denims are the fabrics of choice. Polyester and leisure suits (ugh) are commonplace for men. Lycra stretch disco pants in hot, strident, shiny colors with stretch sequin tops make their gaudy appearance in disco joints.

Steve Rubell and Ian Shrager build the hottest disco ever-Studio 54. It showcases the '70s to the max. Sex, cocaine, and/or amyl nitrate "poppers" seem to be everywhere, but so do bags of cash and. finally, IRS Agents. .

From the first Queen of Disco, Gloria Gaynor, to Chic's "Dance Dance Dance (Yowsah, Yowsah, Yowsah)" and "Everybody Dance," the music is made for dancing. Wild times at Club-Med. Discothèques rule. Jamaican reggae music sung by Bob Marley becomes popular and so does "Jamming." Ya, Mon! *Saturday Night Fever* fuels "disco fever" and sweeps the club scenes. The Bee Gees, the Village People, Donna Summer, and Supertramp make the scene. And Barry White, we "Never, Never Gonna Give You Up." With Sly, we have hot fun in the summertime.

Curt Flood pursues the case known as Flood v. Kuhn (Commissioner Bowie Kuhn) from January 1970 to June 1972 at district, circuit, and Supreme Court levels. Although the Supreme Court ultimately rules against him, upholding baseball's exemption from antitrust statutes, the case sets the stage for the 1975 Messersmith-McNally rulings and the advent of free agency. Thanks to Flood's courageous stand, professional athletes, previously "owned" by their teams, demand and receive the right to free agency. Before 1970, few earned more than $100,000 per year; at the end of the decade, hundreds do. Ali is hailed as a hero, if not a seer, but Flood is just as much a true and righteous hero.

One of the most famous athletes in the seventies is Pete Rose, who breaks Ty Cobb's record of 4,256 hits. Pele is a great soccer player.

．　．　．

**A young and charasmatic Jerry Quarry
(Photo courtesy EastSideBoxing.com)**

In boxing, the '70s later become known as the Golden Age of Boxing Heavyweights with Ali, Foreman, Frazier, Norton, Quarry, Chuvalo, Lyle, Shavers, Patterson, and many other big boppers doing their thing. Ali continues to reign as larger than life, but so does the great Carlos Monzon. Ali fights Frazier in the first of three in the "Fight of the Century." These big guys bring out the best in each other in the division's greatest era. A guy named Wepner ostensibly inspires the invention of a guy named Balboa.

The Bobick brothers, Rodney and Duane, did all of their fighting in the 70s and have a combined record of 85-11. Howard "KO" Smith fights his entire career during the 70s and manages to beat Mike Weaver twice and a bunch of other tough heavies as he finishes with a 17-2 record. Tough Marty Monroe goes 21-0-1 during the 70s.

But there was something about the '70s that stands out like the '50s. These men all fought each other. Frazier fought Foreman twice, Jerry Quarry twice and Ali three times. Big George fought Norton, Jimmy Young and Ali. Young fought Ali, Earnie Shavers, Ron Lyle, Norton and Foreman. Lyle fought Ali, Forman and Quarry. Ali fought everyone (Foreman, Frazier, Norton, Quarry, Young and all the rest). It's an incredible fan–friendly round robin. Surely, no era could ever have so many heavyweight fighters who are so talented at so many different levels.

A young and good looking "Irish" Jerry Quarry is all about charisma. Big boxing matches are televised free on Saturday Afternoons and become events. On the West Coast, Bobby Chacon, Chucho Castillo, Rafael Bazooka" Limon, Ruben Navarro, Mando Ramos and Frankie Baltazar are fighting with an uncommon fury.

The pleasure of watching great boxing free on TV blends well with the other aspects of the pleasure oriented decade.

Big boxing matches are televised free on Saturday afternoons and become events. The operative word is free. Roberto Duran and Danny "Little Red" Lopez become TV favorites. Boxing is becoming big. And so is Don King.

Dementia pugilistica (boxer's dementia or punch-drunk syndrome) becomes more noticeable though it has been around since the beginning of the sport. It is horrific because it develops over a period of years, with the average time of onset being about twelve to sixteen years after the start of a career in boxing. And there is no turning back once it arrives. Many famous fighters eventually become afflicted with it.

·   ·   ·

Elsewhere in sports, the '72 Munich Olympics turn into a bloodbath as nine Israeli athletes are killed at the airport after a long siege. Terrorists claiming to be from a Palestinian guerrilla group called Black September kill two Israelis outright and take others hostage. They then demand the release of 200 Arab guerrillas jailed in Israel. Incredibly, during the siege, the aging Avery Brundage, president of the International Olympic Committee, orders that the Games continue, and his senility rules.

An unusual series of paranoia-inspired events leads to the deaths of more than 900 people in the middle of an African jungle. What happens at Jonestown in Guyana on November 18, 1978, is a mass suicide. The charismatic cult leader of the People's Temple, Jim Jones, gives 912 followers a deadly cocktail of a purple drink mixed with cyanide, sedatives, and tranquilizers, and then apparently shoots himself in the end.

The meltdown accident at the Three Mile Island Nuclear Power Plant begins on March 28, 1979, and is scary as hell. Until Chernobyl seven years later, it is considered the world's worst civilian nuclear accident.

2

AN ODYSSEY

You start winning when you can't lose anymore.
–Anonymous

How much can you know about yourself if you've never been in a fight?
–Tyler Durden, the protagonist in the movie Fight Club

Now I'm a man, And I made twenty one. You know baby,
We can have a lot of fun I'm a man I spell it M A N
–From Muddy Waters/Bo Diddley version of Mannish
Boy (I'm a Man)

1949

He lived on the northwest side of Chicago near the Six Corners and attended a public grammar school, a hugh stone building with two large gravel play grounds that the students used during recess and lunch and on which the bullies staked out their territory and enjoyed tormenting younger kids. In those days, torment cut to the bone, for it was ethnic oriented and God forbid if you were not German or Irish. In this school, it could mean the difference between receiving or avoiding a thrashing.

It had been pretty much going on that way through the seventh grade. He was there to be picked on during recess. Taking lumps was becoming a daily affair and even though he tried to sneak away as best he could, he was an easy target. Bloody noses, chipped teeth and sore ribs were something he was becoming accustomed to, albeit reluctantly. Hell, let's face it; he couldn't fight worth a spit.

Each time, he vowed to himself that he would fight back, but it never seemed to happen. When he got home, he hid in his room in shame. The notion of going to professional fights with his dad was painful as he looked in the mirror at himself and despised what he saw. The tears flowed silently behind closed doors. Dealing with issues of self esteem was not a notion people knew much about back in the late 40's and early 50's. You just suffered through it. You suffered quietly and silently.

One day O'Hoary, a mean and hot tempered Irishman who had flunked and was older than the rest, made the mistake of taking the insults too far. Being called a "little Wop pimp" ("pimp" had a different, less business-like connotation back then) was one thing; being called a son of a Dago bitch was quite another and something stirred in him. This time, he managed to get in a few good shots of his own before the bigger and older 8th Grader prevailed with several blows to the mouth and a few kicks at the end for good measure. What didn't go unnoticed, however, was that the usually large crowd of onlookers actually gave him some encouragement when he fought back. A few even helped him to his feet.

The beatings continued but so did the kid's ability to withstand them with some semblance of resolve. Finally, one of O'Hoary's sycophants started in on the kid after school, but it triggered a real fight with give-and-take. A big crowd gathered as was the custom back then and watched in amazement as the kid held his own before finally succumbing. Bloodied but unbowed, he went home that day, looked in the mirror and vowed that he would never again get his clock cleaned.

Two days later during a basketball game at recess, another of O'Hoary's suck-ups by the name of Ed Stocking tripped him. This time, the kid got up with tears of rage in his eyes and went after Stocking with a vengeance. Instead of throwing wide and looping street fighter shots, he shortened up on his punches as he saw the pros do on TV and got inside Stocking's wild attack. This one turned out to be a savage affair with both suffering deep facial cuts and bruises, and they fought until the onlookers had no alternative but to break it up. Afterwards, the two combatants hugged one another in mutual respect but it was crystal clear who had won.

The next day, he enjoyed something he had never received before; namely, a degree of respect. He was no longer called out during recess or after school and even O'Hoary gave him space. It wasn't exactly swagger, but it did have a bit of weight behind it and it felt good.

He subsequently engaged in his share of brutal street fights and won most of them, gaining a reputation as someone to avoid. Eventually, through his father, he found refuge in a gym and became an excellent amateur boxer. It was safer than fighting in the streets and the acclaim felt good; he could look in the mirror now. He could feel good about himself. The odyssey had begun.

In retrospect, there had been an important lesson in all this. Not a "feel good one," mind you, but one that taught that you can only take so many beatings before you start to learn by them. Pretty soon, you get tougher and gain resolve. Then, one day the tide begins to turn, perhaps imperceptibly at first. More importantly, you don't lose anymore, and that's how it started. You start winning when you can't lose anymore.

> *...How I wish I was a man acting like a man can*
> *Until I start getting bigger, I'll just have to learn to face fear*
> *coz if I did just like you said I never would be scared*
> –Lyrics from "Don't get Scared" by King Pleasure
> and John Hendricks

Fast forward—ten year later.

1959

He was just coming off a tournament in which he had done well early but lost in the finals. He probably should have quit right there and then, but there was this card at the Great Lakes Training Center and he wanted to go out with a win.

Back in the 50's, he loved jazz, particularly West Coast stuff, so when the Herb Geller Sextette was headlining a spring show in nearby Waukegan, he felt compelled to go. Geller, who had returned from Brazil to tour the States after his wife had passed away, could play alto sax with the best and epitomized West Coast "cool." That the kid had a big fight the next day mattered, but this was a real opportunity to groove with his friends and lady and he was not about to miss it. Well, one thing led to another and the great altoist wailed.

The booze flowed freely and he said "why not?" His opponent the next day was an Italian kid out of Stickney, a working class suburb west of Chicago near Cicero. His name was Redondo and his record did not begin to match the kid's, so what the Hell, a few drinks and a couple of Salem Lights couldn't do any harm.

The concert ended at 1:00 A.M. and the group members, buzzed and tired, made their way back to the campus around 2:00. On the way back, he reflected deeply as to whether he was really calling it a career when he had picked up the first of several Dewar's. He also concluded that he just didn't give a damm anymore. He immediately sacked out and slept soundly.

The next morning, he woke up with a headache and an all-around heavy feeling. The fight was scheduled for 4:00 P.M. so he figured he had plenty of time to get ready. Around noon, he lunched on some red meat and salad and then did a few calisthenics to get his system in sync. He got to the gym in North Chicago about two and did some shadow boxing to loosen up. He picked up the pace at 3:30 to get the sweat flowing. He was now ready for the walk-in which amounted to nothing more than getting into the ring with a top wrap on and nothing more. No enswell or rap music. No entourage—hell, he didn't even know what the word meant. It was simply get in there amidst the cheers from your fans and do battle. This was old school amateur fighting in the Midwest.

The referee gave the instructions and the fighters went back to their corners to await the bell. Redondo had veins protruding around his shoulders which suggested he either had done some serious work with the iron or that he had a tough day job. Either way, it gave pause.

Well, the bell finally sounded and the fight began. After exchanging a few blows, the kid was swarmed upon and quickly mugged to the canvas for an 8-count. It was more push than punch. He was not hurt, but he was now wary. All this happened in a matter of seconds. Redondo quickly attacked and hit the kid with a right that straightened him up and then finished with a sharp hook that snapped his head back and sent him down spread eagled. The kid saw little white stars going on and off and then tasted something coppery in his mouth. This time he was hurt.

As he struggled to his feet, the referee asked how he felt. Bleeding from his nose and mouth, he looked up and said, "I'm ok." Redondo then came in fast with a bull rush but was tied up. As the referee broke them apart, the rugged Italian came back jabbing and circling, setting his wary (and weary) opponent up for the finish. He feinted with a right and launched a well leveraged and crunching left hook that connected flush and put the kid down again. As he got to one knee with blood gushing out of his mouth and his nose stinging, the referee again looked down at him, but before he could make a determination, the kid looked up and, as ten years quickly flashed through his mind, said, "I'm done".

The entire affair took less than three minutes and it ended his amateur boxing career, one that spanned a period during which he had enjoyed much adulation.

Later, he mused as to whether he cared all that much given the way he had behaved the night before. Sure, it was not the right thing to do, but maybe he knew it and just didn't want any more. Maybe he was sick of doing road work and going to the gym. Maybe he was tired of the stinging pain and black eyes that resulted when his nose got broken. At least there would be no more training, no more punishment, no more giving out punishment. The blood, sweat and tears would be done and over with. Maybe, just maybe, he decided to call it quits while listening to an altoist wail in a smoky bar in Waukegan. .

He had his run and it was a decent one, but he knew he would never forget the way things ended—and that didn't feel so good, but then, the beginning had been pretty hard as well. Boxing is not about happy endings and he was smart enough to know that. It was time to move on. He was no longer a "Mannish Boy;" he was a man now.

Nature's first green is gold,

Her hardest hue to hold.

Her early leaf's a flower;

But only so an hour.

Then leaf subsides to leaf.

So Eden sank to grief,

So dawn goes down to day.

Nothing gold can stay.

From NOTHING GOLD CAN STAY — by Robert Frost

3

THE TRENCHES

*the rats would eat u allive and the lice would feast of your
rotting corpses whilst diseases like trench foot would rot your
feet away and sometimes they would be amputated if trench foot
was caught then it was almost certain u would loose ur foot /feet
bcoz of the auful conditions*
–Anonymous from England

*We slept in our clothes and cut our hair short so that it would tuck in-
side our caps. Dressing simply meant putting on our boots. There were
times when we had to scrape the lice off with the blunt edge of a knife
and our underclothes stuck to us.*
–Elizabeth de T'Serclaes – a nurse on the front line

*Besides the use of the machine gun, which was the 800-pound
gorilla in trench warfare, other weapons that were used included
bayonets, rifles, grenades and shot guns. Tear gas, mustard gas,
and chlorine gas were also commonly used.*
–Anonymous

Author's father

Back in 1949, we had a pitifully tiny TV set on which my Dad and I (and some of my friends) would watch different programs, but the one that we enjoyed the most were the fights. They were televised from New York or Chicago and names like Madison Square Gardens, St Nicholas Arena or Marigold Gardens were commonplace. Some programs aired boxing matches on Monday. By far the most popular was "Gillette's Cavalcade of Sports," spotlighting the "Friday Night Fights" from Madison Square Garden. The Cavalcade lasted until 1960, a 14-year period which was the longest continuous run of any boxing program in television history. The show's theme song was the "Look Sharp/Be Sharp March by Mahlon Merrick and we would always chime in with Sharpie the Parrot who would squawk, "Look sharp! Feel sharp! Be Sharp! With Gillette razor blades before the fights were telecast. The bell would sound and Jimmy Powers at ringside would announce, "Friday night fights are on the air!"

Fights were so popular that all weight divisions were represented, not just heavyweights, though Jersey Joe Walcott, Rocky Marciano, and Ezzard Charles made their appearances. We used to enjoy watching Jake LaMotta the most because of his savage aura.

These were special family times–huddled around that tiny set and screaming our brains out. They were wonderful times.

My dad was born in 1891 in a City north of Athens, Greece. Since I was born in 1937, there was quite an age gap, but it allowed him to talk about how it was to be an immigrant who, by fighting in World War One, got his citizenship and who learned to read and write on his own. To him, this was nothing special or heroic. It was simply something he needed to do and he did it.

He talked about his war years, but only if someone asked questions first. He had been severely wounded in the Battle of Saint-Mihiel in 1918, and was a decorated veteran of that offensive and also of service in the Ardennes Forest. I was told he had fought "close up" in the trenches and when I pursued this, he would always change the subject in a way that made it clear that everyone else had better as well. Any mention of "the trenches" was a flash point for discomfort and we never did get around to discussing exactly what happened in that "in-close" combat, the stuff that involved situations in which infantry units charged towards the enemy over what they called no-man's land (the area in between the trenches of opposing armies). They called it "no-man's land" because that was a place where no man could survive. Through other family members, I had heard some things about poison gas and something called The Somme, but I was told never to broach the subject.

Well, back to Friday night and pizza, beer, cola and the fights. Two other guys we enjoyed immensely were Teddy "Red Top" Davis and Eugene "Silent" Hairston. One was a top contender; the other just a very good fighter who offered great entertainment to fans who were becoming accustomed to television. Teddy "Red Top" Davis was a crafty and slick fighter who knew all the moves and knew how to go the distance. He fought 146 times and finished with a 68-73- 5 slate.

But it was Hairston, 45-13-5, a rugged fighter who did his best work inside, who was a big fan favorite. Some said he had the style to give Sugar Ray a run for his money. He fought 18 times alone in 1951 giving us many televised opportunities to see him do his magic in the ring. His opposition reads like a Hall of Fame induction list. Among his many accomplishments, he drew with Jake LaMotta, beat Kid Gavilan, out pointed Lee Sala, 61-1 coming in, stopped Paddy Young, and sent Charley Zivic into retirement.

The thing was "Silent" was deaf, though he never asked for special accommodations. Ironically and sadly, an eye injury forced him to give up boxing at age twenty-two and he never got an opportunity to win a World Title or at least to fight the great Sugar Ray.

During one particular fight at St. Nicholas Arena in 1952, "Silent" stopped Al Priest, 43-12-2, by working his body with a furious assault until Al was unable to continue due to bruised ribs. The fight showcased Hairston's ability to fight in-close. In fact, the announcer said that no one could quite fight like "Silent" in the trenches. When he said that, I looked over to my dad who gave me an almost imperceptible wink. It was the closest he would ever come to going in that direction.

*Photos of author's father, John Sares, taken during the First World War.

4

JOEY'S LEGACY

You win, you win. You lose, you still win.
–Joey LaMotta (as played by Joe Pesci in Raging Bull)

**Joey LaMotta (Photo courtesy
of (International
Boxing Research Organization)**

Many families have had more than one member become famous in the sport of boxing. Some even had multiple world champions. Ernie "Indian Red" Lopez was the brother of Danny "Little Red" Lopez. Joe Gatti and Arturo Gatti were well known fighters. Robbie Sims, half brother of Marvelous Marvin Hagler, was a vastly under rated fighter, and Rodney and Duane Bobick both left boxing with a strong legacy. Of course, there were the Fighting Hiltons out of Canada and the Balatazar's from L.A. One of my favorite brother acts was Joey and Jake LaMotta because it featured more twists and ironic turns than most.

Giuseppe "Joey" LaMotta, brother of Giacobe "Jake" LaMotta and not to be confused with Joe Pesci, was 30-1-1 when he fought middleweight Johnny Henry Johnson on March 29, 1946. Many people don't even know that Jake's brother was a fighter. Even fewer knew that his record was 0-0 on June 2, 1945, or just an amazing nine months prior to the Johnson fight. The Bronx native finished his career on November 5, 1946 with a 32-5-2 slate and 22 wins coming by way of KO (see Appendix A).

Joey was born on April 27, 1925, and graduated from the Bronx Vocational School at the age of sixteen. His amateur career was limited to only a few contests. He was honorably discharged from the Army in September 1944 and began serious training in Bobby Gleason's gym under the direction of trainer, Charley Gulota.

He was fighting in main events after participating in only half dozen preliminary contests, as his aggressiveness, speed, and sensational body work made him a fan favorite, but more importantly, captured the attention of promoters. Joe had become a solid attraction in the boxing field. By all accounts, he was a prototype of his brother Jake (stocky and muscular), but faster and more aggressive. Most of his fights ended in a thrilling manner.

Joey fought in such famous venues as Wrigley Field in Chicago, Madison Square Garden in NYC, St. Nicholas Arena in NYC, The Boston Garden, The Chicago Stadium, Comiskey Park in Chicago, and, of course, in arenas throughout New Jersey and New York.

His career was only 21 months long, but over that period, he faced 39 opponents, most of whom, though not great, did not lack experience. Among others, he beat Lew Perez, Lee Black, Ballesandro Carubia and Tony Riccio (who would finish with a record of 55-37-13 and be inducted into the New Jersey Hall of Fame). Joey's KO win over the capable Carubia was indeed impressive as was his draw at the Boston Garden with contender Joe Blackwood, 29-4-1 at the time. Blackwood finished with a final slate of 66-24-8. This was the very same Joe Blackwood who would later upset the great George Benton in Miami Beach in 1953.

He usually had a fight a week. He once had two fights in two days winning both by early KO's! He was one active fighter. Probably the best he ever fought was in a losing effort against Anton Raadik out of Chicago by way of Estonia. Raadik, a favorite among ethnic-minded Chicago fans, fought from 1940–1952. His opponents included the great Marcel Cerdan (whom he knocked down a remarkable three times in losing a highly controversial decision), Jake LaMotta, Carl "Bobo" Olson, Steve Belloise, Danny Nardico, Harry "Kid" Matthews, and Robert Villemain to name a few. Losing to Raadik over ten rounds was no disgrace.

Joey slowed down the pace a bit from March to November of 1946, losing and drawing with Blackwood, outpointing Gene Boland, losing to Raadik and finally dropping two to Freddy Flores against whom he suffered his only stoppage loss. His short but active career reportedly ended because of a nasal ailment

Joey had boxed at an amateur club named Teasdale A.C. The gym was in a loft on the second floor of a movie house on Washington Avenue and was run by Mike Capriano who would later become one of Jake's many managers (though Joey would be, on paper at least, Jake's manager along with Capriano). Joey suggested to Jake that he go there with him to see what it was like, and Jake decided to use the gym's facilities as a way of losing weight. It didn't take very long for Jake to get the bug and the rest, of course, is history.[1]

In the film "Raging Bull," Joey (played by Joe Pesci in a breakout role) comes off as a violent and complex character – part Joey, and a bigger part Jake's best friend, Pete Petrella. Many of the things that happened between Jake and Joey in the film actually took place between Jake and Pete in real life (as Jake reveals in his autobiography) – the arguments and jealousy about women, about the mob, even the breakup and reconciliation with Joey actually happened in real life with Pete.

The fact is Jake overshadowed Joey in just about every way and took care of him as best he could, more like a father than an older brother. But mostly, Joey's role was a background one. At any rate, there is raging disagreement as to the manner in which Joey came off in Raging Bull. Indeed, Joey himself thought so and sued the producer's of the Movie because he thought he was wrongly portrayed.

Joey LaMotta passed away in 1991 at the age of 66 with not much of a legacy except as he is remembered in Raging Bull. But dammit, Joey LaMotta was not Joe Pesci. When you peel the onion, you find that he was a savvy fighter who had fine skills, ring smarts and solid punching power in his own right and who fought a remarkable 39 times in just 21 months. He never let being the young brother of Jake LaMotta be an obstacle; instead, Joey made good on his own.

Let that be a part of his legacy as well.

[1] Hauser, Thomas and Stephen Brunt, The Italian Stallions. Sport Classic Books. 2003

Note: See Appendix A: Career record of Joey LaMotta

5

DAMAGED GOODS

Boxers last only a short time, but managers go on for ever.
–Joe Greb

Gus Dundee and Buddy Brannen met in the movie "The Harder they Fall" and Bunny rendered a terrible beat down on Gus who thereafter suffered from severe headaches going into his next fight with the Argentinean giant, Toro Moreno. With obvious brain damage, the feather-fisted Moreno knocked the helpless Dundee out. He then lapsed into a coma and died. Max Baer was suitably cast as the malefic Brannon. The point being that Gus was terribly badly damaged goods going into the Moreno fight and just about everyone knew it except the naïve Toro.

This was make-believe, of course, and made for great theater. What was not make-believe was that Ernie Schaaf compiled a record of 49-15-1 that included wins over Max Baer, Jim Braddock and Tony Galento. In August 932, he was decisioned by Baer in a rematch. However, he was actually saved by the bell when Baer knocked him out with seconds remaining in the fight. Six months later, an equally feather fisted Primo Carnera, to whom Toro Moreno was compared, knocked out Ernie in 13 rounds. Schaaf died four days later. Many believe the injuries suffered in his bout with Baer (who ironically played the role of Buddy Brannen), contributed to his death. Schaaf, of course, was the fictitious Gus Dundee.

The following are similar chilling fights I recall from the past.

Percy Bassett vs. Sonny Boy West (1950)

Joe Miceli came from the Mulberry Street section of New York's lower east side and was one tough customer from the Golden Age of Boxing. Hell, he fought 12 world champions; namely, Ike Williams, Kid Gavilan, Joey Giardello, Johnny Saxton, Johnny Bratton, Gene

Fullmer, Virgil Akins, Don Jordan, Wallace "Bud" Smith, Curtis Cokes, Luis Rodriguez and Ralph Dupas. He beat Williams 2-out-3, beat Saxton, Akins and Smith, drew with Giardello and lost a split decision to Gavilan.

But back in September of 1950, he fought the rugged Sonny Boy West, a lightweight/welterweight. Miceli, 28-7-2, beat West in Milwaukee by decision.

In an article dated December 21, 2005 and written by Robert Cassidy Jr. entitled "Driving Joe Miceli," which appeared in The Sweet Science, he mentions that the fight was a one-sided affair. In fact, he said that several times throughout the fight Miceli asked the referee to intervene, to stop the beating. But West kept coming and the referee instructed Miceli, "They (fans) pay their money to see you fight." So Miceli kept fighting, kept punching

West then beat Charley Salas, Eddie Giosa, and Billy Justine, but on December 21, 1950, he was knocked out by the great Percy Bassett, 46-2 at the time, at St. Nicholas Arena. West complained of double vision between the 6th and 7th rounds. After he was hurt to the body by Bassett, he was floored by a right hand. As he fell, he landed hard on his head. West died of injuries suffered in this bout on December 21st. The official cause of death was given as an "inter-cerebral hemorrhage resulting from a cerebral concussion."

"I feel like I had something to do with that," says Miceli. "I still feel terrible about that. The beating I gave him."

Sonny Boy West's final record was 46 -8 -1.

Laverne Roach vs. Georgie Small (1950)

Marcel Cerdan savaging Laverne Roach
(Photo from public domain)

Laverne Roach, 26-4, and Georgie Small, 38-6, met in February 1950. Small was a Brooklyn Jewish middleweight who was born in 1925 and frequently fought in Brooklyn. Other outstanding great Jewish athletes out of Brooklyn at that time included the great Max Zaslofsky, Harry Boykoff, Hy Gotkin, Sid Tannenbaum, and boxers Al Davis, Georgie Kaplan, and Davey Feld,

Roach was a tough ex-marine out of Texas. This was a televised fight from St. Nicholas Arena in New York City which, I recall, took place on a Monday night and I believe Don Dunphy may have been at the mike. At any rate and in retrospect, the setting was quintessential 50's.

Roach appeared to be well ahead in the fight and seemingly on his way to an easy points win when suddenly Small uncorked a right out of nowhere in the eighth stanza that landed flush on Roach's jaw. It was more desperation than planned, but the tide of the fight changed just like that. The blow ripped into Roach like a sledge hammer and the blood immediately gushed from his lips and mouth. Bleeding profusely and staggering, he managed to hang on until the bell rang. While he somehow made it through the ninth using every survival trick he knew, he was a bloody mess and the one-sided assault continued through the tenth until a crunching right put Roach down like he had been sapped. Everyone in our house, my Dad, my friends and I, started to yell "Stop it! Stop it." The fans at ring side were doing the same, and Referee Frank Fullam did just that, but simultaneously, another punch sent Roach sprawling. But the damage already had been done.

As Laverne laid glassy eyed on the blood-spattered canvas, he motioned that he was ok, but he was anything but and everyone watching knew it. He went slack eyed and then lapsed into a coma. Fourteen hours later, Laverne Roach, just 24, passed away from a sub-dural hemorrhage in St. Clare's Hospital.

We had watched this one from the safe confines of our living room and it was my first chilling experience witnessing a ring death. Thank God, the fight had been televised in black and white since the amount of blood that flowed was horrific. Though I have seen too many since, this one has stayed with me through the years.

But wait. There is more to the story; there is something else that needs to be said here. Less than two years previously, Roach had been badly beaten by the great Marcel Cerdan, 105-2 at the time.

He had been clubbed to the canvas three times in the second round and four more times in the eighth as Cerdan's monster blows continued to rain down upon him. As he crawled around the ring, the slaughter was finally and mercifully stopped after eight punishing rounds. Clearly, the Texas marine had been brought along too fast to fight the likes of the great Frenchman.

However, two things contributed to his elongated beating. First, he had been slugged and mugged to the canvas in the second round. He was dazed and waited for the count, but timekeeper Jack Watson didn't begin one until the referee ordered him to do so. Watson did and Roach got up at the count of 9 with the entire fiasco using up 32 seconds. As it turned out, Laverne would have been better served had he been counted out.

The second thing was the fact that just when Roach appeared ready to go, he would fight back with just enough skill to stay in the fight. Indeed, he was still countering in the seventh, but things finally ended in the eighth stanza when referee Arthur Donovan put an end to what had become a slaughter. The accumulation of brutal punishment and numerous knockdowns over 8 rounds had been brutal.

Still, up until that beat down, he had been 23-1 with his only loss coming at the hands of rugged New Yorker Artie Towne, a gifted boxer with a great record (who fought as one Henry Johnson when he beat Roach). In fact, Roach had been Ring magazine's Rookie-of-the-Year in 1947.

After the Cerdan massacre, Roach said goodbye to boxing and went back home to sell insurance, but after two years and a few warm-up fights, he was back in the ring, perhaps as badly damaged goods–for one last time.

Kid Paret vs. Emil Griffith (1962)

This fight needs little if any narrative. Most aficionados know what happened, but what many don't know is that The Kid took a horrific beating at the hands of Gene Fullmer just three months prior to this fateful bout.

The Kid, 156¾, was 35-10-3 coming in while Fullmer, 159¾, was 54-4-2. The bullnecked Fullmer was an aggressive and crafty fighter and knocked out 14 of his first 16 opponents. Eventually, in 1957, he won the middleweight title by beating the great Sugar Ray Robinson. His fight with Paret took place at the Convention Center in Las

Vegas, and was for something called the National Boxing Association World middleweight title

Fullmer rendered a tremendous beating on Paret and capped it by putting him down three times in the tenth. The punches he hit Paret with were wind up shots to both his body and head and were difficult to witness given their ferocity. The third time The Kid went down, he stayed down. Gene was a wrecking machine against the game Cuban. Reportedly, he said it was the worse beating he ever gave an opponent.

As for the fight, Paret fought well and dropped the heavily favorite Griffith in the sixth round but eventually Emil was able to dictate the pace and gained control going into the 12th. Then it happened. Griffith (28-3 with only 10 KO's at the time), and never known for having a particularly hard punch or being vicious towards his opponents, drove Paret back on to the ropes with a sharp right. Before not only a live crowd of 8,000 at Madison Square Garden, but a national television audience as well, Griffith unloaded on the cornered "Kid" and fired away perhaps as many as eighteen vicious punches to the head.

Paret was tangled and pinned in the ropes and unable to fall. Griffith punched and punched, the blows landing with tremendous force, one after another. He was beaten into unconsciousness and his body went limp like a rag doll. It all occurred in a matter of seconds, though I do recall screaming at the referee via the television set to stop the fight. Sadly, it would not be the first or last time I would so engage a television set.

The beating resulted in Paret being carried out on a stretcher. He underwent brain surgery that night at Roosevelt Hospital, fell into a coma and died of pneumonia ten days later.

Griffith, a gentleman, was traumatized by Paret's death and would never be the same fighter, though he fought on for another 15 years. The Kid's final professional record was 35-12-3 (10 KOs). Emile would finish with a record of 85-24-2-1 with only 23 KO's. He was inducted into the International Boxing Hall of Fame in 1990 and remains a sensitive and popular personality among his fans and peers. As for Ruby Goldstein, the fight's outcome bothered him greatly and he retired after working just one more fight.

It would be ten years before boxing appeared on television again. Ironically, on the Hall of Fame enshrines page, the following appears:

"EMILE GRIFFITH was a consummate fighter. The only thing he did not do well in the ring, was punch. Aside from that, Griffith did everything well."

The bout had been televised live and I saw it. I was 25 at the time and had witnessed several previous fights that had ended in tragedy though I was by no means inured to them. Sure, there had been bad blood between Emil Griffith and Benny "Kid" Paret prior to their fight, but The Kid had been beaten up even before that fateful fight.

Roy Holloway vs. Miguel Mayan (1975)

Holloway, 8-6, fought Mayan, 33-29-5 coming in, at the Silver Slipper in Las Vegas on November 26, 1975. He was knocked out in the tenth round and died of injuries sustained in this fight. Mayan had fought many top level fighters prior to this fight and even managed to beat a few, but mostly he was a rugged gate keeper.

For his part, Holloway had managed a hugh upset in May 1975 by beating undefeated Leroy Haley on points, but then lost two consecutive knockouts to undefeated Adolfo Viruet and then inexplicitly to untested Concepcion Martinez, 0-0 at the time. He reportedly suffered a head injury during the August bout with Martinez, but stepped into the ring for what would be his last time three months later against the veteran Mayan.[1]

Whether or not Holloway belonged in the ring against Mayan is conjectural. What is factual is that on May 14, 1975, he beat undefeated and future light welterweight world champion Leroy Haley and would get knocked out less than three months later to a fighter with an 0-0 record. As well, Haley went thorough 18 straight bouts without a loss after his upset defeat to Holloway.

Was Holloway damaged goods? I wonder.

Willie Classen vs. Wilford Scypion (1979)

Willie Classen, 15-6-2, was knocked through the ropes on November 23, 1979 by Wilford Scypion, 12-0. He collapsed and the fact no ambulance was parked in the wings of Madison Square Garden and that it reportedly took 30 minutes to flag down an ambulance in the street and take Classen to a hospital, where he died of a brain hemorrhage five days later, is the grist for another story. Nor are the subsequent multiple law suits and eventual settlements the story here.

The story here is that Classen was a middleweight journeyman who had been in the ring with tough competition, guys like Eddie Mustafa Muhammad and Vito Antuofermo. Just a month after being knocked out by Sibson in London, Classen took on unbeaten Scypion at the Felt Forum in New York City. Scypion had destroyed all opposition coming in, but the opposite was true for his doomed opponent.

Prior to the Sibson blow out on October 9, he was KOd in 8 at the felt forum by bomber John LoCicero. He fought Wilford Scypion a little over a month after being iced by Sibson

Classen had been decked a couple of times in the fight from shots from that would have sent other fighters into dreamland. Clearly, he was in very bad, indeed, dangerous condition going into the final round. Hell, after the ninth stanza, he needed the assistance of the ropes to get back to his corner. Then, just seconds after stumbling from his corner for the start of the 10th round, he was knocked out of the ring by Scypion. Ringsiders stood up and hollered for referee Lew Eskin to stop it right there and then, but it was not to be.

After this tragedy, Wilford Scypion would never be the same fighter, the one who fought with fury and even perceived meanness. He had lost the edge. He finished 32-9 and seemed to lose every time he stepped up.

Whether or not Willie Classen was damaged going into this fight is open to debate. What is not is that he had been knocked out by Tony Sibson only one month prior.

Rafael "Bazooka" Limon vs Hector "Macho" Camacho (1983)

When they fought for the vacant WBC super featherweight at Hiram Bithorn Stadium in San Juan, Puerto Rico in August 1983, Camacho was 21-0 coming in. Bazooka was coming in with a strong record of 50-12-2, but one of those losses was to Bobby Chacon in December 10982 in one of the greatest fights in modern boxing history. It was for the WBC super featherweight title, and Chacon was dropped in the 4th and 10th while Limon was decked in the

15th and last round. Both fighters absorbed tremendous amounts of punishment in what would be the 1982 Ring Magazine Fight of the Year.

The effects of this and other fights would later become apparent after Bobby retired, but only after he retired. For Limon, the effects would be more immediate as he was stopped in five rounds by Camacho, who floored the former world champion in the first and third rounds before referee Richard Steele stopped the beating.

Limon would not fight again until 1986 when he was TKOd by Oscar Bejines. In 1987, he knocked out one Santos Moreno, 14-13, but then lost nine of his last ten fights suffering six stoppages. His lone win came against a 6-6- fighter and near the end of his career, he experienced the humiliation of being knocked out by unknown Moises Perches, 1-1 at the time. Limon finished with a slate of 52-23-2 and enjoyed much to celebrate during his long career. However, had he retired after his war with Chacon, he would not have become terribly damaged goods going into the Camacho fight.

As for Chacon, he would win eight of his last nine fights against very good opposition (the last seven in a row), but tragically would acquire the dreaded Pugilistica Dementia after retiring.

David Gonzalez: An Anomaly
1) Rico Velazquez (1988)

On August 21, 1988, a 22-year-old Los Angeles boxer died in a hospital a day after suffering a cerebral hemorrhage while being knocked out by David Gonzales, 18-1-1, as he defended his state lightweight title in a fight at the San Jose Civic Auditorium. Rico Velazquez was declared dead after a life-support system was removed with his family's consent.

Velazquez, 12-3, collapsed seconds after Referee Henry Elespuru finally stepped in to stop the fight in the eighth round Friday night at the San Jose Civic Auditorium against the 19 year old Gonzales.

In an article dated September 12, 2007 in Salon Com, King Kaufman states,

"I interviewed Gonzalez as his next fight approached. He told me he felt bad about Velazquez's death, but not guilty. Serious injury and death were hazards of the trade, he shrugged.

"I asked him how he dealt with that. Having seen first hand the toll his sport could take, how could he climb back through the ropes? He turned the question around on me. "You could get killed every time you get into your car," he said. "You just don't think about it."

"I became fascinated with the question and asked it to pretty much every boxer I met over the next few months, which was a lot of them since I was writing about boxing. Almost all of them gave me a variation on Gonzalez's answer, a mix of fatalism and denial that I found familiar even as I found it strange."[2]

The fight against Rico was a brutal beat down, as he reportedly was decked several times before referee Henry Elesperu halted matters in the eight, as ringsiders pleaded shouted and pleaded for the stoppage. Velazquez had been savaged by Vernon Buchanan back to December 1987, but had mounted a six-fight win streak going into his bout with Gonzalez. The problem was, however, that he had fought in each of the six months leading up to the Gonzalez fight and may well have been shot coming in.

Indeed, boxing writer Pedro Fernandez, in his definitive article dated August 15, 2006 in Ring Talk, states, "…Rico, the defending (sic) California lightweight champion, came into the fight with a broken nose and two black eyes…..The Gonzalez-Velasquez bout was as one-sided a fight as you'll ever imagine, with knockdowns of Rico beginning in the first round. Velasquez, a proud guy whose skills were moderate at best, was 15-5 coming into this San Jose Civic Auditorium bout of August 19, 1988…"[3]

As for Gonzalez, the circumstances of the fight seemed to have no ill effects on him and he actually fought a little over a month later knocking out one Cedric Powell in six rounds and then beat ten other opponents in succession before losing a SD to Anthony Stephens in 1992. He then won ten of his next eleven bouts before his fateful fight with Robert Wangila in 1994.

2) Robert Wangila (1994)

Robert Wangila, alias Wangila Napunyi, a 1988 Olympic boxing gold medalist from Kenya, died on July 23, 1994, from head injuries suffered during a fight with Gonzalez, 38-3-1, of Houston at the Aladdin Hotel in Las Vegas. He was on life support systems with a blood clot on the right side of his head when he pronounced dead at the University Medical Center. He was 26.

About 30 minutes after referee Joe Cortez stopped the bout in the ninth round and declared Gonzalez the winner, Wangila became ill in his dressing room and collapsed. David had rendered a brutal beat down on Wangila pounding on any and all exposed areas of his soon-to-be lifeless body. It was difficult to witness.

Gonzalez then would move to another weight class to meet World 154 lb. champ, Terry Norris in September 16, 1995, but was stopped in nine. He then retired at 40-4-1, with 23 KOs.

When asked if he ever thinks about guys dying at his hands, David seemed stumped, "I never meant to kill anyone."[4]

In the scheme of things, these incidents cannot be easily or readily classified; they are anomalies.

Matthew Hilton (1990) and Robert Hines (1990)

Hilton

Tough Philadelphian Rob "Bam Bam" Hines met Mathew Hilton on November 11, 1988 in Las Vegas with Hilton's IBF light middleweight belt at stake. Hilton was 29-0-0 coming in while Hines sported a fine record of 23-1-1. This promised to be a war and did not disappoint. The opening round featured Hines landing several molar rattling uppercuts while the rugged Canadian worked viciously to Bam Bam's body. Hilton decked Hines in the second and seemed to have him ripe for the picking, but Bam Bam was in fantastic shape and survived the early onslaughts. The Canadian bomber expended too much energy trying to finish off Hines who then took control midway in the fight and inflicted tremendous punishment on an almost helpless and gassed Hilton in the last three rounds. Indeed, referee Carlos Padilla could well have stopped the slaughter in the eleventh stanza and it was amazing that Hilton's corner let him go out for the final round—one in which he absorbed unnecessary punishment. Hell, what part of white towel didn't they get?

Hines won the fight and the title going away as the score cards read 116-110, 112-111, and 114-111.

Hilton would never be the same fighter and when he fought Doug "The Cobra" DeWitt in January 1990 for the WBO middleweight title in Atlantic City, he was a different though still game warrior, as The Cobra won the fight via a TKO in the eleventh stanza. Matthew would then fight on briefly and close out his career with a splendid 32-3-2 slate, but after the brawl with Bam Bam, he was never the same.

Hines

Three months later, Hines defended his newly won crown against upstart Darrin Van Horn in Atlantic City. The "Schoolboy," 38-0 coming in, pulled off an upset by winning a decisive UD win to capture's Bam Bam's title. Given the manner in which Hines fought, it's seem reasonable to conclude that he too may have been damaged going into that fight, particularly so soon after his brawl with Matthew Hilton. And like Hilton, he closed out his career with a win over limited Salim Muhammad and a four round TKO loss to Brett Lally for vacant NABF light middleweight title after which he retired with a record of 25-3-1 and a legacy of having been a quintessential Philadelphia fighter.

Riddick Bowe vs. Andrew Golata (1996)

The signs started showing in 1993 and by 1996, he was a shell of his former self. His brutal trilogy with Evander Holyfield combined with poor training habits and overeating had caught up to him.

After his slaughter of Jorge Luis Gonzalez in 1995, Bowe had his highly anticipated rubber match against Evander Holyfield. Holyfield knocked Bowe down with a left hook but Bowe came back with a knockout in eight.

Bowe was then matched up against the undefeated yet unproven Polish heavyweight contender Andrew Golota at the Garden. Though well ahead on points, Golota suffered his first loss when Bowe went to the floor in round seven after being hit with the last of several low blows throughout the fight. Golota was disqualified and was well on his way to a new nickname.

A Pay Per View rematch was held five months later at the Convention Center in Atlantic City, and Golota once again dominated.

Amazingly, however, he was once again disqualified due to a brutal low blow combination in the ninth stanza. The two Bowe fights earned Golota the nickname "The Foul Pole," though there had been many earlier warnings of his proclivity towards mayhem.

As for Bowe, though he won, he came out of those fights terribly damaged—perhaps as a result of going in damaged.

Bradley Rone (2003)

Bradley Rone met Billy Zumbrun on June 18, 2003. He was fighting to collect the $800 winner's purse so he could help pay for the funeral of his mother, Thelma. Rone, a former sparring partner of both Mike Tyson and Evander Holyfield, accepted the offer to compete just one day earlier – the same day his mother died of heart failure in Cincinnati.

Rone had fought Zumbrun less than a month earlier (on June 30) with Zumbrun having won a UD over six rounds. He weighed 259 for the second encounter

The fight was held at the Cedar City Raceway in Cedar City, Utah. After a non-eventful first round, the two clinched near the end of the round. Zumbrun tapped Rone and the referee separated the two heavyweights as the round ended. Rone took a step towards his corner and then collapsed. Ring doctors came to his aid immediately, and he was taken to Valley View Medical Center, where he was declared dead apparently of a massive heart attack.

Tragically, a double funeral for Rone and his mother was then held back in Ohio. He left a girlfriend and two children behind and was also survived by nine brothers and sisters.

Rone's record according to BoxRec was 7-43, but going into the final fight, he had gone 29 straight without a win (28 losses and one draw). He had a knack for survival which meant he fought a lot of rounds against a lot of very good fighters, and that may have taken a toll on him. In one stretch, he fought Cliif Couser, Jorge Louis Gonzalez, Kelvin Davis, Maurice Harris, Serguei Lyakhovich, Willie Chapman, Balu Sauer, Orlin Norris, Sinan Sam, DaVarryl Williamson, Robert Davis, Danny Eaton and Adolpho Washington. He bookmarked this stretch upfront with fights against the likes of Fres Oquendo and against Javier Mora, Dale Crowe, Chauncey Welliver, and Eric Kirkland toward the finish.

Using what I call a "chill factor" which is the total number of knock-outs (both for and against) divided by the total number of fights, Rone had a reasonable 30%. Still, his record going into that last fight was dismal and may well have contributed to his being shop worn when the bell sounded for the last time.

It's not for me to say whether some commission may have made some mistakes or whether he had been barred by another state just six months earlier. Let the courts sort those items out.

In this connection, his family members say he had no business step-ping into that ring, although he was licensed as a boxer by the Utah Department of Commerce's Athletic Commission, which had regu-lated the fight. In a wrongful-death suit filed against the event orga-nizers and the state of Utah, Rone's sister said athletic commission officials broke several of their own rules in allowing Rone to fight. Among the rules allegedly broken were the fact that Rone had lost more than six consecutive fights, did not have an exam conducted by a physician, and no written certification was provided by a doc-tor saying Rone was fit to compete, despite being visibly overweight. The case has been appealed to the State Supreme Court which will sort out the facts.

What is a fact is that a fighter who had lost 26 straight fights may have been tempting fate when he stepped in the ring on short no-tice under terribly tragic circumstances.

Arturo Gatti vs. Alfonso Gomez (2007)

Most aficionados knew Gatti had taken a brutal beating by Floyd Mayweather on June 25, 2005, but that did not stop him from taking on dangerous Thomas Damgaard in January 2006. Gatti turned in a surprisingly impressive performance dominating and stopping the undefeated Dane, 37-0 coming in. In the process, he won the vacant International Boxing Association welterweight title. In a strange way, he might have been better off losing, as the win set him up for a beat down by Carlos Manuel Baldomir six months later. Gatti was decked twice in the 9th round before the fight was stopped. Tellingly, Baldomir is not know as a heavy handed bomber and only had 12 KO's coming in.

Then, for some reason, he thought he could beat Alfonso Gomez in a "say goodbye" fight, but it was not to be. The Mayweather beating and the Baldomir stoppage combined with all the incredible wars

Gatti has participated in, all caught up with him on the night of July 14, 2007 in Atlantic City. Gomez could not miss and never looked better as he picked apart Gatti in brutal fashion finally ending the slaughter by stoppage in the seventh round. The final straight right tore Gatti's upper lip in two and the blood flowed deeply. It was not a pleasant sight, but then again, he should not have been in that ring.

Oscar Diaz vs. Delvin Rodriguez (July 16, 2008)

A minority of boxing fans enjoy watching someone get beaten up. The rest of us wrestle with this issue from time to time. We ponder not only how a fighter will feel the following morning, but also what the condition of his brain will be ten years from now. We're aware of the fact that a "good fight" means that two boxers have engaged in combat with a brutal ebb and flow and been punched in the head and hurt multiple times.
–Thomas Hauser

This was the biggest night of my life, but also the saddest. I hope I never experience anything like this again…I'm praying for him right now and I'll be praying for him all night.
–Delvin Rodriguez

In my book *Boxing is my Sanctuary*, I wrote a short piece entitled, "Bloodfest at the Alamodome" in which I described a particularly savage fight between Golden Johnson and Oscar "El Torito" Diaz on November 11, 2006, in San Antonio for local bragging rights.

The fight featured ebb and flow brutality the likes of which had not been seen in these parts since Tony Ayala did his nasty thing. This was not one-sided stuff; it was give-and-take the result of which would eventually reduce Diaz's great manager, Lou Duva, to tears. Golden Johnson was a revived and brilliant fighter on this night, showing resiliency, grit, and the ability to close matters.

The ebb and flow action kept the 10,000 fans standing and screaming throughout as Johnson controlled the early part of the fight. Diaz took over in the middle rounds and hurt Johnson badly in the seventh with a vicious body shot. He was poised to take Johnson out when the bell ended the round and arguably saved Johnson. It would be his last chance.

His spirit Rapidly depleting, Oscar then took an unbelievable amount of punishment before a straight Johnson right in the eleventh round caught him flush, sending him staggering against the ropes. After a series of savage and unanswered shots, Referee Ruben Carrion finally stepped in and stopped the slaughter, suggesting once again the possibility that the corner is a lot braver than the fighter. Diaz's one eye was completely closed, and a deep and hideous cut opened over the eyelid of his other eye that even master cut man Joe Souza couldn't close. Blood was coming from his mouth, and his hand may have been broken as well. His face was a bloody mess and triggered some in the crowd yell, "Stop it! Stop it!"

Lou Duva fought back tears at the fight's end. He and the rest of the Diaz camp knew how important it was for their kid to win in San Antonio, but at what cost? Diaz may have been ruined by this fight, even though he fought a valiant one. Even Johnson's corner was critical of Diaz's corner for not stopping the fight sooner.

What part of white towel didn't they get? If ever there was a case of discretion being the better part of valor, this may well have been it. [5]

Fast forward to July 16, 2008

The headlines read: "Soon after collapsing between the tenth and eleventh rounds, Oscar Diaz was transported to a hospital and taken into emergency brain surgery at University Hospital after his fight with Delvin Rodriguez (23-2-1, 14 KO) at the Municipal Auditorium in San Antonio. When ESPN2 went off the air, it was clear something was very wrong."

The fight itself featured some violent ebb and flow (in fact, Diaz had Rodriguez reeling in the fourth), but Rodriguez's punches were sharper, more voluminous and did more damage. Soon, Diaz's face began to break up. In the tenth stanza, a long D-Rod right turned Diaz's head and, after moving to his right, a punishing left jab-double left hook combination landed that had malice written all over it.

Then, between rounds, referee Robert Gonzalez inquired as to Diaz's ability to continue. Just then, Diaz rose to his feet, screamed in pain as his legs went out from under him. Holding his gloves to his head, he was laid out flat on the canvas and quickly and expertly attended to by EMT's, who provided oxygen and secured him to a stretcher. It was a sight all too familiar to serious boxing fans and one that will not be forgotten.

At first, the news seemed grim, but then the following was issued by promoter Donna Duva-Brooks:

Encouraging News

Donna Duva-Brooks, promoter of critically injured boxer Oscar Diaz, has issued a somewhat encouraging update regarding their fighter's condition. "The brain is back to its normal size and position, and the swelling has gone down," said the somewhat relieved promoter from Diaz's bedside at University Hospital Trauma ICU in San Antonio..

Neurosurgeon Dr. David Jimenez performed the two-hour craniotomy on the left side of the fighter's head on Wednesday night and, according to Duva-Brooks, is pleased with Diaz's recovery progress, thus far. "He was operated on within two hours of the injury and the doctor said it was of great benefit how fast they were able to get him to the hospital."

Handling Oscar Diaz's career has been a family affair for the Duvas, who say they've all grown to love the tough little Texan. Tommy Brooks, Donna's husband, serves as Diaz's trainer, her father Lou, his manager. "We're all devastated by this. He's been a son to us for the past 12 years and we hope and pray he recovers from this injury."

The fighter's mother, Theresa, wishes to convey her gratitude to the many who have expressed their well wishes. "We've been overwhelmed by the love and support we've received from everyone. It's helped us stay strong for Oscar during this difficult time."

While Duva-Brooks acknowledges that recovery will require a great deal of time and patience, right now, the outlook seems to be improving. "Oscar's vital signs are good and he has been showing slight improvement each day. Doctors say it could take up to a week to come out of the coma. We are encouraged by the news that the swelling in his brain is gone and we're all praying for him and taking it day by day. We'll release more information when it becomes available."[6]

Hindsight is twenty-twenty vision, and I am not about to play the blame game. This is boxing and these things happen in boxing. I'll leave the issue of "damaged goods" for someone else to pursue.

Oscar Diaz is a warrior and his warrior heart hopefully will pull him though. That is where the focus should be now. The best we can do is pray for his recovery.

[1] Steve Kanigher, "A brutal, vicious sport, 'Sweet science' of the boxing ring results in many brain injuries." October 23, 2005. http://www.lasvegassun.com/sunbin/stories/lv-other/2005/oct/23/519549567.html

[2] King Kaufman, King Kaufman's Sports Daily, September 12, 2007, http://www.salon.com/sports/col/kaufman/2007/09/12/wednesday/

[3] Pedro Fernandez, "BOXER KILLED THREE MEN WITH HIS HANDS!" August 15, 2006, http://www.ringtalk.com:80/index.php?action=fullnews&showcomments=1&id=772

[4] IBID

[5] Sares, Theodore R., *Boxing is my Sanctuary*, iUniverse, Inc. New York Lincoln Shanghai, 2007

[6] "Encouraging News from Oscar Diaz Camp," July 19, 2008. 2009http://www.eastsideboxing.com/news.php?p=16602&more=1

6

JUSTICE IS SERVED

Holman Williams was a great boxer, but he never got the recognition because he wasn't a puncher. He had the finesse of a Ray Robinson, but no punch.
–Eddie Futch

Clever, cunning and skilful, Holman was one of those forever kind of fighters who probably looked like a grizzled old veteran when he came out of the womb.
–Mike Casey

Holman Williams
(photo from public Domain)

I was nine years old and vaguely recall something about my dad wanting to take me to the Chicago Coliseum in April 1946 to see a youthful and popular bomber by the name of Bob Satterfield, 12-1 at the time, go up against a veteran middleweight who boxed with the speed and cleverness of a lightweight. It would be the main event in a card that also included Roy Cadie vs. Torpedo Reed and Tony Musto tangling with Dick Leves.

In 1945, I had seen Satterfield destroy Art McWhorter in one savage round at the Marigold Gardens. He floored McWhorter three times; first from a left hook, second from a volley of shots, and finally from a left hook that dropped him for the count. It was pure but beautiful violence.

The attraction on this 1946 night would be the youth and explosiveness of "Rapid Robert," 168½ and 22, vs. the style and experience of Holman Williams, 34, who was 138-22-10 coming in and a 2 to 1 favorite (his career spanned 1931-1948 and he had 187 fights in all).

Most Chicago fans did their betting under the numerous "no betting" signs that were scattered throughout the Coliseum. This was done as a kind of post-war thing that said "we damm well will do anything we want." That was pure post-war Chicago back in the day and the vets were not to be messed with.

The fight drew 6,500 people, the largest crowd since the 30's, and most were there to see Satterfield unload one of his lethal lefts or crunching rights on a veteran who was considered the quintessential "cutie," and one of the best defensive fighters of the 1940s. The winner stood to fight Jake LaMotta making the fight even more intriguing. Of course, this was an era in which the now devalued title of "'world champion" was accorded to one man only and the stakes of a title fight were much higher.

In his previous duke, the rangy, slick-boxing Williams, who always was in tip top shape, lost to none other than the "Chocolate Kid," Bert Lytell, but prior to that, he put together a 14-fight undefeated streak including two wins over the aforementioned Lytell and one over future Hall-of-Fame inductee Charley Burley. Also included in this streak, were wins over The Cocoa Kid (165-44-8 at the time) and the great Archie Moore. In all, he would go 3-8-2 against The Kid, 3-3-1 against rugged Jose Basora, and 3-3-0-1 against Charley Burley, though I have not been able to verify these figures to the level of exactness I prefer. His career began in 1932 and ended in 1948. He came out of the professional gate fast losing only once in his first 32 fights. Included in this fast start was a win in 1935 for the Negro Lightweight Title.

Back to the Coliseum

Bob Satterfield (Photo from public domain)

Unfortunately, I never did get to that 1946 fight. My dad took my brother instead (he had returned from the War in 1945) and their account of it was that Satterfield gave a great showing but simply could not reach Williams who was able to dodge and deflect the bomber's shots, though it would later be said that even when Bob missed, he could hurt you. As it were, Williams won an entertaining ten round decision with young Bob stalking throughout but never catching the veteran who used a super left jab to keep the bomber at bay. My brother said it seemed impossible for Satterfield to land a clean shot. Little did I know that some 62 years later, Williams would be inducted into the International Boxing Hall of Fame.

Holman would then fight and lose to future Hall of Famers Marcel Cerdan and LaMotta in succession. But these two losses came after he had been a professional fighter for many years and time had caught up to him. He would lose 11 of his remaining 22 fights, as his magnificent reflexes waned. Still, he fought top notch opposition right up to the end in 1948, and some of those defeats were controversial as well. His final record was an amazing 146-30-11. And get this; he was stopped only three times—once on cuts! He fought many times in New Orleans and Chicago, but he was the essence of a road warrior and toiled at his trade in just about every big city in the country.

The legendary trainer, Eddie Futch, has often cited Holman Williams and Charley Burley as the two greatest fighters he ever had the privilege to see and was quoted as saying that he would rather watch Williams shadow box than watch most other fighters in action. (Harry Otty, "Why Holman Williams Belong in the Hall-of-Fame." Wail The CBZ JOURNAL, July 2006).

Williams rated Archie Moore the best he ever fought. As for the hardest puncher, that was Bob Satterfield. He, of course, had high praise for the Cocoa Kid and Charlie Burley as well.

Avoided by many of the higher ranked white fighters (and historically neglected by all except aficionados), this great technical boxing wizard fought the best welterweights, middleweights and light-heavyweights of his time. Inducting him into the International Boxing Hall of Fame in 2008, albeit posthumously, was manifestly the right thing to do.

Tragically, he died in a fire in Akron, Ohio in 1967 at age 52.

However, many others have failed to get their historic due. Yes, the quartet of great black fighters, Williams, Burley, Lytell and The Cocoa Kid, have been the subject of many articles, but others like Jose Basora, Kid Tunero, Joe Carter, Eddie Booker, Jack Chase, Wes Farrell and Aaron Wade have remained on the fringe of appropriate attention. They had to fight often against consistently rugged opposition, often engaging in many bouts against each other.

As boxing writer and historian Angelo Prospero says, "They were shunned by champions and top contenders as being "too good for their own good." Rarely did they fight in the prestigious arenas of the country.""[1]

But for Holman Williams, justice has now been served.

[1] Angelo Prospero, "Around the Boxing Scene- Holman Williams." Feb-2008. Boxing World.

7

TOUGH GUYS FIGHT TOUGH GUYS

Boxing is a tight-knit fraternity. Everybody knows everybody. But a line in the resin will forever be drawn separating those who step into the square ring and those who DON'T. Many, many people make money on a fight, but when the bell sounds, only two people answer it
–Randy Smith, February 2003, Journal Inquirer Newspaper - Manchester, CT

They are men's men. Rocky Marciano was one of them. Oscar Bonavena and Jerry Quarry and George Chuvalo and Gene Fullmer and Carmen Basilio, to name a few...
–Norman Mailer

A guy beating on your head for 10 rounds... I'm lucky to be alive.
–Art Aragon

It's a tough business, man - it's a tough business
–Rocky Graziano

The proof is in the pudding when I get in the ring
–Carl "The Cat" Thompson

Larry Holmes and Evander Holyfield each fought incredibly tough opposition in their time. Maybe Ali fought the toughest. Inexplicitly, Holyfield is still doing it. Ralph Dupas had 135 fights and many were against top level fighters. The same with Willie Pastrano whose opponents have an astounding combined won-loss record. There were (or are) others who would fight just about anyone put in front of them, guys like Beau Jack, Aldo Minelli, Chico Vejar, Holly Mims, Yama Bahama, Kenny Lane, Tony Licata, Vito Antuofermo, Tommy Tibbs (who participated in 139 bouts), and Johnny Cesario. And still more like Guts Ishimatsu, Frank Minton, Jorge Paez (who may be mounting a comeback), James Martinez, Ray Oliveira, Julio Cesar Gonzalez, and Ben Tackie. Oh yes, Dick Tiger was pretty solid as well. He met Champions Emile Griffith, Nino Benvenuti, Jose Torres, Bob Foster, Joey Giardello, Gene Fullmer and Terry Downes. He also fought some impressive contenders like Andy Kendall, Frankie De-Paula, Roger Rouse, Jose Gonzalez, Rubin Carter, Joey Archer, Don Fullmer, Florentino Fernandez, Spider Webb, Henry Hank, Gene Armstrong, Yolande Pompey, Randy Sandy, Holly Mims, Wilf Greaves and Rory Calhoun.

Still, if forced to pick one boxer who fought the very highest level of competition, it would be The Cincinnati Cobra, Ezzard Charles. Here are some others.

Richard Hall: Tough as Teak (1993-present)

I went down to the crossroads, fell down on my knees.
Asked the Lord above for mercy, Save me if you please.
–Robert Johnson

On April 30, 1998, Richard "The Destroyer" Hall stopped South African Gary Ballard in Fort Lauderdale, Florida sending the tough Ballard into retirement. No bid deal except it marked an amazing string of tough fights that Hall would embark on over the next seven years proving, in the proud tradition of Jamaican fighters, that he is tough as teak. The southpaw knockout artist then stopped Anthony Bigeni (for the WBA light heavyweight Interim Title) and Fabian Garcia before stepping in with Roy Jones Junior, 41-1, and being too brave for his own good. The four-time world champion had too much for the game but outclassed Kingston native, as referee Wayne Kelly mercifully ended matters in the eleventh.

The Destroyer then traveled to Germany and fought back-to-back fights against undefeated Dariusz Michalczewski both of which were stopped in the Tiger's favor but both of which were extremely competitive. In fact, The Destroyer had Michalczewski hurt and reeling in both fights.

Hall proceeded to Cape Cod and destroyed none other than "MR. KO," Julian Letterlough, in a two round shoot-out in which both men were down in a raucous round one. The fight lasted three-minutes and forty-seven-seconds but there was enough action for a ten-round affair. He followed this with a win over rugged Rodney Moore in Washington. D.C., but his next foe, Rico Hoye, 16-0 coming in, proved too much for him as he lost in four rounds in Las Vegas.

After a layoff, The Kingston native came back to meet another native born Jamaican, the "Road Warrior," Glen Johnson, at the Seminole Hard Rock Hotel and Casino in Florida. Hall entered the ring to Jr. Gong Marley's "Welcome to Jamrock." The fight was for the Vacant IBA Light Heavyweight Title and both fighters gave 100% in a fiercely fought and exciting war. When the dust settled, Johnson was the new International Boxing Association champion, but his opponent had earned considerable respect and a standing ovation for a gusty showing.

But Hall's career seems to be going south as he recently lost an eight round UD to upstart Shaun George and the prospect of either retiring at 27-7 with 25 KO's or morphing into a gate keeper is now on the table.

If he retires, his legacy will be of having fought the best light heavyweights of his generation (Jones, Michalczewski and Johnson) and of having knocked out almost everyone he's beaten. Should he fight on, his opponents should be wary, for no matter what The Destroyer decides, he will be one very dangerous and tough guy.

PostScript: Richard Hall stopped Bryan Mitchell in four rounds on November 21 in Miami. Mitchell, a two-time super-middleweight world champion who has been inactive since June 2003, survived Hall's early attack but succumbed in the fourth. At 28 (KO 26) - 7 (KO 5) and with a chill factor of 89%, Hall's new nickname could be "Mr. Excitement."

Freddy "Italo" Cruz (1986-2007)

He hails from the Dominican Republic, is 45 years old and is still fighting with a record of 53-37-10 in 100 fights. He fights tough opposition and has won only one in his last 15, so the end is near.

Cruz started out slowly in 1986 going 1-4-1 in his first six outings and losing to Thierry Jacob, 12-0, in the process. Then he settled down and put together a 38 fight undefeated string with all of his fights coming in Italy. The string was broken in a MD loss to the very capable Wilfredo Vazquez in 1992 in a fight for the WBA super bantamweight title. He then won seven straight all but one being held in Santo Domingo, Dominican Republic, but he lost a UD to Steve Robinson in Cardiff, Wales in a bid for the WBO featherweight title. He then fought in France, Austria and lost to undefeated and future champion Prince Naseem Hamed by TKO in Yorkshire, England.

After a six fight undefeated streak, he lost in London to the great Alfred Kotey in a fight for the WBC International super bantamweight title.

After the Kotey fight, he hit bad times, losing 18 out of 20. Some of his conquerors were Victoriano Sosa, 16-1-1, Jose Miguel Cotto (brother of Miguel Cotto), 14-0 at the time, Rocky Martinez, 35-5-1, and Derrick "Smoke" Gainer, 28-4. Other later defeats would come against Gary Balleto, 19-0 coming in, Regilio Tuur, 43-3-1, Luis Villalta, 26-1-1, Lamont Pearson, 17-1-1, and Saul Duran, 33-8-2.

Freddy Cruz really had two careers. Going into his fight with Steve Robinson in Cardiff on June 4, 1994, he was a fine 43-5-5. Going into his most recent fight against Bahamian Meacher Major on August 10, 2007, he was 53-36-10. More to the point, this tough guy went 10-31-5 in his second career. It's just that something happened after the Robinson fight.

Freddy's venues

Bahamas

Florida (5 times)

Dominican Republic (17)

Washington, D.C.

Massachusetts (3)

Illinois (2)

Connecticut

France (6)

New York

Biloxi, Miss

California (3)

Guadeloupe

Germany

Hartford, CT

The UK (3)

Austria (5)

Italy (46 times)

Freddy Cruz was a willing and rugged guy who would fight in any venue.

Eric Holland (1986-2003)

Holland was a rugged super middleweight who fought fifteen fighters with an "0" in their loss column. His final record of 22-33-3 is a misleading one.

In his very first Professional fight, he was pitted against none other than Chris Eubank, 3-0 at the time. Chris would finish at 45-5-2 and achieve legendary status in the UK. That same year, Eric did battle against Darryl Lattimore in Atlantic City, and in i989, he won an MD from Mike Bonislawski.

In 1990, he lost by TKO to Joe Gatti, Arturo's brother, and then to William Bo James, but beat former world IBF light middleweight title holder, Buster Drayton. Holland was 6-12-2 at the time while Buster was 35-13-1 coming in. He then fought undefeated and future NABF welterweight title holder Derrell Coley. He beat undefeated William Jones, 19-0 that same year but lost to Julio Cesar Green and Ronald Winky Wright, 18-0 coming in (in Nordrhein-Westfalen, Germany).He bounced back by ending Scott Smith's undefeated streak at 23 and then put together seven straight wins against tough opposition. One came against "The Outlaw" Jesse James Hughes at the Blue Horizon and was a closet classic featuring savage give-and-take jackhammmer shots throughout. Holland won the battle, but The Outlaw won the war, for Erick's career began to go south thereafter while The Outlaw's soared.

Still, he was able to upset former contender Lupe Aquino in 1997 in Hollywood, California. Later, however, he would lose to former world champion Bronco McKart who was 32-2 while Holland was 20-18-3. He then lost to Kirino Garcia in Chihuahua, Mexico and rugged Merqui Sosa in Las Vegas. Garcia's career is worthy of a separate story as he lost his first 18 and then went on a tear.

Erik then lost to undefeated Cuban Julio Garcia in Rochester, Washington, and to Paul Samuels in Wales for the IBF Inter-Continental light middleweight title. The loss to Samuels was by stoppage, the second of only two Hollnad would suffer in his career.

In 1999, he lost to Lonnie Bradley, 27-0-1, in Washington, D.C. and then to 23-2 Rodney Jones in New Mexico. In fact, Holland lost 11 of his last 12 fights, as he was never the same after his war with Hughes. But the high quality level of his opposition, his durability, and his willingness to fight anywhere in the world qualifies him as a true tough guy who fought other tough guys. And after all, he was born in Philadelphia.

Saoul Mamby (1969-2000-2008)

He was 43 the last time he won a title and 60 at the time
of his last fight.
—Anonymous

A streaking Derrell Coley, 19-0-1, stopped him at age 46 in 1993. He was 42-30-6 at the time and would finish with 84 fights and a record of 45-33-6. This was the only stoppage he ever suffered. Oh yes, it came at age 46. He then won three of his last five fights, his final coming at age 53 against 40 year old Kent Hardee in 2000.

"Sweet" Saoul, a black Jew from Brooklyn, was a savvy and slick fighter with a granite chin and presented a difficult style for his opponents from Lightweight to Welterweight for well over 20 years. After a tour of duty in Vietnam (he served as a grunt and did not participate in any boxing exhibitions), his first pro fight was a loss against Jose Peterson in New York on March 31, 1971. Just nine months later, he fought to a draw with rugged and undefeated Edwin Viruet at the Felt Forum in New York.

In 1977, he lost by a highly controversial SD to Saensak Muangsurin in Korat, Thailand for the WBC light welterweight title. Previously, he had battled to a draw with Harold Weston, lost to Roberto Duran in Miami, and then to the great Antonio Cervantes in Venezuela. After successful fights in Paris and Curacao, he returned to the Garden and beat tough Norman Goins in 1979. His 12-fight win streak included wins over Maurice "Termite" Watkins and Esteban De Jesus, and then against Sang Hyun Kim in Seoul, South Korea for the WBC Light Welterweight crown which he defended successfully in Las Vegas, Detroit, Indonesia and Nigeria. The native New Yorker, Saul, was a road warrior if ever there was one fighting in exotic places throughout the globe. The win over Sang Hyun Kim was particularly gratifying since Kim had previously beaten Muangsurin to whom Mamby had lost in Thailand.

He would lose the crown to LeRoy Haley, 45-2-2, on June 26, 1982 at the Front Row Theatre in Highland Heights, Ohio. Four months later, he beat the crafty and "old school" Monroe Brooks, 48-6-4, in Cleveland, Ohio, but he lost his rematch with Haley and then dropped a UD to Ronnie Shields.

On August 23, 1990, at age 43, he beat undefeated Larry Barnes for the New York State Welterweight Title. But after this moment of glory, he lost 8 straight including dukes with Charlie "White Lightning" Brown, Pat Coleman, and after Javier Castillejo. After his first career stoppage loss to Coley in Largo, Maryland, he then beat one Innocent Mushonga in Zambia, limited George Kellman in Florida and equally limited Darren McGrew in Ocala, Florida. His "last" fight was against the aforementioned Kent Hardee, 20-6-1, in Greensboro, North Carolina.

Not only did Sweet Saul fight just about anyone who was anyone, he usually fought them on their home turf. He did battle in France, Guyana, Canada, Spain, and Zambia. As well, he toiled in Nigeria, Jamaica, Mexico, Indonesia, South Korea, Curacao (Netherlands Antilles), Thailand, Dominican Republic, Venezuela, and Puerto Rico. He also fought in fourteen different states. Since all but one of his 33 losses came by way of decision, God only knows how many were "home cooking."

While the highpoint of his long career was winning a world championship, certainly his stoppage over Roberto Duran conqueror and former WBC lightweight champ, Esteban De Jesus, in July 1980 (on the Holmes-LeDoux under card) has to rank pretty high).

Saul Mamby was a veteran who successfully competed at the highest level, won a world championship, and was a road warrior extraordinaire. He was another very memorable boxer.

Note: Mamby fought again (and lost a UD) on March 8, 2008 in the Cayman Islands. He was 60 years old at the time.

Juan Laporte (1977-1999)

How about Juan Laporte, the World Boxing Council Featherweight Champion from September 15, 1982 – March 31 1984? Laporte, who was born in Guyama, Puerto Rico and raised in New York City, fought the very best during his fine career.

His first noteworthy win was a KO over Jean Lapointe in New York. He then met the great world Featherweight champion (and Boxing Hall of Fame member) Salvador Sanchez and gave "Chava" all he could handle before losing a 15 round unanimous decision, but he gained new respect for his effort..

Laporte then fought future world champion Rocky Lockridge in 1981 at Las Vegas, scoring a second round knockout to become the United States Featherweight champion. Given a second title shot, Laporte met another future member of the Hall, the legendary World featherweight champion Eusebio Pedroza in 1982. He lost a close and controversial split decision. Laporte was given a rematch against Sanchez for the World Boxing Council's world title, but fate would prevent this from happening as "Chava"was fatally injured while driving his Porsche.

Laporte then met Colombian Mario Miranda for the vacant world title in a fight held at Madison Square Garden. Laporte decked the Columbian in the eighth round and forced him to quit on his stool before the start of the 11th. Finally, he had become a world champion.

Laporte defended his title twice against tough Ruben Castillo and Johnny De La Rosa, but then lost it to another Puerto Rican world champion, the legendary Wilfredo "Bazooka" Gomez. A glutton for fighting the very best, he went to Ireland, in 1985 where he lost a ten round decision to future world champion Barry McGuigan. Both Gomez and McGuigan are now in the International Boxing Hall of Fame.

In 1986, Laporte fought future Hall of Famer Julio César Chávez at Madison Square Garden, and gave Chavez almost more than he could handle. In fact, many thought he had won the 12 round decision, but he lost a majority decision in a bid for Chavez's WBC Junior Lightweight title.

Tragically, in 1989, his son died in an accident, and Juan was never really the same.

Still, he fought at the top level against Nicky "Nico" Perez, John John Molina, Azumah Nelson (another future Hall member), Charles

"The Natural" Murray and Zack Padilla. After retiring in 1984, he came back four years later and lost a razor thin SD decision to top contender Teddy "Two Gun" Reid. Then in 1999, he lost another disputed decision, this time against former World Junior Welterweight champion Billy Costello, and finally retired from boxing.

He finished with a fine 40 -17 record and currently works with the New York City athletic department. More importantly, Juan Laporte, a man who defied all odds to become world champion, remains a beloved figure among his peers and fans. He is a credit to the sport of boxing

Doug Dewitt (1980-1992)

His best asset was his fighting spirit. It made him a champion.
–Jim Amato

Doug "Cobra" DeWitt (born Douglas Anthony Italiano) turned professional in 1980 and won his first eight fights before dropping a decision to tough Ben Serrano. He bounced back with three wins including a kayo over Danny McAloon, 29-14 coming in.. He would later fight to a draw with Tony Suero and then lose again to Serrano.

Doug was also beating good fighters like Teddy Mann, 27-10, Mike Tinley, 14-1-1 and Bobby Hoye, 18-4-2. A 1984 first round knockout over Jimmy Sykes led to a match with "Dangerous" Don Lee who had recently stopped highly regarded Tony Sibson. Doug and Don battled to a draw.

Later in 1985, Doug would lose a UD to the vastly underrated Robbie Sims, half brother of Marvin Hagler.

In 1986, Doug beat Charles Boston, but lost decisions to two of the best middleweight punchers in the game, Milt McCrory and Thomas "Hitman" Hearns. Somehow, Dewitt, blessed with a granite chin, suffered a 1987 KO loss to Jose Quinones, but bounced back to beat Tony LaPaglia and then win the USBA middleweight title by edging always tough Tony "The Fighting Postman" Thornton.

After drawing with 13-2 Ronnie Essett in 1988, Dewitt fought the very talented WBA middleweight titleholder Sumbu Kalambay in Monte Carlo. Kalambay held wins over Herol Graham, Mike McCallum, Iran Barkley and Robbie Sims. In a great outing, Kalambay TKOd the "Cobra" in the seventh stanza.

Then, in a 1989 rematch with Robbie Sims for the WBO version of the middleweight title, Doug Dewitt won a well deserved twelve round decision and was crowned the champion. He successfully defended against former IBF junior middleweight champ Matthew Hilton by stopping the hard punching Canadian in the in the eleventh.

In 1990, Doug engaged Bomber Nigel Benn in a savage give and take war that finally ended in the eighth with Dewitt on the losing end— and no longer a world champion.

After taking almost two years off, he returned in 1992 and fought to a draw with Tyrone Frazier, 19-4-3, after which he beat Dan Sherry, 18-3. In his last fight, he was stopped in the sixth round by James Toney ending his distinguished career.

DeWitt finished with a 33-8-5 record and met six other men who were world champions.

Alvaro "Yaqui" López (1972-1984)

We have a good fight for the fans…not like the fights now…they fight for millions, and it's over in a minute and a half
—Lopez

"Yaqui" or "Indian" as he was sometimes called was tough as nails. He was born in Zacatecas, Mexico under a bull ring, but later his family immigrated to Stockton, which is located in California's Central Valley, when he was a youngster. He finished with a fine record of 63-15 (40 KOs), and was inducted into the California Boxing Hall of Fame in Los Angeles on November 9, 2005.

Yaqui, arguably the greatest light heavy never to become world champion, lost five title fights but won the respect of his opponents and fans throughout the world. He was a champion without a belt and nobody had a greater heart than this talented warrior. Campaigning from 1972-84, he went up against a veritable who's who of champions and contenders.

He battled for the Light Heavyweight Title four times and the Cruiserweight Title once. Many observers felt he should have gotten the nod over John Conteh and Victor Galindez (twice). All three fights went to a full 15 round decision the results of which easily could have gone his way. Each fight was held in Europe.

Lopez was never in a bad fight, but none was better than his rematch with Saad Muhammad in 1980. That battle was one of legendary proportions, and is still considered one of the greatest title fights of all time. In fact, Boxing Illustrated ranked Saad Muhammad-Lopez II sixth on a list of the 35 greatest prize fights between 1960 and 1995. The fight was the 1980 Ring Magazine "Fight of the Year" and the eighth round was its "Round of the Year."

Yaqui controlled the first half. Then, in the eighth, he trapped Muhammad in a corner and landed 20 consecutive brutal shots to the Champions head and body. Somehow, Saad survived the onslaught and survived the round. The crowd was in total disbelief. Even referee Waldemar Schmidt seemed in awe. Finally, in the fourteenth stanza, Lopez grew arm weary and simply ran out of gas. The champion jumped on him with a savage attack and that was that. Together, they had made ring history and those who witnessed it still talk about it with reverence.

Sometimes a fighter's record speaks for itself, and that's precisely why Yaqui's is set forth below:

1972

Apr 24 Herman Hampton	Stockton, CA	W 6
Jun 6 Herman Hampton	Carson City, NV	KO 3
Jun 16 Cisco Solorio	Stockton	KO 6
Jul 1 Jesse Burnett	Stockton	L 8
Oct 24 Henry Tavako	San Carlos, CA	W 6
Nov 6 Mark Hearn	Eugene, OR	KO 6
Nov 29 Herman Hampton	Stockton	KO 7
Dec 11 Van Sahib	Eugene, OR	KO 2

1973

| Feb 8 Polo Ramirez | Stockton | KO 7 |
| Mar 15 Al Bolden | Seattle | L 10 |

Apr 21 Hildo Silva	Santa Ros	W 10
Jun 9 Ron Wilson	Santa Rosa	W 10
Jul 6 Dave Rogers	Gardnerville	KO 5
Aug 3 Ron Wilson	Reno	KO 6
Aug 22 Herman Hampton	acoma, WA	KO 6
Sep 20 Budda Brooks	Stockton	KO 5
Nov 1 Alfonso Gonzalez	Portland, OR	KO 2
Dec 6 Al Bolden	Portland, OR	W 10

1974

Feb 14 Andy Kendall	Portland, OR	KO 5
Mar 7 Willie Warren	Reno	W 10
May 10 Hildo Silva	Stockton	W 12
Jul 7 Joe Cokes	Gardnerville	W 12
Oct 11 Bobby Rascon	Portland, OR	KO 6
Nov 13 Hildo Silva	Stockton	W 10

1975

Mar 4 Terry Lee	Sacramento, CA	KO 9
Apr 8 Lee Mitchell	Sacramento	KO 6
May 14 Mike Quarry	Stockton	W 10
Jul 3 Gary Summerhays	Gardnerville, CA	W 10
Jul 31 Jesse Burnett	Stockton	L 12
Sep 24 Jesse Burnett	Stockton	W 12

1976

Feb 12 Terry Lee	Portland, OR	W 10
May 3 David Smith	Stockton	W 10
Jun 30 Karl Zurheide	Stockton	KO 6
Jul 17 Larry Castaneda	Stockton	KO 9
Oct 9 John Conteh	Copenhagen	L 15
(For WBC Light Heavyweight Title)		
Nov 18 Clarence Geigger	Stateline, NV	TKO 5

1977

Feb 18 Danny Brewer	Stateline	TKO 6
Mar 7 Larry Castaneda	Stockton	KO 8
Apr 5 Ron White	Incline, CA	KO 8
Apr 22 Lonnie Bennett	Indianapolis	TKO by 3
Jun 17 Bobby Lloyd	Miami Beach	KO 5
Jul 20 Manuel Fierro	Stockton	KO 3
Jul 27 Benny Barra	Las Vegas	KO 5
Sep 17 Victor	Galindez Rome	L 15
(For WBA Light Heavyweight Title)		
Oct 27 Chuck Warfield	Stockton	KO 4
Dec 15 Clarence Geigger	Stockton	KO 4

1978

Jan 12 Fabian Falconette Los	Angeles	KO 2
Mar 2 Mike Rossman	New York	TKO 6

Mar 17 Ned Hallacy	Las Vegas	W 10
May 6 Victor Galindez via	Reggio, Italy	L 15
(For WBA Light Heavyweight Title)		
Jul 2 Jesse Burnett	Stockton	W 15
(Wins US Light Heavyweight Title)		
Oct 24 Matthew Franklin	Philadelphia	TKO by 11
(For NABF Light Heavyweight Title)		

1979

Jan 18 Wilfred Albers	Stockton	KO 3
Feb 27 Ivy Brown	Sacramento, CA	KO 3
Sep 12 Ernie Barr	Stockton	KO 4
Oct 4 Bash Ali	San Carlos, CA	W 10
Dec 1 James Scott Rahway	State Prison	L 10

1980

Apr 16 Pete McIntyre	Fresno, CA	KO 8
May 20 Bobby	Lloyd Fresno	KO 8
Jul 13 Matthew Franklin	McAfee, NJ	TKO by 14
(For WBC Light Heavyweight Title)		
Oct 18 Michael Spinks	Atlantic City	TKO by 7
Nov 29 Carl Ivy	Lake Tahoe, NV	KO 3

1981

Feb 14 Grover Robinson	Lake Tahoe	KO 4
May 18 George O'Mara	San Carlos	TKO 10

May 27 Willie Taylor	Stockton	KO 7
Jul 24 S.T. Gordon	Reno	TKO by 7

(For NABF Light Heavyweight Title)

Nov 21 Tony Mundine	Brisbane, Australia	TKO 3

1982

Jan 14 Johnny Davis	Atlantic City	L 10
May 5 Alvin Dominey	Stockton	TKO 6
Jun 1 "King David" Smith	Sacramento	W 12
Jul 31 Ken Arlt Lake	Tahoe	W 10
Sep 9 Roger Braxton	Stateline	W 10
Nov 27 James Williams	Lake Tahoe	W 10

1983

Feb 19 Mike Jameson	Incline, CA	W 10
May 7 Eddie Gonzalez	Stateline	W 10
Sep 21 Carlos DeLeon	San Jose, CA	TKO by 4

(For WBC Cruiserweight Title)

1984

Sep 12 Bash Ali	Stockton	L 12

Alvaro "Yaqui" López is a humble, kind and thoughtful person, but in the ring, he defined what the word warrior was all about. Along with Jerry Quarry, George Chuvalo, Earnie Shavers, South African Pierre Fourie, Argentinean Jorge Ahumada, Bad Bennie Briscoe, Armando "Mando" Muniz and Canadian Clyde Gray, he was an "almost champion," but with aficionados and other fighters, he will always remain a champion warrior

Scott LeDoux (1974-1983)

If I'm gonna fight in the alley, I want LeDoux with me.
–Pat Summerall.

Scott LeDoux was a rough, tough, 6'2", 220 lb road warrior out of Minnesota who fought the very best during the golden age of heavyweights in the 70s. Big boppers like Frazier, Ali, Quarry, Norton, Foreman, Shavers, Chuvalo, Terrell, Mike Weaver, Jeff Merritt, Mac Foster, Joe Bugner, Leroy Jones, Jimmy Young, and Jimmy Ellis, among many others, roamed the landscape.

Known as the 'Fighting Frenchman," he toiled at his trade from 1974 to 1983. During the earlier part of his career, he met Roy "Cookie" Wallace, Rodney Bobick, Terry Daniels, George "Scrap Iron" Johnson, Ron "The Butcher" Stander and Larry Middleton. Aside from a cut eye stoppage to Cookie Wallace in 1975, Scott ran his record to a fine 18-1-1 going into a bout against rugged Duane Bobick, 34-0 coming in.

The fight between these two Minnesota born fighters was held at the Metropolitan Sports Center, Bloomington, MN on April 22, 1976. The attendance was a record 13,789. LeDoux lost a UD and then went on to lose to tough John "Dino" Dennis, 27-0-1, at the time, and Big George Foreman, 42-1 coming in.

After "losing" to Johnny Boudreaux, 19-1-1, in a horrendous decision that prompted a grand jury investigation and rivaled Toney-Tiberi in its unfairness, he stepped up to a higher level of opposition. He beat Pedro Soto and Tom Prater before losing a rematch to Duane Bobick, 38-1. Then, after consecutive draws with Leon Spinks and Bill Sharkey, LeDoux ran off four KOs including a stoppage of tough "Big Jim" Beattie, 41-7.

Amazingly, LeDoux stepped up to an even higher level of competition meeting Ron Lyle, Ken Norton, Mike Weaver, undefeated bomber Marty Monroe, and then Larry Holmes, 34-0, in 1980 for the WBC Heavyweight Title. After his stoppage loss to Holmes, he would go on to fight Greg Page, Gerrie Coetzee, Gordon Racette, Ken Arlt, and closed out his career in 1983 with a TKO loss to Frank Bruno in London.

His final slate was 33-13-4, but more significantly, he fought seven opponents who were heavyweight champion of the world at some point in their career. He also fought top contenders on their home turf. He fought tough guys because he was a tough guy during an era of tough heavyweights.

If Minnesota has a Boxing Hall of Fame, I am sure Scott is in it. More importantly, he has been a credit to the sport.

"I beat Rodney [Bobick] in a 10 rounder. I also beat him once as an amateur. Then I beat him as a pro. Then I lost to Duane [Bobick], and there was a period there when I had three losses in a row and every-body was bad mouthing me saying I couldn't fight. I said wait a minute – these guys got a combined record of like 104-1 and the only loss was Foreman's to Ali. It's not like I'm in bad company here." [Scott was referring to his losses to Duane Bobick, Dino Dennis, and George Foreman.] THE CYBER BOXING ZONE JOURNAL, April 2000.

Jose Monon Gonzalez (1959-1974)

I'm not intimidated by any man.
–Jose Monon Gonzalez

Jose Monon Gonzalez fought virtually every tough guy available as he grew through each weight class beating some and losing to fewer. His final record was 42-21-2, but that hardly tells the story of the man who may well have faced the toughest opponents of any boxer I can remember.

Here are some of the fighters with whom he did battle:

Jorge Ahumada

Joey Archer (twice)

Yama Bahama

Tom Bogs

Bennie Briscoe (twice)

Rubin Hurricane Carter

Bobby Cassidy

Joe DeNucci

Billy Douglas

Ferd Hernandez (twice)

Florentino Fernandez (twice)

Don Fullmer

Victor Galindez Hall of Fame member

Emile Griffith Hall of Fame member

Eugene Cyclone Hart

Richie Kates

Isaac Logart

Willie Monroe

Eddie Owens

Juan Carlos Rivero

Luis Manuel Rodriguez (thrice) Hall of Fame member

Vincente Rondon

Dick Tiger Hall of Fame member

Jose Torres Hall of Fame member

Chico Vejar

Ted Wright

Five were inducted into the International Boxing Hall of Fame. Florentino Fernandez could hit like an ox and that was his nickname. Joey Archer was a crafty spoiler who knew his way around a boxing ring like a lawyer knows the courtroom. Tom Boggs, the great Danish fighter, finished with a record of 77-8-1-1. Chico Vejar fought 116 times against extremely stiff competition and won 92.

Jorge Ahumada was from Argentina and handled by Gil Clancy. He met Bob Foster for the title in 1974 and they battled to a disputed draw. He then met John Conteh for the vacated WBC title, and lost a fifteen round decision. He then fought fellow Argentinean Victor Galindez for the WBA version of the crown and was outpointed over fifteen.

Bennie Briscoe may have been the best middleweight never to win the title. He finally received a long overdue shot at Carlos Monzon and almost pulled out the upset when he hurt Monzon in the ninth round. Carlos rallied to win the decision.

Many of the aforementioned fighters surely would have won a "title" under today's sanctioning bodies, rules and regulations. They were top class fighters.

Monon turned pro in 1959 at the age of 19, starting out as a welterweight and fought 27 bouts through 1961, beating tough Ted Wright in a 10-round decision (a nonstop, slam-bang affair in which Jose got the decision on October 17, 1960 in New York), Issac Logart in 10, and iced Victor Zalazar. Then at 16-3-1 coming in, he lost a razor thin 10 round decision to popular Chico Vejar, 90-20-4. He beat Charley Scott in 10, and became the first to beat the clever Joey Archer. (Jose is still bitter about the rematch with Archer in which he dropped a 10-round decision). Jose had lost a shocker in 1961 to Luis "Feo" Rodriguez in Miami but went on to beat "Feo" in 1970 by decision. He beat Don Fullmer for the WBA American middleweight title in 12 in March 1966, and went on to defend that title against tough Ferd Hernandez in 12 rounds four months later. He knocked out future light-heavyweight champion Vicente Rondon in eight rounds in April 1968

Beating Florentine " The Ox" Fernandez twice (everyone thought he would knock Monon out), beating southpaw Bobby Cassidy via an eighth-round TKO in New York in May 1972, and losing close 10-round decisions to the great Jose Torres and Emile Griffith have to be career highlights for this fierce warrior.

About Griffith, he says "We knew each other's styles so well from boxing together in the gym, so it wasn't the most exciting fight, but it was close." [1]

Former referee, author, and friend of Monon, Ron Lipton, describes him as follows:

"Never was there a more striking total appearance that God had blessed a fighter with than what was given to this young man. His face was a ruggedly handsome mask of controlled ferocity with high prominent cheekbones; his taunt skin the color of coffee, rippled with muscle like a big hunting cat as he warmed up in the ring. His thighs and calves, front and back, were developed into the shape and hardness of diamonds. But his eyes, even when not focused on an opponent, burned like two obsidian stones set into his skull.

"His shoulders were packed with the thick, gnarled rope of usable fighter's muscle that belongs only to a seasoned professional, but the most amazing things were his forearms and his neck. Never was a bodybuilder of any weight blessed with the shape, thickness, and vascularity of this man's forearms and neck. This was not a slow, lumbering, pumped up bodybuilder who had ventured into the world of boxing, but a skilled professional prize fighter I had seen destroy the great fighters in his division in one fearless swap session after another." [2]

He closed out his career by losing to four typically tough opponents in Victor Galindez (at the Estadio Luna Park in Buenos Aires in June 1974), Richie Kates, Jorge Victor Ahumada, and Willie Monroe. His last win came in April 1973 when he TKO'd Eugene Cyclone Hart in Hart's home turf of Philadelphia.

Monon was not just another fighter; he was cut in the same cloth as other great Puerto Rican warriors, ones like Jose Torres, Edwin "Chapo" Rosario, Wilfred "Bazooka" Gomez, Wilfred Benitez, Tito Trinidad, Miguel Cotto and many others.

Joey Giardello (1948-1967)

He turned pro in 1948 and fought primarily in Philadelphia where he built his reputation. In 1951 he entered the world rankings with a 10-round decision win over contender Ernie "The Rock" Durando. Except for 1955, Giardello would fight and beat at least one ranked contender every year until 1966.

He went to war with Hall Of Famers like Sugar Ray Robinson, Gene Fullmer, Dick Tiger and Billy Graham. Joey defeated such men as the great "Sugar" Ray Robinson, Dick Tiger, Billy Graham, Harold Green, Joey Giambra, Peter Mueller, Ruben "Hurricane" Carter, Harold Green, Gil Turner and Pierre Langlois. Also among his victims were Henry Hank, Holly Mims, Randy Sandy, Walter Cartier, Garth Panter, Rory Calhoun, Rocky Castellani, Bobby Dykes, Georgie Small, Chico Vejar, Del Flanagan, and Ralph "Tiger" Jones. He also fought the aforementioned Johnny Saxton, George Benton, Spider Webb, Ralph Dupas, Wilfred Greaves, Joe DeNucci and beat undefeated Jack Rodgers in his final fight in 1967. He fought many of these rugged opponents more than once and in some cases three and four times.

He retired with a record of 100-25-7 and a reputation as a fighter that never ducked anyone in his long career. Indeed, if one added up the won-lost records of his opponents, the result would be astounding and perhaps without peer.

He was inducted into the International Boxing Hall of Fame in 1993 and had a record of 5-3-1 against fellow Hall-of-Famers including a 2-2 mark against Dick Tiger.

Joey Giardello may well have been the "toughest of the tough."

Randy Sandy: The Best 500 Hitter Ever (1951-1963)

Freddie "Babe" Herman came close at 48-46-8, and so did rugged Ray Charley Cato, 32-36-7, Tony Masciarelli, 49-47-6, Charley Scott, 34-32, and Ed Pollard, 23-24. Etienne Whitaker is at 32-29-2, but has lost 15 in a row and needs to reconsider his career options. Derrick Whitley is at 24-25-3.

Ray Perz hit it at 26-26-7 as did Bill McMurray, 24-24-3, the limited Tom Tarantino at 24-24-3 and Tim "The Evangelist" Shocks, 26-26-4. Jerome Artis tallied a 27-27-4 slate but lost 17 of his last 18. The following are guys who evened things out against particularly high level opposition:

There was one guy back in the 50's that was tough as nails. He was a clever former national amateur champion by the name of Randy Sandy. The quintessential, 1950's fighter, He finished with a final record of 24-24 -2 which is nothing special—that is, unless you take a look at the opposition. In just his third fight, he beat Bobby Rosado, 43-12-2 at the time, at the St. Nicholas Arena. Two fights later, he beat Henry Jordan, 42-56-12 coming in, at Madison Square Garden. Amazingly, Jordan was the only fighter Sandy ever did battle with who had a losing record and Jordan had won 42 fights coming in.

But it gets even better. In July 1953, Randy met and beat the formidable Lee Sala, 76-5, at the Eastern Parkway Arena in Brooklyn. He suffered two KO losses to red-hot Willie Troy, but drew with Ernie "The Rock" Durando before losing a decision to Walter Cartier and being stopped by the undefeated Rory Calhoun, After icing Bobby Roaado, he dropped a razor thin SD to the great Joey Giradello, 70-13-5, at the Chicago Stadium in 1957. Losses to undefeated Spider

Webb, tough Franz Szuzina and a SD defeat to Rory Calhoun followed.

Sandy was far ahead on points, when he was disqualified for low blows against Hans-Werner Wohlers in 1959 in a fight that tellingly took place at the Arena Westfalenhalle in Dortmund, Germany. A month later, Sandy beat the great Dick Tiger in the UK but lost the rematch. He then lost by decision to Peter Mueller, 103-16-13, in Cologne, Germany. After losing to rugged Jimmy Beechaam, he turned around and gave the great Emile Griffith his first loss in a bout held at the Academy of Music in New York City. He then lost two decisions to the great Jose Torres and one to Henry Hank. In 1963, he lost a points battle to the great and undefeated Laszlo Papp and was then stopped in one by another great, Cuban bomber Florentino Fernandez. Randy Sandy's last fight was against a road warrior by the ironic name of Jack Johnson, 5-1 at the time. This fight took place in Curacao, Netherlands Antilles and marked the end of Randy Sandy's remarkable career.

In summary, he beat Griffith and Tiger and fought Torres, Papp and Giardello. All five are Hall of Fame members. He beat Lee Sala. He only fought one guy with a losing record. He was something else.

Ted Lowry (alias Tiger Lowry)

To be fair, there was another pretty good 500 hitter who fought between 1939 and 1955. He did battle with fighters who had colorful monikers including Italian Jack Dempsey, Young Dempsey, Irish Johnny Smith, Charley "Hobo" Williams, Deacon Johnny Brown, Jimmy "Gunboat" Davis, Charley 'Doc' Williams, Saint Paul, and Young Gene Buffalo. But he also fought the likes of Tiger Jack Fox, Lee Savold, Lee Oma, Archie Moore, Billy Fox, Phil Muscato, Roland LaStarza, Jimmy Bivins, Bernie Reynolds, Cesar Brion, Joey Maxim, and Harry Kid Matthews. Oh yes, he fought a young and up and coming heavyweight by the name of Rocky Marciano twice in Providence, Rhode Island and lost both times by UD. He was one of only four fighters to last the distance against The Rock and the only one to do it twice. Indeed, he gave the Rock all he could handle. He also held a nail tough and prime Roland LaStarza to decision wins twice.

During a four month period beginning in November 1950, he fought Marciano (29-0), LaStarza (41-1), Bivins (74-18-1) and Brion (28-5).

He last fought on July 7, 1955 and retired with a record of 67 (43)-67 (3)-10. Yes, out of 144 fights, he was only stopped three times.

He finished with a record of 67 (KO 43) - 67 (KO 3)-10 in 144 bouts. Ted Lowry could represent at least half of the time; he was as tough as it gets.

Chief Crazy Horse

Chief Crazy Horse (a.k.a, Frankie Martin) was a member of the Chippewa Tribe and fought from 1936-1954. This 500 hitter was a staple in the early and more successful part of his career at the Legion Stadium in Hollywood, California and at the Olympic Auditorium in Los Angeles. Around 1941, he took his show on the road and fought on the East Coast but ran up against stiffer competition. Toward the end of his active and long career, he fought frequently in the Miami Beach area. His propensity to fight on equal terms was borne out by his final record 47-47-19, yes, and 19 draws. One of his wins came against a young Charley Salas in 1946

Eduardo Lausse (1947-1960)

The thing about "Zurdo" was that after serving his apprenticeship in Buenos Aires, he became that rare Argentinean who ventured to other countries where he did some of his best work. Amazingly, he held wins in 1955 over Milo Savage, Johnny Sullivan, Gene Fullmer Kid Gavilan, Ralph Jones and Georgie Small all in the States. He also iced Joe Ridone in Madison Square Garden and Chico Varona at St. Nicholas Arena. Completing the NYC venues, he beat Jesse Turner at the Eastern Parkway Arena in 1954. And in 1953, he KO'd Gus Mell at the Westchester County Center in White Plains, New York. In all, his record in the United States against excellent opposition was 12-2-1 with tens wins coming buy KO.

Attesting to his toughness, two of his losses came against the great Andres Antonio Selpa, alias El Cacique de Bragado), who ran up a remarkable tally of 136 (KO 80)-51 (KO 6)-30 in 220 fights. Unlike Lausse, however, he did most of his fighting in Argentina, with occasional forays into nearby countries.

Whether fighting in the premier venues in New York or at the fabled Estadio Luna Park, Buenos Aires, "Zurdo" was a force to be reckoned with in the 50's and finished with an outstanding 75 (KO 62)-10 (3)-2 record. He was another great fighter few ever heard of.

Johnny Saxton (1949-1958)

Johnny Saxton was a good fighter, a colorful fighter…He beat Kid Gavilan and he beat Carmen Basilio - who beat me by the way - and he fought other champions. He fought Gil Turner. Joey Giardello he fought too, the middleweight champion. He beat Virgil Akins, who also beat me. So Saxton was no stumblebum.
–Tony DeMarco

Just when you have found the toughest guy out there, along comes another. This time his name is Johnny Saxon and he finished with a fine 55-9-2 mark, but it's not his record that stands out as much as whom the opponents he fought. Saxon fought through the 50's and I caught him on TV many times.

In 1947, he won the New York City Golden Gloves title and the 147 lb. National AAU title. In 1949, he again won the National AAU 147 lb. Title. He finished his amateur career with a record of 31-2.

He boxed as a professional from 1949 to 1958 and in just his third fight; he took on and beat Dave Andrews, 53-29-2, something that would be unheard of today. He was 39-0-1 when he lost his first fight by SD to the great Gil Turner in 1953. During the streak, he beat such rugged opponents as Ralph Tiger Jones, Johnny Bratton, Virgil Atkins, Luther Rawlings, Lester Felton, Livio Minelli, Charlie Salas (who was 103-34-11 at the time), Charley 'Red' Williams (twice), Freddie Dawson, Joe Miceli, Joey Carkido and Tony Pellone.

After the loss to Turner, he beat Charley "Red Top" Williams for the third time and then took the measure of super tough Joey Giardello before losing to the great Del Flanagan by split decision on December 12, 1953.

After beating the always exciting Johnny Bratton in 1954, he went on to claim the World Welterweight Title by beating the great Kid Gavilan that same year in a dull fight, with little early action.

By the time he fought and lost to Ronnie Delaney, 54-1-3, in February 1955, he sported a 46-2-2 slate. That same year, he lost his title by late stoppage to Tony DeMarco, 45-5-1 coming in. He then launched an 8-fight win streak which included victories over Jackie

O'Brien, 64-14-8, Ralph Jones, 37-14-3, Carmen Basilio, 48-11-7, and Gil Turner, 50-11-1. He regained the title with his win over Basilio, but would lose it to Carmen in 1956 in Ring Magazine's Fight of the Year.

By 1956, all of the wars caught up with him, as he lost two by stoppage to Carmen Basilio and another to Joe Miceli, 53-28-7. After beating Barry Allison, he closed out his career by losing to two undefeated fighters at the time, Denny Moyer and Willie Green.

Out of boxing and penniless (after having earned over $250,000 in the ring), he became despondent and was arrested for house breaking with the slim proceeds of $5.20 in his pocket. When asked by the judge "Where did your money go?" he replied in a slurred, barely audible voice, "I didn't get much of it." "Why did you give up fighting?" Saxton responded, "They didn't need me any more." He then attempted to commit suicide and was committed to an asylum for a short period. Several years later, he worked as a security guard at a community center. Today, he is living in a nursing home in Magnolia Park, Florida (Edward J. Healey Rehab) where he reportedly suffers from pugilistic dementia. He apparently has no one to visit him and is basically all alone. He deserved better. As a minimum, he deserves a legacy of being one of the toughest fighters who toiled in one of the toughest eras of boxing.

Johnny Saxton passed away on October 4, 2008.. He was 78. May he rest in peace

Ezzard Mack Charles (1940-1959)

Some day, maybe, the public is going to abandon comparisons with Joe Louis and accept Ezzard Charles for what he was—the best fist-fighter of his particular time.
–Red Smith

If forced to pick just one boxer who fought at the very highest level of competition, it would be difficult not to select the great "Cincinnati Cobra," Ezzard Mack Charles.

Charles was a 1939 Chicago Golden Gloves Champion and National AAU titleholder (reportedly his amateur record was 42-0) who turned pro the following year and fought until 1959 finishing with a record of 90-25-1 (58 KOs). But it's not so much his record that stands out as it was his opponents. For example, in 1954 alone, he fought Rocky Marciano twice – grueling fights that arguably "ruined" him (after the first fight, referee Ruby Goldstein said he did not have to say "Break" at any time during the bout). He iced both bomber Bob Satterfield and Coley Wallace, lost two decisions to Harlod Johnson (41-5) and Nino Valdes, and beat Billy Gilliam, Rex Layne, Tommy Harrison (of' "Resurrecting the Champ" fame) and rugged Wes Bascom. The following year, he fought teak-tough Charley Norkus and Tommy "Hurricane" Jackson (twic).

Prior to 1954

But the Cincinnati Cobra did his best work prior to 1952. He beat Joe Maxim five times (in all, they fought 62 rounds), Layne, Jersey Joe Walcott twice, mean Lee Oma, Nick "The Fighting Marine" Barone, the one and only Joe Louis , Freddie Beshore (in a classic), Gus Lesnevitch (a member of the WBHF), Archie Moore thrice (88-13-8 coming in), and the great Jimmy Bivins twice.

Charles won his first fourteen out of the professional gate but then lost to Ken Overlin (120-19-6) in 1941. He later drew with Overlin who finished with a record of 133-19-9. After losing to the very capable Kid Tunero (75-23-12) in 1942, he beat legendary Charley Burley (52-6-1) in back-to-back fights. Among other subsequent victims was Lloyd Marshall (59-13-3) twice. Marshall was no slouch, and defeated eight fighters who held World Titles. While he lost to Charles twice, he did KO him in 1943 decking him an astounding eight times in the process.

Charles also whipped Oakland Billy Smith twice, but lost to hard punching Elmer"Kid Violent" Ray in 1947 in a truly terrible decisions. Ring Magazine said Charles "…was the faster, the better boxer, and the sharper hitter." (From The Ring, October 1947, page 42).

In 1948, The Cobra knocked out Sam Baroudi and avenged his "defeat" to Ray by icing him in Chicago. Baroudi died from injuries sustained in his bout at the Chicago Sadium. Some boxing observers later thought that the devastated Charles had become overly cautious afterwards – even to the point of trying not to hurt his opponents. Where previously, the slick Cobra was a ultra-dangerous fighting machine who had a complete tool chest of skills, he now appeared to have lost much of his venom and desire. But his post - Baroudi record does not bear this out. In fact, he went on a long winning streak following the fateful Chicago fight.

Toward his career end, he lost seven of his last nine bouts, but still fought top opposition including Harry "Kid" Matthews (88-7-6), Donnie Fleeman (24-2), and Pat McMurtry (20-0-1). Like many greats who hang on too long, he faded into obscurity, especially after his last draining fight against Marciano. And from 1955 until his retirement in 1959, he fought twenty four times, winning only ten which, of course, diluted his legacy insofar as his record was concerned, but nothing can ever dilute the following encapsulation:

Rocky Marciano (twice)	IBHF/WBHF
Joe Louis	IBHF/WBHF
Jersey Joe Walcott (four times)	IBHF/WBHF
Archie Moore (thrice)	IBHF/WBHF
Rex Layne (thrice)	
Joe Maxim (five times)	IBHF/WBHF
Jimmy Bivins (four times)	IBHF/WBHF
Charley Burley (twice)	IBHF/WBHF
Lloyd Marshall (thrice)	WBHF
Gus Lesnevich	WBHF
Ken Overlin (twice)	
Elmer Ray (twice)	
Harold Johnson	IBHF/WBHF
Bob Satterfield	

Names like Moore, Burley and Bivins are mentioned in conversations reserved only for the legendary, but when you add Marciano, Walcott, and Joe Louis into the mix, well, maybe "legendary" becomes "immortal." Charles fought them all.

Hall of Fame

Ezzard Mack Charles died in 1975 from (ALS) also known as Lou Gerhig's Disease at 53, In1976, Cincinnati honored him by changing the name of Lincoln Park Drive to Ezzard Charles Drive. This was the street of his residence during the height of his career. He was inducted into the World Boxing Hall of Fame in 1983 and the International Boxing Hall of Fame in 1990.

Charles was indeed one very tough customer; maybe the toughest ever. While he was too early for television to fully capture his greatness, this noble fighting machine made enough appearances in Chicago for me to know what he was all about.

[1] Ron Lipton, "Divorced but not Forgotten: Jose Monon Gonzales," March 1995. http://www.cyberboxingzone.com/boxing/w0305-Lipton.html

[2] IBID.

8

A BIG MAN WILL HURT YOU, A LITTLE MAN WILL KILL YOU

Guest article courtesy of Ron Lipton*

The Arena gym known as Mooksie's was a famous Newark boxing landmark which used to be located at 230 Market Street. I heard about it one day while training at the East Orange YMCA in New Jersey in the early 1960's.

While training at the East Orange "Y" for hours on end hitting the speed bag and the one heavy bag they had in the weight room, I ran into the famous bodybuilder Bill Grant who later held the IFBB title "Mr. World."

We became friends and he and I had some gut busting workouts together having contests to see who could do the most free dips on the dipping bars without weight and the most wide grip chin ups to the upper pecs.

While sipping the small cans of apple juice from the vending machine, I would glean whatever knowledge I could from him about sets, reps, diet and technique. It later helped me in boxing tremendously and when I became a physical culturist and trainer at Figuretone in West Orange working for Mr. North America, Robert Sorge.

It amused Bill Grant to watch me intently hitting the bag and one day he asked me if I wanted to be a fighter, a real fighter. He told me that his father used to box and there was a boxing gym called "Mooksie's" in Newark near Broad and Market Street. He told me to go down there and check it out, but to be careful as it was in a rough area of Newark.

I always got along with most folks by being very quiet, showing respect and always minding my business but at the same time I was too head strong, foolish and confident in myself to be smart enough to be afraid of anything. I decided however to ask someone who I thought would know, about this Newark boxing gym.

I had a much older buddy I used to visit in Newark, a pretty tough and solid brother named Al Andrews, not the famous fighter but the man had the same name. He had a beautiful wife who was a nurse and a little boy named Val.

I was having some real bad problems at home, and despite the love I had for both parents things were getting worse and worse and I was spending less time at home, and trying to survive on my own while making it through school.

I took whatever work I could get, delivering Pizza's for Ralph Rafanelo's Capri restaurant in West Orange, and breaking my back loading heavy wooden soda cases onto trucks at Hoffman Soda Company in Cranford NJ for $2.66 an hour.

I hungered to try and channel my street fighting skills and the speed and balance I absorbed from Judo into the sport of boxing, and armed with Bill Grant's suggestion I was hot to trot to check out Mooksie's.

Al Andrews knew everything going on in Newark as he had lived there all his life. This guy had respect on the street from everyone wherever he went and when he spoke he always made sense to me.

He was one of the most street wise guys I ever met in my life and we both had the ability to make each other laugh with raw honest humor regarding our daily outlook on anything and everything.

This guy was like Richard Pryor times 10 with his wit and every word out of his mouth had me breaking up so bad I would beg him to just shut up so my ribs would stop hurting.

He was about 5'7" and 165lbs with very strong arms and a good street fighter, but not a skilled boxer.

He had to have a good sense of humor to stay alive. He worked packing parachutes in a factory while his wife worked nights at the hospital. Little Val was the love of their life and he would go everywhere with me and Al.

The little boy had played with matches one day and burned himself up so badly, it required a series of operations, skin grafts, burn center treatments and Al was beside himself with grief over it.

Val survived and Al showed me the massive medical bills he was hit with. He would work himself to the bone to help pay the ongoing medical bills to continue the boy's treatments.

His only love and relaxation was watching boxing and with me he had the right guy with him. He told me to go down there to 230 Market Street by myself and check it out. He was always trying to stay out of any kind of trouble so Val would have a father to take care of him. I respected that. And he avoided being in places where trouble would find him, while always placing his family's welfare over any wandering wolf calls of the wild that might whip at him now and then hanging out with a roughneck like me.

So I had to go it alone, but he said I should be ok down there if I just zipped in and out of the gym and did not hang out too long on the streets.

With his advice, I decided to go to the gym by myself and see if I could find a trainer. My hunger for boxing had been sparked by a variety of things that happened to me in my life which is another story, but this was the first step of a long journey into that world.

Ron Lipton 140 lbs in the Ring at Channel 47 TV, Symphony Hall Newark, awaits the entrance of Lt. Heavy Steve Quinn, who is filling in for Mike Riley of Cliffside Park. Lipton stopped Quinn in 6 seconds of the 1st Round plus the 10 count. George Branch mentioned in the article is in Lipton's corner. (Photo courtesy of Ron Lipton).

In doing my research for this article on the old gym, I recently spoke to NJ Hall of Fame member George "Buddy Gee" Branch. He is a former Newark Councilman and my old trainer, who was one of the first men I met in the gym back in the early 60's and who went partners with Tommy Parks calling their stable of fighters, "Park's Branch." I fought many hard and bloody fights with one or the other in my corner mostly scoring quick knockouts over the years.

According to George, it had formerly been run by a man named Tom Garner and was taken over by the new owner, Mr. Mooksie Daniels around 1945.

If the walls of that old building could talk, they would tell you that some of the toughest fighters in the NY and NJ area were melded into pieces of steel inside that ancient and dilapidated fistic oven.

Guys like Arnold Cream better known to you as Jersey Joe Walcott trained there along with men like heavyweight Bill Gilliam who beat Nino Valdes and went 10 rounds with Ezzard Charles.

I took the long bus ride from West Orange and walked there from Broad and Market Street all the while getting looks that said I must be crazy for even being there alone.

Walking past Ken's Famous Flame Steak House, I had to fight the urge to go in while the colorful sign overhead called out to my hungry belly to come on in and partake of their famous $1.29 sizzling steak dinner. I breezed by Chock Full of Nuts with their tempting buttered grilled frankfurters and coffee, and passed the famous elite men's clothing store in Newark called "Cornwall's."

You had to walk several long city blocks from Cornwall's Clothier down to the gym's entrance passing by an atmosphere reminiscent of 42nd street and Broadway in New York City.

I remember Cornwall's Men's Shop as the sharpest place I have ever seen to this day. The suits, sweaters, shirts, ties, pants and accessories they had there, were so unique that if you purchased anything there, no one anywhere would be wearing the same thing.

Like in the movie the Whiz, the color of the day would change, and the color of the day then was an intoxicating purple. The brand new and shocking availability of clothing items in that color was blowing people's minds back then. It was a new age of clothing changes with the advent of shirts in Orange and bright electric colors, that were only now being offered to the color hungry public who had been forced for too long to wear only limited and mundane apparel.

Suits, V-neck sweaters and ties in dark Royal purples and electric violets graced the panorama of their windows, along with vests and flashy ties and cufflinks that made you want to take your rent and food money and give it all to them for the enchanting garments they had inside.

I had to pass it all up as I cared for nothing but boxing and getting the right equipment.

Wall to wall hustlers, grifters, thugs, hookers, head knockers and pimps lined the walkway along with any brave shoppers who loved the streets like I did. They risked their lives just to be around the action. It was all in Lady Luck's hands whether you made it there and back to the bus without a fight or a mugging.

I tempted her everyday for years and had my share of both kinds of luck until finally I was known and left alone, but the first scary time I visited the gym this is what happened.

If you drove a car, which I did in later years, you could park right around the corner in a small parking lot and risk walking at night around the corner. If you were lucky you would make it alive up the stairs. A cafeteria was downstairs next door and guys were always hanging around outside looking for trouble.

I entered 230 Market Street and gazed up the long set of staircases. By the time you got to the top floor of the three long and steep steps, you were lucky not to have a nosebleed from the altitude.

I soon found out that there were wonderful gentleman waiting up inside for you with delight in their hearts to give you that nosebleed by other violent means as soon as possible.

When I finally made it up the stairs and turned right into the gym, I could not believe my eyes as to what I saw. It was smaller inside than I expected and it was jammed packed with loud activity.

By the time I had arrived there for the first time, the real alumni of the gym were part of it's internal fabric and their territories were staked out as definitively as a State Prison yard with fighters, trainers, managers and cliques ruling every square inch of wall space.

Back then in the Newark NJ of the 60's what went down inside those walls would make the gym wars at Detroit's Kronk gym look like pillow fights at the YWCA. There was a constant air of danger and tension in the gym between rival factions. It came from the turmoil and turbulence of the times and here in the gym, was a catharsis available for all who carried chained lightning in their fists and anger in their souls. It was the place where left hooker Joe Louis Adair from Wichita, Kansas knocked out Rubin Carter as surely as Chico Rollins did years before in the Army.

Territory was a daily issue, as was use of the gym equipment and the heated rivalries in the strangling battle for advancement in this world of boxing inflamed the atmosphere as much as the sweat. This tension would soon erupt into one of the worst bloodbaths I had ever witnessed.

At that time, I was the only white fighter in the gym along with Hungarian born Freddie (Ferenc) Martinovich. No one bothered me in the gym other than standing in line to blast my novice ass to pieces in the ring.

As I went through the entrance to the right at the top of the stairs, Mooksie's domain was directly to the left. If you dared to enter his little room without permission and ventured through the portals of this particular bucket of blood, you trespassed where devil's feared to visit, his inner sanctum.

Later Archie Moore would call his San Diego gym by that very name, "The Bucket of Blood," and later a West Orange gym copied that, but this gym had our blood in its buckets back then before anyone else.

In his room which contained a cot like bed, a low ceiling and the aroma of all the jails in NJ combined, was a large Steamer Pirate's trunk which would have been appropriate to take on a sea voyage.

In it contained all the brand new boxing equipment a fighter could dream of having in the 60's. Brand new leather ball bearing jump ropes with hand carved wooden handles, and a variety of satin boxing trunks made in the color combinations of the day, along with exquisitely beautiful black and white high top leather boxing shoes for sale.

The great color combinations available for boxing trunks and the variety of modern boxing equipment which would later become the trademark of Ringside Products over 40 years later were not even a dream in a fighter's imagination yet. But I was determined to find a place that would make them up for me in different colors, like G&S at 43 Essex Street in Manhattan.

It was the day of black and white television and fighters invariably wore black trunks with a white stripe or the reverse of that. Since the days of Joe Louis wearing his Royal Purple Ben-Lee trunks, there were few choices to make in those days from the Everlast, Spartan and Tuf-Wear trunks Mooksie had to sell.

If you were Irish, you could choose the Kelley Green and white trunks, or Red satin with white trim, and there were still the blue trunks with gold trim too that I took into battle in my lightweight fight with Elizabeth's tough Billy Beam in the Elizabeth Elks Auditorium February 5, 1965. I dressed with black woolen tights with the trunks worn over them trying to look like the Pioneer fighters like Jack Johnson, just to be different.

He also had very long and short skin tight black, green or red woolen Spartan trunks for sale along with black kangaroo leather speed bags, ball bearing speed bag swivels and anything else you might need if you had the dough.

He had black Tuf-Wear heavy bag gloves and brown leather Everlast speed bag gloves and absolutely beautiful 12 oz sparring gloves too.

If you bought something from him, which I always did, his demeanor softened a bit.

The only nourishment ever supplied that I can remember was a table with clear glass mugs of hot tea with lemon for sale for a nickel, for the famished fighters at the end of a grueling workout. The tea there was nectar of the God's and the price was right.

Two fixed metal high speed bag braces with strong heavy and professional circular wooden platforms hung over in the right hand corner and 3 or 4 heavy bags hung from the rotten ceiling on long swinging chains. The heavy bags were taped up from being ripped to pieces from the constant blasting of some of the hardest hitting fighters active in NJ.

Some bleachers surrounded the ring where everyone could come in and watch the fighters spar. The blood and sweat was constantly flying from the elevated ring more often than the water at The Shamu show in Sea world and it represented the price you paid for watching the action too close.

The spray of those unpleasant body fluids would back up the hustlers more than once and it later would amuse me to see them cringe at getting nailed. Every betting man was always cataloging everything each fighter did and the wagering at the fights was as serious as a winter on welfare. This is where they got their edge if they knew how to study tendencies, and I learned that art to perfection.

If you wanted to take a shower and risk getting athlete's foot or worse, you were welcome to try your luck all the way in the back of the gym. I always passed on that area.

The whole gym was simply one of the only boxing factories in the area other than the Newark Dukers AC. It produced the most hard core gladiators, who asked for no quarter and gave none, but the best in NJ trained there and each day was a war zone with much to see and to learn for the brave of heart.

The gym was fraught with talent and some incredible things happened there that I witnessed.

Lou Stillman, who had ruled his roost in New York City with an iron fist and the heavy duty gun in his shoulder holster, had nothing on Newark's Mooksie.

Like they say in England when they yell instructions to a fighter from the corner, urging him to take over the fight, they urge the fighter to

"Be the Governor." This guy governed his realm totally and no one gave Mooksie any trouble, not twice anyway if you wanted to stay, and many wanted to and needed to stay.

My social life had taken me through some nasty street fights before I arrived at the door of Mooksie's University of higher learning to seek out some real boxing instruction and sparring for the first time.

I had experienced some nasty street fights at this time and was very strong for my weight. I had taken a few shots in those fights but always got those battles over with quickly with fast straight hard punches to the jaw or temple or with hip and shoulder throws, foot sweeps and Judo chokes.

I learned my mixed martial arts in Jerome Mackay's Judo for Boys in New York City. I had a good background from training with Sensei George Hamlin and Yoshisada Yonezsuka, the young Japanese Judo champion from Japan, who I still write to today. He became the coach for the U.S. Olympic Judo team and his school in now in Cranford NJ. Yet nothing on this earth prepared me for what I would endure this day and later in the week.

The first day I climbed those stairs, looking for a trainer, I ran into Roscoe Manning an elderly looking black man who had 55 pro fights under his belt. He had fought a draw with Ben Jeby the former middleweight champ, and won an 8 round decision over one the hardest hitting light heavyweights I ever heard about, Mr. Frankie Zamoris. Zamoris had stopped Melio Bettina in 6 rounds and was a legend of punching power in Orange NJ.

Roscoe also fought a draw with Solly Krieger another 160lb champ and lost on a fifth round TKO to Billy Conn, so this guy was not exactly cherry.

He showed me how to hold my hands and charged me $5 which I paid. I told him I could not afford that each time but that was his fee. He put a pair of boxing gloves on me and put me in the ring with a borrowed foul proof cub to box with a rugged looking black fighter who resembled the scowling panthers I so admired and was my lucky charm since I was a boy.

Another trainer stood on the ring apron named George Branch, about 5'6" and a former pro fighter in the late 40's and 50's. Manning got his permission to let me box with Branch's fighter. Little did I know it was Lloyd Marshall the deadly lightweight who would go on to beat Maruice Cullen in England and go 10 rounds with Ishmael Laguna, the lightweight champion of the world.

Lloyd was a killer and the terror of Newark. I think he went to Weequaic High School where he was a fighting legend. He later became a good mentor and pal and would eat with me in the cafeteria downstairs on occasion while helping me train.

He did not speak much and neither did I. He was very taciturn, melancholy and serious with his black goatee and was always in shape, but meant no one any harm. He had the goods to be champion of the world but for the likes of Laguna and Roberto Duran who he later lost to.

That day of our first meeting, I tried to kill him and he had been told to take it easy on me.

That soon changed as I forced the agenda into a different category.

I came after him like I caught him sneaking out of my woman's bedroom window and within seconds he bloodied my nose with jabs. He put some right hands behind it and he was stunning me with shots that I was taking flatfooted without rolling my head or shoulders, but I was an animal pursuing him and each punch landed on his shoulders knocked him back two feet and I had the fastest hands imaginable and always did, but was crude, unrefined and reckless. My punches were falling short and the snap at the empty air hurt my elbows.

His pro moves nullified all my extreme power and he moved with the grace of the big cats I admired so much, and would later strive to become in my learning process.

We tore up the ring as the slats in the ring's floorboards were thumping with the heavy fast action as he timed me and caved my face in for me with every step. Yet later, Manning told me the whole gym stopped and was watching me try to hurt him everywhere with each punch just grazing him.

When he opened up on me Branch yelled for him to take it easy, but Marshall yelled back at George through his mouthpiece, "Bullshit," as I kept hot on him and made him fight me off of him.

The whole thing did not turn out too cool, as Buddy Gee was upset with Manning as he suspected him of turning me loose like that, which he did not do, as I looked like I was trying to kill his fighter who after all was supposed to take it easy on me.

Manning was upset with me for going berserk and Lloyd wanted to go another one to knock this crazy white boy's privates in his watch pocket.

They finally rang the bell and my nose and cheekbones had taken a pounding like I had never felt before in my life. I could see in Lloyd's eyes that they were ablaze with a bloodlust at being forced into condition Red and into 5th gear so quickly and his inner warrior was fully awake chomping at the bit and chafing at his chains to break loose and tear my head off. It was beautiful!

The others standing around the ring, looked like they knew they had witnessed some real raw fury that wasn't just sloppy and crude but a force that given the right direction would be interesting to see again.

I climbed out of the high ring with shaky legs. I felt like my lungs would explode, and the pain in my head and taste in my mouth was very strange to me and unpleasant like a mouth full of dirty copper pennies and my swollen nose was full of blood. But somehow, it all ignited a fury in my spirit that was not even close to being sated and was also the greatest catharsis I had ever felt, and I wanted more. I was home!

As I climbed down from the ring and tried to hold my head high while my bloody headgear was removed, I noticed a very distinct and different looking black man staring at me while leaning against the wall in a white tee shirt. He was not a big man and was kind of slim and wiry and he had the fiery and deadly eyes I would see glaring back at me now and then when I looked into a mirror at my own reflection when the world was young and I was full of anger.

He had a pencil thin moustache over his upper lip and his whole slinky and restless body language just radiated danger. His name was Mark Murray. He had been a fighter and was now a trainer and had a reputation of someone never to trifle with on the street. I of course did not know this at the time.

He had fought from 1957-58 as a welterweight, with a 2-2 record. He won two 4 round bouts by decision and lost two fights. He was knocked down twice and stopped in one round by Joe Shaw at St. Nicks Arena in NY and lost a 6 round decision in Mass to Tony Veranis.

I will never forget his stare as long as I live or the powerful and deadly menace of the man that radiated from him up close.

In my young mind it looked for a second like unbridled hatred, maybe racial hatred directed at me, but I was wrong. He had a toothpick hanging loosely from his tough looking mouth, and as I walked slowly by, I thought he was going to pick a fight with me.

I was ready to fight again if I had to, but as I passed him, he looked as deep into my heart, as the Sphinx in the "Never Ending Story." And he nodded his head to me with a respect and awe at the anger and fury that came out of me in the ring while a novice against a pro. You could see he not only liked it but seemed to understand it more than anyone I ever saw in my life.

He glanced once more very quickly into my eyes searching for what I thought was weakness, I made sure that I showed him none and just kept walking. I had the strangest feeling that we had something in common that only he understood as an older man.

It was like someone who was secretly possessed by the same fiery fight demons as me that lurked in my raging abused spirit ready to pounce at the slightest disrespect. It was a look from one hunting cat to another, transmitting that he understood what had just happened in there and why. It was eerie, but for some strange reason I instinctively admired this guy for his instantaneous observation of understanding and appreciation of me that he communicated so quickly and knowingly.

The encounter with him stuck in my mind more than the sparring and I left the gym kind of quick to make the bus back home. While I rode home nursing my swollen face, I could only think of coming back to do better.

I was still curiously haunted on the bus by the thought of that bizarre encounter and puzzled how someone could smile like that and see right through me and know how much I liked the violence of the ring, not winning or losing but the turning loose of the fury.

I kept coming back each day as my home life was horrible. There were more fights in my house than in the gym and all I cared about was getting back to the boxing. Reading about it, studying it and being around it.

So I went back to Mooksie's everyday and waited until he opened the door and then stayed there not saying a word to anyone but watching everything.

I had never been prepared or could have imagined the bizarre feeling and horrible taste in my mouth from getting hit in the nose and face, side of the head and gut from a pro fighter over and over again in a sparring match. I thought I was in good shape and finding out I wasn't even close was a rude and humbling awakening.

That first experience with a pro fighter made me want to quit forever but just the thought that other guys were sparring and surviving made me feel like a "Back to The Future," Marty McFly chicken, to even contemplate not coming back. The hatred and loathing I would have had for myself would have been intolerable and was something I feared much more than anything they could have done to my physically in that ring.

I was determined that I could face the only terrifying horror of boxing itself, and that to me was not the pain, or the fatigue but the specter of possibly looking bad in that ring. I would learn that not being in shape was the only thing to fear.

Many years later my future daughter as a child would refer to the movie "Apocalypse Now," as "Pocket Lips Now," and Brando's quote always stuck with me, "To make a friend of horror," so it would not frighten and cripple you when it showed it's petrifying face.

Little did I know that life would show me very soon to be very careful of who you make friends with and what you let into your heart to admire in the foolishness of youth.

Between learning my fighting skills and being beaten half to death by the non ending list of experienced fighters in the gym, stood George Branch. He was always there standing on the ring apron telling guys like Lloyd Marshall, Joe Louis Adair and Martinovich to ease up a bit when my eyes started swelling or the blood flowed too much.

I finally started to learn how to slip punches and stayed there all day and night watching all the sparring sessions and trainers teach. George was going to night school and always had the perennial book under his arm when he left at night and was a good role model.

Finally, Branch took pity on me and started training me everyday but I was still a babe in the woods. I still had to go home everyday into a world with my Father, Mother and two brothers who all fought so much among themselves they knew nothing about me, nor ever asked where I was or cared at all.

If the dinner table was not turned over in screaming anger, it remained totally silent while we ate, until one final explosive day the family finally broke up and I ended up sleeping at Mooksie's on a cot.

Yet right before that happened something much worse went down at the gym.

I came in one day and worked out in the late afternoon. I was leaning against the wall by the speed bag braces watching a big heavyweight by the name of Thurman Johnson move around the ring.

His hands were wrapped with ace bandages and he was shadow boxing by himself in his ring togs as the bell and three minute timer clocked his movements.

He was a big 6'4" heavyweight who weighed close to 220lbs, who did not take boxing too seriously and he ended his career with no wins and one 6 round loss to a guy named Phil Smith.

The usual guys were there in the gym staying busy while ripping shots into the heavy bags, stepping and pivoting around them while the rusty ceiling chains creaked as the bags were driven back and forth with power shots. I was far off to the side while firing up the speed bag and the black leather tear drop little bag was slamming into the wooden platform with a machine gun staccato rhythm as the ball bearing swivel was smoking with the sound of the thunder.

Then as the rounds timer went off everyone stood still, sweating, heaving and waiting for the minute's rest to end and the new round to begin.

It was during this last minute that time stood still and the Devil let death itself silently slip into Mooksie's and glide like a hooded dark shadow into the far corner of the poorly lit gym. It found it's spot of power against a paint peeled wall and the unholy wraith stood there waiting patiently eating life savers while it's sister fate decided who to send him.

Mark Murray called up to the big heavyweight in the ring. "Finish up, Man, we're gloved up here." Murray's fighter he was training had his headgear on, Vaseline on his face and his foul proof cup was laced and tied tight over his sweatpants. He was ready to go and was starting to cool off. The other trainer on the far side of the ring had his fighter set to get in there and go and he was jiggling in place to keep his rhythm going.

It was an unwritten rule as it is in most boxing gyms, that actual sparring takes precedent over anyone just moving by themselves in the ring, shadow boxing.

Thurman Johnson yelled back, "I'm gonna move one more man," "The fuck you are," shot back Murray and he jumped up onto the ring apron and slipped through the ropes.

The big heavyweight met him head on and grabbed his arms pinning them and picked him up placing him outside the ring onto the apron like a feather. A brief heated scuffle broke out and vicious words and a push were exchanged.

Mark Murray left the gym quickly and the sound of his frenzied footsteps flying down the staircase out of the building sent up red flags of danger cutting through the silence. Several fighters, trainers and regulars grabbed their coats and left. Someone yelled to Thurman Johnson to get the f...k out of the gym as fast as he could. He ignored that suggestion and stayed.

I kept hitting the speed bag as I had two more rounds to go. The other fighter who was supposed to spar with Mark Murray's guy had his trainer escort him quickly out of the gym into the cold night.

Too many people were leaving too quickly and I was told to get out of there too. I was riveted to the bag work and ignored the warning.

While Thurman Johnson was still up in the ring, Mark Murray returned. This time he was wearing a long rain coat. He had one hand behind his back and the other hand inside the long coat. He covered the ground to the big heavyweight as fast as an Olympic sprinter and the big man tried to back up into the corner at the side of the ring.

He never made it. He was hit with a lug wrench and a meat cleaver. His screams and the blood spray were mixed with the horrible sound of the lug wrench smashing into his skull over and over again. The meat cleaver sunk into his neck and then took his fingers off and they lay on the floor in a pool of spreading dark blood which stained the old wooden floor for eons afterward.

His punishment for manhandling the smaller man came in waves of savagery until he lay still on the floor broken and mangled. Finally, his bloodlust for revenge ended, Murray stopped and took hold of himself. No one moved, no one tried to stop it except for the screams, "You're killing the man," "God Damn, brother, enough is enough."

His eyes were glazed with a vengeance sated, as he walked around the heavy bags guys were jumping out of his way with cringing fear.

He ignored all the brothers on the way out and then he passed me slowly standing by the speed bags.

Long before this happened I knew that life had painted me into a corner. I had been bullied long before by many bigger foes while sick and helpless and endured many years of torture in and out of hospitals until I got better and stronger.

While the carnage was going on, I was hypnotized and fascinated by only one thing. How big the other guy was and how fast this other man took him down with weapons, speed and a vicious attack.

I felt terrible for the fallen man, but the realization that such violence existed was new to me as a boy. As he walked by, I neither admired what he did, nor feared it, nor feared him, I understood why he did it, and seeing it was possible held my macabre interest and in that moment, he passed me again and stopped. He looked at me, saw the look in my eyes again that he saw in me when I came out of the ring and growled softly and without any menace at all, "You, You, know, don't you."

He gave me that same smile and split into the night. The police aftermath was expected. I heard that most everyone in the gym, all the "Tough" fighters and some guys who went on to hold high positions in boxing, told the cops everything they saw. They were visited by the cops and told them everything. With hindsight, they did right and told the truth.

I went home that night, a long bus ride home. I made it inside the house while everyone was finishing up at the dinner table. I came through the garage and made it quickly into a hallway bathroom to wash up. I could hear the family at the dinner table inside getting ready for my Father's coffee and desert which I never ate.

I heard my Mother ask my brother Bobby who was three years younger than me what was new, he said, that he had to finish a report for English class and wanted her to type it. My brother Jamie, 8 years younger who would later become a Dr. and Commander in the Navy taking care of the S.E.A.L.S. was talking to my father about bringing him home a gift he wanted that he saw in my Father's store in New York City.

I looked into the mirror and there was blood on my shirt. It was blood from the arterial spray from Thurman getting hit in the neck with the meat cleaver. I could not get it out.

I sat down at the table. No one noticed it. No one asked. Finally little Jamie said, "Why doesn't someone ask Ronnie how he is?" An embarrassed silence followed. Finally, my mother said, "Who's having desert, and what's new with you?" "Nothing" I said and I got up and went upstairs.

I called Al Andrews. It was late, but he listened to the whole story. When I was done, he was quiet for a long time. I said, "Well, what do you think?" He said, "What I always knew, a big man will hurt you but a little man will kill you."

The Newark cops finally came to my home about a week later after getting every name in the gym from someone. I told them I knew nothing. I did not want to rat out anyone for anything and my misplaced sense of justice had a long way to evolve, but I felt stronger and tougher than all the guys who told on him.

I was told that he was convicted and did some time. Thurman had a bunch of operations on his hand and never fought again after an excruciating recovery.

I made many more mistakes in my life in respecting the wrong kind of guys at times, but I came to understand them, the streets and how important it is always to know where your children are and what they are doing. It all helped me to end up being a good cop and understand why things happen and how to prevent them.

I also learned how to show love to your kids everyday they are with you and to listen to them.

Boxing, the love of my life, is controlled violence, beautiful, ugly and visceral, it is the jungle itself come alive in a sporting arena, it has it's Charlie "The Devil" Greens, Rubin Carter's, James Butlers and it's Joe Louis.' Sometimes they meet and like Sonny Liston used to say, "Sometimes the Bad Guy wins".

Referee Ron Lipton checks Tracy Patterson's gloves. (Photo courtesy of Ron Lipton)

I learned something from all of them, all their personalities, what can happen in a split second from disrespect, or how sometimes, just sometimes something tragic that is in the works can be prevented with intelligence, kindness and reason.

I read a long time ago in my favorite book the original classic by Rudyard Kipling, The Jungle Book, that Mowgli knew how to speak to the Tiger, Shere Khan, and how to speak to the great Black Panther Bagheera in their tongue. They spared him, let him walk among them and showed him the respect of life.

I used what I learned to spot things bad before they happen, I am proud of all the work I do with kids, wild kids that I have saved because I know how they think.

You see, I went to that University of higher learning; I have a Doctorate from Mooksie's in Newark.

* Ron Lipton is a retired police officer and former Investigator with the Hudson County, NJ Prosecutor's Officer. He was a former

fighter who set records for fast knockouts and was a paid spar-ring partner to the greats like Ali, Hurricane Carter, Dick Tiger and Carlos Ortiz.and later became an international professional boxing referee. He worked big fights on HBO, and Pay Per view featur-ing Oscar De La Hoya, Evander Holyfield, Roy Jones Jr. and Pernell Whittaker. In 2000, he won the Black Prestige Lifetime Civil Rights Award presented by the Mayor of Poughkeepsie, NY and an Award for a Lifetime of Service to Boxing. On Oct 27, 2007, he won the NAACP's Man of Distinction Award. He trains fighters full time and has taught boxing at Marist college for the past 7 years. As well, he is a Senior Boxing Historian and staff writer for a leading on-line boxing site (CBZ), and has been a published boxing writer since the 60's.

9

GENERATIONAL BIAS

...if we compare either the fight itself or each of the two men [PBF and De La Hoya] involved with the glory days of pugilist masters like Ray Robinson and the almost unbelievable fights he had, we are going way too far with the hype... Look at the facts, Robinson had over two hundred fights as a pro - over twice as many as both Oscar and Floyd combined. And Ray was never once legitimately KO'd. Fighters were just tougher back in Robbie's day. It's that simple
—James Slater

I have always adhered to two principles. The first one is to train hard and get in the best possible physical condition. The second is to forget all about the other fellow until you face him in the ring and the bell sounds for the fight.
—Rocky Marciano

The latest is the greatest
—Anonymous

Rocky Marciano

I loved Rocky Marciano for any number of reasons not the least of which is that he was from my era and my generation. That he was an Italian didn't hurt much either. I also thought he was a great fighter who did what he had to do against everyone they put in from of him. After all, 49-0 is a perfect record.

Of course, looking through the prism of nostalgia makes everything seem better and I like to play out old school memories just like other old timers. However, I also try to be thoughtful and objective when making comparisons between the past and the present—and that's where the issue of generational prejudice comes in (some call it "era" prejudice). And that's where comparisons between The Rock and modern fighters come in as well.

Should he be compared to recent heavyweights in the mold of Ali, George Foreman or Wladimir Klitchko? Of course not. He simply was not big enough, but how about comparing him to the likes of the following who fight at Cruiserweight (175-200 lb (90.72 kg) :

O'Neil Bell

Enzo Maccarinelli

Vadim Tokarev

Jean Marc Mormeck

David Haye

Emmanuel Nwodo

Matt Godfrey

Steve Cunningham

Rico Hoye

Krzysztof Wlodarczyk

Marco Huck

Grigory Drozd

Pietro Aurino

Johnathon Banks

BJ Flores

Felix Cora Jr.

Dale Brown

Valery Brudov

Wayne Braithwaite

Guillermo Jones

Chris Bryd

Rocky fought at a disciplined 183-188 for the most part which places him in the middle of the cruiserweight limit. Looking back, how would he have done against guys like Marvin Camel, Lee Roy Murphy, Carlos Deleon, Dwight Braxton, Boone Pultz, Ralf Rocchigiani Bobby Czyz, Orlin Norris, Fabrice Tiozzo, Vassily Jirov, Virgil Hill, and James Toney? Perhaps the best matches would have been against Evander Holyfield (when he was a cruiserweight champion) and Dariuz Michalczewski.

When I compare Marciano to the top cruiserweights, I am comparing apples to apples except for the difference in era. The task, however, is to engage facts before nostalgia. The lesson is to take into account all essential variables when making comparisons between old and modern. Variable such as number of fights, era (for example, the 70's were a great time for heavyweights and the 80's for middleweights), stamina, training techniques and methodology, records, style, chin, KO percentages, skill-sets, entire body of work, quality of opposition, management, etc. When this is done, myth is stripped away from facts. When this is done, you are not engaging generational prejudice. Of course, I must confess when I do this; Rocky Marciano quickly becomes the greatest cruiserweight in history.

Sugar Ray Robinson vs. Floyd Mayweather Jr.

I confess to being an unabashed Robinson fan. In my book *Boxing is my Sanctuary*, I included a piece (Chapter 50) on the top 100 fighters since 1950 and had Ray a firm number one. Here is what I said about him:

"1. Sugar Ray Robinson's final record was a gaudy 175-19-6-2 with 109 KOs. In a career that spanned three decades, Sugar Ray embodied the essence of the Sweet Science. He was a world welterweight champion and held the middleweight title five times. He never lost to a welterweight. When he gave up the 147- pound title to challenge Jake LaMotta for the middleweight championship in 1951, his record was 121-1-2. The lone loss was to LaMotta and both draws were against middleweights. Incredibly, he was so great for so long that he won his first Fighter of the Year award in 1942 and his second award in 1951. Talk about book ends! The fact that I don't have to say much says it all. In 201 fights over an amazing twenty-five-year career, Robinson failed to finish a fight only once when he was felled by heat prostration against Joey Maxim in a fight he was winning handily."[1]

He is considered by the majority of boxing historians as the greatest of all time. He started his career at lightweight but could knock out middleweights with one punch from either hand. Completely dominant at welterweight, His peak record was 128-1-2. He had a 91 bout winning streak against first class competition. He could do it all. He had speed, power, fluid boxing skills, and could take a tremendous punch. He was never physically knocked out in over 200 fights. He was as close to perfection as it gets in boxing. Ray received 60% of the Boxing Historian's first place votes. 27 of 30 placed him inside the top three, and he is the only fighter who did not receive a vote outside of the top 10.

I'm not going to make skills comparison here except to state below how I see a mythical fight between the two playing out at a particular point in time.

"When PBF fights Sugar Ray, the PPV is the largest in boxing history. Mayweather comes in at 40-0 while Sugar is at 128-1-2. The fight, however, turns out to be less than sizzling; in fact, it's a boring encounter. Once again, styles make fights and their two styles are too similar to make this one interesting. Nevertheless, Robinson does enough to win a close UD. Neither fighter was in any trouble during the fight. As they hugged, both seemed pleased with the result even though its Pretty Boy's first career loss."

Note that Sugar was 128-1-2 coming in. That was not the fictional ramblings of a nostalgic old timer who refuses to recognize the goodness of modern fighters. No, that was plain fact. PBF will probably retire with fewer than 45 fights under his belt and a frequency of fights index that doesn't even begin to compare with that of Ray's. "Cherry picking" and PPV mega-purses were not in vogue back then. Maybe that's why Oscar de La Hoya and Mayweather do what they do. Maybe that's why Fernando Vargas retired with only 31 fights under his belt. Maybe that's why Sugar Ray (and Willie Pep, for that matter) had to fight as long as they did.

Sugar Ray Robinson vs. Sugar Ray Leonard

Sugar Ray Leonard (Photo courtesy of ESB)

Again, in my book *Boxing is my Sanctuary*, I rated another Sugar, Ray Leonard, number seven and here is what I had to say about him:

"7. Sugar Ray Leonard's record was 36-3-1 with 25 KOs. Like Ali, he was equipped with super speed, ability, and charisma. Leonard filled the boxing void left when Muhammad Ali retired in 1981. With the American public in search of a new superstar, he came along at just the right moment. Like Ali, he was another right person for the right time. An Olympic gold medal winner, he was named Fighter of the Decade for the 1980s. He won an unprecedented five world titles in five weight classes and competed in some of the era's most memorable bouts. He won the unofficial round robin of his era by beating Benitez, Duran, Hearns and Hagler which is enough of a platform for entry into any Boxing Hall of Fame. No one could exploit an opponent's weaknesses better than Leonard and there were few better and more ruthless closers in boxing history."

Like Muhammad Ali before him, Leonard was the right man for the right time. His amateur record was pristine and he carried it over into the pros. He seldom fought low level opposition (for example, his second opponent, Willie Rodriguez, was 10-1 coming in), and competed in some of the era's most memorable contests.

Here is how I see a mythical fight between the two playing out at a particular point in time (about 65% into their respective careers).

"When SRL fights SRR, there is no PPV, but the welterweight fight is seen as one of the most important in boxing history. The promoters bill it as: "Whose Sugar is Sweeter." Leonard comes in at 27-0 while Sugar is at 128-1-2. The fight is a sizzler as Leonard tries to bully Robinson and punished him in the clinches with sharp body shots. While their respective styles are similar on paper, Leonard tries to take early control by pressing matters and backing Robinson up. Robinson, however, begins to counter Leonard, slows him down, and then takes control in the 7th stanza. Going in to the championship rounds of this fifteen round match, the fight is extremely close, but Robinson asserts himself with cute maneuvers and quick leads that seem to confuse and frustrate SRL. This continues into the 15th where they both let it all hang out, engaging in furious exchanges and all-out action. Robinson does enough down the stretch to win a razor thin UD, but both fighters know they were in a great fight. And so does the MSG crowd as it stands as one and roars its approval. As they hug, both seem pleased with the result even though its Leonard's first career loss."[2]

Note that Sugar had 104 more fights than Leonard coming in. Leonard retired with 40 fights under his belt and a frequency of fights index that doesn't even begin to compare with that of Ray's, though he did fight excellent opposition. On balance, they both fought excellent competition coming into their fight, but I give the strong nod to Robinson here. Heck, he had fought Jake LaMotta four times by then, not to mention the great Marty Servo, rugged (as in dirty) Frtizie Zivic, California Jackie Wilson, Maxie Shapiro and future Hall of Famer Sammy Angott. There were so many more.

Once again, the lesson here is to take into account all essential variables when making comparisons between old and modern. When this is done, nostalgia and myth is stripped away from fact. When this is done, you are not engaging in generational prejudice. Of course, as with PBF, when I do this, I again affirm that Sugar Ray was the greatest.

Sugar Ray Leonard vs. Floyd Mayweather Jr.

To complete this exercise, what about Sugar Ray Leonard fighting Mayweather on a prime vs. prime basis at a weight of 145 pounds?

The facts

Leonard comes in at 31-1 while Mayweather is a perfect 39-0. Mayweather is 100% into his record while Leonard is 83% into his. Mayweather has a KO percentage of 64%; SRL'S is at 69%. SRL is coming off his great win over Thomas Hearns for the WBC and WBA welterweight titles in a 1981 Ring Magazine Fight of the Year followed by a brutal KO of Bruce Finch in 1982. PBF's last fight was his superb icing of Ricky Hatton for the WBC welterweight title. Indeed, if your moniker is the "Hitman," it does not pay to fight these two greats multiple title holders.

The Fight

Both fighters have extremely high ring IQ's. They know their way around the ring as if they were born in it. Both have skill sets that include everything from great defense and body punching to crisp counterpunching and ring movement and stamina. Still, Leonard's style is a bit more ferocious than Mayweather's in that he has always been willing to take risks by initiating and/or engaging in furious exchanges.

Unlike the other fights in this series, this one turns out to be a ebb and flow war as Leonard refuses to allow Mayweather to hit and run and continually catches him with sharp combinations that have PBF retreating in the early going. With 30 seconds to go in each round, Leonard steps up the pressure to impress both "Pretty Boy" and the Judges.

Going into the mid rounds, Mayweather changes his strategy by clinching and roughing up Leonard in close, but Ray responds with straight rights which shockingly land and neutralize Mayweather's attack. A short right hurts and backs up PBF and Leonard raises his hand (as he did against Hearns and others when he sensed a ready prey). As he moves in for the kill, the crowd rise and roars with anticipation, but Mayweather is playing possum and meets him with a left hook from Hell which both surprises and hurts Sugar who now backs off as the bell rings. While that last surprise shot may have turned the fight, Mayweather seems behind in the bout.

However, knowing that he can hurt Sugar Ray, a rejuvenated Mayweather becomes more aggressive and begins to dictate the action with more punch volume and savvy movement. As the fight heads into the final rounds, both fighters engage in mid-round flurries that are incredible to witness. Then, the flurries become heavy exchanges and the punches do more damage. Both trade violently. While both are badly bruised around the eyes and cheeks, cuts are not a factor.

In the tenth (a round Leonard is winning), Mayweather lands a solid left and a second shorter one that appears to stun Leonard. In the ensuing clinch, Leonard seems to be holding on. As the bell rang, PBF connects with a wide left, a sharp right and a parting left that leaves SRL shaking his head as he goes back to his corner. No one has ever seen Mayweather fight the way he does in these late rounds and maybe it takes a SRL to bring such ferocity to the fore.

It is now crossroads time, but instead of both fighters letting it all hang out, Mayweather inexplicitly goes back to what he does best by attempting to land one lead shot after another and then moving out of Sugar's range. This strategic adjustment backfires as Leonard, catching the judges riveting eyes, goes after him like a Jaguar after a Gazelle. The fight is up for grabs and both combatants know it, but SRL seems to know it just a bit better.

When the bell rings ending the fight, the crowd stands as one and cheers for several minutes. Mayweather had fought in an atypically violent and risky manner in several rounds while an always aggressive Leonard answered each onslaught with a malefic one of his own. Still, Mayweather's strange shift is strategy may well have been his downfall. The cards will tell the story.

The Result

After a lengthy delay, the scores are finally read to a hushed crowd and are as follows: 115-113, 115-113 and 113-115. It is a razor thin split decision win for Sugar Ray Leonard.

That's not exactly the way I thought it would come out, but when you keep "era or generational prejudice" out of the equation, that's how I reasoned it would play out.

[1] Sares, Theodore R., Boxing is my Sanctuary. (iUniverse 2007).

[2] IBID

10

CONCUSSIVE MAYHEM

Eddie Machen was only forty years old when he left this world. It was only five years after his last fight but he left a legacy that will live forever
–Jim Amato

I was a fighter for almost thirteen years. It was hard for me to walk into something else after all that time.
–Eddie Machen

Ingemar Johansson, 20-0 met Eddie Machen, 24-0-1, in 1958 and the outcome was worse than the 1981 Cooney-Norton slaughter. The Machen-Johansson bout is on youtube.com. Viewers can judge for themselves. In fact, Machen was lucky to escape with his life, though the "smart money" had him a favorite going in.

Johansson was born in Sweden and won a silver medal in the heavyweight division at the 1952 Olympics. He turned pro in December of that year. A good boxer, he carried a tremendous knockout punch in his right hand, affectionately dubbed the "Hammer of Thor." He captured the European heavyweight title in 1956 and successfully retained it twice, including a win over Henry Cooper.

A win over Machen would put Johansson in line for a shot at Floyd Patterson's heavyweight title, but the same held true for Machen.

The fight lasted but one round and Machen was floored three times before he inexplicably was counted out by Referee Andrew Smyth. I say inexplicably because Machen was out cold on the ring apron and there was absolutely no need to waste 10 seconds counting. He needed help as fast as he could get it, but I'm getting ahead of myself.

The first knockdown came as a result of one of Ingo's patented "Toonder" right hands following a feint with his left shoulder and it sent Machen down hard. The second came from a five-punch combination ending with a sharp left that hurt the American slugger badly. If the fight had been stopped right there and then, there would have been little to complain about. Amazingly, just before the second knockdown, referee Smyth appears to be waving to someone in the audience.

The worse was yet to come. After Machen got up and staggered badly, the big Swede trapped him in a corner ala Cooney-Norton and blasted away with at least 17 unanswered shots. For reasons that only Smyth apparently knows, he let the assault continue. To this day, I don't know how Machen was able to get up. As for the Swede, suddenly the boxing world became aware of a hard puncher known as "The Hammer of Thor".

After this devastating loss, Eddie Machen embarked on a 7-fight win streak, but during this time, struggled with many demons and issues including alcohol and depression. On December 12, 1962, disturbed over financial issues and his ability to get a fight, he was found sitting in his car with a gun and a suicide note. Shortly thereafter, he was admitted to the Napa State Hospital where he was declared "schizophrenic." Upon his release at the end of the year and from 1964 to 1966, he went 4-5-1, but one of his wins came against an up-and-coming young fighter by the name of Jerry Quarry.

Machen was always an overly cautious fighter and many of his fights were fan-unfriendly, if not downright ugly.

After becoming a stepping stone, he finished out his career in 1967 with a 50-11-3 record against incredibly tough opposition, including champions Sonny Liston, Patterson, Johansson, Ernie Terrell, Joe Frazier, Joey Maxim and Harold Johnson.

In 1968, his erratic behavior once again surfaced as did another severe bout with depression. He was financially bankrupt, divorced, and undergoing the ever-difficult transition from boxing to life after boxing.

Sadly, Machen passed away at the young age of 40 in San Francisco where he had been working as a longshoreman. The Coroner's office said he had either fallen or jumped from his second floor apartment in the Mission District. The police said they did not know if he had any immediate survivors. [1]

As for Ingo, he went on to win the Heavyweight title from Patterson and eventually was inducted into the International Boxing Hall of Fame. His final slate was 26-2.

Johansson's ventures after boxing included boxing promotions, owning a fishing boat called "Ingo", owning a bar in Gothenburg called "Ingo's," and some other activities. He moved to the US where he operated a hotel in Florida, and began running in the Stockholm Marathon 1985. He then started a career as TV commentator during the 90´s, but it became apparent that something wasn't quite right with him.

Though financially secure, he now resides in a nursing home outside of Gothenburg diagnosed with Alzheimer's disease and dementia.

Ironically, his great friend Floyd Patterson passed away in New Paltz, N.Y. on May 11, 2006, suffering from Alzheimer's (or perhaps dementia) as well. He also had prostate cancer. He was 71.

As for Referee Andrew Smyth, he would be the referee in fights featuring such greats as such as Sugar Ray Robinson, Willie Pastrano, Carlos Ortiz, Jersey Joe Walcott, and Floyd Patterson.

[1] From Mr. Machen's obituary dated August 7, 1972. (UPI)

11

REELIN' IN THE YEARS: PART TWO

The 80's

After the election in which Republican Ronald Reagan wins the American presidency and the Republicans also take control of the U.S. Senate for the first time since 1956, successful negotiations with Iran begin. On Jan. 20, 1981, the day of President Reagan's inauguration, the U.S. releases almost $8 billion in Iranian assets and the hostages are freed after 444 days in Iranian detention. It seems to be interesting timing.

Nixon, the Vietnam War, Watergate, Carter, the energy crisis, and disco are soon relegated to memory as President Ronald Wilson Reagan takes charge.

The 80's are about Reagan and Madonna and everything in between. It is a decade of free enterprise, materialism and shameless self promotion, of which Madonna is the queen. She is a material girl in a material world.

The first test tube baby is born. An AIDS virus is discovered, and Prozac is introduced as an anti-depressant. Psychopharmacology helps millions. First implantable heart defibrillator appears. Biotechnology comes into its own.

Movies like Ordinary People chill and actors like Robert De Niro rule. The Fonda's, one of whom remains unforgiven, spend time On Golden Pond and Meryl Streep struts her talented stuff. Kingsley is Gandhi and Dustin Hoffman is the Rain Man, Cher is Moonstruck and Michael Douglas says greed is good. Richard Gere is no Officer and Gentleman. From the Killing Fields to Platoon to Daniel Day-Lewis's incredible acting in My Left Foot, the 80's offer great entertainment. Here come the Untouchables, The Last Emperor and a

Fish Called Wanda. Morgan Freeman drives Miss Daisy. Cher does her 99th final tour and Arnie flexes. Kathleen Turner sizzles in Body Heat and many are thrilled by Michael Jackson's Thriller. Everybody wonders just how short Danny DiVito is? People watch Miami Vice and dig the music.

The Name of the Rose by Umberto Eco, Earthly Powers by Anthony Burgess, The Hotel New Hampshire by John Irving., Megatrends by John Naisbitt, Lincoln by Gore Vidal: Foreign Affairs by Alison Lurie, and Billy Bathgate by E.L. Doctorow make darn good reads but, Paris Trout by Pete Dexter and Beloved by Toni Morrison are real sleepers.

Major U.S. banks increase their prime lending rate to a record high 20%. Are you kidding me? Inflation continues in the U.S. as prices rise 12.4%..... 125,262 Cubans leave their country, with most heading for the United States. This mass migration ends when Castro shuts down the port of Mariel. It's humiliation for Jimmy Carter.

In 1981, Israel bombs and destroys a French-built nuclear plant near Baghdad, asserting it is designed to make nuclear weapons to destroy Israel. It is the world's first air strike against a nuclear plant. No more weapons of mass destruction in Iraq, but 20 years later nobody seems to notice what Israel accomplished.

Yugoslavia's President Tito dies and is a precursor to Yugoslavia splintering into Croatia, Bosnia, Serbia, Montenegro, Slovenia and Herzegovina. It's also a precursor to horrific war and a return to "ethnic cleansing." Serial killer Andrei Chikatilo does his own brand of killing in Russia which says it can't be so.

Still more humiliation for President Carter as his brother Billy becomes a registered foreign agent of the Libyan government after receiving a $220,000 "loan" from the Libyans.

Shipyard workers in Gdansk, Poland, quit working in protest of rising meat prices. The strike includes 350,000 workers who demand the right to form self-governing unions independent of the ruling Communist Party. They are led by 37-year-old electrician named Lech Walesa. Solidarity, the new independent federation of Polish trade unions, is soon given legal status by a Warsaw court. It's the beginning of the end for the Communist Party.

A fire in the MGM Grand Hotel in Las Vegas claims 84 souls. Helicopters lift more than one thousand guests to safety.

Iranian and Iraqi air and naval forces clash as a conflict over disputed territory escalates into a war that will last most of the decade.

Mark David Chapman shoots and kills Beatle John Lennon. Why should all assassinations be limited to the 60's?

Major U.S. banks raise their prime lending rate to 21.5%, a new record, as the U.S. economy continues to suffer from rising inflation and high unemployment.

The 80's are all about "The Great Communicator" and the Reagan years; all about Budget battles, Reaganomics and Star Wars and supply and demand. Qaddafi and Khomeini are despicable. Americans swelled with Pride as Reagan says, "Come here to this gate! Mr. Gorbachev, open this gate! Mr. Gorbachev, tear down this wall!" He helps us get through the grief of the Space shuttle tragedy and pays tribute to the memory of Astronauts Ellison S. Onizuka, Christa McAuliffe, Gregory B. Jarvis, Judith A. Resnik, Michael J. Smith, Francis R. Scobee and Ronald E. McNair. He reduces taxes and also reduces big government, but the price is to turn loose on the streets many who might be better off institutionalized, as the 80's vibe homelessness. Reagan says the Department of Energy "never produced one barrel of oil."

He bonds with Thatcher and directs a massive effort to define a long-term research and development program to eliminate the threat posed by strategic nuclear missiles. He scares the hell out of Russia; he wins the Cold War.

A savage and brutal 36-hour riot takes place at the New Mexico State Penitentiary; 33 inmates die and 100 are seriously wounded, most at the hands of fellow inmates.

Mount St. Helens in the state of Washington erupts for the first time since 1857. Another eruption occurs on May 18, killing 34 persons.

The high-tech industry really takes off in the 80's. Fortunes are made but not before a savage Stock Market implosion shakes thing up in 1987. Names like Apple, Data General, Digital, HP, IBM, Wang, Prime, Microsoft, Oracle and countless others offer opportunities of a life time. Many will later disappear. Silicon Valley duplicates itself around the country. Get it while you can. Think exit strategy while you enter. Buy and hold, but who holds when a stock doubles?

The Chicago Bears and "The Refrigerator" beat New England 46-10 in Superbowl XX, but the decade belongs to the San Francisco 49ers. The Heisman Trophy goes to Bo Jackson who can-do. Jerry

Rice and "LT" stand out and so does a Rookie of the Year by the name of Mark McGwire. "Dr. J" makes his presence felt, along with Kareem Abdul-Jabbar.

• • •

Light heavyweight Bob Foster is the sheriff in town. Bantamweight Ruben Olivares has a happy smile and devastating power. Napoles, Monzon, Chacon, Benvenuti, and Griffith thrill fans everywhere. Bennie Briscoe lurks and is BAD.

Names like Fletcher, Roldan, Parker, Scypion, Ramos, Green and Mugabi provide great entertainment in the middleweight division. When John "The Beast" Mugabi knocks out Frank "The Animal" Fletcher in 1984, the monikers are closer to reality than one might think. Another animal type, Tony "El Torito" Ayala Jr makes it all too real and his next fiight is not until 1999. What could have been.....

The decade is a memorable time in boxing. Marvin Hagler destroys Alan Minter in 1980. The boxing world waits for Leonard and Hearns in 1981, Holmes-Cooney in 1982, Hagler-Hearns in 1985 and Sugar Ray Leonard-Hagler in 1987. No PPV back then. Wow! It's free. Leonard, Duran, Hearns, Hagler and LaLonde were all in the 80's. Great fights include Hagler-Mugabi, Mancini-Arguello, Holmes-Spinks and Ali's final fight against Berbick. Duran-Barkley and Chacon-Boza-Edwards were also in the 1980's. Wow!

Leonard replaces Ali as the right man for the right time. His charisma permeates. Hagler, Hearns, Duran and Leonard face off against one another in an unofficial round robin and Sugar comes out on top. Mega fights are now held and the participants get mega bucks. Arguello and Pryor go to the brink in a savage battle. Deuk Koo Kim and Ray Mancini go beyond the brink. Only one returns.

Big boppers like Cobb, Shavers and Norton do a round robin. It's frightful stuff, but the heavyweight division belongs to Larry Holmes and Mike Tyson, as the World Boxing Association (WBA), the World Boxing Council (WBC), and the International Boxing Federation (IBF) compete for which truly produces the world's heavyweight champion. Tyson is to the 80's what Liston was to the 60's. He terrorizes and becomes a lightning rod in plain sight. Tony Tucker holds an IBF title for a short while, but surley that does not mean he is a better fighter than Jerry Quarry of the 70's who never did?

**A young Tommy Morrison
(photo courtesy of ESB)**

Boxing experiences turmoil from 1980 through 1989. The end of universally recognized champions comes in the late 1970s, as the WBC and WBA begin to recognize different champions and top contenders. This becomes the era of multiple champions, unworthy mandatory challengers, and general corruption and confusion that come to be associated with sanctioning bodies in later years. Boxing morphs toward the casino industry, and public broadcasts begin to be replaced by closed-circuit. Can pay-per-view be far away?

• • •

Donald Trump promotes deal making. Yuppie success becomes bile inducing, but non-yuppies yearn for and copy yuppie success.

On December 21, 1988, Pan Am Flight 103 explodes over Lockerbie, Scotland, killing all 259 people on board as well as 11 on the ground. Wars have been started for less. HIV/AIDS continues to make its ugly presence and thousands die. Is it payback time for the reckless sexual abandon of the 70's? Whatever it is, it changes the way people live. But if anything symbolized the 80's, it was the Material Girl, Madonna. The clothes, the hairstyles, the music and the attitude were pure 80's.

The 90's

Iraqi violates Kuwait's territorial integrity. We intervene. The importance in the region as a key supplier of oil is critical. The Carter Doctrine states in part that, "...an attempt by any outside force to gain control of the Persian Gulf region will be regarded as an assault on the vital interests of the United States of America, and such an assault will be repelled by any means necessary, including military force."

The 1991 war (or the "First Gulf War)"as distinguished from the 2003 invasion of Iraq, is "won" big time and restores our pride. Colin Powell and "Stormin" Norman Schwarzkopf shine as heroes for a nation badly in need of heroes. President Bush's popularity rating soared until the apparent success of the military operations becomes just that, apparent. It falls dramatically because of an economic recession. When taxes are raised after "Read my lips." The Skull and Bones President is done.

Now it's William Jefferson Clinton's turn. Eight years of prosperity under "Bubba." There is more peace and economic well being than at any time in history. Then, on April 19, 1995, the Oklahoma City bombing claims 168 souls and reflects the evil men can do. Tim McVeigh was a decorated veteran of the US Army, having served in the Gulf War, where he was awarded a Bronze Star. Tim is bad juju. Bill helps us get through this.

Despite Monica, he apologizes and continues to have unprecedented popular approval ratings. Bill rules; Hillary lurks. At the end of the day, oral sex is no big deal-not even during the day.

Rodney King gets beaten by police officers in L.A in the early 90s when resisting arrest. Somebody films it and all hell breaks loose. The police officers are handed a verdict of not guilty by the first review board resulting in deadly riots breaking out in south central L.A. Several days of anarchy ensue. "Can't we all just get along?" The O.J. Simpson case in 1994-95 carried with it an undercurrent as well. He was found innocent—in plain sight! Jeffrey Dahmer shocks the entire country. Andrew Cunanan is a "serial rampage killer" and slays Versace.

The nineties featured Schindler's List, Saving Private Ryan, Philadelphia, Forrest Gump, Silence of the Lambs, Good Will Hunting, Pulp Fiction, Sling Blade, Fight Club, Shawshank Redemption, Gladiator, Unforgiven, Braveheart, and Glengarry Glen Ross (with its depressing edge). Clint Eastwood, Tom Hanks and new kid on the block, Russell Crow, do their thing. Ellen announces to the whole world that she is a lesbian. Who cares? VP Quayle attacks Murphy Brown for being a single mother. Who cares? CBS News fires co-anchor Connie Chung. No one cares. British Monarchy divorces. Nobody cares. Quebec votes to remain part of Canada. People care. John Gotti is convicted. Wow! Everybody cares.

People read Seven Habits of Highly Effective People and Smilla's Sense of Snow by Peter Hoeg. They watch The Simpson's, Cheers, Charles Barkley and Mark McGwire. They watch the Red Wings win the Stanley Cup in 1997 and 98 and the Bills lose the Super Bowl four years in a row. Say what? The NY Yankees win the World Series in 1996 and 1998 with Jeter, Williams, David Cone, David Wells, Clemens and George Steinbrenner. Barcelona wins the Europe Cup. They watch the Cowboys win the Super Bowl in 1993, 1994 and 1996. They watch the Chicago Bulls with Michael Jordan, Scottie Pippen and Dennis Rodman dazzle their way as NBA Champions for six years. The bulls are all about Zen, strange hair colors, hatred, greed, magic and greatness. Phil Jackson's weirdness is part of the deal.

A potpourri of slang, styles and clothes permeates. Mary Janes, baggy jeans and baseball caps that still have the tags on them are in. Getting your tongue, belly button, eyebrow, and nipples pierced is cool. Everyone has piercings. People buy Polar Fleece. Spiral Perms. Tattoos were formerly the preserve of gang members, jailbirds and other rebels; tatts now are so common even the Spice Girls have them. You used to get a tattoo to stand out, now you avoid one to stand out. Bling-Bling, blazed and back in the day. Chill out, chillin' and "What up Dawg!" Hoochie, it's all good, jack you up, pimpin and props. Guys say "Wassup" or just plain "sup." Yadda Yadda Yadda, You be trippin fool, hottie.

People listen to Wannabe by the Spice Girls. They dig Nirvana, Mariah Carey, Beck, Dr. Dre, DJ Shadow, Wu-Tang Clan and more Nirvana. They check out Underworld, the Beastie Boys and Metallica. They dig rap and by the end of the 90s, hip-hop becomes widely accepted. Kenny G plays fusion (not so cool). If I could play like Kenny G, I might not. Miles discovers jazz fusion (cool). Miles leaves us in the nineties.

So does John Candy, Chris Farley, Kurt Cobain, George C. Scott, Mother Teresa, John Denver, Sonny Bono, Tupac Shakur, Aaron Copland, Margaux Hemingway Linda McCartney and Ralph Bellamy.

And oh my God, so did Princess Di. We said goodbye to Walter Payton, Stanley Kubric, Mario Puzo, JFK Jr. and Wilt "The Stilt."

Frederik Willem de Klerk and Nelson Mandela reach out to end apartheid. Both receive Nobel Peace Prizes in 1993. Both deserve them.

The 90s is about the "dot-com bubble" about to burst on Bush's watch in 2000. Bubba dodges the bullet. The period marked by the founding (and in many cases, spectacular failure) of a group of new Internet-based companies referred to as dot.coms. Rapidly increasing stock prices, individual speculation in stocks and widely available venture capital creates an exuberant economic environment. Standard business models are replaced by a focus on increasing market share. Greenspan calls it "irrational exuberance" in 1996 and the markets rumble. Buffet says that if a B School student could explain it, he would fail him.

•   •   •

One of my favorite pieces of film is of George at Jerry Quarry's testimonial dinner, with a tear coming down his cheek while Jerry speaks, and then giving him a big hug. The sweetest person God ever put breath zinto is George Chuvalo.
—Ron Lipton

Boxing becomes a microcosm of the decade. As in the '80s but unlike the '70s, boxing's popularity focuses on all divisions. Oscar De La Hoya becomes synonymous with Pay Per View and vibes mega fights. He replaces Sugar Ray with his charisma and good looks but fights his image among his own people. He beat Chavez twice. He rules.

Bully boy Mike Tyson gets his ass whipped by 42-1 underdog Buster Douglass. Evander Holyfield then takes over and fights a trilogy with Riddick Bowe. Pernell Whitaker, Julio Cesar Chavez. Oscar De La Hoya, Tito Trinidad and Roy Jones Jr. dazzle us in the ring. The later 90's are dominated by Lennox Lewis. In July 1992, Tyson is sentenced to 6 years in prison.

In 1992, after nine years of inactivity and at age forty-seven, Jerry Quarry fights and loses to unknown Ron Cranmer in Colorado and takes tremendous punishment. Early in 1999, he passes away at age 53. The cause of death is pugilistic dementia.

There is controversy as referee Richard Steele stops Meldrick Taylor with two seconds to go against Chavez and Taylor ahead on the scorecards. Terry Norris soundly defeats come-backing Sugar Ray Leonard. Big George Foreman, at 45, becomes the oldest heavyweight champion knocking out Michael Moorer. Roy Jones Jr. defeats James Toney by a lopsided unanimous decision to win the IBF super middleweight championship

English fighters Eubank and Watson take it beyond the brink and so do McClellan and Benn in savage battles that leave the losers in comas and permanently damaged. .

A man parachutes to the corner of the ring during a Bowe -Holyfield fight and starts a mini riot. The intruder is labeled The Fan Man. Years later he commits suicide. Holyfield wins by disqualification over Tyson after Iron Mike bites Holyfield's ear twice. Andrew Golata is disqualified for low blows against Riddick Bowe in the Garden. With no police in sight, a massive riot ensues. Golata becomes known as the "foul pole." Incredibly, he again gets disqualified against Bowe for low blows in their rematch. His nickname is affirmed. Oliver McCall breaks down and cries against Lennox Lewis. The 90's feature bizarre happenings.

As the Cold War ends, Russian boxers loom and are poised to make their mark.

• • •

BTK stands for "Bind, Torture and Kill." Dennis L. Rader, the BTK Killer is later caught. So is The Green River Killer, Gary Leon Ridgway. So is Aileen Wuornos who violently kills strangers, all men, along Florida highways in 1989 and 1990. Damm good police work.

The religious right adopts God's values for families and rearing children. It becomes a strong political force.

The new millennium looms. Like the 50s moving to the 60s, things will get worse, far worse

12

THE FEN TIGER AND THE LUTON LIGHTWEIGHT

Dave "Boy" Green

On March 31, 1980, Green came to America to challenge Sugar Ray Leonard and was knocked cold in round four by one of the most devastating left hooks ever seen. It was generated by Leonard's super hand speed and full leverage, and many at ring side wondered if it had killed Green. It was that scary.

Unfortunately, too many American fight fans remember Dave from this fight, but there is much more to him. Early in his career, his all-out and aggressive style earned him the nickname the 'Fen Tiger.' His innocent boyish face gave him his other nickname of "Boy"

He was born in a small Fenland town in 1953 and had 105 amateur contests winning 74 with 33 inside the distance and turned professional in 1974. In a short time, he became a serious contender for the welterweight title. Taking England by storm, he won his first 24 fights. In 1976, he stopped Joey Singleton to win the British title. That year continued to be big as he defeated veterans Ramiro Bolanos and the active Jimmy Heair. Green capped 1976 by knocking out Jean Baptiste Piedvache to win the European 140 pound title.

Fans were now calling for a match between Green and John H. Stracey, 44-4-1 at the time. Finally, in March 1977, they met at Wembley and the fight ended with Green the winner in the tenth round by stoppage. Stracey, a former WBC world champion from the mean streets of the East End of London, had his left eye closed. Clearly, Boy had now earned a shot at the WBC title.

He then got a shot at Carlos Palomino, 21-1-3, and the WBC welterweight crown. This fight took place in June 1977 and w hat a fight it was. Green pressed the action from the get-go, but Palomino's counter punching began to beat a tattoo on Green. Still, Green held his own and then some in the early rounds, but the tough future Hall of Famer worked his way back in. Then it happened. One punch left Green out on the canvas. Palomino had retained his title and Green had suffered his first defeat.

Green bounced right back to decision Andy "The Hawk" Price who had wins over Palomino and WBA champion Pipino Cuevas. That win began a seven fight win streak until Dave was stopped by Denmark's Joergen Hansen in the third round for the European welterweight title. This was a big upset.

The gritty Green came back again to win two fights. He then challenged for the WBC welterweight title, this time against the great Sugar Ray Leonard. The rest, of course, is history, even though Green put together four wins to stay in contention. Finally, on November 3, 1981, he lost to Reggie Ford, a fighter with an 8-7-1 record. The end had come.

When the Editor of the UK's trade paper, 'Boxing News', the late Harry Mullan, was searching for a way to describe the aggressive style of 1980s featherweight, Barry McGuigan, he commented that not since the days of Dave 'Boy' Green had a British fighter brought such an attacking spirit into the ring.

Dave 'Boy' Green's biography, 'Fen Tiger' has been written by respected author and Green friend, Bob Lonkhurst. The foreword is written by none other than all-time great Sugar Ray Leonard.

Green has made a great transition to life after boxing and is Chairman of Renoak Limited in Chatteris, a company he founded with Bob Emerson. He takes part in charity golf events and is a respected member of the local community. Dave never gave less than one hundred per cent and was a tough, game and rugged competitor in the tradition of gritty English fighters.

Here is what respected English trainer and author Brian Hughes has to say about Dave Boy Green in an email message to the author:

"Dave 'Boy' Green was a two-fisted attacking fighter but had little defensive techniques. He was a huge crowd pleaser and drew huge support from the people in his area. Mickey Duff and Harry Levene featured him on their big tournaments in London and he never failed to please. He was trained by Joe Bugner's former trainer, the late Andy Smith. Mr. Smith did a masterful job on Dave and brought him to the top of the mountain. He fought Sugar Ray Leonard after he reached his peak and got beaten badly. But fans remember this man for his willingness to fight anybody at any time. He also had a fierce attitude and was a credit to his trainer and family. The nicest thing for me about him is that he seems to have used his ring earnings quite sensibly something more boxers should copy. I don't think he will reach the Hall of Fame, but he was exciting and honest."

And this email from noted English writer Mike Casey:

"Like that other famous 'Boy', Eric Boon, Green hailed from the Cambridge town of Chatteris, and his style of fighting left you in no doubt as to why he was known as the 'Fen Tiger'.

"From the very beginning, he was full of fire and brimstone, a tough, aggressive box-fighter who never stopped coming forward. His overhand, windmill-like right was affectionately known as 'The Muckspreader'.

"Although he scored many quick victories early in his career, Green was not a true knockout puncher against top class men, but rather a persistent and hurtful hitter who ground down opponents by the sheer accumulative effect of his blows."

Green ended his career with 37 wins in 41 fights. He was stopped in each of his losses, but in turn won 29 by stoppage. He was a tough and game, and was among the best welterweights in the world in an era when the welterweight division was loaded with talent, a time when Leonard, Hearns and Duran were doing their thing. Many will remember Green from his devastating knockout loss to Leonard, but had he fought at any other time, he likely would have been a World Champion.

Billy Schwer

One day you are someone and the next you are basically nothing.
—former great jockey Richard Dunwoody

One minute you are a world-class athlete. Walking down the road.
Holding your head up. Feeling bulletproof. Billy the boxer. Then, in
an instant, you're just Billy.
—Billy Schwer

Within the boxing community, there was little solace. 'You don't have a great deal of friends in boxing. There's no real closeness. We're trained not to show emotion. We're tough and macho, not depressed, lonely and

lost. I had no idea about the emotional stuff that would happen when I quit. That has been the hardest stuff to deal with. [1]
–Billy Schwer

I'm far from perfect. Actually, me and perfection don't belong in the same town. But I just have methods to clean up the mess.
–Billy Schwer

When your life has been boxing - the discipline, the training, the prepa-ration for fights - giving it all up is a very hard thing to do. Boredom. That's the main thing you face and it's what you've got to get out of your head. Boredom.
–Frank Bruno

I thought boxing was hard. But life in the real world is much tougher. I had no training for it. Silly, isn't it?' [2]
–Billy Schwer

A lovely lad was Billy. I hope he made a lot of money and still has it.
–Brian Hughes

The fighters that aren't doing so well, they didn't look ahead. They've got to prepare themselves for it while they're fighting.
–Carmen Basilio

This lightweight scrapper out of Luton was my kind of fighter. He would leave it all in the ring and fight with uncommon courage in the gritty tradition of so many other fighters from the Common-wealth—guys like Alan Minter, Dave Boy Green, Nigel Benn, Michael Watson, and Chris Eubank— guys who displayed sharp skills, courage and determination in the ring. A boxer at first, he later became a boxer/brawler.

He held the British, Commonwealth and European titles, before he finally realized his dream in 2001 by winning the IBO light welter-weight title by beating Columbian Newton Villarreal, 18-2. He was a clear winner on the judges' scorecards - 111-118, 112-116 and 110-117 - but it was the heart he displayed in the final three rounds which was most remarkable. It was his fifth attempt at a world title and this time he got it, but it was clear to most keen observers that he may have been to the well once too often.

He finished his fine career shortly thereafter with a mark of 39 (KO 30)-6 (KO 4), but the manner in which he fought took a tremen-dous toll both physically and mentally. In short, it had taken his body to the limits. He lost his title to Argentina's Pablo Sarmiento in the eleventh stanza in a grueling affair at Wembley. He was admitted to a Hospital in north London and was given a brain scan, which thankfully proved negative.

Eleven more hard rounds against Sarmiento meant that Billy had fought 47 bruising rounds in the space of 20 months, 35 in the last nine months. "Age and all the hard fights caught up with Billy on Saturday night," said his father. "I'm glad that Pablo Sarmiento was not a chilling puncher who could have knocked Billy's head off. A year ago Sarmiento would not have laced Billy's gloves."[2]

And then, like many other fighters, his transition from boxing would not be easy. Before earning his living from boxing, he was a carpenter and then sold pensions and insurance. This time, going back proved difficult. His 18-month marriage disintegrated, much of his hard-earned money was lost in poor investments, and he ignored advice. He said the phone stopped ringing and that people he had known disappeared. Not an unfamiliar story in the grueling business of boxing.

Now, after a period of enormous turmoil, he works as a personal mentor, executive coach and motivational speaker. Thanks in large part to his experiences with Landmark Education, a life-transforming organization that gave him purpose and "the tools to deal with life," he is up and running again, having found his vocation as a personal mentor and executive coach, giving talks around the country, but mainly in London. His script is entitled 3D Methodology: the Science of Success and focuses on desire, discipline, dedication, doubt, distraction and disappointment, all of which can bring about pleasure or pain. Billy uses his boxing experiences to inspire his audiences. None of this came easily, and it is to Billy's credit that he stayed with it.

Billy at work (photo from public domain)

Sure, there is still some lingering, albeit justified anger, particularly at how American Stevie Johnston beat him for the WBC lightweight title in 1999, and then when nothing was done after Johnson failed a post-fight drugs test. Billy felt the fight should have been declared a no-contest because he believed Johnston cheated. It was the second time a world title had eluded "The Luton Lightweight," but far from the first time he had finished a bout with his face a bloody mess.

Still, when he beat Villarreal for the title, he felt joy and satisfaction, even though he is the first to admit the IBO crown didn't compare with the WBC.

These days a visit to his website reveal the multitude of activities with which he is now involved. Among them, he gives riveting speeches that describe his journey as a boxer from Luton who was determined to come out on top. He leaves nothing out as he talks about his rise to the top, his career end, a spiral into post-boxing depression, and his gritty fight back to his new career where he is now rewarded for helping people improve.

[1] Xan Rice, "When the Music Stops-Part 2," Billy Schwer. The Observer, May 9, 2004 http://observer.guardian.co.uk:80/osm/story/0,,1210207,00.html

[2] Bryn Cooper, "Schwer is sent home after scan." July 17, 2001. The Independent. http://www.independent.co.uk/sport/general/schwer-is-sent-home-after-scan-678019.html

13

"DANNY!"

Chacon breaks my heart. When I see him at the fights or the gym, his eyes light up and he gives me a big hug 'n' kiss – like a little child.
–Joe Rein

When I last saw "Little Red" at an HOF luncheon, if one didn't know what he'd done – the warrior he was, he'd have passed for an accountant, sitting quietly.
–Joe Rein

The year Bobby was inducted, we happened to be inside the HOF building at the same time, and when I introduced myself I told him I was the guy who made his VHS tapes for him. His eyes lit up in recognition, he flashed that brilliant smile, and then came over and kissed me on the cheek. It was a bit startling, but it was priceless. It was just Bobby being Bobby
–Lee Groves

Chacon vs. Lopez (Photo courtesy Of ESB)

They had been sparring partners and had both been on the same amateur team, but this was different. It was May 24, 1974, at the smoky Sports Arena in Los Angeles and it was a long awaited meeting for West Coast boxing fans. These two warriors fought like, well warriors, but in the end "The Schoolboy," Bobby Chacon, took out Danny "Little Red" Lopez with a savage onslaught that ended at the 48 second mark of the ninth stanza. The final punches landed with full leverage rendering Lopez helpless and giving the referee no alternative but to stop the fight.

Several decades later, they would meet again at the World Boxing Hall of Fame in California and when "The Schoolboy," dressed handsomely in a blue grey suit, saw" Little Red," he yelled out in an almost child-like voice, "Danny" and ran across the hall to hug him. Those who witnessed this emotional reunion will never forget this rare moment.

The late and great Mando Ramos, Bobby Chacon and Danny Lopez (Photo courtesy of Frank Baltazar)

What had happened to these two West Coast warriors between the years is the stuff movies are made of, but in Bobby's case, the story is so melodramatic, no one would believe it. Bobby Chacon was World Featherweight Champion from 1974 - 75 and World Super Featherweight Champion from 1982 - 84. Danny "Little Red" Lopez was the World Featherweight Champion from 1976-80

Bobby, a Hispanic-American, was born on November 18, 1951 in North Hollywood, CA. Danny, a German/Mexican/ American Indian, was born on July 6, 1952. He came off a Ute Indian Reservation in Utah and moved to Southern California.

Bobby

I had it all, and I threw it all away
–Bobby Chacon

Bobby Chacon went from shiftless, gang-banging street punk to the top, but he had trouble staying there. After a great amateur career, he turned pro on April 17, 1972, and ran up 26 wins (23 by Kayo) in his first 27 bouts. Along the way, he beat Tury Pineda (KO 5), Irish Frankie Crawford (W 10), Chucho Castillo (KO 10), and the aforementioned "Little Ped" Lopez. He stopped Venezuela's Alfredo Marcano in nine rounds to win the WBC featherweight title on September 7, 1974, and followed with an easy (KO 2) defense against Jesus "Papelero" Estrada

But things began to unravel. Firing his manager manager-trainer Joe Ponce soon after becoming champion, he showed up for a title defense against the great Ruben Olivares overweight and in poor shape. Things you just don't do if you are fighting the likes of Olivares who made him an ex-champ within two rounds.

Downtrodden, he quietly relocated to Northern California. Meanwhile, Valorie, his beautiful Chinese-Irish wife, pleaded with him to quit fighting. Tragically, her suicide in 1982 was blamed in part on his decision to continue fighting.

While battling personal demons, he continued his quest for another shot at the title he once had taken for granted. He managed to keep winning, but he was not the Chacon of old. His first bid to regain the title ended in a bloody technical draw with "Bazooka" Limon in 1979. He then lost to the great Alexis Arguello. Cornelius Boza-Edwards spoiled his third challenge for a title in 1981.

It finally happened when he outlasted bitter rival Limon to take the WBC super featherweight title before a national TV audience in the 1982 Ring Magazine Fight of the Year. He also was named Ring Magazine's Comeback Fighter of the Year in 1982. This was one of the great fights of all time.

Five months later, he came from behind in explosive fashion to beat Boza-Edwards in boxing's 1983 Fight of the Year. Two fights; both were Fights of the Year. After losing to a heavier Ray "Boom-Boom" Mancini in 1984, Bobby ran off seven straight wins against very good opposition before retiring in 1988 with a reputation of being one of the most exciting fighters in boxing. Unfortunately, however, the physical damage had been done.

Today, he suffers from the dreaded dementia pugilistica (boxer's syndrome) and his considerable fortune has vanished, but his sense of humor remains intact as does his trademark smile. While monitored by a nurse employed by the state of California, he continues to receive the affection of fans whenever he attends a fight or a benefit.

His final record was 59-7-1. He has been inducted into both the World Boxing Hall of Fame and the International Boxing Hall of Fame.

Bobby's life story likely will never be made into a movie. Who would believe it?

Danny

It's great to know that I left an impression
–Danny Lopez

I loved Danny 'Little Red' Lopez. I loved the way he fought and I loved the way he looked with that tall and rangy frame and that eternal glint in his eye of the natural born hunter. The moustache that later accompanied the famous shock of bushy red hair would perfectly complement the appearance of an old-style gunfighter out of time, blazing a trail with flesh and bone instead of pig iron.
–Mike Casey

Little Red was "Mr. Excitement;" he was never in a dull fight and was most dangerous if he had been decked—which was often. Soft-spoken and humble, he was ferocious and unrelenting once the bell rang. In an era in which fights were regularly seen free on television, he was one of the greatest of the television fighters and his name guaranteed big ratings. Danny was a high volume puncher who worked hard to set up his knockout blow. His fights often turned into melodramas in which he overcame knock-downs, severe punishment, and adversity to score sudden and spectacular knockouts. In this regard, he was like Matthew Saad Muhammad. He would get off the canvas and roar back. Turning predator, he would hunt down and take out his opponent in savage fashion. He was heavy-handed and if he connected flush, it usually spelled the end for his opponent.

Managed by Hall of Famer Howie Steindler and Benny Georgino, he was an incredible power puncher with either hand, and bombed his first 23 foes into submission.

Against the equally popular Chacon, 23-1 coming in, and before over 16, 00 fans at the Sports Arena in Los Angeles, Little Red, 23-0 at the time, would lose his first fight. The fast, dangerous and more talented "Schoolboy", who was always tough inside, prevailed on this night. Lopez had lost for the first time in 24 fights. He was just 21 and had yet to reach maturity. He was under the featherweight limit at 123 1/2lbs and knew the problem. He needed to come in at a heavier weight; he needed to be stronger. Lopez did just that. Improved and became a World Champion just two years later.

He kayoed "Chucho" Castillo, Ruben Olivares, Raul Cruz, Sean O'Grady, Famoso Gomez, and Art Hafey en route to the featherweight title which he won by beating David "Poison" Kotey in the latter's home town of Accra, Ghana in front of over 100,000 hostile fans. He defended the title successfully eight times against outstanding challengers. In 1979, he fought in a Ring Magazine Fight of the Year against Mike Ayala winning by a dramatic 15th round knockout.

Finally, he lost his championship to the legendary Salvador Sanchez. After failing to regain it, he retired with a 42–6 record and a KO percentage of 81%, extremely impressive given the level of his opposition. He also left boxing with a reputation of being one of the most exciting fighters to toil in the square circle.

Lee groves had this to say about "Little Red" in an email message to the author dated December 25, 2007:

"Danny Lopez, in the brief times that I've met and talked with him, seems to be the same humble guy that he projected in his numerous TV interviews. It's always been said that it's the quiet ones that you have to watch out for, and Lopez certainly fit the bill. He didn't engage in pre-fight histrionics at press conferences or spew venom about his opponents. The only flair he demonstrated outwardly was the Native American headdress he wore into the ring and the way he laid out his opponents during his time in the ring.

"Though he spoke with a soft monotone, he was a man of immense pride. Benny Georgino once told me that whenever Lopez was knocked down he would get up and stand in the neutral corner, his legs constantly moving in a way that suggested he wanted to pay his opponent back in the quickest way possible. Then he would go out and do just that. He was always a sucker for overhand rights, but his fighting heart made suckers out of all of us – for him."

Danny was inducted into the World Boxing Hall of Fame at age 35, the youngest man ever elected. But inexplicitly he is not in the International Boxing Hall of Fame and that is just pain wrong.

14

INSPIRATION

Fighters are the ones taking the punches and doing the work not pro-moters, managers, or commentators.
–Sean O'Grady

It really can't be measured but you recognize it when you see it; it's palpable. On any number of occasions, I saw fighters win against great odds seemingly inspired to go beyond their self-imposed limi-tations–to stretch parameters of possibilities beyond the norm.

"Lightning" Lonnie Smith (1985)

On August 8, 1985, I watched an inspired underdog by the name of "Lightning" Lonnie Smith dethrone WBC Light Welterweight light-weight Champion Billy Costello at Madison Square Garden. Smith was decked in the first round but returned the favor five times until referee Louis River finally stopped the fight in round eight. What made this fight memorable was that Costello was 30-0 coming in, had successfully defended his title three times against top opposi-tion, and was a heavy favorite to beat the little-known Smith.

Smith would lose his next fight and title to tough Rene Arredondo. His final record was 45-6-2 (27 KO's), but on the this particular evening in New York City, Lonnie Smith was the "Baddest man on the planet" much like Buster Douglas would be five years later. It was all about inspiration and fighting beyond one's limits. He was simply incredible.

James "Buster" Douglas's tenth-round KO of Mike Tyson in Tokyo on February 10, 1990, was a thing to behold. I recall Douglas's fabulous conditioning. Tyson, a 42-1 favorite, was ill-prepared and overconfi-dent. But what made this the perfect storm was Douglas's almost spiritual motivation, inspired by the recent death of his mother, Lula Pearl. There was an aura about him that bordered on the surreal as he looked up to the Heavens while the instructions were being

given by referee Octavio Meyran. He was the perfect fighting machine on that memorable night, and he would not be denied. No
man alive could have beaten him. After the fight, Buster simply said,
"My mother, my Mother! God bless her heart!"

Diosbelys "The Oriental Kid" Hurtado (1997)

Hurtado is fighting) like a jazz musician at a rock concert...
–HBO color commentator George Foreman

"The Kid" (Photo courtesy of ESB)

Hurtado, known as "The Oriental Kid," began his professional
career in 1994, and in 1997 challenged WBC welterweight title
holder Pernell Whitaker. He was 20-0 at the time while Pernell was
39-1-1.

An inspired Hurtado started fast and dropped the champ with a right to his jaw which had been exposed by a sharp body shot only five seconds into the fight. Whitaker's wide smile perhaps belied what was ahead. Hurtado proceeded to fight with uncommon savvy and courage hitting the champion with two shots for every one he received and never backing down. He also threw lead rights and combinations from awkward positions confusing Pernell and forcing him to attack. This was a masterful strategy because it took him out of his defensive game. In addition to his effective hit-and-run tactics, the Cuban did more than his fair share of roughhousing which shook up the champ.

In the eighth round, Hurtado again shocked everyone but himself as he launched a fast left to jaw that dropped Whitaker to one knee. In an act of theatrics, Whitaker grabbed the sides of his head and shouted an agonized "no!" but Arthur Mercante Junior would have none of it and administered his second eight-count. Whitaker was now behind and the crowd sensed major upset.

Point deductions resulted for both fighters as the roughhousing continued into the late rounds. This Cuban was turning out to be one tough customer.

Going into the eleventh stanza, most thought (and correctly so) that Whitaker needed a stoppage to win. Ronnie Shields said, "You need a knockout to win the fight." Then, with 1:23 remaining in the 11th round, Whitaker proved his worth as a champion. He let go a vicious left that that snapped Hurtado's head and sagged his legs. For all practical purposes, the fight was over.

With memories of Paret-Griffith lurking, the totally gassed challenger got snagged between the second and third strands of rope and "Sweet Pete" unleashed nine or ten murderous overhand lefts. Whitaker, with the WBC welterweight title and a mega pay day with Oscar De La Hoya at stake, had pulled it out. Hurtado, who was leading on all three judges' cards by 93-92, 94-92 and 96-91, was fortunate to come out of that fight without serious damage (or worse). Many, including the HBO commentators, made quite a point over the helpless Cuban taking too many unnecessary shots as he absorbed one potentially lethal power punch after another with no way to defend himself. It was as if Whittaker was pounding nails into a piece of wood. These were monster shots the accumulation of which could well have caused permanent damage. Still, Hurtado amazingly went on an 8 fight winning streak and seemingly has suffered no lasting effects from the fight. In fact, just 5 months later he iced Mexican bomber Jaime Balboa, 64 (KO 58)-23-1. He retired in

2004 but has since mounted a comeback and is 39-3-1, winning two recent fights in Spain against poor opposition.

For his part, Whitaker also fought with inspiration, but it almost came too late, for the Cuban warrior came a hair from winning the title in a major upset. Indeed, the Hurtado fight would prove to be the last official win of his career.

Whitaker fought many formidable foes but none ever fought with more inspiration than "The Oriental Kid" on January 24, 1997 at the Convention Center in Atlantic City.

Sean O'Grady (1981)

Sean O'Grady holds the distinction of being the only world champion boxer from Oklahoma and for placing that state on the boxing map. He turned professional at the age of fifteen in 1975, after a brief amateur boxing career.

He won the United States Boxing Association lightweight title in 1980 and the World Boxing Association lightweight championship title in 1981.

Because of the controversy surrounding the his fight with Jim Watt in Scotland, WBA Lightweight champion, Hilmer Kenty, gave him another opportunity at the title. They met on April 12, 1881 at Bally's Park Place, Atlantic City, New Jersey and O' Grady suffered a severe cut early in the bout, but he dropped Kenty, 20-0, in round eight and pummeled him throughout winning a unanimous decision. The fight was hailed as one of the ten best fights of 1981. The scoring was 146-139, 146-138 and 147-137.

Up until the Watt fight and despite his amazing record, the young and innocent looking lad fought most of his early bouts in Oklahoma which hardly conjured up confidence that he could fight, much less win a World Title. But against Kenty, he left no doubt that he could in fact fight and he turned in what can only be described as an inspiring performance. With blood covering his face from a bad cut and in one of the most brutal Lightweight slugfests of the 1980's, he systematically took control of the fight and emerged with the title.

Sean O'Grady would never duplicate that performance, which further attests to just how much inspiration was involved.

O' Grady, a member of the exclusive group of boxers with 50 or more career knockout wins (he had 70), has made a successful transition to life after boxing, He retired with an 81-5 record, many of his wins coming by clean knock out.

Mike Rossman (1978)

A bull in the ring, Vicious Victor Galindez captured both the Argentine and South American light heavyweight titles in 1972. Along the way up, he beat tough Argentine fighters like Juan Aguilar and Jorge Ahumada. In 1974, he challenged for the vacant WBA light heavyweight championship and TKO'd Len "The Pumper" Hutchins in 13 rounds. A busy champion, Galindez traveled the world defending his title 10 times over formidable foes.

But he lost the crown in 1978 when he met a distinct underdog by the name of Mike Rossman. Mike may not have been the best light heavyweight of all time but he was a solid and formidable professional, having fought top flight competition. He prided himself as a Jewish fighter who fought with a Jewish Star on his trunks. He was very ethnic being Italian on his father's side and Jewish on his mother's.

Positioning himself for the Galindez battle, Rossman lost a verdict to the crafty Tony Licata in June 1976, but then halted Christy Elliot in three rounds. A few weeks letter Rossman and Elliot battled to a draw. Rossman then outscored rugged Mike Quarry. Then he halted Akron, Ohio's long time contender Ray Anderson in four rounds. Mike Quarry tried again but was stopped in six. Marcel Clay went in one and Gary Summerhays went the route.

But then he met one of the best fighters who never won a title in Alvaro "Yaqui" Lopez on March 2, 1978 at the Garden in New York City. Lopez took Rossman to school that night and battered him for a sixth round KO, but to Mike's credit he bounced back with knockouts over Lonnie Bennett and Matt Ross.

On September 15, 1978, Mike met Victor Galindez for the WBA light heavyweight title in New Orleans. In a tremendous upset that had to be seen to be believed, he hammered, bloodied, and outfought the champion to win the title on a thirteenth round TKO. You could feel Rossman's energy and knew that on this night he would not be denied.

In the rematch, Galindez fought like the "Vicious Victor" of old and regained the title in ten dominant rounds. Five months later, Rossman lost on stunning kayo at the hands of unknown Ramon Ranquello, and for all practical purposes, his run was over.

March 2008: A Month that Defined Inspiration

If it wasn't for God putting me into boxing, then I wouldn't be here today. I would probably be locked up or dead.
–Cornelius Bundrage

During this amazing month, five boxers fought with uncommon inspiration.

On March 8, Nate "The Galaxxy Warrior" Campbell schooled and shocked Juan Diaz with superb focus and a great fight plan. The 36 years old beat the seemingly indestructible Diaz, 24, to win the IBF, WBA and WBO lightweight titles in what was his final grab for the brass ring. He stretched his own limits to stay with his plan and break the much younger champion down.

On the Under card, even heavyweight John Ruiz fought with rare inspiration as he beat Jameel McCline aggressively and decisively in an important crossroads battle. Ruiz got back into the mix with his win.

On March 21 in Connecticut, Brian Vera shocked over-hyped Andy Lee by stopping him in the seventh with a series of crunching rights. Representative posts from the online forums expected Lee to ice Vera based on what Emanuel Steward was saying about him. They also referred to his opponent as a "contender wannabe," wannabe indeed. Vera came in inspired and determined. This was a big opportunity and he made the most of it over the ill-prepared Irishman who had no back-up plan when hurt.

The next night in Cabazon, California, Michael "The Great" Katsidis, 27, met Joel "El Cepillo" Casamayor and many thought the 36 year old Cuban slickster was ripe for the picking off of a dismal showing in his last fight. But "El Cepillo" proved them wrong by reverting to his old skilled self. After some sizzling ebb and flow, including four knockdowns, he put the guy from down under well, down under, with a rattling left hook.

On March 27, mandatory veteran challenger Verno Phillips, 42-11-1, won the IBF Junior middleweight title with an upset twelve-round decision over Cory Spinks, 36-5. Phillips won over the slick Spinks by SD. Verno is 38; Corey is 30. Phillips regained the belt he lost to Ouma in 2004 in an inspired performance by the "old" warrior.

The next night, Kasim Ouma, 25-4-1, met Cornelius "K9" Bundrage, 27-3, in a crossroads battle which Bundrage, 34, won. "The Dream" is 29, albeit an "old" 29. K9 took control down the stretch and won a close UD getting him right back into contention while giving Ouma his third straight defeat and career-decision time.

Guys like Casamayor, Campbell and Bundrage all share something besides being older than their opponents (by an average of 8.5 years). They climbed the mountain the hard way by overcoming serious personal obstacles. When these guys fight, the mere fact they step into the ring is inspiring.

March 2008 was the Month that Was.

Bernard Hopkins (2008)

Bernard Hopkins turned back the clock on October 18, 2008, when he "schooled" Kelly Pavlik. The 43 year old turned in a dominant performance. A great description of what took place is the following eye witness account from fellow writer, Ronald "Old Yank" Schneider which he was kind enough to share with me via email dated October 21, 2008 as follows:

"On this night, the best was saved for last. It was a genuinely moving experience to watch Hopkins as he wept after the bout – there was not an unmanly moment in the moment. A piece of creation will forever be owned by Bernard and nothing for the remainder of eternity can ever take that away."

"Hopkins was literally driven to tears following the bout – it was more than a simple emotionally charged evening where an old man fought better than expected. You have been to enough lives fights to know when the ozone levels are low in an auditorium and, by contrast, when you don't dare touch anything metal for fear of a shock from the electricity in the room. It was a special night. Hopkins will NEVER be a perfect human being – but he may have had a "perfect" moment. The neighborhood of his youth that set a boy on a dangerous path was erased for a moment. The building of a career while on "vacation" behind razor wire was erased for a moment. Broken promises to a dead mother were erased for a moment. Back-to-back suspect performances were erased for a moment. The ticking of time was erased for a moment. The feeling from inside Boardwalk Hall slowly began to change from about 30 seconds into the 1st round. Where once a small, dim fleck existed there was a spark. The spark began to glow. That glow began to flame. That flame began to blaze. It was like an old-fashioned revival meeting in a waxed tent from the 1950's. The preacher was working the tent into an ever-increasing pitch. Heathen were converted before my very eyes. And I got to watch a fighter walk on water."

15

HOW SOON THEY FORGET

Pound for pound, Willie Pep may have been the best boxer
who ever lived
—Joe Duffy

His were classic victories, rarely bloody; more the incredibly skilled
surgeon, operating on his foe with the cool dispassionate dispatch
of the antiseptic clinic.
—Don Riley

Sometimes there seemed to be music playing for him alone and he
danced to his private orchestra and the ring became a ballroom.
—Jimmy Cannon

Let me tell you something about boxing,...I was champion of the world
and there's three things that go and that's how a fighter knows that
he's all done. First, your legs go, but if you got reflexes, you can see the
punches coming, and you can bob and weave. The second thing is that
your reflexes go, and the third thing is that your friends go, and you
know you're all done when there's nobody hangin' 'round no more.
—Willie Pep

If a man dies, what he can truly take with him is what he gives away...
Willie Pep was a giver. Willie Pep was a gentleman. Willie Pep was a
gentle man. Willie Pep was a champion.
—Deacon English in his eulogy

They don't make 'em like this anymore.
—Boxing historian Craig Parrish

In my 2007 book, *Boxing is my Sanctuary*, I rate the top 100 fighters since 1959. My second choice is as follows:

"2. Guglielmo Papaleo, a.k.a. Willie Pep had an incredible record of 230-11-1 with 65 KOs. Nicknamed "Will o' the Wisp" for his elusiveness, Pep is considered, along with Nicolino Locche, one of boxing's all-time great defensive artists. He held the featherweight title for six years and out boxed all comers. He is best remembered for his physical and dirty series of fights against fellow Hall of Famer Sandy Saddler. He turned pro in 1940 and won his first sixty-three fights. In 1952, he won the featherweight title by decision over Chalky Wright. His first loss came the following year when he dropped a non-title fight to former lightweight champion Sammy Angott. He died in 2006."

Born Guglielmo Papaleo in Middletown, CT, he learned to fight while protecting his turf as a shoeshine boy on the tough street corners of Hartford's North End. From there, the elusive featherweight danced and dodged to the top of the boxing world

He became featherweight champion of the world in 1942 at the age of 20. His speed was legendary, as was his fluid movement in the ring. Red Smith once called him the "Artful Dodger." He was a prodigy when he burst onto the New England boxing scene in 1940, winning 63 times before losing a fight, and then winning another 72 straight before his next loss. In 1942 alone, he fought 24 of his 242 career bouts. His four-fight series with Sandy Saddler may be the greatest boxing rivalry of all time, epic in its ferocity and roughhousing (a nice word for "dirty").

Was he the greatest fighter pound-for-pound in history? To this day, many boxing aficionados rank the colorful featherweight as just that. Clearly, he was the best and most popular featherweight of all time.

At the turn of the century, the Associated Press named Willie the greatest featherweight ever. Sadly, at that same time, he was diagnosed with dementia.

Willie Pep belonged to Connecticut and he put the Capital City of Hartford on the map, having grown up there and having learned to fight there, but his death (advanced Alzheimer's disease) went virtually unnoticed by the people of the Nutmeg State. He died on November 23, 2006 at the Alzheimer's unit of Haven Health Center, a nursing home in Rocky Hill, Connecticut, where he'd been confined since 2001. He was 84.

The following article appeared in the Hartford Courant - Hartford, Connecticut on November 29, 2006 and is reproduced here with the author's permission:

OUR GREATEST DESERVES BETTER

Author: JEFF JACOBS

Date: Nov 29, 2006

The Rev. Thomas B. Campion said his father – his biological one, not the heavenly one – was a huge Willie Pep fan.

"He was an avid boxing enthusiast," the co-pastor at Corpus Christi Church said Tuesday morning. "He loved Willie Pep."

After Campion had finished celebrating a funeral mass for arguably the greatest pound-for-pound boxer in history, he couldn't resist looking up and telling the 100 mourners about his own dad.

Campion is only five years younger than Pep, who died Thanksgiving morning at 84, but his eyes lit up like a little boy's when he retold the story of his dad taking him to Braves Field in Boston.

The date was June 8, 1943.

Pep's featherweight crown was on the line against Sal Bartolo of Boston. More than 14,000 fans, many from Hartford, arrived for an all- New England title bout.

"I'll never forget it," said Campion, whose own calling took him to the seminary rather than a minor league contract with the Brooklyn Dodgers. "Willie won that one in 15 rounds, as he won all his fights in those days."

Father Campion was on a roll now. He talked about how he used to go to fights at Capitol Park at the end of the trolley line on Wethersfield Avenue. He grew up in West Hartford, but he went to school at St. Joe's Cathedral in Hartford and, even as a kid, he'd go to the gym on Main Street just to watch Pep work out.

"He was so graceful, a master boxer," Campion said. "There was nobody like him. He could go 15 rounds and barely get touched. He was that deft. He was that artistic."

They laid Willie Pep to rest Tuesday in Rose Hill Memorial Park in Rocky Hill and decades before they did, those who knew boxing best had used many of the same words Campion did on Tuesday. Red Smith called Pep the artful dodger. With a 134-1-1 record after 136 fights, he was nicknamed Will o' the Wisp. Catching Willie, it was said, was like catching moonbeams in a jar. Pep hung with the big names in those days. They knew him at Toots Shor's place in New York. He knew DiMaggio. He knew Sinatra and Sammy Davis Jr. He knew all the big stars, back when Manhattan was Hollywood, back when boxing was second only to baseball in importance to a sports nation.

There were only eight weight divisions in those days and no alphabet-soup divisions among sanctioning bodies. Eight world champs and everyone knew their names. Sugar Ray. The Brown Bomber. Will o' the Wisp.

Willie Pep was named the fifth greatest fighter of the 20th century by an elite Associated Press panel. For some perspective, do you know who No. 5 was in baseball? Ty Cobb. He was sandwiched by Ted Williams and Joe DiMaggio.

If the plane crash that nearly killed Willie in a 1947 snowstorm really did kill him, Corpus Christi Church would have been overrun by hundreds and hundreds of mourners ... celebrities, sports icons - - heck, given some of the accusations, maybe even the FBI. Those were the days when Hartford was Willie's town and anybody with a road map to greatness knew he was from here. He was U Conn basketball in a pair of leather gloves.

"Willie didn't just do something great for Connecticut, he did something great for the world," said former welterweight champion Marlon Starling, hobbling from Corpus Christi on a crutch. "This is a sad day, but it's a day that Willie can go home. He won't hurt anymore. He'll be there with a lot of his friends."

It's a shame more of them couldn't be there for the wake and the funeral. Willie used to joke that first, your legs go, then your reflexes go and then your friends go. Only that joke didn't seem so funny Tuesday morning. We live in a what-have-you-done-for-me- lately world and Willie hadn't won a fight in more than 40 years. Looking back in The Courant archives on his immortal victory over Sandy Saddler in 1949, you see a big, unsettling headline that Pep beat the "Harlem Negro" and you realize how long ago this was.

There are probably 100 reasons why only 100 people attended his funeral. Some had gone to the wake the previous night, generously estimated at 300 visitors. The hardest truth, of course, is that Willie outlived most of his contemporaries. Of those living, many are infirmed and called with their condolences. Willie, too, had been sick for years; Alzheimer's hammering away at his precious memories.

But what about boxing? John Scully, a young man with a noble sense of the sport's history, was a pallbearer. He cornered Pep's attorney Michael Georgetti to tell him how touched he was by the honor. Starling, who said he had hurt his ankle running to do his laundry, hobbled into church on a crutc.

It is improper and careless to start pointing at individuals who didn't show. But there are so many big-name promoters, big-name boxers, big-time announcers, officials from international sanctioning bodies. Where were they?

'I couldn't tell you' Starling said. 'But I can tell you one thing: I'm here. I'm here out of respect for Willie Pep. And I'm here out of respect for boxing.'

A cruel, disorganized sport, boxing is dying on the vine and on days such as this you begin to understand how it is poisoning itself.

"I am stunned by the number of ordinary people who didn't know him, new and old fans, who did feel compelled to show their respects and bid him farewell," said Georgetti, also a pallbearer. "There were so many familiar faces, too, simple and gentle people from his era.

He was an amazing boxer. Connecticut was his home. Typically, when a person is famous, politicians are out in droves. Where was the city of Hartford? Where was the state of Connecticut and the state legislature? The thing that I find so sad is that there was no real political presence at all. I don't know ... maybe he was just out of circulation for too long."

Maybe there's no political gain in showing up for an old pug's funeral. Maybe there's no political gain climbing into the same church pew as boxing anymore. Because the absence of the top state and city leaders is stupefying.

There was a blessing in Willie's death, however, a blessing no public shower of emotion could ever provide. The Papaleo family has been locked in some pretty fierce squabbles over the years and the last few days could have gone badly.

"The family came together and they embraced to pay tribute to Willie," Georgetti said. "They put aside their feelings and their anger. There's something wonderful in that. There is something beautiful in that."

It's a shame more people couldn't find the time to bid farewell to the greatest athlete Hartford has ever known. [1]

Among those attending the wake were Superior Court Judges E. Curtissa R. Cofield and Christina G. Dunnell; and John J. Woodcock III, a lawyer and former state legislator. Michael Kostrzewa of the

Department of Public Safety, which oversees amateur and professional boxing in Connecticut, attended the funeral.

Pep was buried at Rose Hill Memorial Park in Rocky Hill. His pall bearers were Scully; his brother, Nick, of East Hartford; his attorney, Michael A. Georgetti, of Hartford; boxing writer Kirk Lang; his grandson, Bill Papaleo of Farmington; and a man identified as "the

"Iceman" John Scully and Marlon "Moochie" Starling were the only ex-professional fighters there. No promoters, managers, or commentators.

How soon they forget.

[1] Jeff Jacobs,"OUR GREATEST DESERVES BETTER."'" Hartford Courant. November 29, 2006. http://icemanjohnscully.com/phpBB2/viewtopic.php?t=797

Note: See Appendix B: Career Record of Willie Pep

16

THE SURVIVORS

We all saw the new Andrew Golota tonight. He looked like he was thirty years old", stated the promoter extraordinaire. "Jabs, combinations, wow! He (Golota) was the best fighter on the card tonight.
–Don King

You know what I think? I think he's [Golota] a great, great, GREAT fighter who had some misfortunes in his career. That's probably why I admire and like him so much. I love the kid. I really do.
–Jameel McCline

My goal is to get myself in a title eliminator fight. I get that unheralded quote that they had in front of my name; unheralded Mike Mollo de-feated Kevin McBride. What do I got to do to get heralded?
–Mike Mollo

Golota in a combustible state of mind.
(Photo courtesy of ESB)

The first sign of trouble probably occurred on the back streets of Warsaw, Poland, but no one here knew about it. He won Bronze at the 1988 Olympics and a number of Polish national championships, and unlike most "stand up" Eastern European boxers during that period, he could flat out fight with great moves for a 6'4" heavyweight.

The first sign of trouble I witnessed was in his fight against Samson Po'uha in which he stopped the portly fighter from Tonga in 5 at Atlantic City. Andrzej "Andrew" Golota preceded the stoppage by taking a sizable bite out of Po'uha's shoulder, an early warning of what was to come.

His propensity towards mayhem continued the following year when he stopped Danell "Doc" Nicholson, 24-1 coming in. Well ahead on the scorecards, he intentionally head butted Doc who, after figuring out he might get a DQ, did a delayed swan dive but no one fell for it (except, of course, Doc), and Golata dodged the bullet. The thing was, he didn't have to do it as the cards read 74-78, 74-77 and 73-77 all in his favor. Andrew was 27-0 at the time and may have been at his peak going into his July 1996 battle with Champion Riddick Bowe.

Golota demonstrated uncommon skills as he took Bowe apart and was well and on his way to victory when, after several warnings, he launched a wicked low blow combo at "Big Daddy's" testicles, and was disqualified by referee Wayne Kelly in the seventh round. Golota had suffered his first loss and was on his way to a new nickname.

The riot that ensued resulted in the injury of some 22 people including police officers as well as the arrests of 17 people, three of whom were part of Bowe's entourage. Golota was hit on the back of the head by some goon who used a cell phone, while Lou Duva hyperventilated on the canvas. The entire scene was bizarre.

A Pay Per View rematch was held five months later at the Convention Center in Atlantic City, and Golota again dominated. Ahead 75-71, 75-73 and 74-72 on the cards, the big Pole was administering a huge beating to Bowe, but amazingly once again launched a savage combo to Bowe's lower region and was DQ'd, this time in the 9th round. This ending earned Golota the nickname The Foul Pole, notwithstanding the aforementioned earlier warnings.

That Andrew inflicted neurological damage on Big Daddy Bowe may be subject to conjecture, but what I saw of Bowe thereafter was not pretty. At any rate, even though he lost the fights, he earned himself a shot at Lennox Lewis in October 1997 at Caesars Hotel & Casino in Atlantic City.

There was no time for bizarre behavior as the WBC heavyweight champion, 32-1 with 26 KO's coming in, demolished the Pole with a volley of brutal shots that knocked him down twice in the first round. Referee Joe Cortez, being "fair and firm," halted the massacre at the 1:35 mark. Clearly, Golota was neither properly warmed up or in the right frame of mind to win the heavyweight title.

The "Foul Pole" then went on a 6-fight win streak against decent opposition setting him up for a major fight with the much bally-hooed Michael Grant, 30-0. Golota shattered the myth and chin of the "Heir Apparent" by sending him to the canvas twice in the first stanza. Sure, Lewis had an easy time with him, but Andrew exposed him badly and Grant was never the same following this fight. Still, his strange behavior took hold when he himself was rocked and floored in the tenth. For reasons known only to him, he imploded once again and told referee Randy Neumann that he did not want to continue.

Many thought at the time it was a career-ending loss, but boxing allows numerous "comebacks." Andrew somehow would survive this humiliation. He beat Marcus Rhode and Orlin Norris positioning him for a fight with none other than Mike Tyson at the Palace in Auburn Hills, Michigan in October 2000. Asked how long he expected the fight to last, Tyson answered, "However long it takes to kill somebody." Golota, for his part, joked that he couldn't hit below the belt Friday night because the 5-10 Tyson was too short. "It's physically impossible for me to throw a punch that low," he said.

This time, both fighters contributed to the mondo bizarro ending as Golota, down in first, once again refused to go out and fight. Former two-time world champion Mike Tyson registered a TKO after Golata refused to answer the bell for the third round. But the Michigan Commission changed the result from a TKO after 2 for Tyson to a NC, due to Tyson's testing positive for marijuana after the fight. Golota complained of dizziness and nausea, and may have suffered a concussion, but was the target for many brutal insults that were heard on national T.V. from his trainer Al Certo. Despite pleas from Al that, "You're going to disgrace yourself," Golota struggled with Al to keep him from putting his mouthpiece back in and forcing him to continue fighting

Andrew seemed like a man with a broken spirit after the bout and expressed great dissatisfaction to referee Frank Garza, whom he believed had let Tyson repeatedly head butt him, which, in all fairness, he appeared to have done. At the 42-second mark, Tyson stepped inside and caught Golota with his skull just above the Pole's left eye. Golota emerged from the exchange with a deep cut in his left eyebrow and began dabbing at the gash with his glove. With just seconds remaining in the opening stanza, Tyson clocked Golota with a clean overhand right to the head. Golota, 32, hit the deck on all fours but was up almost immediately on very shaky legs. Tyson opened the second with a volley of withering shots that Golota was able to survive. He then hit the Pole with a sharp right hand up top followed by a whistling left hook to the ribs. After Golota scored with a long right, he was head butted once again while Garza did nothing. He then quit.

He was pelted with objects by the crowd as he left the arena in Auburn Hills in Detroit. Certo later claimed his fighter had been badly injured in the fight, while some suggested, albeit cruelly, that he should have been arrested for impersonating a boxer.

In 2002, while taking a three-year layoff to get regrouped, he reportedly was charged with impersonating a police officer after being stopped in his car. Prosecutors said Golota was pulled over for allegedly driving past a stop sign in a black Mercedes Benz, but they added he had been given the honorary badge by a police department in New Jersey, for performing charity work. [1]

Finally, in August 2003, he returned to the ring with a TKO over Brian Nix and followed it up with stoppage of Terrence Lewis at the Turning Stone Casino in Verona New York. On April 17, 2004, he met Chris Byrd for the IBF heavyweight title at Madison Square Garden and turned in one of his best career performances as he fought to a draw in a fight that most thought he had won. Yes, Andrew had come that close to a world title. He fought his heart out against a superior boxer, using his size and power, and keeping his focus on a great fight plan strategy. This time, there was no sign of the combustible persona.

That same year in a fight for the WBA Title with John Ruiz, he lost a UD despite putting Ruiz down twice with thundering shots. Again, there were some who thought he had been stiffed. The score cards read 111-114, 112-113 and 111-114. It was another close call for the resurging Pole. "I thought I won the fight. I am confused," Golota said the defeat. "I don't agree that he beat me, that's the thing about boxing."

In May 2005, he got still another opportunity at a heavyweight title with a fight against Lamon Brewster in the friendly home confines of the United Center in Chicago. A city populated by millions of Poles. 20,126 fans, many of them pro-Golota, packed the Center. Brewster, coming off a poor performance against Kali Meehan, seemed ready for the taking. It marked the third straight fight in which Golota received a world title shot.

Unfortunately for Andrew, Brewster had done a great job of studying the tapes and came out bombing ala Lennox Lewis

After a stunning knockdown 10 seconds into the first round, Brewster kept firing and the Pole continued to catch shots with his jaw. The second knockdown drove him halfway through the ropes where he almost landed on top of the photographers. A final flurry of brutal leather including a sharp and punishing left hook to the chin floored Andrew for the final time. Referee Genaro Rodriguez finally waved off the malefic mugging at the 52-second mark of round one. It was over before you could say "Pulaski Avenue."

The Road to Redemption

"Let's get it on." (Photo courtesy of ESB)

Golota waited two years before he would fight again. Most had written him off. After a lengthy lay off, he took on limited journeyman Jeremy "The Beast" Bates in Spodek, Slaskie, Poland and tamed him in two with a savage attack. Four months later, he was in with the Clones Colossus, Kevin McBride, 35-4-1, for the Vacant IBF North American Heavyweight Title. This fight was held at Madison Square Garden and featured punishing exchanges between two very big men. In an intriguing match up, this was a real crowd pleaser. Both were hurt at different times until Golota, who survived an opening-round assault, rendered a terrible cut under the game Irishman's left eye forcing referee Arthur Mercante Jr (continuing to show great improvement) to stop the carnage at the 2:42 mark in round six of the scheduled twelve round bout.

Both turned in a rock solid effort. Golota, who improved to 40-6-1, exhibited a focused and professional approach. McBride, who certainly did not disgrace himself, slipped to 34-6-1.

Then on January 19, 2008, Andrew affirmed his resurgence by beating tough fellow Chicagoan "Merciless" Mike Mollo, 19-1 coming in, over 12 grueling rounds for the WBA Fedelatin heavyweight title at Madison Square Garden. Mollo had iced Kevin McBride in brutal fashion coming into the fight and was no pushover. Again showing great focus and discipline, Andrew withstood his opponent's early bull rushes to win a UD going away (with Mollo holding on for dear life at the end). This time, however, Golata showed something else. Finding redemption, he showed courage and an abundance of heart as he fought with an eye hideously closed.

What's next?

What's next for the "rejuvenated" Golota? Will we see the one who gave two champions a run for their money, arguably winning at least one and maybe both? Or will we see the one who was blown away by Lamon Brewster? Will we see a train wreck or will we see a disciplined fighter. Whatever the case, there is no denying that the Polish pugilist has charisma and is an intriguing personality. Andrew Golota adds needed excitement to a division beset with boredom.

Most are now history. Mike Tyson is gone. Riddick Bowe is gone (or should be). Doc Nicholson and Samson Po'uha are long gone, and perhaps Lamon Brewster, with an eye injury, may be done. Michael Grant struggles to get back into the mix but fights poor competition in small venues. Byrd is near the end after his stoppage loss to Shaun George. Only two, Golota and John Ruiz, still seem to have a shot at the brass ring, but only one seems to have survived through an incredible number of ups and downs.

Golota's loyal fan base and unpredictable behavior makes him extremely marketable as one of the most exciting attractions in the heavyweight division. Despite his advanced age and noticeable lack of speed, many feel he still could be competitive against many top fighters, including some reigning champions.

Yes, Andrzej "Andrew" Golota is still a viable candidate to fight for one of the many titles out there. And imagine if he should win. Say what you will about him, he is a survivor.

John Ruiz

My main thing is to go out there and win. That is what boxing is. You go out there and you fight and you win. It is not about looking pretty.
–John Ruiz

Be more concerned with your character than your reputation, because your character is what you really are; your reputation is merely what others think you are."
–John Wooden

The Quiet Man" (Photo courtesy of ESB)

John Ruiz is neither pretty nor pleasing to watch, but he IS determined and gutsy. More importantly, he also is a survivor. Some even feel he still could be competitive against many top fighters, including reigning champions. And just like that, he may be back in the mix with others like Golota, Toney, Danny Williams, the Eastern Europeans, Peter, Rahman, Tua, etc.

John "The Quite Man" Ruiz, 43-7-1-1, was 25-2 when he met undefeated David Tua in 1996 for the WBC International heavyweight title in Atlantic City. Tua was 22-0 at the time. Ruiz came out cold and was cold cocked by a particularly vicious and fully leveraged series of left hooks in just 19 seconds. It was the kind of brain-scanning inducer that could end a career, but to Ruiz's credit, he regrouped. Three months later, he launched an unbeaten string of eleven fights including a stoppage of Tony Tucker and a SD of Jimmy Thunder for the vacant NABF heavyweight title. He also iced tough Ray Anis in one.

Then, on August 12, 2000, he fought the first of three consecutive big fights with Evander Holyfield going 1-1-1 but seemingly having the best of it over the more popular Holyfield during the course of the matches. However, the fights were not fan friendly and for many, Ruiz had a horrible style to watch with his continual clinching, sneaky short rights and roughhousing tactics. Ruiz's unspectacular style makes it difficult for an opponent to look good, but against "The Real Deal," he did what he had to do and jumped back into the mix.

He successfully defended his WBA heavyweight title belt against rugged Kirk Johnson whom he defeated by DQ (Johnson virtually handed the fight to Ruiz by going low 5 or more times). He then lost the belt decisively and soundly to Roy Jones Junior in their historic fight on March 1, 2003.

By now, Ruiz had become the heavyweight fighter most fans did not want to watch. He had been winning close and ugly fights, but against Jones, his time finally seemed to run out.

To his credit, he came back to beat Hasim Rahman for the interim WBA heavyweight title, and defended it successfully against Fres Oquendo (TKO win) and Andrew Golota (a close UD). He then met a rotund but still highly skilled James Toney who rolled his shoulders, slipped punches and countered with brutal accuracy in scoring a 12 round unanimous decision over The "Quiet Man." Following this bout, Toney tested positive for a banned substance and the decision was changed to a "No Contest" by the New York State Athletic Commission.

Ruiz then tested the risky German Boxing scene and surrendered his title to the undefeated "Russian Giant," Nikolay Valuev, in a hotly disputed MD loss that many felt was a bad decision. The bout was held at Max Schmeling Halle, in Berlin where many Russian and other Eastern European fighters are often considered the home fighter. In September 2006, Ruiz announced he would be managed by Wilfried Sauerland, the very same man who manages Valuev. His former manager, the volatile Norman Stone, retired in December 2005 stating that the unjust decision in the loss to Valuev was the last straw. However, his departure from Ruiz became bitter.

Undaunted, John then fought undefeated Ruslan Chagaev in November 2006 in Dusseldorf, Germany and this time lost a close SD in a WBA Heavyweight Title Eliminator.

Shaking free of domestic and managerial problems hanging over his head, "The Quite Man," now a Las Vegas resident and far from the tough streets of blue collar Chelsea, MA, made a decision to fight on and try to get back into the heavyweight picture. On October 13, 2007, he scored a smashing second round TKO over journeyman Otis Tisdale in Chicago and looked surprisingly aggressive in the process.

Then, in a crossroads battle and a WBC Heavyweight Title Eliminator, he took on big Jameel McCline on the under card of the Maskaev-Peter heavyweight bout in Cancun on March 8, 2008 and won a convincing decision over "Big Time." Judges Guillermo Ayon had it 117-111, Manual Cervantes 118-110 and Julie Lederman 119-109. Ruiz was more active and accurate in nearly every round, though every round included the expected and unwanted shoving matches and clutching and grabbing. Curiously, however, McCline seemed to be the one who initiated the clinching and holding tactics. It was almost as if he knew he was going to be KOd and knew the only way to finish was to hold and lean on Ruiz.

John Ruiz lacks Golota's loyal fan base and is not nearly as marketable, but he IS determined and gutsy. More importantly, he also is a survivor. Some even feel he still could be competitive against many top fighters, including reigning champions.

And like Golata, he is be back into the thick of things with others like Danny Williams, the Eastern Europeans, Samuel Peter, Hasim Rahman, David Tua, David Haye and others waiting for the call. In fact, he is scheduled to fight the Russian Giant Nikolay Valuev (48-1) on August 30, 2008 at the Max Schmeling Halle in Berlin, Germany. At stake will be the vacant WBA heavyweight title. Win or lose, John Ruiz is the quintessential survivor.

Postscript: John lost a close decision to the Russain Giant on August 30, 2008. He felt he had won and so did many others in the Halle who roundly booed the decision. Will it mean the end of Ruiz's career? Don't bet on it.

[1] "Golota cops a load of trouble," BBC Sport, February 6, 2002 Wednesday, 6

February, 2002, 19:45 GMT BBC Sport

http://news.bbc.co.uk/sport1/hi/funny_old_game/1805338.stm

17

BEYOND THE BRINK

Win or die
–Quote attributed to Duk Koo Kim

I'm not thinking, 'What's next?' I have to see what happens to Kim …
though I know the inevitable. It could have easily been me … What's to
say it couldn't be me next time?
–Ray Mancini

Boxing is war, and in war you have to be prepared to die
–Gerald McClellan

Some go to the very edge. Michael Watson, Paul Ingle, Kid Akeem, and Spencer Oliver went there. So did Gerald McClellan and Greg Page. Bobby Chacon and Bazooka Limon did it to a lesser degree. This is about those who go beyond never to return. This is about the darker side of the sport of boxing.

Mancini-Kim (1982)

"Boom Boom" (Photo from ESB)

I am always amazed at how many people forget about this savage battle. I say savage because it was not a one-sided beat down as many have been led to believe, though Mancini landed an inordinate amount of head shots throughout the fight but particularly in the 13th round. I saw it "live" on TV on November 13, 1982 (though I cannot recall where I was at the time).

Deuk Koo Kim was 17-1-1 coming in and had fought all but one of his fights in Seoul, South Korea. He needed to lose several pounds before the fight to make the weight and many claimed he was dehydrated going in. Ray "Boom Boom" Mancini was 24-1 at the time and was the World Boxing Association lightweight title holder. Mancini was a real life Rocky Balboa.

The fight featured incredible give and take action early on with Kim showing unexpected heart and courage. Throughout the first 11 rounds, Mancini and the southpaw Kim went toe to toe landing big shots with neither fighter taking a step back. Kim's bravery was never in question. However, the body punching of Mancini's began to take its toll on Kim and by the twelfth round; he was showing signs of fatigue as he began to stumble at times. The thirteenth round began with Boom Boom pummeling the game South Korean with a voluminous barrage of punches and it appeared the end was near, but incredibly, Kim rallied with his own big shots thus nullifying any notion of stopping the action. What began as a one-sided round for Boom Boom became a close one. Kim fought back with an uncommon ferocity and inflicted powerful blows on Mancini. While Kim looked battered, he was not yet ready to surrender. The crowd stood up as one and roared its approval for both combatants as the round ended. These were two gamecocks going at it non-stop. Ray had suffered a cut over one eye and one of Kim's eyes was swollen.

Kim (Photo from UBS)

By the fourteenth stanza, the valiant Korean warrior was spent and Mancini attacked immediately. After missing two lethal shots, he floored him with a straight right from hell. Somehow, Kim got up with the assistance of the ropes, but he was done. He staggered back to his corner and onto his stool. In the end, his courage cost him dearly.

As Ray celebrated his hard-earned win in the ring, one could tell something was not right in Kim's corner as his seconds were motioning wildly and there was a sense of urgency. Even Ray sensed something was not quite right. As it turned out, Deuk Koo Kim had sustained brain injuries and then lapsed into a coma. He was carried away by stretcher never to recover. He died a few days later in a hospital.

The aftermath of this tragic bout (with its dramatic twists and turns) is the stuff of screenplays and books, but this is more about two very game fighters who took it beyond the brink; sadly, only one came back. This is about giving both their due.

The story goes that Kim, in an eerie premonition, proclaimed in a note prior to the fight: "Kill or be killed." If so (and I have never corroborated this), it played out that way.

The Aftermath

The death of Deuk Koo Kim also had terrible collateral damage.

- Kim's mother committed suicide four months after the fight.

- Richard Greene, referee for the fight, also committed suicide in 1983.

- Kim's pregnant girlfriend changed her name and lives in an undisclosed location.

- Mancini went to the funeral in South Korea, but fell into a deep depression afterwards. Never the same, he lost his title to Livingstone Bramble in 1984 and retired early from boxing going 4-4 in his final 8 bouts to pursue an acting career in Hollywood.

- Word boxing organizations began operating 12-round championship bouts instead of 15 as doctors determined that most fatal injuries occur inside of those rounds.

- Some states adopted the standing eight count and the referee giving the mandatory eight count. Other changes required that electrocardiograms, blood tests, and other physical tests be performed before and after bouts to avoid at-risk fighters from stepping into the ring

Years later, pop musician Warren Zevon wrote a song called "Boom Boom Mancini." Among the line are the following:

When they asked him who was responsible

For the death of Duk Koo Kim

He said, "Someone should have stopped the fight," and told me it was him.

They made hypocrite judgments after the fact

But the name of the game is be hit and hit back

Hurry home early – hurry on home

Boom Boom Mancini's fighting Bobby Chacon.

Yo-Sam Choi vs. Heri Amol (2007)

After losing a cow, one repairs the barn. Only after a
big disaster, you fix the problem.
–Korean Proverb

Yo-Sam Choi, 32-5, was a little known South Korean fighter who won his first world championship in his 22nd professional fight. Choi did not have great power, but had good boxing skills and relied on those skills to win fights. He traditionally fought in the Far East.

When he went to war against Indonesian Heri Amol, 22-8-, in Seoul on Christmas 2007 for Choi's WBO Inter-Continental flyweight title, he may have been physically fit, but there was something else that was in the mix.

In the fight which Choi controlled, there had been several clashes of heads. Suddenly, Choi was dropped by a right to the jaw with five seconds remaining in the twelfth and last round and he barely beat the count. But just before being hit, he reportedly gestured to the right side of his head. He was declared the winner by unanimous decision, but collapsed and lost consciousness immediately after the decision was announced. He was then rushed to the Soonchunhyang University Hospital in Hannam-dong and had brain surgery.

"Right now we are relying on drugs to relieve intra-cranial pressure and stop the bleeding but we can't say he is in any better condition than he was (on Tuesday)," Dr. Park Hyeong-ki told The Korea Times. "It will take at least a week to tell whether he will ever regain consciousness."

Since losing his title to Jorge Arce in 2002 by TKO, he had gone 8-3 but his wins have come against limited opposition and his losses have come when he has stepped up. Perhaps this was a precursor to what was to come, but Choi's diary is far more revealing and describes a deeply troubled man.

Sam Kim, a reporter for Korea's Yonhap News Service, described the log as crude and written in black pen. The diary reveals Choi's feelings of isolation in the aftermath of the Asian financial crisis of nearly ten years ago that nearly ruined boxing in the country and which prevented fighters from being paid. Many of Choi's friends reportedly left because of the financial collapse.

He goes on to lament that the parting of his friends led to mental illness that required medical attention. "There are wounds in my heart, I need treatment," he writes, alarmingly.

The final entry reads of being ready to give his all to retain his championship and one day realize his dream of living a more simple life.

"One step back, then I die. This is a match on the brink. I just want to live a simple life in a pretty house on a green landscape with someone I love. Now, I don't like the smell of blood anymore. I'm just afraid of tomorrow." (Hurley, Matthew, "Yo Sam Choi: Diary of Stricken Boxer Reveals Troubled Young Man," Eastsideboxing.com. December 29, 2007)

Postscript

Sadly, on January 2, 2008, Ko Seung-kwan, a spokesman for the Seoul Asan Hospital, said that a panel of nine doctors led by a neurosurgeon determined the fighter to be brain dead after two examinations. Upon notification of the diagnosis, Choi's relatives said that thirty-three year old former champion would be disconnected from a life support system on Thursday night, January 3rd, the anniversary of the death of his father.

Many came close; Choi went beyond.

Grant to him eternal rest, O Lord, and let perpetual light shine upon him. May he rest in peace. Amen.

18

THE SPOILER

There are cuties, there are bombers and there are closers, but what about spoilers? A spoiler to me is a boxer who derails a potential or favored contender and thwarts his chances, at least temporarily, of staying hot or even winning a championship.

The late Tony "The Rock" LaRosa beat Trevor Berbick, Dwight Muhammad Qawi, Iran Barkley, and Lenny LaPaglia. Sure, they were all upsets, but "The Rock" did some serious dererailing with these wins and was a serial spoiler.

Had Kevin Howard beaten a come-backing Ray Leonard, he would have been a spoiler. He even had so nicknamed himself. Gene "Mad Dog" Hatcher spoiled many a streaking boxer's record– something to which Joe Manley, Alfredo Escalera, and Johnny Bumphus can all attest. Mike "The Bounty" Hunter certainly did some serious spoiling. He could turn a fight between himself and some flashier, stronger, and faster opponent into a battle of limited exchanges. Jose Maria Flores Burlon, Jimmy Thunder, Pinklon Thomas, Dwight Muhammad Qawi, Oliver McCall, Alexander Zolkin and Buster Mathis Jr. can verify the "Bounty Hunter's" propensity to spoil expectations. When Jimmy Young derailed George Foreman, he was a both a "cutie" and a "spoiler."

When Tommy Morrison was upset by Michael Bentt in 1993 thus depriving the "Duke" of a hugh payday against Lennox Lewis, some called Bentt a spoiler, but one upset does not make a spoiler. No, a spoiler in my view must have a propensity to pull off upsets with some degree of regularity while still remaining at a lower level than those he beats. Of course, when a fighter has a large number of "upsets" during the course of his career, that may be another story.

Emanuel Augustus (Burton), 36-29-6, fills the bill as he upset Courtney Burton, Ray Olivera, Alex Trujillo (a prospect with a 23-1 record), Carlos Wilfredo Viliches 37-1-2 (Augustus took the fight on 2 days notice), Mike Griffith (who gave Paul Spadafora all he could handle, and Terrel Finger, 21-0, whom he KOd in 8. He also derailed Fred

Ladd, 45-1, coming in, Soren "Mr. Perfect" Sonderrgrad, 38-1, (the fight was ruled a draw though most thought Augustus had won), and David Toledo, 25-1 at the time. He also fought to a draw with the late Leavander Johnson. That's impressive spoiling.

With wins over Freddy Italo Rojas, 48-1, Tony Lopez, 45-5-1, Darryl Tyson, 45-6,, Jorge Paez, 46-5-4, Tracy Spann, 27-1-1, Livingston Bramble, 26-2-2, Tyrone Price 12-0, most by stoppages, "Fearless" Freddie Pendleton fit the mold as well as anyone. In March 1986, "Fearless" Freddie, who was (14-13) at the time, shocked the boxing world by knocking out Roger Mayweather, 23-3, in the 6th round at the Sahara Hotel in Las Vegas.

In 78 bouts, he finished with a 47 (KO 34) - 26 (KO 7)- 5 record and was always an exciting performer who gave the fans more than their money's worth.

Another is Derek Whitley, 24-25-2, who fought Kirino Garcia to a draw in Garcia's hometown in Mexico. He has NEVER been stopped and pulled big upsets over the likes of James Coker, George Walton, Dana Rucker, and Bawa Adime (17-0 at the time).

Big Dee Collier iced (yes, iced) Tex Cobb, but he also Iced Mark Wills who himself stopped Greg Page twice. That's some serious spoiling all the way around.

Among others, Gus Dorazio, 72-22-1-1, Joey Archer, 45-4, Ralph "Tiger" Jones, 52-32-1, Ellsworth "Spider" Webb, 34-6, Bob Benoit, 37 -8, and Mike "Hercules" Weaver, 41-18-1 were representative. So were Ted Sanders and Darryl Pinckney.

Joey Archer (1956-1967)

Archer, a master boxer who stayed within the perimeter of victory in each and every contest he fought, was one of the last of the great Irish boxers. He was a beautifully skilled fighter and there was only one guy he could not beat, Emile Griffith. However, his losses to Griffith were both razor thin decisions and controversial.

A month before his bout with Don Fullmer in December 1965, he beat none other than Sugar Ray Robinson in Pittsburgh before 9,234 fans. It would be Robinson's last fight. Sugar was floored for a 9-count in round four, and Archer was the aggressor throughout. The three officials scored it 49-40, 50-39, and 48-41. Joey, a "cutie" if ever there was one, admitted that it was one the few times he had knocked an opponent down. The year before, he had beaten Dick Tiger over ten rounds in the Garden.

But it's not so much who beat him as much as whom he vanquished (almost all by way of decision as he lacked the knockout punch but was blessed with a slickter's tool chest). He was 30-0 before losing by SD to Jose Monon Gonzalez in 1962. He would avenge this defeat two months later and then run up a streak of 15 straight wins.

He retired in 1967 following a controversial 15 round loss to Griffith. But he could look back at spoiling the party for many notable fighters. The list included future Hall of Famer Dick Tiger, Holly Mims, malefic Rubin "Hurricane" Carter, rugged Jose Monon Gonzalez, tough Denny Moyer, the skilled Farid Salim, Don Fullmer (with whom he split a pair as he did with Monon Gonzalez), Canadian Blair Richardson, Englishman Mick Leahy and Tony Dupas (twice and when Dupas was at his peak). Seventeen of his bouts were fought at Madison Square Garden attesting to his popularity with New York City aficionados.

Like Marlon Starling, Joey Archer, 45-4, never lost a "bad" fight. And like Marlon Starling, he is not in the International Boxing Hall of Fame! Thankfully, he was inducted into the World Boxing Hall of Fame in 2005.

Bob Benoit (1966-1974)

**Benoit (on right) attacks George Holden at
The Boston Garden in 1971. (Photo courtesy of
Bob Benoit)**

It started when he beat undefeated Carter Williams aka Johnny Gil-lio in Walpole, MA in 1968. Williams would go 6-8 over the remain-der of his career reflecting the beginning of a pattern that emerged when Benoit, who was a very fine fighter in his own right, beat guys with good records coming in. They would never be the same.

Josh Hall (1968)

Hall, an exciting and heavy handed fighter, was 10-0 when he met Benoit at the Steelworkers Hall in Baltimore in 1968. Hall gave it his all in the first five rounds as he took the fight to Benoit, but then got gassed in the sixth round and Benoit came on like gangbusters winning over the Baltimore fans in the process. It was a good old fashioned barn burner and the Massachusetts native ended Hall's 10 fight win streak by taking a razor thin split decision over eight rounds.

Irish Bobby Cassidy (1969)

Irish Bobby Cassidy was 28-8-2 and well regarded when he met Benoit at the Auditorium in Worcester, Massachusetts in 1969. Ben-oit was decked in the first round but, fighting cleverly, managed to beat the heavily favored Cassidy by SD over ten rounds. It was an upset that shocked the boxing world.

Larry Carney (1970)

Benoit was again an underdog when he met Carney, 26-7-2, in Portland, Maine, but he managed a UD victory over 10 stanzas. Using his crisp jab, he popped it into Carney's face throughout the fight to win handily. Carney never stopped trying but Benoit proved too slick and shifty, mixing up his punches nicely. He almost took out his Lowell, Massachusetts opponent in the eighth when he launched punches from all angles. Carney, who went 1-0-2 against tough Joe DeNucci, would never be the same after his loss to Benoit.

Jose Roberto Chirino (1971)

This time it would be the heavily favored Chirino's turn to be upset in one of most exciting fights ever witnessed at the Embassy Hall in North Bergen, NJ. It was Chirino the slugger, 18-3-4, vs. Benoit the boxer. Benoit took the early rounds and even decked and hurt the Argentinean in the fifth with a beautiful uppercut. But Chirino took the sixth in convincing fashion only to have the red-headed Benoit take the next two stanzas as the large crowd roared its approval. The final two rounds saw Chirino land some crunching hooks while Benoit kept him at bay with crisp jabs. At the end of this thriller, Benoit's hand was raised in victory.

Jose beat legendary Nino Benvenuti, 82-5-1 at the time, in his very next fight less than two months later in Italy, but his career quickly went downhill as he lost seven of his last eight fights, and many believe it was his loss to Benoit that started things going in the wrong direction.

Macka Foley (1974)

In Bob's last fight, the very same thing happened to Foley. Benoit gained a lop-sided decision over Foley in Worcester, MA by being the aggressor throughout and smothering most of Foley's futile counters with great defensive work. Foley was 26-8-1 coming in, but would lose ten of his last sixteen against tough competition and finish with a slate of 32-20-1.

Bob Benoit not only spoiled the records of many opponents, he also spoiled their careers. He finished out his own fine career with a fine record of 37 -8.

Ted Sanders (1977-1983)

When Sanders fought Alex Ramos in 1982, he was 8-14-4 and was picked as a designated loser, but he was having none of it against the undefeated Ramos who was 15-0 at the time and a rising star in the middleweight ranks. In a shocking upset "The Sandman" knocked out Ramos in the eighth round. Alex managed to regroup, but this upset derailed his title plans.

In his very next (and last) fight, Sanders shocked I.W. Johnson, 10-1-1- coming in, by icing him in the sixth stanza in San Jose. This loss sent Johnson's career on a downward spiral.

Teddy showed his propensity as a spoiler in earlier fights including a draw in 1981 with the very capable Bernard Mays who was 19-0 at the time. A year earlier, he ruined Ronnie Brown's perfect record with a points win at the Silver Slipper in Las Vegas. In 1979 at the Dunes, he won a shocking ten rounder against power punching Mickey Goodwin, 17-0 at the time and a prohibitive favorite to dispatch The Sandman who was 2-9-2 coming in. Goodwin would finish his career with a 40-2-1 slate thus reflecting the enormity of this win.

What made Sanders so remarkable was that he won only one fight in his first eleven, though true to form, a draw came against an undefeated fighter by the name of Russell Pope. When Sanders iced Chris Black at the Silver Slipper in 1979, he was 3-10-2. This defeat ended Black's career.

Teddy would then go 6-5-2 and close out his short career with a 10-15-4 record. Nine of his opponents had perfect records coming in; only five remained so going out. Ted Sanders was a spoiler deluxe.

Mike Weaver (1972-2000)

I was a fighter who stepped in the ring and gave his best. I never came into the ring overweight or out of shape in my career. I wanted to give the crowd their money's worth and never talked bad about anyone
–Mike Weaver

He was beating the hell out of me...
–Larry Holmes

Mike "Hercules" Weaver, 46 (KOs 33)-18-1, won his first United States Heavyweight title against Stan Ward in Las Vegas knocking him out in the 9th round. Blessed with a fabulous physique, he was nicknamed "Hercules" by Ken Norton while working as his sparring partner.

On March 31, 1980, he challenged John Tate on Tate's home turf in Knoxville, Tennessee for the World Boxing Association title, and won when he knocked Tate, 20-0, cold in the 15th round with one of the greatest left hooks ever launched in a heavyweight championship fight.

James Pritchard met chill-or-be-chilled Weaver in Pritchard's hometown of Louisville, Kentucky, in August 1987. Pritchard was 16-0-1 going in and was the favorite. The unpredictable and heavy-handed Weaver (29-13-1) bombed Pritchard out in six. Pritchard quickly proceeded to go south, finishing 15-17 and losing his last four fights. He finished with a 31-18-2 (26 KOs) record, but, to his credit, he fought extremely tough opponents over the years, yet it was the fight with Hercules that sent his career in the wrong direction.

For his part, Weaver was fast becoming a destroyer of careers. He did the same to undefeated Bill Sharkey ten years earlier. Mike garnered serious attention when he iced power punching Bernardo Mercado, 20-1, in 1978 and almost pulled off a giant upset when he decked and hurt undefeated Larry Holmes, 30-0, in 1979. After beating Tate, Hercules defended his title by knocking out Gerrie Coetzee, 3-1 and beating undefeated James Tillis. The Coetzee win came in South Africa and reflected Mike's propensity to spoil parties that were hosted in unfriendly locales.

He did not help Carl "the Truth" Williams, 17-1 coming in, when he KO'd him in two in 1986, and contributed greatly to Harry Terrell's change in career direction. Phil Brown lost seven in a row after losing to Weaver. Another Weaver victim, Bill Corrigan, lost eight out of ten and retired. In 1987, he traveled to Johannesburg and knocked out undefeated South African Johnny DuPlooy in seven.

Call him a career-ender or a spoiler, Mike Weaver meant big time trouble for those he fought. The soft-spoken, sensitive Weaver once revealed that he really didn't like hurting his opponents. Nevertheless, he always brought great excitement into the ring.

Smokin' Bert Cooper (1984-2002)

With a final record of 36 (KO 30) - 22 (KO 14), Cooper was another ice-or-be-iced kind of fighter, but he also spoiled the dreams of many an up and comer. In his second to last fight, he beat Craig Tomlinson, 23-9, for the Vacant Pennsylvania State Heavyweight Title. In 1997, he KO'd undefeated but terribly over-hyped Richie "The Bull" Melito for something called the vacant WBF heavyweight title. In 1991, he came within a hair of knocking out Evander Holyfield for the WBA and IBF heavyweight titles, but Holyfield held on and finally TKO'd the dangerous Cooper in the 7th round. Having suffered the first knockdown of his pro career as a result of a strong counter right hook in Round 3, Holyfield regrouped and administered a terrible beating that left Cooper unable to defend himself.

In 1990, he stopped Orlin Norris, 22-1, for the NABF heavy-weight title. Andre "Big Daddy" McCall was 13-0-1 when he met Smokin' Bert in 1987 in Atlantic City. After being iced by Cooper, McCall finished out his spoiled career with a 14-7-1 slate.

That same year, Bert fought undefeated favorite Willie DeWitt in Saskatchewan, Canada and took him out in two. The win against the highly touted DeWitt was perhaps his crowning role as a spoiler. The Canadian had an outstanding amateur career that peaked in the 1984 Olympic Games when he won a Silver Medal. He then turned pro and won the Canadian Heavyweight Title. However, he received a rude shock when he met the vicious-hit-ting Philadelphian who hit him flush and often dropping him four times in two rounds en route to the quick stoppage win. It would be Willie's only career defeat as he retired with a 20-1-1 record. He now lives comfortably as a lawyer in Canada.

Bert Cooper was the quintessential spoiler and no matter who he fought, his heavy hands and lethal Philadelphia style hooks always posed a threat

Manning "The Spoiler" Galloway (1978-2006)

Manning "The Spoiler" Galloway, 62-19-1, is another who quickly comes to mind. This aptly nicknamed light middleweight, who fought from 1978-2006, beat upstart Ricardo Williams Jr. in 2004. Williams won a Silver Medal at the 2000 Olympic Games, and was immediately touted as a future star and the best fighter to come out of the 2000 games. He also stopped Anthony Jones, 34-5-1, in Puerto Rico in 1994, took heavily favored Pat Barrett's measure in 1992, beat the legendary Australian Jeff "Falsh" Malcolm. 79-21-10 coming in, in Australia in 1991, stopped Gert Bo Jacobsen, 29-2, in Randers, Denmark by TKO also in 1991, and defeated Al Hamza, 23-3-2, in Yabucoa, Puerto Rico, in 1989 for the vacant WBO welterweight title. These high profile fights were won far from the friendly confines of "The Spoiler's" home state of Ohio thus affirming his moniker.

Darryl Pinckney (1985-2006)

Before he took a deep slide south starting in 1997, "The Nightmare," 21-21-2 at the time, was the quintessential spoiler when he shocked and stopped undeafted Guty Espadas Jr. in 1996. A year earlier, he KOd undefeated Louie Leija.

In 1994 and with a record of 18-18-2, he shocked and stopped 33-1 Junior Jones in 3 rounds at Bally's Park Place Hotel in Atlantic City. Two years earlier, he iced Prudencio Cardona, 40-22-1 at the time.

He lost 21 of his last 24 fights including 12 at the tail end and finished with 24-42-3 record, but he had plenty to brag about with some early, high profile surprise wins—all by clean stoppage and all against heavily favored fighters coming in.

In many instances and like Freddie Pendleton, he was able to level the playing field over more obviously talented opponents. Darryl Pinckney ruined expectations and was a spoiler's spoiler.

19

WHAT MAKES A CLOSET CLASSIC?

Quite simply, when an exceptionally great fight is not widley tele-vised or professionally taped and the details are thereafter passed on by word of mouth, the fight can gain closet classic and even cult status (or both such as the case of Murphy vs. Mutti). Foreman-Lyle, Castillo-Corrales, Moorer-Cooper, Somsak Sithchatchawal vs. Mahyar Monshipour and Durelle-Moore were classics in the true sense, but they were seen in plain sight. Closet classics stand the test of time; they are talked about decades after they happened. Aficionados continue to talk about Brooks-Curry as if it happened yesterday.

Let's review some closet classics of yore.

Danny Nardico vs. Charley Norkus (1954)

Danny Nardico (50-13-4, 35 KOs), was an ex-Marine who had been awarded multiple Purple Hearts in WWII. He holds the distinction of being the only man in boxing history to put Jake LaMotta on the deck (in a 1952 fight in Florida, LaMotta was knocked down in the 7th by a right hand and his corner stopped the bout between the 7th and 8th rounds). Nardico put together a string of wins and knockouts to move into middleweight contention during the 1950s. Not unlike Charlie Norkus, he fit into an exciting mold of a hard-hitting, aggressive puncher without much defense. He never did get a title shot, but he entertained as a rugged combatant and fought very tough opposition.

Charley Norkus out of Queens, New York, was also a top ranked heavyweight fighter. In a professional career that began in 1948, he amassed a record of 33-19 (22 KOs). He was undefeated as a boxer in the US Marines in 1946–1947. He became known as "the Bay-onne Bomber." He possessed a lethal left hook that also produced a string of KO victories.

One of his friends and stable mates was fellow New Jersey Hall of Famer Ernie "the Rock" Durando, a personal friend of mine back in the 70s. I mention this because I had many opportunities to discuss Norkus with Ernie and to learn some interesting things about his war with Nardico.

By 1955, Charlie was a highly ranked heavyweight, beating such notables as Roland LaStarza, Cesar Brion, and an undefeated Charlie Powell to whom he lost in a rematch. Charlie had notable non-title fights against champions Archie Moore, Willie Pastrano and Ezzard Charles, but his most talked about and perhaps career-defining fight was against the aforementioned and highly touted Nardico.

The Fight

Here it was, two ex-Marines, both possessing paralyzing power, meeting in the square ring in Miami Beach in 1954 and there was palpable anticipation of a brawl. What the fans got was something that went beyond.

Both fighters were ripped with monster biceps and broad backs. Norkus looked much bigger and actually outweighed his opponent by 16 pounds (197-181). He controlled the early action and put Nardico down in the second with a long and thunderous right. Nardico was hurt again and decked in the third, and was also thrown to the canvas twice by the stronger Norkus who fought in an old-timer standup sort of way reminiscent of James J. Corbett. Nardico used good movement and a counter left to keep Norkus away and survive the round.

In the fourth, Nardico turned the tables on Norkus and hurt him badly with his trademark left hook. Both fighters forgot about body shots and exchanged simultaneous head shots that would have KOd most. These were haymakers and each was meant to end the fight. And one almost did as Norkus caught one of Nardico's patented left hooks and went down like he had been sapped. He was on Queer Street but Nardico could not finish him off.

Both fighters continued to exchange sizzling shots in the fifth and sixth and both were wobbled. The brutal battle continued into the seventh when Charlie unloaded a number of crunching overhand rights on Nardico's head, but right at the bell, Danny floored Norkus with a sharp and sneaky right to win the round.

Then in the ninth, Nardico attacked at the bell with a sense of urgency and Norkus met the intended onslaught with a brutal straight right

WHAT MAKES A CLOSET CLASSIC?

that sent Danny down and for all practical purposes out. Somehow, he got up and was sent down again by a flurry of Charlie's clubbing shots. The referee inexplicably let the fight continue and Norkus attacked again with crunching shots that left Nardico helpless. This time the referee had no alternative but to stop the slaughter.

The fight was an incredible and savage pier six affair yielding eight knockdowns and several pushes to the deck that could have been ruled knockdowns. It was full-tilt boogie violence featuring a total disregard for defense on the part of both fighters. Officially, Nardico went down six times (3 in the ninth) and Norkus twice.

This was a 1950s fight at its very best; a thrilling rocker in which both fighters gave their all. The fight is still written and talked about today, though few have seen it. A rematch on national TV had no knock downs but was a toe-to-toe affair with Norkus the victor again

Postscript: I have a video of the action which just might be worth a fortune.

Hector Carrasquilla vs. Soo Hwan Hong (1977)

The Lead Up

Hong was 38-4-3 coming in while Carrasquilla was 10-0 with all wins coming by KO. The fight was for the vacant WBA super bantamweight title (a newly created title) and was held in Panama City, Panama

The Panamanian challenger, at 17 years 186 days, was attempting to become history's second-youngest world champion. Wilfred Benitez was 17 years 180 days old when he won the WBA junior welterweight championship by beating the great Antonio Cervantes in March 1976.

The bout took place in Hector's hometown of Panama City and most thought it was the perfect time for the veteran, Hong, to taste bitter defeat since none of Carrasquilla's fights lasted more than three rounds

At 27, Hong was somewhat battle worn, but had experienced much success coming into this frey. After winning a number of South Korean titles, he stepped up the level of competition. He knocked out future world title challenger Thanomchit Sukothai in eight and a three-round KO of Susumu Inuoe was followed by his biggest win to date, a 10-round decision over former WBA flyweight champion Berkrerk Chartvanchai. He then beat Arnold Taylor by 15-round decision to capture the WBA bantamweight title in Durban, South Africa in an exciting fight in its own right, but he would later lose the WBA belt to legendary Alfonso Zamora, who, like Carrasquilla, was both young and powerful at the time.

Hong earned a rematch with Zamora by going 9-0-1 in his next 10 fights. The fight took place in October 1976 in historic Inchon. Hong fought competitively before the fight was stopped controversially in the 12th, prompting the pro-Hong crowd to riot.

Following his two disappointing stoppage losses to Zamora, he earned a spot in the WBA elimination tournament. Carrasquilla had already earned his spot by knocking out Jesus Esparragoza. Hong grabbed the other final slot by decision over Futaro Tanaka thus setting up the battle.

The Fight

The excitement was incredible as the fans sensed something special was in the offing, but nobody could have anticipated what they were about to see.

In round one, the young Panamanian showed uncommon composure by sizing up Hong who, for his part, blended shots to the body followed by sharp uppercuts upstairs. Carrasquilla landed three rights to Hong's head late in the round and that stopped the Korean's momentum immediately. All in all, the first round showcased a volume puncher and a lanky stylist.

Carrasquilla began the second using his jab while Hong, in classic Korean fashion, dug to the body from long range. The two began exchanging heavy shots and the crowd was up and screaming. Then the Panamanian unloaded three short, jackhammer hooks, and Hong hit the canvas as the crowd roared its encouragement. The fireworks had started.

Hong took the 8-count and tried to smother Carrasquilla's lethal shots, but was hit again by picture perfect combinations of straight rights followed by hooks. Finally, he was decked by one such combo and when he got up, he was on wobbly legs.

Carrasquilla was not through with the onslaught as he sent Hong down for a third time with a right to the body and a right to the jaw. The crowd sensed the fight was over since this had been the third knockdown, but referee Jay Edson let it continue superimposing his own discretion over the three knockdown rule.

Hong's legs could barely hold him upright. Ten, while groggy and on Queer Street, he went into survival mode. He then hit the canvas from still another lethal right-left to the chin, and the crowd thought the fight now would surely be halted, but the gutsy Hong, fighting with the "never-say-die" tradition of Koreans, incredibly arose, this time at six. The slaughter continued, and Hong was then rocked by a rainstorm of power shots from Carrasquilla who smelled championship on every punch. Two hooks and a right crashed off Hong's jaw as the round mercifully (for Hong) came to an end.

Round three started and the teenage bomber was met by Hong, who surprisingly charged out of his corner two thirds of the way across the ring. Somehow, Hong looked fresh as he circled Carrasquilla and bounced up and down on legs that now seemed okay. Then, incredibly, he hurt Carrasquilla with a page out of the young Panamanian's own book; namely, a hook to the body and a right to the temple. Something was going on here and the crowd suddenly became quiet. Hong started to press the action using a high punch volume that was his signature style. The tide had now turned.

Hong then let it all hang out as he launched an all-out attack using bruising uppercuts and ripping hooks to the body as Carrasquilla's legs began to wobble. Hong then positioned himself to lower the boom on the badly hurt youngster. And then it happened.

The Korean snapped Carrasquilla's head straight back with a sledge-hammer hook and then hit him again with a hook that caught Hector as he was falling to the canvas. Carrasquilla was flat on his back along the ropes and barely moved. Edson couinted to ten and Hong miraculously became the WBA's first junior featherweight champion.

Carrasquilla was never the same fighter after this remarkable bout later losing to fellow Panamanian Eusebio Pedroza for the WBA featherweight title—and then to undefeated Ruben Castillo in a short but thrilling affair in 1981. He was 21 when he retired with a slate of 17-5 with 15 KOs.

Soo Hwan Hong fought just three more times after his classic with Carrasquilla. He defended his new belt against Yu Kasahara in February 1978, scoring five knockdowns en route to an impressive 15-round decision in another seldom talked about but sizzling fight. He was then stopped in 12 by Ricardo Cardona in Seoul. His final fight was a rematch with tough Dong Kyun Yum in 1980 and it ended in a 10-round draw. Hong's final record was fine 40-5-4 (13 KOs), but his greatest moment would come on November 26, 1977 in Panama City when he displayed the courage of a true South Korean warrior. If you like cult classics, you will love this one.

Lee Roy Murphy vs. Chisanda Mutti (1985)

Lee Roy Murphy, known as "Solid Gold," was one of the greatest amateur fighters to come out of Chicago with a record of 157-17 and the 1979 Light Heavyweight National Golden Gloves title. I saw him fight many times in the amateurs and can attest to his brilliance. Only President Jimmy Carter's senseless boycott of the 1980 Moscow Olympics (see list below) prevented him from reaching his true amateur acclaim and a possible Gold Medal.

106: Robert Shannon, Edmonds, Wash.

112: Richard Sandoval, Pomona, Calif.

119: Jackie Beard, Jackson, Tenn.

125: Bernard Taylor, Charlotte, N.C.

132: Joe Manley, Army

139: Johnny Bumphus, Nashville, Tenn.

157: Donald Curry, Fort Worth, Texas

156: James Shuler, Philadelphia, Pa.

165: Charles Carter, Yakima, Wash.

178: Leroy Murphy, Chicago, Ill.

+178: James Broad, Army

Turning pro in 1980, he ran off 24 straight wins before suffering his first defeat. In 1984, he won the IBF cruiserweight title with a dramatic 14th round KO of Marvin Camel in Montana. After taking out Joe Louis in the twelfth stanza, he was set to meet Zambian Chisana Mutti in Monte Carlo.

Mutti was a tough customer who had fought at a high level almost from the start of his career. In fact, he fought Englishman Tony Sibson in just his fourth pro outing. Only two of his 35 career opponents had a losing record.

This October 19, 1985 shootout would end up being a closet classic, and because of the way it ended, a cult classic as well.

The Fight

The first seven rounds involved incredible seesaw action with both fighters exchanging bombs that had dreamland printed all over them. Neither dominated for sustained periods of time and the fight became a classic ebb and flow war of attrition. The number of punishing head shots each absorbed was frankly alarming. Moreover, both warriors were fast becoming exhausted. Mutti used vicious jab-hook-cross combos that quickly served notice he would not be an easy mark.

Here is what fellow writer Lee Groves had to say:

"The crowd heartily applauded the action, and why not? For a division originally created to accommodate too-fat light heavies and too-small heavyweights, this fight represented the best of both worlds – the power of the big boys and the speed of the smaller men. Both combatants were intent on inflicting damage in the eighth and both succeeded as they teed off on each other and continually traded the momentum. Neither man made much of an effort to evade the incoming bombs as they concentrated on loading up and letting the bullets scatter wherever they may."[1]

In the ninth, Mutti decked Murphy with a volley of vicious shots begun with a left that turned Murphy's back to him. It appeared he would be taken out forthwith, but somehow he survived the round. He then returned the favor with a series of molar rattling rights in the eleventh and now it was Mutti's turn to make it to the bell. Both guys had been down; both were ready for the taking going into the championship rounds.

Again, Groves captures it perfectly,

"But Murphy was too strong for Mutti to hold off for long. A one-two and a double right snapped Mutti's head after which the champion moved in for the kill. But Mutti again turned the tables when a hook and a right to the temple made Murphy slump into the ropes. Both men stood on the precipice of victory and defeat simultaneously, each just a punch or two away from ending the fight, and as the bell rang Mutti had trouble finding his corner while Murphy trudged toward his. With three rounds remaining, this already action-packed bout was building toward an unforgettable crescendo."[2]

The fight turned into something else in the twelfth when both fighters exchanged bombs in a neutral corner and then they threw lightening fast rights simultaneously and both landed simultaneous. They both fell together in a heap hanging on to each other with Mutti landing atop Murphy before sliding to the floor. Glancing at Murphy who was struggling to get up (and keeping tabs on the progress of both), referee Larry Hazzard began the count over Mutti. Murphy was badly hurt and barely made it up at the seven count, but Hazzard proceeded to count out Mutti at the 1:53 mark. Mutti then stayed down a full three minutes. Behind on the scorecards at the time, Murphy had retained his title in what can only be described as a surreal fight.

Neither fighter would ever be the same after this grueling fight. "Solid Gold" would lose his title by TKO to Ricky Parkey a year later. Mutti would go 2-4-1 before retiring in 1989. But for 12 rounds on October 19, 1985, in Monte Carlo, Monaco, these two would provide fireworks that have seldom been witnessed before or after in the square circle.

Oh Kon Son vs. Myung-Woo Yuh (1986)

These two Koreans met in Seoul on September 8, 1986 in a fight that featured head to head exchanges without let up and which had Son's face a bloody mess by the sixth round.

Son suffered two standing 8-counts during the first six rounds, but gave as well as he took against the more skilled Myung-Woo Yuh who used sharp combos to slice and dice Son. Finally, in the seventh stanza, he dropped Son with a body shot and the fight was wisely halted. Son, as is the case with most Korean fighters, is one of those who must be saved from himself.

In March 2006, Somsak Sithchatchawal took part in what would later win Ring Magazine's Fight of the Year laurels. He challenged WBA Super Bantamweight champion Mahyar Monshipour. Sithchatchawal dropped Monshipour in the first round, and won via TKO in the 10th round to capture the belt.

Somsak Sithchatchawal vs. Mahyar Monshipour was an incredible fight; a true classic. While it flew somewhat under the radar, it was named Ring Magazine's 2006 Fight of the Year thus precluding it from being called a Closet Classic. Here is what fellow writer James Slater had to say about it: "...The 9th round was especially mind-blowing. In this session, with the two rivals beginning to tire, they traded blow after blow with absolutely no regard for defense. Both swinging for the fences, the spectacle was like few others ever seen inside a boxing ring. Finally, as round number ten approached its end, the stubbornness was drained from the man from France. As Sithchatchawal teed off, making Monshipour head visibly reel as he did so, British referee John Coyle dived in to call a halt. One of, if not the best-ever, fights in boxing history had ended."[3]

The Son-Yuh savagery was every bit as good, but went unnoticed and thus achieved true cult classic status.

And speaking of Myung-Woo Yuh, who finished with a 38-1 record, he made 17 successful title defenses during his first reign, the record for the 108 pound division. He avenged his only loss to Hiroki Ioka. The question remains, however, why is he not in the International Boxing Hall of Fame?

Leland Hardy vs. Ike Padilla (1989)

While televised, this one was not witnessed by many people and there has been sparse discussion about it. This epic battle was the Madison Square Garden "Fight of the Year" in 1989 and was listed by Boxing Scene Magazine as one of the "Top 20 Fights of the 80's." Reminiscent of Foreman vs. Lyle, Hardy vs. Padilla is considered by most pundits of the sport to be the single greatest non-main event bouts of all time. You want ooooes and aaaas? This will give you ooooes and aaaas.

Hardy was a tall, skinny heavyweight with good hand speed, a hell of a punch, and a glass jaw. Padilla was a physically strong former NYC Golden Gloves champ who was undefeated and untested as a pro. The match was supposed to be a record-building showcase for the better-known Padilla, but instead, it signaled the beginning of the end of his pro dream.

Following a tough, rather non-committal first round, won by Padilla, Ike came out blasting in the second and quickly sent Hardy down with a thud. In most of his previous losses, Leland seldom rose from the first knockdown, but this time he dragged himself off the canvas, weathered some hellish moments, and slowly worked his way back into the action before dropping a shocked Padilla near the bell.

In the third, it was time for Hardy to rush wildly forward in an effort to end it all. In so doing, he ran face-first into the best overhand right that the still wobbly Padilla could throw and went to the floor as if sapped by a Chicago cop. Commentator Gil Clancy stated that he didn't think Leland could have been hit harder than that. The fragile-chinned Hardy might as well have been a body pulled from a bus crash, for all of the life he showed upon going down, but again he somehow willed himself up and convinced the referee that he could continue. Though rejuvenated by this second knockdown, Ike was still in a world of trouble himself, yet he stumbled forward and threw everything in his arsenal in an effort to finish Hardy.

Hardy leaned against the ropes, took some flush shots while swaying out of the path of others (almost accidentally, it seemed), and eventually began to counter instinctively. It was enough. With Padilla on the verge of recovering completely and crushing Leland, the latter crossed over a right which splattered the local favorite so forcefully on the deck that the referee stopped the match instantly not even bothering to count. Clancy called the event a "great, great heavyweight fight." Each man was down twice in fewer than three full rounds.

Padilla's career never re-ignited, and he retired soon afterwards. Hardy won a few more times and was knocked out a few more times before retiring and going into his far more lucrative second calling as a high-level sports agent/financier, eventually being instrumental in the pro football career of talented but under-achieving Ricky Williams.

Note: Great gratitude extended to Pete Leonitis for much of the above report.

Tommy Morrison-Joe Hipp (1992)

I was up screaming at the screen. You find a fighter today that can finish a fight with a broken jaw and two broken hands and come out a winner.
    —Tommy Morrison's mother, Diana "Flossie" Good

A prime Tommy "The Duke" Morrison was a powerful fighter who possessed a great left hook; however, he was "chinny" and that factor made him an exciting fighter though it cost him against stiff punchers.

Joe "The Boss" Hipp, a fringe contender and a member of the Black-foot Tribe, was a rough, tough heavyweight out of Yakima, Washington and the type of guy you didn't want to meet in an unfriendly bar.

While Tommy had the punch but a suspect chin, Joe was gritty with solid whiskers at that point in his career.

On a three-fight winning streak and 24-2 coming in, Hipp met "The Duke" in Reno, Nevada on a hot sunny afternoon on June 27, 1992. After suffering a devastating KO loss to Ray Mercer in 1991, Tommy, 32-1, was on a 4-fight winning streak of his own. Both had fought Harry Terrell and both had iced him early. Still, Morrison was the clear favorite in what promised to be a barroom brawl for as long as it lasted. As it turned out, the fight was all of that and more.

The Fight

In what was one of the most brutal wars of the 90's, The Boss gave The Duke all he could handle for nine rounds. Joe was a south-paw on top of being a durable fighter, and south paws gave Tommy trouble. Morrison suffered a broken jaw thanks to a savage Hipp right in the second stanza. As a result, he began breathing through his mouth and was soon sucking air like a fish out of water. He also broke one hand and fractured the other one by the halfway point. To compliment these dangerous injuries, he sustained a severe cut over his right eye (it would later require 20 stitches). The barroom brawl was going on in earnest.

Morrison put Hipp down in the fifth with a combo that featured a thundering right, a vicious uppercut, and then another straight right combination, but the durable Indian survived and got back into the fight. However, he had sustained shattered cheek bones in these exchanges. By the middle of the ninth, Morrison appeared to be fading rapidly. He looked gassed and in pain, badly cut above one eye and bleeding from the mouth. His jaw was hanging wide-open.

Hipp was now coming on strong and the fight clearly was up for grabs, but then, like a bolt of lightening, The Duke staggered Hipp with a crushing right hand and took him out with a right-left-right combo that had assault and battery written all over it. Blood and sweat splattered with the force of the blows. The fight was immediately halted by referee Vic Drakulich as Hipp was just rising inside the count.

Joe Hipp had put Tommy through pure hell. At the time of stoppage, judges Keith McDonald and Herb Santos had it for Morrison both by the slim margin of 76-75 while Doug Tucker had it 75-76 for the Boss.

Here is what The Boss had to say about the fight in a 20008 interview with James Slater:

"Oh, the Morrison fight, that was a great war! I lost the first 3 rounds when he was trying his best to take me outta there. But then I thought, if I'm gonna lose, I'm not gonna lose backing up (laughs). So I stood and traded with him. I felt good after the fight; I knew I'd given my all and that it was a good fight. There are no good heavyweight fights like that today. I felt it was a bad stoppage, I was up at the count of 6 (after being decked in round 9), but the ref stopped it. In a way that fight did more good for me than it did for Tommy, I actually went up higher in the world rankings than him afterwards. It was hard fight though, I broke his jaw, he broke my cheek bone!" [4]

The fight was televised ABC's Wide World of Sports, but it was an afternoon show in the spring and many fans missed it. Yet the video footage affirmed what those who were lucky enough to witness it live knew; namely, it was a classic in every sense of the word—one that featured broken bones and blood and guts.

Philadelphia Mayhem (1992)

The Setting

On March 10, 1992, welterweight Tim Rabon met Philadelphian William "The Hammer" Jones at the Blue Horizon in Philadelphia in a 4-rounder that was televised on Tuesday Night fights as part of a bigger venue. Those who were fortunate enough to see this one will never forget it. Rabon was 13-7-2 at the time. Jones was 18-0 but his only notable win was a KO over Rafael Williams, and his overall level of opposition was very poor. In fact, only five opponents had winning records. As well, most of the Hammer's fights took place in the friendly confines of the Blue Horizon Rabon, out of Broussard, Louisiana, had duked with much better fighters, but had just fair success. He was knocked out by Santos Cardona and Tyrone Moore, fought a draw with then undefeated Chad Parker (19-0), split a pair of SD's with Jason Watters, and lost on points to Kevin Pompey,

Reggie Miller and the very capable Aussie Jeff "Flash" Malcom (for the IBC Welterweight Title). Malcom was 77-21-10 at the time. One other thing, Rabon was a National Golden Gloves Champion in 1984 (along with such notables as Ronnie Essett, Virgil Hill, Evander Holyfield and Mike Tyson). On paper, the undefeated Jones looked ripe for the picking.

The Fight

The fight was a barnburner during the first two rounds with both tall and skinny fighters wasted no time as they teed off on each other with long and looping shots that had deadly intentions written all over them. The punishment absorbed by both fighters was alarming, and those at ringside were sprayed by the sweat as each thundering shot came down the pike. Then, in the incredible third round, things heated up fast as "The Hammer" lived up to his nickname by flooring and punishing Rabon in the early going and appeared to be on his way to a crunching finish.

But miraculously, Rabon caught Jones with a solid hook that had him hurt and hanging on. He then floored him and when he got up, stalked him down like a Tiger sensing a fresh kill and floored him again. But in so doing, he used up serious energy and Jones knew it. Indeed, Rabon had punched himself out and was now helpless and ready to be hammered into submission, but time was running out. With seconds to go in the round, Jones backed Rabon into a corner and took him out with a single debilitating shot to the liver. The bell had rung but Tim could not get up. He was counted out four seconds after the round was over. These nine minutes of unmitigated mayhem featured everything: give and take, ebb and flow, courage, determination and ferocity.

Rabon would lose most of his remaining fights against very creditable opposition and finished with a slate of 14-12-2. Jones would never be the same losing two of his next four. Both defeats came at the hands of another Philadelphian, ultra tough Eric Holland. His final record was 21-2 and he retired in 1994 after being KOd by Holland in 1995.

The career of both would be defined by what happened at the Blue Horizon on March 10, 1992. They call it the "Legendary Blue Horizon" and fights like this contributed greatly to that Moniker.

Postscript: Beau Williford, Tim's proud manager/trainer, recently shared this poignant email message:

"My boxer Timmy Rabon (MAY HE REST IN PEACE) who passed away a few months ago from Lou Gehrig's disease, was one of the most fun guys I ever had the opportunity to work with. Timmy [a two-time National Golden Gloves Champion] said the reason he lost to Jones was the altitude, the ring was very high he joked. He jokingly said he was not in shape to climb five steps.

One Christmas Eve, (1989 I think) Timmy called me to borrow some money to buy presents for his children. He wanted to borrow $50.00 and I told him NO! Astonished he said Beau I promise to pay you back. I then told him I would not loan him $50.00, but would loan him $300.00. I waited for over two hours for him to show up but he never did. He phoned me to tell me he had two dollars when he left to come to my house and stopped at a gas station to put a dollars worth of gas in his car and then decided to take a chance on a $10,000.00 lottery ticket. He purchased the winning lottery ticket and asked me if I needed any Christmas money!!!

A truly wonderful guy who I am sure is entertaining the angels with his great stories."

Other solid candidates for "Closet Classic" status (winner on left):

Ezzard Charles vs. Nick Barone (1950)	— Barone off his feet and out for first time in career
Bob Baker vs. Sid Peaks (1950)	— Baker down for first time in career pulls it out in 5th
Bob Satterfield vs. Lee Oma (1950)	— Bob ices Oma after almost being iced himself
Jake LaMotta vs Laurent Dauthuille (1950)	— KO win for Jake in last 13 seconds of 15th round
Bob Satterfield vs. Tommy Gomez (1950)	— Gutsy Gomez down 4 times but refuses to give up
Georgie Small vs. Laverne Roach (1950)	— bloody battle that ends tragically for Laverne
Rex Layne vs. Bob Satterfield (1951)	— Layne comes from behind to KO "Rapid Robert" late.
Bob Murphy vs. Jake LaMotta (1951)	— Jake could not answer the bell for the 8th round!
Gil Turner vs. Kid Gavilan (1952)	— The "Keed" wins it with a late round KO before 39,000 fans
Robert Villemain vs. Joey DeJohn (1952)	— both down but Joey is down 5 times and out in 9th
Roland LaStarza vs. Dan Bucceroni (1952)	— Dan down 5 times but survives the 10-round limit
Ike Thomas vs. Charley Norkus (1953)	— Norkus mauled and stopped after leaing early
Charley Norkus vs. Charley Powell (1954)	— both down until Powell drops three times in 7th
Peter Muller vs. Ernie Durando (1954)	— Muller down thrice, Durando twice and iced in war
Marty Marshall vs. Herbie Moore (1954)	— One of the most unusual fights ever held. Two in one

Sid Peaks vs.
Bob Jackson (1954)

— Jackson way ahead then gets dropped thrice in 9th to lose

Eduardo Lausse vs.
Gene Fullmer (1955)

— Lausse decks Fullmer in route to UD win

Bob Satterfiield vs
Johnny Summerlin (1956)

— Johnny knocked out of ring but survives

Bob Satterfiield vs.
Warnell Lester (1956)

— Trailing, Bob wins it with last round knockout.

Sid Peaks vs.
Ernie Cab (1956)

— Peaks down twice in 1st rallies to take a SD

Bob Satterfiield vs.
Garvin Sawyer (1957)

— Bob pulls it out with knock down in last round

Rocky Castellani vs.
Felix Benson (1957)

— both down but Rocky wins UD near end of career

Gene Armstrong vs.
Rory Calhoun (1958)

— Rory down in the 1st, 2nd, 4th, and 9th rounds

Spider Webb vs.
Rory Calhoun (1958)

— Webb down twice; then ices Rory

Cleveland Williams vs.
Curley Lee Chapman (1959)

— Williams says it's his "toughest fight"

Marcel Pigou vs.
Eduardo Lausse (1960)

— Gatti-Ward type battle royal of the 60's

Curtis Cokes vs. Luis
Manuel Rodriguez (1961)

— El Feo is dropped in 5TH and loses SD

Denny Moyer vs.
Sugar Ray Robinson (1962)

— Moyer almost iced the great Sugar, almost

Ruben Carter vs.
Emile Griffith (1963)

— Hurricane suddenly blows away Griffith in one

Flash Elorde vs.
Teruo Kosaka (1964)

— Kosaka leading at time of stop page in 12th

Flash Elorde vs.
Teruo Kosaka (1965)

— Kosaka down 5 times and fi nally out in 15th

Flash Elorde vs. Ismael Laguna (1966)	— Laguna down in the 4th and 9th rounds
Emile Griffith vs. Nino Benvenuti (1967)	— Griffith aveneges "Fight of Year" loss that same year
Vincente Saldivar vs. Howard Winstone (1967)	— razor thin win in thrilling 15 rounder in Wales
Shozo Saijo vs — Flash Besande (1968)	— Saijo snuffs out Flash in brutal outing
Bob Benoit vs. Josh Hall (1968)	— Benoit rallies and wins over his opponent's fans in barnburner
Chartchai Chionoi vs. Efrem Torres bouts (1968, 69, 70)	— "wow" for all 3! Chionoi in others too
Bob Foster vs. Andy Kendall (1969)	— a war from the opening bell but Foster was a great finisher
Mac Foster vs. Roger Rischer (1969)	— Roger downn 7 times before done in fourth
Leotis Martin vs Sonny Liston (1969)	— As Howard Cossel said, a crushing and compelling KO
Mando Ramos vs Sugar Ramos (1970)	— bloody classic between a the Rmos's
Ruben Olivares vs Kazuyoshi Kanazawa (1971)	—brutal fight, Kanazawa down thrice in 14th
Bob Benoit vs Jose Roberto Chirino (1971)	— ebb and flow thriller as Bob takes upset win
Masao Ohba vs Orlando Amores (1972)	— come-from-behind in for the great Ohba
Masao Ohba vs Chartchai Chionoi (1973)	— another and maybe the best of his career
Danny Lopez vs. Genzo Kurosaw (1974)	— "Little Red" launches 1,791 punches over 10 rounds.
Jerry Quarry vs Joe Alexander (1974)	— Quarry in early trouble wakes up and ices Joe in 2nd

Ron Lyle vs Eranie
Shavers (1975)

– both down until Lyle ends
matters

Danny Lopez vs
Ruben Olivares (1975)

– high energy thriller; is Little
Red in any other kind?

Victor Galindez vs.
Richie Kates (1976)

– Fight stopped with just one
second left in the 15th. Why?!

Earnie Shavers vs Roy
"Tiger" Williams (1976)

– incredible late round action

Bennie Brisco vs Eugene
Cyclone Hart (1976)

– seldom mentioned war ends in
draw

Matthew Saad
Muhammad vs
Marvin Johnson (1977)

– savage 12 rounds until Saad
ends it

Jorge Lujan vs.
Alfonzon Zamora (1977)

– Dramatic late round icing wins
it for "Mocho."

Danny Lopez vs.
Juan Malvarez (1978)

– Two-round shoot-out win for
"Little Red"

Carlos Palomino vs.
Armando Muniz (1978)

– Carlos down in 1st stops
Mando in 15th!

Bruce Curry vs
Monroe Brooks (1978)

– epic ebb and flow closet classic
with everthing in it

Soo Hwan Hong vs
Yu Kasahara (1978)

– Hong scores 5 knockdowns in
route to 15 round win

Luis Resto (yes, that Resto) vs
Pat Hallacy (1979)

– two-way mayhem

Matthew Saad Muhammad vs
Marvin Johnson (1979)

– another Saad barnburner

Randall Tex Cobb vs
Earnie Shavers (1980)

– big bombs away as both gives
and takes beatings

Saoul Mamby vs
Estaban De Jesus (1980)

– 13th round stoppage wins it
for road warrior Sauol

Leo Randolph vs Ricardo
Cardona (1980)

– Olympian wins via TKO in the
15th round

Bill "Caveman" Lee vs John LoCicero (1981)	– back and forth brutality; an all time great
Frank "The Animal" Fletcher vs Ernie Singletary (1981)	– both hospitalized
Rolando "Bad Boy from Dadiangas" Navarette vs Chung-il Choi (1982)	– both down
Bazooka Limon vs Rolando Navarette (1982)	– uppercut ends it at 3:08 mark of round 12
Alexis Arguello vs, Andrew Ganigan (1982)	– real war until the 5th when Andy is iced at end of round
Ray Mancini vs Arturo Frias (1982)	– 2.54 seconds of pure back-and-forth fury
Frank Fletcher vs James Green (1982)	– wild, give-and-take win for Animal
Frank Fletcher vs. Curtis Ramsey (1983)	– another wild, give-and-take win for the Animal
Juan Domingo Roldan vs Frank Flether (1983)	– Roldan sends Frank to Animal Dreamland
Juan LaPorte vs Ruben Castillo (1983)	– 12 rounds of war at Roberto Clemente Coliseum in PR
Dujuan Johnson vs Brian Janssen (1984)	– incredible come-from–behind icing by Johnson
Alex Ramos vs. Curtis Parker (1984)	– A pure masterpiec; Arguably Alex's finest fight
Carl Williams vs. Jesse Furguson (1985)	– Williams down more than once but still wins.
Jorge Garcia vs. Tommy Cordova (1985)	– The first of two brutal draws between these two.
Mark Kaylor vs Errol Christie (1985)	– Brit grudge match
Harry Arroyo vs Terrence Alli (1985)	– maybe a pure classic; it was that exciting
Robin Blake vs Adolfo Medel (1985)	– an under-the-radar war with give-and-take all the way

Renaldo Snipes vs.
Bobby Crabtree (1986)
— Snipes wins with KO in 5th after crunching action

Antonio Avelar vs
Wilfredo Vazquez (1986)
— unforgettable fifth round in come-from-behind win

Bobby Czyz vs Willie
Edwards (1987)
— see-saw battle that ends in Bobby's favor in 2nd

Thomas Hearns vs
Juan Roldan (1987)
— great 4th as both trade bombs before Hearns lands big

Kelvin Seabrooks vs
Thierry Jacob (1987)
— Seabrooks down thrice, Jacob once

Lloyd Christie vs
Mo Hussein (1987)
— dramatic 12th round TKO ends matters

Thomas Hearns vs
Dennis Andries (1987)
— Brit down 5 times (only 3 official) but brave in loss

Renaldo Snipes vs
Lionel Washington (1988)
— Rated "most fun fight" of the year by *Ring*

Julian Jackson vs
Buster Drayton (1988)
— no one ever manhandled Buster like this before

Mo Hussein vs
Mark Reefer (1988)
— TKO wins it in 10th round, this time Mo wins

Jorge Paez vs
Calvin Grove (1988)
— 3 knockdowns in 15th wins it for "The Clown"

Nigel Benn vs
Anthony Loagan (1988)
— Benn getting hammered in 2nd wins with monster hook

Belaid Khaldi vs
Mark Reefer (1988)
— Khaldi down first; Reefer three times and done

Roger Mayweather vs
Harold Brazier (1988)
— had him; then let him off the hook. So close.

John Meekins vs
Mohammed Kawoya (1988)
— Meekins iced split second after stoppage win

Fidel Bassa vs.
Dave "Boy" McCauley I (1988)
— rough encounter for "Boy"

Jeff Harding vs Dennis Andries (1988-89-90)	– all 3 are classics; both ice each other in process
Fidel Bassa vs Dave "Boy" McCauley I (1989)	– brutal encounter for Boy
Rocky Lockridge vs Mike Zena (1989)	– Zena down 4 times, Lockridge down once
Trevor Smith vs Ian John-Lewis (1989)	– Lewis down 5 times, Smith once in TKO finish
Nigel Benn vs Iran Barkley (1990)	– wild for as long it lasts which is one contaversial round
Derrick Jefferson vs Maurice Harris (1990)	– near decapitaion KO of Harris after give and take
Simon Brown vs Tyrone Trice (1990)	– all-out action until dramatic 14th round KO
Paul Banke vs Ki-Jun Lee (1990)	– tough Korean down thrice before being stopped in 11th
Jorge Paez vs Tracey Spann (1991)	– all-out action throughout
Katsuya "Spanky-E" Onizuka vs Suzuhara Kitazawa (1991)	– Asian war, Katsuya by TKO
Sung-Kil Moon vs Nana Konadu (1991)	– another Asian war. Konadu down thrice, Moon twice
Muangchai Kittikasem vs Jung-Koo Chang (1991)	– down thrice, Thai comes back to ice Chang
Morris East vs. Akinobu Hiranaka (1992)	– 11th round KO in Tokyko wins WBA titlet for East
Yuri Arbachakov vs Yun Un Chin (1992)	– Chin's chin finally gives out
Zck Padilla vs. Ray Oliviera (1993)	– two punch machines break CompuBox records in punch fest
Tony Lopez vs, Joey Gamache	– bloody back-and-forth war until Lopez takes control in 11th

Kevin Kelley vs   — over 2,000 punches thrown in
Troy Dorsey (1992)   nonstop action

Andy Till vs   — epic British dust up
Charley Swift Jr. (1993)

Yuri Arbachakov vs   — dramatic late TKO win by
Muangchai Kittikasem (1993)   Russian great

Junior Jones vs Jorge   — both down in still
Eliecer Julio (1993)   another brawl invoving Jones

John Michael Johnson vs.   — Johnson upsets Jones and takes
Junior Jones (1994)   title in process'

Freddie Pendleton vs.   — Ruelas down twice in 1st round
Rafael Ruelas (1994)   wins 12 round UD

"Jesse" James Hughes vs   — dramatic come-from-behind
Anthony Stephens (1994)   KO

Erik Holland vs   — savage and punishing give-and-
"Jesse" James Hughes (1994)   take battle

Jorge Luis Roman vs.   — Roman edges Scotty after
Scotty Olson (1994)   having been floored.

Kenny Keene vs.   — two gladiators in 12-round blood
Terry Ray (1994)   fest. Kenny wins it.

Bronco McKart vs.   — Kelp takes career-altering
Skipper Kelp (1994)   punishment in savage affair

Freddie Pendleton vs   — Freddie down, Lopez 4 times
Tony Lopez (1995)   before being TKO'd

"Jesse" James Hughes vs   — another Hughes's come-from-
Adrian Stone (1995)   behind win

Vincent Pettway vs   — Brutal fight with
Simon Brown (1995)   very, very scary KO ending

Merqui Sosa vs.   — tremendous punishmentt,
Charles Williams (1995, two)   stretcher used at end

Merqui Sosa vs.   — Incredible double knockout,
Charles Williams (1995, one)   simply amazing

Shinji Takehara vs. Sung-Chun Yi (1995)	– savage Asian dust up including double knockdown
Alejandro Gonzalez vs. Kevin Kelley (1995)	– "Flushing Flash" retires after 10th in San Antonio
Kevin Kelley vs. Ricardo Rivera (1995)	– Kelley down in rounds 2 & 4, wins by KO in 9th
Wilfredo Vázquez vs. Eloy Rojas (1996)	– Dramatic KO of Year wns it for Elroy
Tony Martin vs. Kip Diggs (1996)	– 10th round come-from-behind KO wins it for Tony
Kevin Kelley vs Derrick Gainer (1996)	– Four knockdowns as Flash blows Smoke in the 8th
Frankie Liles vs Tim Littles II (1996)	– Wild one!! 4 knockdowns and lots of fouls
Kevin Leushing vs Chris Saunders (1996)	– Brit shootout with TKO win for Kevin
Marco Antonio Barrera vs Kennedy McKinney (1996)	– both down, in real brawl
Spener Oliver vs) Patrick Mullings (1997	– dramatic 10th round KO but Oliver wins it
Kennedy McKinney vs Junior Jones (1997)	– both down as Mac wins by TKO in fourth
Ray Annis vs Bobby Harris (1997)	– very scary as the two wail away at each other non-stop
Darroll Wilson vs Courage Tshabalala (1997)	– Wilson down twice miraculously wins by KO
Derrell Coley vs Kippy Diggs (1997)	– Coley down thrice wins by 11th round KO
Ed Mahone vs Cody Koch (1998)	– another last round KO wins it via sudden lightening
Shea Neary vs. Andy Holligan (1998)	– Neary in still another exciting Brit dust up.

Dave Hilton vs Stephane Ouellet (1998) — last second KO win

Charles Brewer vs Herol Graham (1998) — Brewer rallies to win in 10th by TKO

Paul Ingle vs Manuel Medina (1999) — both down, Ingle holds on to squeak out win for title

Micky Ward vs Reggie Green (1999) — Come-from-behind, blood & guts all-time classic

Micky Ward vs. Shea Neary (2000) — Competitive until Irish Micky opens up and ends matters.

Ray Oliviera vs. Vince Phillips (2000) — 463 total punches thrown in one round by both guys!

Julian Letterlogh vs. Demetrius Jenkin (2000) — Both at each other with ferocity until KO wins it.

Stevie Johnston vs Jose Luis Castillo (2000) — Stevie wins. It's a draw! Make up your minds

Ben Tackie vs, Roberto Garcia (2000) — Tackie behind on all scorecards before 10th round TKO

David Reid vs Kirino Garcia (2000) — Garcia exposes Reid and almost takes him out

Hasim Rahman vs Corrie Sanders (2000) — back-and-forth brawl until The Rock ends matters

Danny Williams vs Mark Potter (2000) — badly injured Williams pulls it out with one arm

Thomas Tate vs Omar Sheika (2001) — gut crunching action before Sheika stopped on cuts

Paul Spadafora vs Victoriano Sosa (2000) — Paul down twice comes back strong to pull it out

Mauricio Martinez vs. Lester Fuentes (2000) — Martinez down 3 times in first four rounds, wins!

Antwun Echols vs Charles Brewer (2001) — Echols down 3 times ices "The Hatchet."

Ezra Seller vs Carl Thompson (2001) — Cat down four times, Sellers twice

Julio Gonzalez vs Julian Letterlough (2001) — 5 knockdowns; maybe best one on this list!

Ben Tackie vs. Ray Oliviera (2001) — Punch-fest by two guys with more stamina than porn stars

Elvir Muriqi vs Sam Ahmad (2002) — 4 rounds 8 knockdowns. Maybe this is the best one on list!

Charles Brewer vs Scott Pemberton (2002) — both guys punish each other without mercy

Rich LaMontagne vs Michael Bennett (2002) — "Mountain" behind, wins with specatacular KO

Antonio Margarito vs. Antoniio Diaz (2002) — toe-to-toe battle of attrition which Margo wins.

Michael Gomez vs. Alex Arthur (2003) — Undefeated Arthur down 3 times before brutal end.

Acelino Freitas vs Jorge Rodrigo Barrios (2003) — both down twice, "Hiena" stays down in 12th

Paul Spadafora vs Leonard Dorin (2003) — brutal ebb and flow non-stop action ends in draw

Ebo Elder vs Courtney Burton (2004) — Ebo pulls it out in last round after both fight savagely

Danny Hunt vs Lee Meager (2004) — another Brit dust up with English title at stake

Scott Pemberton vs Omar Sheika (2004) — blood and guts and more in closet classic deluxe

Brian "the Beast" Minto vs Vinny Maddalone (2004) — the very essence of a closet classic

Carl Thompson vs Sebastiaan Rothmann (2004) — "Cat" down in 4th, Rothmann in 5th and 9th

Carl Thompson vs David Haye (2004) — veteran bomber rallies to whip favored upstart

Chris McInerney vs Anterio Vines (2005)	– both down in wild one that ends in 4-round draw
Jason Litzau vs John Nolasco (2005)	– both on verge of being iced
Jamie Moore vs Mathew Macklin (2006)	– Violent ebb and flow war disguised as boxing
Anotnio Escalante vs. Jose Hernandez (2006)	– Tonio gets off floor to win this non'stop thriller.
Takefumi Sakata vs. Roberto Vazquez (2007)	– Sakata avenges defeat by outworking The Spider
Carl Johanneson vs. Michale Gomez (2007)	– Corker with Gomez staring out well but fading fast
Louis Turner vs. Angel Hernandez (2007)	– An action packed war that was a Fight of Year type.
Michael Katsidis vs Graham Earle 2007)	– all-out shoot-out as Earle is courageous in loss
Darrell Woods vs Samuel Miller (2007)	– vet upsets upstart in thrilling Fight of Year type war
Jesse Feliciano vs Delvin Rodriguez (2007)	– thrilling stoppage as Delvin gasses late
Darnell 'DingB-A-Ling Man' Wilson vs Emmanuel Nwodo (2007)	– crunching and scary KO
Michael "The Great" Katsidis vs Czar Amonsot (2007)	– Czar badly hurt in gory war
Danell Jiles Jr. vs Henry Lundy 2008)	– 4 rounds of jackhammer shots ends in draw. Wild one
Andrew Golata vs Mike Mollo (2008)	– uncommon courage and heart displayed by both
Alfredo Angulo vs Richard Gutierrez (2008)	– both guys engage in all-out two-fisted attack
Ali Oubali vs Chris Fernandez (2008)	– incredible punch volume by both; Ali wins on cuts

Chartchai at work. (Photo from Public domain)

Many fights have been excluded because they have received featured treatment in this and in my first book, *Boxing is my Sanctuary*.

Note: I believe writer Lee Groves coined the phrase "Closet Classic" and in my opinion is the best authority on such fights. Some of his early favorites and ones that hold the most significance in his heart are:

Danny Lopez-Juan Malvarez

Antonio Avelar-Wilfredo Vazquez,

Victor Callejas-Loris Stecca II,

Leland Hardy-Ike Padilla (see above)

Thomas Hearns-Juan Roldan (see above).

He has many, many more and I can't wait to read them.

---

[1] Lee Groves, "Closet Classic - Lee Roy Murphy vs. Chisanda Mutti." March 25, 2008. http://www.maxboxing.com:80/Groves/Groves032508.asp

[2] IBID

[3] James Slater, "Somsak Sithchatchawal vs. Mahyar Monshipour - Could It Be The Greatest Prize Fight Ever Captured on Film?" March 21, 2008. http://www.eastsideboxing.com/news.php?p=14923&more=1

[4]. James Slater, "Exclusive Interview with Joe Hipp - "The Morrison Fight? That Was A Great War!" April 22, 2008. http://www.eastside-boxing.com/news.php?p=15350&more=1

20

A JAPANESE FLYWEIGHT AND A MEXICAN FEATHERWEIGHT

Masao Ohba should be in the IBHOF and the WBHOF and it is almost criminal that he has been overlooked....
–Ken 'KSTAT' Pollitt

Masao Ohba could very well have become one of the greatest "little guys "in boxing history. He was only 23 years old and just entering the prime of his career when he tragically passed away
–Jim Amato

Masao Ohba was born in Tokyo, Japan in 1949 and became a professional boxer in 1966 knocking out one Kazuyoshi Watanabe in the first round. He would go on to compile a 35-2-1 record and in the process, win the WBA flyweight title with a dramatic thirteenth round icing of Berkrerk Chartvanchai in 1970 at the Nihon University Auditorium in Tokyo becoming the 8th Japanese boxer to capture a world title. He was 25-2-1 at the time and would never lose another fight

His first title defense came in 1971 when he beat the very capable Betulio Gonzalez, 25-2 coming in. Two months later, he stopped limited Constancio Garcia in, of all places, San Antonio, Texas–a strange place for a Japanese champion to fight. Indeed, it was rare for a Japanese fighter to do battle in any country other than South Korea, Thailand or Japan.

After two successful defenses against Fernando Cabanella and future world champion Susumu Hanagata, he was positioned to fight Panamanian Orlando Amores and future world champion Chartchai Chionoi, the legendary brawler from Thailand. His fights with Amores and Chionoi would cement his cult status among boxing aficionados.

Ohba vs. Amores (June 20, 1972)

Masao Ohba possessed a great left jab combined with a warrior's proclivity. Clearly, he was a top pound for pound fighter when he fought Panama's Orlando Amores. The tough and stylish Panamanian had a 25-1 (18) record but was given little chance against the young and skilled Japanese champion.

Orlando surprised Ohba in the first, exposing a pattern of Ohba's vulnerability in the early rounds, and suddenly landed a savage left hook that sent him to the canvass. Ohba was hurt and Amores quickly launched punishing combinations as Masao, now in survival mode, hung on until the bell saved him from the surprise onslaught.

Amores again came out winging in the second round, but this time Ohba held off the Panamanian with his great left jabs. Finally, a straight right following a jackhammer jab floored Amores. While not badly hurt, Ohba poured it on with his patented two-punch combos until the bell rang.

After round three (which both fighters appeared to take off), Amores resumed the sudden attack that proved successful for him in the first stanza, Ohba was backed up by the Panamanian's all-out attack. As the bell rang ending the fourth, he looked worried as he returned to his corner

The fight was quickly taking on the aura of a classic as both fighters engaged in furious give and take. In the fifth and final round, Amores was not able to sustain the success he had in round four, as he was banged continuously with brutal and damaging straight lefts. Finally, he was backed up and trapped on the ropes where Ohba stunned him with a ripping right. Sensing that his prey was now ready for the kill, Ohba launched a volley of two dozen unanswered punches which rendered Amores helpless. Before the fight could be halted, Ohba went for the kill with two vicious rights that left the challenger in a heap. Taking the full count was simply a formality, as the Champion raised his hands in triumph and the crowd roared "Obha Obha, Obha."

Ohba vs. Chionoi (January 2, 1973)

Ohba faced Chionoi for his fifth defense and, affirming his pattern of early vulnerability, was knocked down hard with a right hook in the first round. He injured his right ankle while falling to the canvas, but managed to get up. Receiving ice for his ankle in between rounds, he limped out and began savage exchanges with Chionoi. He took control in the middle rounds, and finally decked the fearsome Thai challenger in the twelfth stanza. Chionoi staggered into the ropes, as his opponent launched a vicious volley that decked him. Getting up too fast, it was clear he was hurt, but the fight was allowed to continue, and the Champion seized the opportunity launching another more vicious assault that caused the Thai to drop in a corner. Somehow, the brawler got to his feet, but for all practical purposes, the fight was over. Ohba finished matters with a final multi-punch assault that rendered Chionoi helpless. Even with a badly injured ankle, Ohba had scored a dramatic KO for his fifth and most dramatic title defense. It was a great ending for a great warrior

Ohba made five defenses of his world title. Three of his victims would go on to become champions. With his prime years still to come, one can only wonder how he would have fared had he fought the great Miguel Canto. Still, he conquered rugged fighters like Bernabe Villacampo, Hanagata, Betulio (who probably belongs in the Hall of Fame), Fritz Chevert, Gonzalez and Cabanella—all world class boxers.

January 24, 1973

Ohba, like the legendary Mexican fighter Salvador Sanchez, seemed destined for greatness but it was not to be. Twenty-two days after his last title defense against Chionoi, he died tragically in a car accident involving his new Corvette. Like Sanchez, he was just entering the prime of his career bringing a sad end to the reign of a most exciting flyweight, one who could well have become one of the greatest in boxing history.

Still, based on the accomplishments of his abbreviated career, a strong case could be made for his induction into The International Boxing Hall of Fame.

August 12, 1982

Sanchez died in a car crash just a few weeks after his tenth and final title defense against future Hall of Famer Azumah Nelson. He crashed on the early morning while driving his brand new Porsche sports car, dying instantly. He too was just 23 years old.

But unlike Ohba, Sánchez was posthumously inducted into the International Boxing Hall of Fame in 1991. Perhaps it is time to put together the last piece of symmetry to this remarkable comparison and induct Masao Ohba.

In a weird twist of fate, Panama's Orlando Amores would beat Mexican Antonio Becerra in 1976 by third round KO in Culiacan, Mexico. Becerra would go on to beat Sanchez by SD in 1977 giving "Chava" his only career defeat.

2 I

REMEMBERING ROGER PHILLIPS

The world of boxing that Roger Phillips knew, the world of $40 paydays and bus trips to small arenas and dressing rooms the size of closets, was very real. In his world, club fighters did not wind up in champion-ship bouts
—Michael Katz

There'll always be opponents, there's got to be opponents - they're a necessity.'
—John Gagliardi, Promoter

My manager once told me, whether they say good or bad things about you is not the problem. The problem comes when they say nothing about you at all.
—Mustafa Hamsho

This middleweight fought from 1971 to 1981 and toted up a record of 6-34 (KO 22)-2. He was TKO'd in his last fight by highly skilled contender Vinnie Curto, 44-5-3 coming in. He had lost 22 straight at the time. Remarkably, he lost two bouts to Al Romano by DQ both in the second round but beat Romano, 53-15-1, in 1972 (his last win). Earlier, he split a pair with Jose Pagan Rivera who would finish with a 30-93-8 slate suffering 39 losses by KO along the way.

Phillips fought in armories and union halls throughout the country providing fodder for those anxious to get a win on their record. He even fought in Brazil in 1973 against Miguel de Oliveira, 32-0. Phillips was 6-17-2 and was dispatched in three rounds.

Two days after his final bout with the overmatched Curto, Roger Phillips hanged himself in a cell of his hometown jail in Pittsfield, MA. He was 29. However, it does not appear that loss was the trigger for this tragedy.

While his brother and former boxer, Joe Phillips, reportedly blames boxing, others blame personal problems. Whatever the cause, what is not in dispute is that on March 6, 1981, Roger Phillips, with a 6-33-3 record, was allowed to box a tough contender, even though his home-state license reportedly had been revoked.

Indeed, there had been a lot of contaversy about whether or not he had a valid license. Apparently, his Massachusetts license had been revoked in 1973 after he had allegedly struck a referee. It was his second such offense. And he hadn't won a fight in almost nine years.[1] What is not in dispute is that Vinnie Curto beat someone by the name of "Bad" Bennie Briscoe, 64-20-5, at the Hynes Memorial Auditorium in Boston just three months before his fight with Phillips. What is not in dispute is that Curto was in the middle of a 28 fight undefeated streak.

As for Curto, raised in a rough, low-income neighborhood in Boston, he became one of the better super middleweight fighters of his era (which was a great one for middleweight) finishing with a 62-10-3 record, though 5 of the losses came in his last 14 fights. This Boston cutie who knew all the tricks started out with 17 straight wins and seemed destined for greatness, but never fulfilled his promise. He lost two against the great Korean Chong Pal Park, but claimed he was robbed in the first that was fought in Seoul in 1985 (one which I witnessed live while living in Seoul)). Between 1976 and 1984, he lost only one fight while winning 34 with one draw (against Willie Classen in 1978).

Curto fought many of the best fighters of his era, including the aforementioned Briscoe and Park (twice each), Vito Antuofermo, Tony Chiaverini, Rodrigo Valdez, Chucho Garcia and Tony Licata. While he came close to winning the Super Middleweight Title, in another strange twist of events, he actually did win the WBF Super Cruiserweight Title against one Jimmy Haynes in his very last fight in 1996—and in the unlikely spot of Lincoln, Nebraska.

Today, Vinnie Curto is a professional actor and has appeared in movies such as Stealing Harvard and Equinox and TV shows including Walker, Texas Ranger. He has also written a screenplay about his life that reveals an extremely compelling story and tragic in its own right. Plans are in the offing to make it into a film entitled, "Out on My Feet."

But men like Roger Phillips need to be remembered too. Not because of their boxing exploits (or, in Roger's case, lack therof); not because their end came under tragic circumstances. No, Roger had the courage and nobility to enter the ring in the first place. In the end, boxing was his only strength in life; it was his anchor. He needs to be remembered for that.

[1] Michael Katz, "The Tragedy of a Middleweight Loser." March 9, 2008. http://query.nytimes.com/gst/fullpage.html?sec=health&res=9 F04EFDE103BF934A3575AC0A967948260

22

FOURTEEN YEARS LATER (FICTION)

David "Tino" Meza had grown up in the hardscrabble environs of East LA and never really learned how to box until he was in High School. His venues for fights were the streets and he gained a reputation accordingly. But once he started fighting amateur, his skills developed exponentially and he was soon one of the best amateur middleweights on the West Coast and considered a prime prospect for the Olympics.

Meza soon caught the eye of the professional boxing people who believed his persona as a power boxer in the mold of Sugar Ray Leonard would be the kind of thing that sells tickets. He was an extremely handsome kid who finished high school with good grades despite the disadvantages of growing up in the barrio. Attending college at night and majoring in business, he had looks, brains and skills. Now all he needed was some national attention and he got it when he was selected to the Olympic squad and became a distinct favorite to win a medal. He did not disappoint.

He won the Gold Medal in a close decision against a tough Argentinean fighter. His amateur record was 175-9. All the bruising rounds he had spared in the gym, all the blows that had rained down upon him during these gym wars, all the grueling fights he had participated in had paid off. He was ready; he had paid his dues.

From that point forward, it was not if but when he would become a world champion. Of course, Tino needed to get through a number of hand fed professional opponents to build up a record and soon he was 15-0 with 12 KOs. He then stepped up and began fighting world class competition winning a scintillating battle in England against the Commonwealth's Middleweight Champion and then doing the same in Italy and France. With these three impressive international conquests under his belt and an Olympic Gold Medal, he quickly became something like the Dallas Cowboys Football Team; he became America's boxer and the fans fell in love with him.

By this time, he had made enough money to get his family out of LA and into a new house and in a much nicer area closer to San Diego. He also had the atypical savvy to hook up with a financial planner who began investing his earnings into annuities, real estate and mutual funds. Meza was determined he would not end up like so many other great fighters from the West Coast who either were in dire financial straits or were suffering from the ravages of the dreaded pugilistica dementia or both. It is horrific because it develops over a period of years, with the average time of onset being about 12-16 years after the start of a career in boxing. Looking for aluminum cans in alleyways to turn in for a few bucks while suffering from this dementia was not on Tino's wish list nor was dying in a rest home while on life support.

Soon the opportunity to fight the top ranked middleweight presented itself with the winner fighting for the unified championship of the World in a mega-fight to be booked in Las Vegas. But first things first, and Meza went to camp with his team of trainers and nutritionists to prepare. As popular as he was, his opponent, 44-2-1 with 39 KOs, was an East Coast bomber out of Brooklyn with a great following as well. In fact, he was a slight favorite going into this battle at Madison Square Garden. The Garden billboard flashed:

"David 'Tino' Meza, 21-0 vs. Mike Ramos, 44-2-1: En Latino Explosivo."

The packed house was not disappointed as both fighters engaged in a war. Meza was pressed in the early going and was rocked and decked by a Ramos right in the third. But around the 5th stanza, he turned the tide with a combo that stunned his Puerto Rican foe and forced him back into the ropes. Suddenly, the crowd was chanting "Tino, Tino, Tino." Soon he was dictating the action, though the two hit each other with jack hammer shots and both were wobbled. Finally, in the eleventh, he trapped Ramos in a corner and peppered him with a dozen unanswered shots before the referee stepped in and "saved" Mike who sagged against the ropes like a rag doll.

The crowd was mostly Puerto Rican and the noise level equaled the nights when Trinidad and Cotto had fought under the banner of the Puerto Rican flag. But this time it was not to be, as the popular Chicano's hand was raised at the end. He had emerged as the top contender and was now ready to assume the mantle of World Champion.

The championship fight was almost anti-climatic when compared to the Meza-Ramos brawl which was being hailed as a classic. "Tino" made short work of the Champ, Bobby Harris, and, after two boring rounds, knocked him unconscious with a savage left hook from hell 20 seconds into the third. David Meza was now the unified Middleweight Champion of the world and was ready to defend his title for as long as it would take to make the necessary money to move into other endeavors.

Yes, he wanted a legacy worthy of the Hall, but he also knew about guys like Julio Caesar Chavez and Evander Holyfield who stayed around too long. He witnessed the unlikely sight of Roy Jones Jr. getting knocked unconscious. David would fight only as long as he could make enough money to finance his dreams of being a serious player in the glitterati of the Las Vegas business world where he now made his home.

He successfully defended his title seven straight times before suffering his first and only defeat at the hands of a crafty Venezuelan named Eduardo Palencia in a fight where Meza's reflexes seemed off and where his punching was sluggish. It was as if he had grown old overnight and he knew it better than anyone. Still, he was able to reignite his passion and avenge the defeat in a rematch six months later. But it was not an easy win, as he engaged in a number of brutal exchanges that hurt both combatants.

After the fight, he announced his retirement to a shocked but skeptical fandom given that he was only 30-1 at the time. His professional career had been one of the shortest, albeit most successful ones on record. Most thought he could fight on for several more years.

Meza shocked the boxer world again by remaining retired, and soon became the partner in a large casino operation in Laughlin, Nevada. This would be the start of several such ventures in that state, as he ventured into real estate and other activities as well. His successes were manifest and he was a man who seemed to have it all.

He was invited to the International Boxing Hall of Fame to have his fist cast and while there, ran into his old foe Mike Ramos. They hugged and talked, but David was bothered by Mike's inability to put his words together coherently and by what appeared to be a difficulty to remember things. It haunted David on the way back to Vegas.

Things prospered for the Meza management team for the next several years and David often reflected upon how fortunate he had been to quit at just the right time. He also reflected at times on whether he really enjoyed boxing given his desire to get out as fast as he did. Marciano, Hagler, Fighting Harada, Yoko Gushiken, Jiro Watanabe and Khaosai Galaxy all knew when the time was right. Eder Jofre and Ricardo "Finito" Lopez walked away with no regrets. He had done it as well; he had outsmarted an unforgiving system that was difficult to outsmart. Maybe that was it, maybe beating the system was just as important as beating his opponents.

Finally, after having been away from the ring for five years, he received a call from one of the sports writers that he had been nominated for induction into the Boxing Hall of Fame in June. He was thrilled by the news as was his family and friends. This would be an honor that not only would cement his ring legacy but would also turbo charge his many business operations.

As the induction ceremonies loomed, David decided he would touch base with some people in New York City and then fly upstate where he would meet his wife, Sarah, in Syracuse for some private time before the ceremonies began.

Sarah arrived in Syracuse and waited for David's call. She waited and she waited but it never came. She then moved to a hotel in Verona near the Hall. Then, just before the Hall of Fame weekend began, one of David's friends called the Hall to say that "Machito" had just left for Canastota.

Upon his arrival, Sarah asked what had happened and David replied, "what do you mean?" She asked why he had not called to cancel their meeting in Syracuse and he said "what meeting? Now terribly disturbed, she asked her husband why he even bothered to be here. With a dull and glazed look, he replied that he was there to have his fist cast............

23

ALL THINGS BOXING

*It's hard to get away from that feeling. I think a lot of people don't
understand it. They see a Sugar Ray Leonard making a comeback and
they are almost aggravated. They say "Ahh, man, why does that guy
want to fight again?" And they don't understand it because they have
never been fighters. When you are a fighter, it's hard to shake that feeling. It's like they say the boxing bug, that's legitimate, that's a good way
to describe it… once you've tasted it, it is just so hard to get that taste
out of your mouth. You want to box as long as you are able to walk*
–Iceman John Scully

*I never turn down an interview request now because I find it pretty
funny, it's really a trip that you even care enough what I have to say to
ask me.*
–Iceman John Scully

I plan on training fighters for as long as I am alive on this earth
–Iceman John Scully

*You go to an amateur tournament," says Scully. "You get an inner-city, re-
ally rough, hard-core black kid, and you get a white kid from Minnesota.
Maybe they never even say 'hi' to each other all week. But they fight
each other, and after the fight, they hug.*
–Iceman John Scully

Hartford, Connecticut's John Scully is indeed all things boxing. Let's
look at just some of them:

A Great Amateur Fighter: Seemingly destined to be a boxer
from age 12 (when his father took him to his first professional fight),
he won numerous tournaments and was in one with Roy Jones and
other fighters of Roy's caliber and was present when Gerald Mc-
Clellan beat Jones in the nationals. He fought many great fighters like
Lamar Parks, Otis Grant, Melvin Foster, Joe Lipsey and Darren Allen,
who was the world amateur champion. His career peak may well
have been when he beat Allen to qualify for the 1988 U.S. Olympic
trials. As an aside, he once beat Omaha's Terry Christianson by a 5-0

decision in Terry's hometown. Christianson beat Gerald McClellan at the nationals and gave the fearsome G-Man a standing 8 count at 156 pounds.

Writer: He is a frequent on-line boxing writer and is currently completing a book, *The Iceman's Diaries,* which chronicles his 13 years of professional boxing experiences in the ring.

Commentator: You can catch him announcing on the televised fight classics alongside Joe Tessitori where his insights are invaluable. Someday, it would not be surprising to see Scully as a regular commentator on one of the big networks.

Historian: John Scully knows the history of boxing better than most boxers, and few know the ins and out of the sport as intimately as he does. A student of Muhammad Ali whom he idolizes, he discovered early on that Ali was a non-substance abuser and that this may have been the secret to his success. He views Ali as one who translated his values to action and even rationalizes Ali's "trash talking" as more fun than disrespect. Scully tries to emulate Ali by living out his values, but having fun in the process.

Scully and his champs
(Photo courtesy of John Scully)

Trainer: He is a leading trainer as well. In a way, he had been bred to be a trainer since he had been training boxers since he was an amateur himself back in the 1980's. He trained several national champions including the Armed Forces champion, PAL, Junior Olympic, Golden Gloves, and Ohio State Fair champions

These days, he counts Matt Godfrey and Mike Oliver among his charges and both seem headed for the top. As well, he guided Liz

Mueller to the women's world lightweight title in 2001 with a UD-10 over tough Jaime Clampitt at Foxwoods Casino. They fought twice and Liz won both times.

In all, "The Iceman" has worked with six champions as a trainer. They include WBA 154 pound world champion Jose Antonio Rivera, former NABF/USBA 135 pound champion Israel "Pito" Cardona, USBA 122 pound champion Mike-Mike Oliver, IBA intercontinental heavyweight champion Lawrence Clay-Bey, WIBF female 135 pound world champion Liz Mueller and WBC Youth 130 pound champion Matt "Sharpshooter" Remillard (for whom he was the assistant trainer/cornerman). As well, he did not train Cardona at the time he actually won his titles.

Scully still spars on occasion with current fighters such as Rivera, Matt Godfrey, Scott Pemberton, Peter Manfredo, and Eric Harding.

Former Top ten Contender: With a final slate of 38-11 in the professional ranks against very solid opposition, John got his shot at the brass ring when he fought Henry Maske in Germany for a world title in May of 1996. The year before in what may have been his best performance; he lost a decision to Michael Nunn, but gave Nunn all he could handle. He fought in a southpaw stance rather than in a conventional one. And was successful using a right hook, both to the head and a to Michael's body. Even the compubox numbers had him well ahead in power punches landed. (Actual punch stat numbers for the fight were 1291 thrown, 373 landed at 29% for Nunn vs. 689 thrown, 389 landed at 48% for Scully).

In his next bout, he stayed in Germany and fought the former IBF super middleweight title holder, Graciano Rocchigiani. Graciano would win a split decision against Nunn in his very next fight to capture the vacant WBC light heavyweight title.

Scully closed out his career by beating Cleveland Nelson (13-1) in June 2001.

A complex soul, you can throw a dart at his won-lost record and come up with a compelling story wherever it lands. Whether it involves his disappointing TKO loss to Drake Thadzi or his courageous outing with Sam Ahmad at the Blue Horizon or his 13 fight win streak right out of the professional gate, there is plenty of drama and grist for the writing mill.

Webmaster: He has his own active on line site where he never refuses to answer a reasonable question and is most approachable.

As well, he provides uniquely professional insights for those who post on his site.

Community activist: In 1998, he was presented with the "Commissioners Award" by the Connecticut state health department for his work as an expert in the field of AIDS prevention and awareness. His interest in this activity came about because one of his boxing friends, Lamar Parks, contacted the virus. In 1997, the Connecticut Sports Writers Guild presented him with their highest honor, the "Connecticut Sports Writers Presidential Award." The award was based on his athletic career and community service.

He frequently goes to schools and talks about the value of getting an education and doing the right thing. John has made an amazing connection with street kids in some of Hartford's tougher areas. His nickname belies the fact that he is a humble, decent person with a big heart.

"Iceman" John Scully is the rare total package and one hellava guy to boot. But merely listing his achievements and activities really fails to peel the onion. There is more to this man, much more.

A Mother's son; a caretaker:

In May 1996, the following article written by Terry Price appeared in the Hartford (Ct) Courant and reveals someone else:

"HE'S A GOOD SON...EVERYBODY SHOULD BE SO LUCKY"

TOUGH GUY, DEVOTED CARETAKER

"The downstairs den in John Scully's house is a shrine of boxing memorabilia. Scores of posters and photos, including Muhammad Ali, Sugar Ray Leonard and Mike Tyson in poses with Scully, are plastered on every inch of the walls. A table to one side is covered with trophies, medals and gloves commemorating conquests. There is no mistaking it, this is the home of a fighter. A few steps up to the living room, Carol Scully lies propped up in a hospital bed. Beneath the covers, her thin torso barely creates a rumple. Both legs have been amputated from just above the knees. Moving her head side to side is difficult and, at times, painful, from surgery to remove a cancerous growth on her neck. There is an IV in her left arm dripping antibodies to combat infection. She is hooked up to a catheter, permanently. There is no mistaking this is the home of someone locked in conflict with serious illness.

`Pound for pound, the toughest fighter in the world,' John Scully said.

"Carol Scully will not be in Leipzig, Germany, May 25 when the younger of her two sons will fight Henry Maske, the International Boxing Federation light heavyweight champion. This is no different than any of his fights. She never goes. She loves him too much. Carol Scully will wait for the videotape and for the souvenir miniature bell her John-John always brings back from his trips. `He's a good son," she said. `Everybody should be so lucky. I've never heard anybody say a bad word about John. That pleases me." Pausing to find the breath to continue, she added, ``He gets it from his mother.'

"Scully, 28, lives at home with his mother and his brother, Jerry Jr. Carol and Jerry Sr. have been divorced for years, but he moved back in to help care for her when she became ill nearly a year-and-a-half ago. A nurse comes in every day for two hours to help. But it has been John who has kept a vigil throughout her ordeal. It was he who carried her into the emergency room when she woke up one morning and couldn't get out of bed. It was he who bought her a television set for her convalescence. It is he who brings home ice cream sundaes for her after he finishes training at the gym. The only time Scully is not home with his mother is when he's at the gym or away for a fight, as he is now. Scully left May 5 to train in Tampa, Fla., before heading to Germany May 16. Whenever he leaves town, he makes arrangements to ensure his mother is properly attended. ``I couldn't have made it without him," she said. ``I'd fall apart."

"The Scully home also includes four dogs and the occasional visitor. Andy Sarkozy, a fighter from Bethlehem, Pa., stayed there recently. He also accompanied Scully to Tampa and Germany. ``John is an unbelievably special kid," said Sarkozy, 25. ``His mother has problems, it doesn't take a genius to figure that out, and he's here with his mother. That's amazing. He's got kind of celebrity status, and he could be living on his own having a blast. Instead he's living here with his mother. His mother needs him, and there he is. It's rare to say, especially for a fighter, but it's rare to see a kid like John. He's got this heart of gold."

"Scully said his mother's resilience has kept the situation from becoming depressing. ``My mother is a real strong person," he said. ``She's never complained once. I try to make it as comfortable for her as possible. She's not sad and crying all the time," Scully said. ``She's always, `What's happening? What are you doing today?' You wouldn't know she's bedridden. You just think she's there watching TV. Her being that way makes it kind of easy. I don't leave the house thinking, `Man, look at her, she's miserable.' I leave the house and she's like, `Talk to you later.' She's made the transition so smooth, it's not something you think about. It's almost like you don't even notice it. It's like she had a tooth pulled. I go. She can't. It sounds like a regular thing. But that's something she can never do again for the rest of her life."

"Scully remembers the day his mother started having problems. It was January 11, 1995. He was leaving for Detroit that day to spar with James Toney. That morning his mother awoke at 7 a.m. to prepare for work at The Travelers. But she couldn't get up; her legs refused to work. Scully took her to the hospital, but the people in the emergency room couldn't find anything wrong. So he carried his mother home again, and took a later flight. He figured she'd be OK in a day or so. But late that night she had to be taken back to the hospital. The next morning, Scully called home and learned his mother had undergone surgery on her neck to remove the cancer that had invaded her spine and caused paralysis in her legs. Carol Scully spent the next seven weeks at Hartford Hospital with her head held in place by a ``halo.'' Then she was moved to a nursing home, where she spent six months. She had to be rushed back to the hospital at least twice, once when she developed pneumonia and once when she stopped breathing because of a problem with her medication. After she left the nursing home -actually, she fled with the help of her family- Carol Scully developed gangrene in her left leg. It was removed just before Christmas. A month later, the same thing happened to her right leg. `There were a lot of times it seemed like it was it,' John said. `But they pulled her through, and she pulled herself through.'

"Carol Scully has spent precious little time feeling sorry for herself. ``You always say, Why me?' I was always very healthy, active, on the go. But the cards were dealt this way.'' She's even been able to appreciate the humor in her travails. The episode at the nursing home was like some scene from a movie. The Scully family, all four of them, attended a meeting with the nursing staff to discuss her release. The home argued the family would not be able to provide for all her needs. The Scully's said they could.

"About two minutes into the meeting, John's older brother, Jerry, banged the table, jumped up and said he'd heard enough. He took his mother in her wheelchair and rolled her out of the room, out of the building and into the parking lot, all the while the staff of the home followed behind, protesting, ``But sir. But sir.''

"The Scullys never looked back. Nor do they look too far ahead. If there is a long-term prognosis for Carol Scully, she hasn't heard it, refuses to believe it, or isn't saying. ``What comes, comes," she said. Although his mother's illness has come as his boxing career is approaching a zenith, Scully has shown no sign it is affecting him professionally. If anything, he's performed better.

"He earned the shot against Maske because of an impressive performance, albeit a losing one, against Michael Nunn last December. Scully, who has a ring record of 36-5 with 19 knockouts, admits fighting Maske in his homeland will be tough. He'd like to bring back the International Boxing Federation belt and maybe he will. His mother would like that, but it's not very important to her. She just wants her son to come home safely. And Carol Scully wants one more thing from him.

``Don't forget my bell from Germany."

Epilogue: Mrs. Carol Scully passed away on September 4, 1996 with her son John by her side. The bell collection has continued to grow and will be passed on to his daughter, her granddaughter, Sarita Carol Scully."

She would be proud, indeed.

Unlike many in the periphery of boxing who have a disproportionate sense of self importance, John Scully is real, well grounded and brutally honest.

24

COURAGE

Many fighters are respected for the courageous way they fight. Michael Katsidis and Jamie Moore, as just two examples, are warriors and get respect accordingly. Some, like Jameel "Big Time" McCline and Zab Judah gained it in losing but courageous efforts. Paulie Malignaggi even used the newly earned respect he gained in his loss to Miguel Cotto as a launching pad to a title.

The beatings Ricardo Mayorga and Fernando Vargas took against Tito Trinidad were horrific, but both just kept getting back up in an incredible display of courage and heart. They were willing to die in that ring rather than quit. Warriors like George Chuvalo, Matthew Saad Muhammad, Danny "Little Red" Lopez, Carl Thompson, Arthur Abraham, and Arturo Gatti were in numerous fights in which they took real beatings, but somehow, someway managed to come back and win those fights.

It may not be easy to measure this quality, but one can sure as hell recognize it when it presents itself. Sometimes it's displayed unexpectedly and that makes it even more scintillating.

Danny Williams

Danny Williams (Photo courtesy of ESB)

Heavens knows Danny Williams has had his ups and downs. Losing to Sinan Samil Sam was certainly not a highlight nor was being stopped by Audley Harrison in 2006. Certainly one of his "ups" was taking out heavily favored Mike Tyson in shocking and decisive manner when they met in Louisville, Kentucky in 2004 setting up a fight with Vitali Klitschko in which he himself was brutally stopped.

Of course, beating Tyson has to be the pinnacle of his career, but there may have been a fight back in 2000 that was even more remarkable; a fight in which he fought Mark Potter, 14-2 coming in, for the vacant BBB of C British heavyweight title and the Commonwealth (British Empire) heavyweight title

Both fighters appeared fit and ready, but Williams badly injured his right shoulder in one of the early rounds and Potter took advantage by pressing the action with Danny trying to hold him off as best he could. Then in the sixth round, Williams missed with a right that had "ending" written all over it. In so doing, he grotesquely dislocated his already injured shoulder and was in terrible pain. His right arm sagged and he grimaced, but he hung on and managed to keep Potter at bay with his left jabs. Some of the fans at ring side looked on in horror.

Potter inexplicably let Danny off the hook by not launching an all-out attack. Then midway in the round, the "Brixton Bomber" caught Potter with an astonishing left hook (some called it an uppercut) that sent him down and almost out. Danny jumped on the badly hurt Potter and decked him two more times before Referee John Coyle called a halt to this amazing fight. Now the crowd was up and roaring in disbelief.

Attesting to the seriousness of the injury, Williams underwent surgery and was out for eight months. He came back and fought unbeaten New Zealander Kali Meehan at Bethnal Green. It took him just 32 seconds to dispatch the same fighter who almost beat Lamon Brewster over twelve rounds and who would later stop slugger DaVarryl Williamson.

Danny Williams has been inconsistent, but the way he fought through pain in the sixth round at the Conference Centre in Wembley on October 21, 2000 defined courage. Anyone who thinks there is no such thing as a puncher's chance needs to see a video of this fight. Anyone who wants to know about not giving up when the odds are stacked against you needs to watch this fight. Others have demonstrated courage in the ring, but this was Danny's turn to do it.

In March 2007, the affable and deeply religious Williams once again achieved an "up" when he KO'd Scott Gammer, 17-0-1 coming in, in Wales for the BBBofC British heavyweight title in a crossroads fight for both fighters. In an interview after the fight, Danny, 37-6, talked about retiring on a high, but the Brixton Bomber came back on April, 12, 2008 to beat American Marcus McGee. Danny is still very much in the mix.

Zuri Lawrence

Courage is the discovery that you may not win, and trying when you know you can lose.
—Tom Krause

On November 15, 2007, Zuri Lawrence, 23-12-4, met former two-time world heavyweight champion Haseem "The Rock" Rahman, 45-6-2, in Reading, Pennsylvania for the NABF heavyweight title.

Yes, the same Zuri Lawrence who almost was decapitated by Calvin Brock in 2006 and was blown away in brutal fashion by Dominic Guinn in two rounds this past year. Here is a feather fisted guy with a so-so record who slaps instead of punches, and has never stopped a professional opponent. Here is a guy with a porcelain chin who took this fight with Rahman on short notice and was a distinct underdog.

In his first seven professional fights, Lawrence's record was 1-2 -3-1. It was not very promising start, though he did dominate Jameel McCline in 2005 winning a UD and extended future champion Sultan Ibragimov to the eleventh round before being stopped in 2005.

This one shaped up to be an important bout for Rahman who was looking for a major outing in early 2008. Rahman appeared to be strong and in good shape during his training camp at Kings Gym in Reading, Pa.

The fight had all the earmarks of a blow out and who would have guessed it would go beyond the first round let alone into the tenth? As it turned out, Zuri was stopped (but still on his feet) with seconds to go in the tenth and was even leading on one of the cards.

Even more remarkable, he was mugged clear out of the ring in the mid-rounds much as Rahman had been in his first fight with Oleg Makiev. He hit a chair hard and was on his back looking up at the ring while laying flat on his back. Many other fighters likely would have asked themselves at that moment whether it was worth trying to crawl back in rather than simply staying down and go home with a payday. Not Lawrence. He managed to crawl under the bottom rope in time and get back in to fight competitively until the end of the round. The crowd roared its approval for his show of courage. Zuri Lawrence displayed the essence of heart and courage.

The fight was reasonably close until the stoppage (which was a good one by Referee Gary Rosato) as Lawrence fought in spurts displaying superior technical skills, great hand speed and fast combos. The Rock, however, was able to bully him onto the loose ropes where he did his best work with superior strength. He also threw more punches, albeit ponderous ones until the tenth round when some clean rights finally did the trick.

At the end of the fight, Rahman's face looked like it had gone through a shredder with bad cuts over each eye and facial bruises as well. But even he gave props to Lawrence during the post-fight interview admitting he underestimated him and extolling his skills. The 6'4" Zuri's face was unmarked and he was articulate in the interview.

The Rock used a one dimensional attack and may be coming to the end. While in good physical shape, he needs to go back to the drawing board and come up with a more varied attack and better use of his once vaunted jab or his days clearly will be numbered.

But the story here is about a guy who most likely will never fight for a world championship, but showed a champion's heart in Reading, Pennsylvania on this November night and in so doing, won the respect of all who witnessed it.

Jesse Feliciano

I was a 20-1 underdog...No one expected me to even go the first two rounds with Cintron, but I proved everybody wrong.
—Jesse Feliciano

Yes, welterweight Kermit Cintron, 29-1 beat him, but it was Jesse Feliciano, 15-6-3 who gained the most respect in this entertaining fight for the IBF welterweight title. 10,365 fans were on their feet rooting for Feliciano at the end of this fight at the Staples Center. All were on their feet begging for more of his never-say-die ferociousness.

Perhaps those who witnessed Jesse's come-from-behind destruction of highly touted Delvin Rodriguez were not all that surprised by his gusty showing that gave Cintron almost more than he could handle. Maybe those who knew that Jesse had come out even in his trilogy with tough Alfonzo Gomez were not surprised by his stamina and ability to absorb punishment. And perhaps those who were astonished by his game and courageous showing did not realize the level of opposition he had fought against in a relatively short career. Opposition that included such names as Oscar Diaz, Mike Arnaoutis, Mohamad Abdulaev, Freddie Cadena, Jermaine Marks, Vince Phillips, and Demetrius Hopkins—no cherry picking on Feliciano's charts. What they might not have known about was his heart, grit, determination and granite chin.

It was Zuri Lawrence who gained respect for a game but losing effort against heavily favored Haseem Rahman. This time it was Jesse's turn, and wow, did he ever gain it!

Cintron had no answer or fall-back strategies for Feliciano's incredible punch volume and incoming style. In the end, a savage volley stopped Jesse, but he was still standing.

"Jesse Feliciano displayed all that's great about the sport of boxing" said Star Boxing's CEO Joe DeGuardia. "A true underdog, Jesse showed the will, character and determination of a true warrior". Jesse earned the respect of all the fans who watched and of all of us involved in the sport of boxing."[1]

Sadly, however, Jesse may well fall into the category of a fighter who is just too tough for his own good, and his best days appear to be behind him. Still, he comes pretty darn close to being a real-life Rocky.

[1] "10,365 FANS ON THEIR FEET ROOTING FOR FELICIANO AT STAPLES CENTER!" EASTSIDEBOXING.COM, November 27, 2007; http://www.eastsideboxing.com/news.php?p=13423&more=1

25

WINNERS, OPPONENTS, AND THOSE AT RISK

The Most important thing in the Olympic Games is not to win but to take part, just as the most important thing in life is not the triumph but the struggle. The essential thing is not to have conquered but to have fought well.
–Olympic creed, by Pierre de Coubertin

Without losers, there would be no winners.
–Denise Grollmus

Some say a "tomato can" is a guy who is picked because he has no chance of winning, but he looks good doing it. Maybe so, but tomato can, paid punching bags, tanker, pasty, stiff, bum, or palooka are derogatory terms that show disrespect for those who risk their lives entertaining the fans, and I refuse to use such terms.

However, some on the lowest level of the quality tier often play the role of designated loser–and 'loser" is not meant here in a pejorative sense. Perhaps opponent is a better word. These are fighters who have a high predictability and likelihood of losing and, as such, can be matched for that purpose. Quite simply, they lose far more fights than they win. Some even say their sole purpose is to provide fighters that are more promising a chance to pad their records and enhance their careers.

While club fighters have a gambler's chance to win, those who are matched to lose are so matched because if the number of their losses is divided by the number of their total fights, the resultant percentage is usually high. And numbers don't lie. Yet, every time they enter the ring, they are by definition noble and courageous. No fighter dreams of lacing up to soak up punishment. Let there be no doubt of that. No one goes in there with the intention to lose–at least I don't believe that. Of course, there are the occasional "the fix is in" fights, but this is not about that. This is about mismatches or fighters who engage in them; it's not about rigged fights– and the distinction is essential.

Sometimes, the mismatch can be dangerous; for example, when a fighter who has lost most of his fights by KO is pitted against a bomber who has won most of his fights the same way.

Jerry Strickland, with his horrendous slate of 13-122 (KO 78) in 136 fights, was a designated loser. His likelihood of losing (and by knockout) was always extremely high, but his brother, Reggie, warrants special mention.

Reggie Strickland

Reggie (Photo courtesy of Ringside Report)

Strickland's amazing record is 66-276 (KO 25)-17. Yes, he has had 363 fights, but wait. Reggie may lose, but his excitement index (total knockouts divided by total fights) was a paltry 10.7% which suggests he could go the distance just about every time out, and he did just that with many tough fighters. His KO percentage was a flimsy 3.86, and according to BoxRec, he boxed an incredible 2033 rounds. He last fought in 2005, a six round loss to Dante Craig, and his career (which dates to 1987) is now over. But while he fought, he was a promoter's dream; he was a designated loser (and a barnstormer as well) because his likelihood of lasting the distance, though in a losing effort, was so high.

Donnie Penelton

Donnie "The Spoiler" Penelton has a slate of 13-164-5 and, like Strickland, a low excitement index. Penelton knew how to survive and come back to fight another day, but his likelihood of losing was even higher than that of Reggie Strickland, and if anything, he was no "Spoiler."

Marris "Midnight" Virgil

Virgil, however, may have tempted fate, for his record was 15 (KO 10) - 63 (KO 42)-3. 42 KOs in 63 losses is just too many for comfort.

Still, every once and a while, the unexpected happens. On March 15, 2003, "Midnight" Virgil met Jonathan "the Native Sensation" Corn at the Ho-Chunk Casino in Baraboo, Wisconsin. Virgil was 14-53-3 at the time while Corn came in at 42-5-1 with most of his wins coming against terrible opposition. However, a close look at his record indicated that in 1988, while 18-0-1, he beat Harold Brazier, 104-15-1, in Baraboo for something called the WAA Middleweight Title. Brazier would fight just three more times, but a win is a win.

Thus, Corn was a big favorite to take out Virgil, but things didn't work out that way as "Midnight" took a six-rounder in what has to be the zenith of his career. Corn would never be the same, and Virgil lost his net ten bouts before retiring in 2004 with 81 fights under his belt.

It's seems fair to conclude that when the excitement factor is low, the level of survival is high. Conversely, where it is high, the ability to avoid a stoppage becomes less probable and, far more importantly, the potential for a dangerous mismatch exists.

Brian Yates

Upholding Indiana's distinction for producing fighters with dubious records, Brian "B-52" Yates flew to a record of 13-86-3, and also knew how to go the distance putting him on a promoter's wish list as well. He battled 102 times between 1992 and 2001 which computes to a righteous work rate. His slate included losses to Iran Barkley, Oliver McCall, Dicky Ryan (twice), Donovan Ruddock, Bert Cooper, Orlin Norris, and Derrick Jefferson In his career highlight, he KOd Earnie Shavers in the second round ending Shaver's ill-advised comeback in 1995. He also beat the very beatable Reggie Strickland in 2001. "B-52" did the Midwest circuit proud by fighting the best and going the distance many times, though most ended in defeat.

John Basil Jackson

"JJ" was another Hoosier-type who could stay the distance. His record is 4-75 (KO 13)-2 in 81 outings. One of his wins came against David Payne, 1-18. Shannon Briggs, Lou Savarese, John Ruiz, Jose Ribalta, Michael Grant, Danell Nicholson and Dicky Ryan all took easy wins from JJ. So did the aforementioned Brian Yates and so did "Hurricane" Peter McNeeley (twice).

Obie Garnett et al

Sometimes a record warrants a retake. Obie Garnett was neither a designated loser nor barnstormer. He was someone who risked his life while fighting 11 times between October 1978 and September 1981; he mounted a short-lived one- fight comeback in 1986. Fighting in such cities as Louisville, Detroit, Chicago, and Indianapolis, he finished with 12 bouts, 12 defeats and 12 defeats by first round KO. Willie "Sandman" Edwards and heavy handed Luke Capuano were among his conquerors. Just how many total seconds Obie fought could not be ascertained, but the suspicion is that it was not many.

Joe "Tank" Mooney did his part by losing each of his 12 by KO. Eric Crumble's professional boxing record stands at 0-31-0-1. All losses have been by knockout in either the first or second rounds. Crumble has become somewhat of an Internet legend, and has been tabbed with such nicknames as "The Anti-Marciano" or "The Ultimate Tomato Can." He was even KOd by Donnie Penelton, 8-95-2 coming in. Matching crumble is Ed Strickland (alias Ed Carter) who went 0-30- (KO 30), but at least his competition was pretty stiff.

Lonzie Pembleton fighting in the Midwest from 1997-2002 ran up a 0-24 (KO 21) tab losing his last eight by KO. He suffered 11 first round stoppages in all.

Heavyweight Gary Butler is a global barnstormer of sorts based out of Texas and has fought everywhere from Denmark to Japan. Unfortunately, he has been KOd in most of those locales. 21 of his last 22 losses have come by way of stoppage, 11 in the first round. Remarkably, one of his UD losses came to bomber Iran Barkley in 1994. Fighting since 1990, his last loss was to Ron Aubrey, 1-1 coming in, when he was iced in the first round in Oklahoma City. Though most of his opposition has been marginal, going up against the likes of Ike Ibeabuchi 1996), Frank Tate (1997) and Chris Henry (2005) could have been an accident waiting to happen. Milwaukeean James Wilder, at 3-53-1, did beat Leon Spinks but then lost 19 in a row to round out his career. Another Wisconsin product, Jeff May book-ended his 2-16 record with wins, the first coming against former heavyweight contender, Ron Stander. However, Jeff's 16 defeats were all by way of KO, 7 seven in the fitst round.

Southern Designees

For whatever reason, the south always contributes a great number of fighters who lose far more times than they win.

Light heavyweight Kenneth Bentley fought mostly out of Dixie during the past four decades and ran up a record of 9-95 (KO 31)-1. He closed out his career winning just two of his last 67 fights. Eric Rhinehart also toiled on the southern circuit and closed with a 16-52-2 mark, but suffered 29 defeats by way of stoppage. The fact these two did not meet defies logic, though Rhinehart did meet Carlton Brown, 2-48, and Caseny Truesdale, 10-61-3 with 37 losses coming by KO. Cruiserweight Richard Wilson finished at 14-63 (KO 14)-3. He was 0-13-1 against Rob Bleakley and went the distance each time.

Roy Bedwell also got into the Dixie mix fighting out of Tennessee during roughly the same time frame and running up a record of 15-71 (KO 43)-1. He did manage to beat Bentley in 1990 and Gary "Tiger" Thomas, 4-51-1, in 1989—perhaps the highlights of a career that saw him lose 59 of his last 61 bouts, many by first round knockout. Danny Lee Wofford, 17-102 (KO 23)-2 fought just about everyone, but unfortunately lost to just about everyone.

Benji "Bad News" Singleton (who was good news for his opponents when he stepped up) chips in with a 26 (KO 18) - 107 (KO 18)-5 tally in 139 outings. Among his wins was his last in 2002, a KO over Travis "The Scrapyard Dawg" Clybourn, 5-23 coming in. He is now on a long winless streak, but when he steps down, it's usually bad news for his opponents

Billy Outley, a light middleweight who fights in Dixie, has a poor record of 13 (13)-48 (37)-2, though when he wins, he wins by KO. Billy won his first fight in 1989 by DQ and then went winless in 35 straight losing 28 by stoppage. Thirty seven KO losses out of 47 total losses is a statistic that bears watching. Robert Woods (alias Alvin Brooks) was another Dixie fighter who compiled an astounding 1-48 (KO 42) record between 1986 and 1985. His lone win came by dramatic 12th round KO against one Tim Turner, 4-5 coming in, for the North Carolina State Lightweight Title!

James Mullins, working mostly out of Nashville, last fought in 2006. His record now stands at 7-68 (KO 39)-2, though he did beat

Jerome Hill, 1-48-9 (KO 30) and Trib Perry, 1-25 (KO 20). Middleweight Carlton "Speedy" Brown ran up a 2-48 (KO 30) mark while doing Dixie, while Lopez McGee tallied a slate of 9-60. Jerry Barnes fought all of his 19 fights in Tennessee and lost all of them, 17 by stoppage 9 in the first round.

Two Jakes

Jake Torrance fought in and around Indiana until 2000 and owned a mark of 22-79 (KO 16)-2.

Winless in his last 29, southpaw Jake "The Snake" Riley tallied a 1-34-2 record while fighting in New England.

Others

Jose Pagan Rivera, a New England welterweight, toiled from 1970 to 1985 participating in 131 bouts and compiling a 30-93 (KO 39)-8 record. According to BoxRec, he fought 35 times in 1971 and 32 times the following year. Scott Sala, a cruiserweight out of Cincinnati, toted a record of 5-56 (KO 29), winning just one in his last 43.

Terrence Wright did the Midwest circuit and toted up a 4-51 (KO 31) - 2 record from 1983-1999. I witnessed his last fight when he was stopped by Bobby Harris in Leominster, Massachusetts in a less than compelling duke. Andre Crowder, a road warrior of sorts, matched Wright's record during just about the same exact time. He finished with a slate of 8- 55 (KO 32)-4 in 67 fights.

Jordan Keepers never fought outside of the heartland; he was quintessential Midwest and finished with a 3-53 (KO 27)-2 record. Only a draw "ruined" Andre Smiley's perfect record of 0-25 (KO 19)-1 as he also worked the arenas and venues of the Midwest.

Unlike the journeyman who not only believes he can win but sometimes does, a record of 1-48 or 17-102 reflects something perhaps quite different in terms of a fighters chances.

Other Countries

But so much for American fighters who, based on their records, had a high likelihood of losing but also had a high likelihood of staying out of harm's way. What about situations in which the designated loser can find himself in situations where the risk factor is higher? These situations just might exist in Slovakia and Romania–and maybe Brazil and Paraguay (not to mention, Indonesia, Thailand, Tanzania and the Philippines). This is not about throwing darts to see if they always land on horrendous records; it's more about determining if there are patterns—ones that sometimes place a fighter in a highly vulnerable situation based on a dangerous mismatch.

Mexico

Joel Yocupicio, fighting out of Mexico, is at 0-16 (KO 12) and evidences the fact that even in that macho country, some tempt fate. He has fought only one opponent with a losing record–Guadalupe "Lobito" Arce who is currently at 2-35 (KO 32). Eduardo "Lalo" Gutierrez sports an unhealthy 1-38 (KO 31) mark and has lost his last 34 in a row, most by early stoppage.

Jorge "Koki" Romero is at 7-39-1 and his level of opposition is alarmingly high. Having lost 30 in a row, he needs to step down—or perhaps step out,. though he did beat one Romulo "Olmeca" Juarez, 1-15 (KO 14).

Dominican Julio "El Cangrejo" Jerez. 1-29 (KO 21) warrants mention as well. His lone win came against hapless Dionisio Moreno, 0-16 (KO 12). And so it goes on and on and on.

The strange record of "El Monstuo"

Juan Ramon Perez, alias El Monstuo, had his first pofessional fight in the Olympic Auditorium against rugged David "Maceton" Cabrera, 36-9 coming in. Cabrerea had won 7 of his last 8 all by KO and was clearly on a different level than the debuting "El Montruo." He had gone up against the likes of Marvin Camel, Marcus Geraldo (twice), Johnny Baldwin, and Ramon Ranquello and was poised for an early icing of Perez. Unfortunaely for "Maceton," it was Perez who did the icing with a stunning first round knockout of Cabrerea, who would successfully defend his Mexican light heavyweight title in his very next fight against Gerado Valero.

For his part, Perez (seemingly on the verge of a great career), would go winless in his next 27 bouts finishing with a dismal 1-26-1 mark. To his credit, he fought high level competition, but that may well have been the rub–and his downfall.

Romania

Marius Petre Sorin has been fighting since 1997. His record is 0-37-2. He fought to a draw in his first fight, and then went winless in the next 37. He has been KOd 22 times. Only six of his fights have been held in his home country. He recently was TKOd by Kobal Alpayi, 0-0 coming in.

Cristian Nicolae, 2-49, a super bantamweight, was stopped in his first professional fight in 2002, but won his next bout against 0-0 Leon Adrian who has not fought since. Nicolae then lost his next 48, most recently on September 6, 2008. He is a road warrior extraordinaire fighting in different venues throughout Europe, but has only done battle in Romania twice. He is reasonably durable having been stopped ten times. His likelihood of losing is now an eye popping 96%. Not looking to "pad" his record, he has never fought fellow Romanians Marius Sorin, 0-37-2, Constantin Stan, 0-29-2 or Ionel Ilie, 0-16. Maybe he should. But wait! On February 19, 2008, he KOd Samir Kasmi of France and book-ended 41 losses with two wins. As an aside, and in what can only have been a bad omen, Iiie lost his last bout to Thomas Bastard in November 2995. Sorin also lost (twice) to the well- traveled Bastard.

A Romanian Contrast

Fourty-one year old Peter Simko has only won two fights out of 41 and has suffered 30 stoppage losses. He is tempting fate. Eugen Stan has an equally poor won-loss record of 4-40-1 in 45 outings, but wait, Stan has never been stopped, not even by rugged Diosbelys Hurtado, a classic case of never judging a book by its cover. As well, Gheorghe Ghiompirica has an 8-37 mark but has only been halted once.

Slovakia

Slovakians are useful road warriors who are willing to travel throughout Europe seemingly as designated losers. This is fine and dandy as long as their KOd-by-percentage is not high, but chill-or-be-chilled Stefan Stanko is chilled far more than he chills. His record is a mind-boggling 6 (KO 6)-58 (50)-1, and when he fights someone like rugged Pole Krzysztof Wlodarczyk (41-2), he is tempting fate. Wlodarczyk beat IBF cruiserweight Champion Steve Cunningham by SD before losing the rematch by MD.

Robert Zsemberi, a featherweight, is 6-46-2, and his record is distinguished by the fact he has been sent to dreamland 37 times. That's just plain dangerous. There are many others with similar dreadful records including none other than the "Slovak Rambo," Vlado Szabo, 2-34 (not to be confused with Hungarian Titusz Szabo at 2-29). Also included are Anton Vontszemu at 2-26 (KO 18), Josef Holub at 1-28, Slavomir Dendis at 2- 35 (KO 26), Peter Batora at 1-21 who was beaten by Stefan Berza, 3-34, Richard Remen, 2-29, Zoltan Horvath, with a "perfect" 0-26 (KO 22), Jozef Gabris, 0-20-2, and Vladimir Varhegyi, 20-69-3 (who amazingly has won five of his last six all by KO). There are many, many more but these are representative of what can be found in Slovakia.

Active Laszlo Paszterko (29-34-7) is somewhat of an anomaly. After losing to Hermann Bendl by TKO in 1997, his record went to a dismal 11-31-4. But then he turned things around and has gone 18-3-3 since that loss to Bendll. .Along the way, be beat hapless Belgium, Frank Wuestenberghs, 1-42 at the time and now a risky 3-65-1. (Frank is about even with Brazilian Jose Claudio Da Silva, at 5-63 with 31 alarming defeats coming by stoppage). He has lost his last 55 in a row! Rudolf Murko, from the Czech Republic, warrants mention for his less than enviable 2-39 mark, but he has done better than Joseph Sovijus who risks his health with a mark of 2-44-2.

But globe trotting Slovakian Peter Balazs has a record that warrants immediate attention. He is 0-20 and 16 of his losses have come by way of stoppage. Losing to Sandor Fekete (1-24-1) by early TKO suggests someone needs to intervene before a tragedy occurs. After all, that's what this is all about.

Jozef Kubovsky (13-101-14)

Jozef Kubovsky, a Slovakian Welterweight, deserves special mention as he has fought 96 times since 1999. During that time, he managed to win only six. One came against fellow Slovakian, hapless Imrich Parlagi now 2-67-3. Another rare win came against the dreadful Anton Glofak, 2-77-8. Kubovsky has won only once in his last 83 fights—count 'em 83! After losing 61 in a row and sporting a 76% likelihood of losing, he fought against Domingos Nascimento Monteiro for something called the "International Championship of Luxemburg for Welterweights." Of course, he lost.

Hungary

It's no better in nearby Hungary where Cruiserweight Csaba Olah owns a staggering 3-71-3 record, while Bela Sandor is at 10-56-3. One of his wins came against Slovakian Amboz Horvath, 0-18. Should Amboz ever do battle with super featherweight Zoltan Horvath, 0-26, or Szabolcs Gergely, 0-27, there will be a new twist on the saying, "someone's 'O' must go!"

Gabor "Rocco" Balogh just misses this round robin with a mark of 1- 40-5 and so does Miklos Toldi who sparks a "better" mark of 2-31. Toldi lost to the active Zoltan Beres (38-40-2) five times. Beres is another who always loses when he steps up, but wins when he fights the likes of Toldi, Csaba Olah, Szabolcs Gergely, and, of course, the "Wolfman," Janos Somogyi (8-39-2). Finally, with a dismal mark of 8-49-3, Hungarian road warrior extraordinaire, Attila Kiss, needs some serious love.

Every once in a while a promoter gets it right as evidenced by the following venue of fights held on April 19 2008 at the City Hall in Komárno, Slovakia

Flyweight Klaudia Ferenci	1 - 1	W Sim Pencakova	0-14 (5)-1 PTS
Welterweight Julius Rafael	2 - 16 (5) – 1	W Sandor Fekete	1-20 (3) -1 PTS
Super Bantam Elemir Rafael	2 - 18 (7) – 1	W Anton Walter	0-1 - PTS
Middleweight Antal Kubicsek	5 - 13 (3) - 4	D Gabor Balogh	1-30 (17) - PTS
Heavyweight	3 - 19 (12)-1	NC Stefan Kusnier Stefan Cirok	0-19 (16) –

But then on May 18, 2008, at the Sturovo City Hall in Slovakia, the following Hungarian boxers were on the losing end:

Szabolcs Gergely - 0-24

Attila Nemeth - 0-8

Gabor Czinke - 0-25

Janos Somogyi - 8-33

Slovakian Vlado Szabo at 2-30 completed the card.

Mexico and Japan do a great job when it comes to matching up fighters with relatively equal records. The following venue from Mexico affirms this:

Thursday 8 May 2008 Root's, Lomas de Sotelo, Distrito Federal, Mexico

Weight	Opponent	Winner	Record/Result
Lightweight	Fermin Uruzquieta 1 (1)-0	W Marco Sanchez	1 (0)-1 (1) TKO 1
Bantamweight	Jaime Aguilar 2 (0)	W Guadalupe Cuadros	1 (1) - 1 (0) - 0 UD 4
Lightweight	Eric Malagon 2 (2) - 2 (2)	W Guillermo Vidal	1 (1) - 2 (2) - 0 TKO 1
Bantamweight	Noe Barron 4 (1) - 3 (0)	W Bernardo Rodriguez	1 (1) - 5 (3) - 0 UD 4
Bantamweight	Gustavo Morales 1 (0) - 0	W Hector Morales	1 (1) - 1 (0) - 0 UD 4
Bantamweight	Cuatlayotl Romero 1 (0)-0	W Oscar Rojas	0 (0) - 4 (2) - 0 UD 4
Bantamweight	Virgilio Ramirez 1 (1) – 0	W Alfredo Garrido	1 (0) - 1 (1) - 0 KO 2
Bantamweight	Jose Gonzalez 1 (0) - 0	W Adrian Ramirez	0 (0) - 2 (0) - 1 SD 4
Bantamweight	Octavio Hernandez 3 (2)-1 (0)	W Eric Morin	1 (1) - 1 (1) - 0 KO 1
Lightweight	Mario Cuevas 1 (1) - 1 (1)	W Roberto Alavez	0 (0) - 1 (1) - 0 KO 2
Lightweight	Alejandro Cortes 1 (1)-0	W Edgar Bolanos	0 (0) - 1 (1) - 0 KO 2
Lightweight	Noe Chavez 1 (1)-0	W Eliuth Coronel	0 (0) - 1 (1) - 0 KO 3
Lightweight	Ivan Cano 2 (1) - 1	W Martin Garcia	0 (0) - 1 (1) - 0 TKO 2

However, Thailand never seems to get it quite right as this typical venue (April 2008) from Chiang Mai Shows:

Minimumweight Kwanthai Pattaling 20-0-1 W Zang Yuan Boau 0-1 TKO 1 11

For PABA minimumweight title ~

Flyweight Denkaosan Kaovichit 43 (18)-1-1 W Wang Jun Hui 5 (1)-8 (3) -TKO 2 10

Yes, there are winners and losers—and some in between, which brings us to Feliciano Dario Azuaga Ledezma, alias "El Indio de Oro," who fights out of Paraguay

"El Indio": The Record behind the Record

The issue of deceptive records is a global phenomenon as well. As one of a multitude of examples, let's look at the interesting record of Feliciano "El Indio de Oro" Ledezma who fights out of Paraguay. This bantam weight has an eye popping slate of 72 (KO 61) - 12 (KO 8) - in 88 outings. Ledezma has a chill factor ("excitement factor") of 78%. He gets you or you get him. The problem is that with almost mathematical certainty, he gets "gotten" when he steps up, and does the "getting" when he steps down.

El Indio was KOd by Simphiwe Nongqayi in August 2007 in a bid for the WBF super flyweight title. He has since won three fights, all by knockouts. Two were over Walter "El Coyote" Satler, now 0-7. In fact, of the Coyote's seven career defeats, four have come at the hands of "El Indio." The combined record of his last three opponents is 0-32.

Ledezma has also taken a liking to Arnaldo "Polvorita" Orrabalis, also from Paraguay. Ledezma has beaten Polvorita, 2-23-2, seven times. He also stopped Argentineans Enrique "Chirolita" Ocampo, 0-27 (KO 17)-2, twice.

El Indio also found time to dispatch the Brazilian Jose Carlos Amaral twice. Jose, fighting since 1993, currently has a record of 1-52 with 29 losses coming by way of knockout. That's 1-52!

However, when Ledezma fights better opposition, he gets into big time trouble. Tough "Rocky" Medina, 30-1, iced him twice. In fact, the last time he beat a fighter with a winning record was in December 2003 when he KOd Erich "Chispita" Franco, then 14-8-1. In 2002, he stopped Julio Cesar Garibaldi, 1-0. In 2001, he beat Bolivian "Sugar" Castro, 4-2-3. In 2000, he stopped Argentinean Julio "Clerico" Oliva in 25 seconds of the first round.

Maybe his career best came in a SD loss to Argentinean Juan Domingo "Panza" Cordoba, 33-5-3 in a 2001 fight held in Mendoza, Argentina. Ledezma was 49-1-2 coming in.

On March 15, 2008, he again moved down and stopped Basilio "El Mono" Mendiola in the second round. It was his fourth win over the hapless "El Mono" who now has an alarming record of 0-20 (KO 18).

But then on May 9, 2008, he stepped up against Franklin Teran, 25-2, and was stopped in the 4rth round in Galicia, Spain. And in October 2008, he was stopped in two by Canadian Sebastien Gauthier (14-1).

Thailand: The Vulnerable

Thailand is a country where all kinds of boxing is extremely popular. But it is a country where fighters are often placed into situations where obvious mismatches raise the stakes of the outcomes. Take the well documented case of Lito Sisnorio.

Filipino Angelito "Lito" Sisnorio, twenty-four, was coming off a fourth-round TKO loss to reigning WBC Flyweight Champion Pong-saklek Wonjongkam, 63-2, on January 26, 2007. It was Lito's third consecutive defeat. Then on March 30, 2007, he fought former WBC Flyweight Champion Chatchai Sasakul, then 58-3 (now 64-3), again in Thailand. Sasakul had won his last six fights, four by stoppage, since losing to Kuniyuki Aizawa in Tokyo. Lito, who reportedly was not licensed to fight in Thailand, had won only five of his eleven fights.

Sasakul is truly one of the great Thai fighters. He battered—yes, battered—Manny Pacquiao for six rounds before Manny caught him with a devastating combination to win the title by a sensational eighth-round knockout in 1998. One of his other losses came against the great Yuri Arbachakov in 1995. He avenged this loss by upsetting Arbachakov two years later for the WBC flyweight title. It would be Arbachakov's only career defeat and final fight.

Fighting at a catch weight of 116 pounds, the vastly-experienced Sasakul predictably ended the fight via a fourth-round stoppage. He landed a series of vicious right hooks, decking Lito, who had absorbed tremendous punishment. The referee then stopped the contest at the 2:35 mark as a badly-cut Sisnorio came under a sustained barrage and could no longer defend himself. Later, he fell unconscious and was rushed to Bangkok's Piyamin Hospital where he underwent emergency brain surgery to remove a blood clot. Sadly, he failed to regain consciousness.

Kaennakorn Bangbuathong

An equally dangerous mismatch occurred when world class Thai fighter, Sirimongkol Singwancha, 57-2, took on Kaennakorn Bangbuathong in the latter's very first professional fight on September 14, 2007. In 2005, Singwancha beat Michael Clark in a WBC Lightweight Title Eliminator in Las Vegas. Prior to that, he lost to the very tough Jesus Chavez in Austin, Texas in a fight for the WBC super featherweight title. His only other defeat came at the hands of Joichiro Tatsuyoshi when he lost his WBC bantamweight title by seventh round KO.

Maybe Bangbuathong had an extensive amateur career or maybe he crossed over from Muay Thai boxing, but I could not corroborate either. Fighters with 0-0 records fighting seasoned pros is not an unusual occurrence in Thailand, but it should be. And so a 57-2 ex-champion fights a guy in his first pro bout and sometimes, this can have a tragic ending.

Others at Risk

Why was Filipino Roger Monserto, 0-3 at the time allowed to fight the very same Chatchai Sasakul, then 60-3 (now 64-3), in July 2007 in a steaming hot arena in Bangkok? Heck, why did he Roger fight Ratanachai Sor Vorapin, then 69-9 and now 72-9 with 48 stoppages? Monserto, now 0-6, has fought against opponents with a combined won-loss record of 308-27-1. This is crazy.

Veeraphol Sahaprom, now 61-3 with 43 KO wins, won a recent fight over Richard Laano, 4-3-1. In 2006, Sahaprom beat three boxers from the unlikely locale of Tanzania: Maiko Yombayomba, 0-0, Maiko Yombayomba, 0-1, and Scari Korori, 0-0. One of Sahaprom's victims, Indonesian super bantamweight Hasan Ambon, finished with an 0-9 record. His losses came against rugged Fahsan 3K Battery (twice), one -time WBF super bantamweight title holder Somsak Sithchatchawal, future WBA featherweight champion Chris John, the great Ratanachai Sor Vorapin, contender Andrian Kaspari, and Rachman Kili Kili, now 10-2. Ambon has to be one tough customer.

Speaking of tough customers, why was Medgoen "3K Battery" Singsurat, 55-5 with 39 KOs, allowed to step into the ring with Denpayak Sor Pisanu, 0-0-0, on January 25, 2008 and with 0-0 Yodkumarn Chitraladagym on February 29, 2008? This was the same Singsurat who knocked out Manny Pacquiao (then 26-1) in 1999 for the WBC flyweight title. The same Singsurat who fought eleven fighters with a combined record of 1-5 before he was TKO'd in one by Jorge Arce just prior to his fight with Pisanu.

Following his UD loss to tough Steve Molitor, Fahsan 3K Battery, 59 (35)-9 (1), beat Filipino designee Roldan Malinao, 3-13., in February 2008. Poonsawat Kratingdaenggym, 32-1, beat hapless featherweight Almaz Assanov of Kazakhstan, 1-4, on February 27, 2007 but hell, Assanov who is now 1-7 has fought Sod Looknongyangtoy, Saohin Srithai Condo, Somsak Sithchatchawal and Ratanachai Sor Vorapin. Their total won-lost record coming against Assanov was an eye-popping 199-24-1.

Like the aforementioned Hasan Ambon, Almaz Assanov has to be the toughest fighter in the world with a 1-7 record.

And why was Yodsanan Sor Nanthachai, 53 (42)-3-1, in the ring with Mar Suvanichev, 0-1, in January 2008 and Omid Gholizadeh, 0-5 in December 2006 when he was 49-3-1? Why was Gholizadeh in against Yoddamrong Sithyodthong, 43-2-1, when he was 0-1?

As recently as March 21, 2008, Denkaosan Kaovichit, 41-1-1 beat Filipino Rey "Kid" Orais. The Kid had a 9-14 mark coming in and was iced in 3. His record is 1-8 when fighting in Thailand.

Yodsanan Sor "3-K Battery" Nanthachai, 54 (KO 43)-3, KOd Dennapa Bigshotcamp, 2-17 (KO 8) a week later in Bangkok. "Bigshot" is that rare Thai fighter who does most of his work outside of Thailand. He has lost his last 12, mostly in Australia.

In other glaring mismatches, Thai flyweight Wandee Singwancha, 55-8-1 fought and beat Indonesian Dan Nafsadan, 0-0 coming in, on March 31, 2008. After being iced by Vic Darchinyan twice in 2003, Wandee went on a 17 fight unbeaten streak going into his six round bout with the untested Nafsadan. The streak included a stoppage in 2004 over Ernesto "Hard Rock" Rubillar for the vacant WBC

International light flyweight title. He also beat Juanito Rubillar in 2006 for the interim WBC light flyweight title. Despite these high profile fights, he fought Nauldy Falazona and Jang Peng Gai, both 0-0 coming in 2007. These could have been accidents waiting to happen.

On April 18, 2008, Napapol Kiatisakchokchai, 45-2-1 with 39 wins coming by way of KO fought Indonesian Ewan Borne, 0-0 coming in. This was just plain wrong.

Sadly, these seem to be the norm, but what these kinds of matches fail to take into account is that not all designated losers know how to lose safely. Sure, mismatches will occur from time to time; that's the nature of the beast. However, when patterns manifest themselves, the amber light should be flashing.

26

HAVE GLOVES WILL TRAVEL

As long as I come out of the fight OK and I'm able to count my money when it's over, I'm fine…I'm ahead of where I was before I got there.
–Reggie Strickland

I won't lie to you: I still miss it sometimes. But boxing's always been a part of me, and it always will be.
–Reggie Strickland

'I'm not in it for the recognition…'I fight, I get paid, and I go home, that's all I do. I don't really have a story to tell.
–Verdell Smith

I'm the last of a dead breed.
–Bruce "The Mouse" Strauss

… there's always been a curious mystique surrounding Opponents
–Marc Gerald

The only thing that you owe the public is a good performance.
–Humphrey Bogart

Some of these guys give prospects a win but they thwart those who want to pad their knockout totals at their expense.
–Anonymous

Boxing Encyclopedia defines barnstormers as follows: A barnstormer (or 'barnstorming') is a term used to describe a boxer who goes from small town to small town, taking fights, often against local heroes, for cheap, but frequent paydays. Barnstorming was common among black fighters before 1940. It was also done by heavyweight champions such as Jack Dempsey, in the form of exhibition tours. In some instances the barnstormer, if already well known, would come to town with his hand-picked opponent. Although this would usually provide him with a safe foe, it often provided for a mismatch and a disappointed crowd. [1]

The definition fits well. These barnstormers made a decent living with predictable and ultra frequent activity. Some did it by being a designated loser, often against each other. Others were winners who had gloves and were willing to travel as road warriors.

Let's look at some.

Reggie Strickland

Many scribes have written about Reggie. After all, it's not every fighter who sported a record of 66 (KO 14) - 276 (KO 25)-17 in 363 outings. That's right, 363 fights! Reggie, like many others, played the role of both a barnstormer and designated loser simultaneously. He did his losing while barnstorming just as Buck Smith did his winning while barnstorming. Sometimes, they did it together.

One wire service called Strickland, a/k/a Reggie Buse, a/k/a Reggie Raglin a "legendary Midwest campaigner." Reggie Strickland just loves boxing. Having last fought in 2005, he has now made a transition from boxer to a busy matchmaker in the Midwest. Reportedly, he has also joined the North American Boxing Council sanctioning body as Commissioner and Chairman of the NABC Ratings Committee.

His amazing career included matches with Derrick Harmon, Hugo Pineda, Keith Holmes Randall Bailey, James Butler and Corey Spinks. He also duked it out with Anthony Bonsante, Raul Marquez, Troy Weida, Joe Hutchinson, Alex Bunema Rubin Williams, Charles Brewer, James Crawford, and Derrick Harmon. Also included among his opponents were Tony Menefee, Lonnie Smith, Todd Foster, Tony Marshall, Syd Vanderpool, Manning Galloway, Harold Brazier, Gary Kirkland, Alex Ramos, Marty Jakubowski, Tocker Pudwill, Anthony Stephens and others too numerous to mention.

Perhaps his career highlight occurred in 2002 when he beat Conley Person, 1-15 coming in, by 6 round TKO. The fight was held at Farm Bureau Building, Indianapolis, Indiana. Something called the vacant Global Boxing Federation super middleweight title was at stake.

But what is compelling about Reggie is the record behind the record. With a 76% losing percentage, he was a promoter's dream, for the likelihood of his losing was predictable and reliable, and if there is anything a promoter likes, its predictability. In this regard, he too was a designated loser. That was his role pure and simple.

However, the real oddity about Strickland's final slate is the excitement factor which is derived by dividing the total number of fights into the total number of knockouts. In his case, the factor works out to an extremely low 11% which suggests Strickland knew how to go the distance. It further suggests that the amount of rounds he fought was simply astounding.

Look, if it's excitement you crave, try Herbie Hide (98% excitement factor), Alejandro Berrio (97%) or Tommy Morrison (86%), all members of the chill-or-be-chilled brigade. Two "Julian's," Jackson and Letterlough, were members of this club as well. But guys like Strickland come in and give you the full number of round. In the process, they perform adequately enough so hat people buy the tickets.

As Russ Greenspan wrote in a neat July 12 2007 piece entitled "Reggie Strickland: Boxing's All-Time Leading Also-Ran,

"It was not uncommon for Strickland et al. to compete in bingo halls, state fairgrounds or auditoriums before double digit sized audiences, for paydays ranging from $500 to $2,000; any place with a boxing ring and some metal folding chairs would suffice, as long as there was up front cash available." [2]

He was banned in many states, but found a sanctuary in Indiana where he became notorious, if not a notorious curiosity. Benchmarked against Milwaukee's Donnie Pendelton, Benji Singleton from Charlotte, N.C., 26-106-5 and Danny Wofford from Columbia, S.C., 17-102-2, he arguably was the best of the worst. Donnie "the Black Battle Cat" Pendelton, by the way, was Gerald McClellan's first cousin but that's where the similarities end.

Reggie and others traveled the back streets in vans and cars; it was the circuit that ran from Indiana, Ohio, Wisconsin, Minnesota, Nebraska, North Dakota, South Dakota and Montana. By frequently fighting in small towns under aliases and crossing state borders for multiple fights (often against each other) in a span of a few days, these barnstormers were able to beat a system that was poorly regulated at best. Hell, this was all about "Have gloves, Will travel."

Remarkably, Reggie shows few signs of wear and tear, speaks extremely well, and his face, adorned with a neat Mandrake the Magician mustache, belies the astounding number of fights in which he has participated. He avoided serious medical risk because he fought defensively and knew how to hang on. He also had a knack of dropping to the canvas and getting out of harm's way when engaging incoming pressure.

On October 3, 2000, at the Farm Bureau Building in Indianapolis, Indiana, Reggie Strickland, won an eight round unanimous decision over Donnie Penelton. The two fighters had a combined won-loss record of 62-334-19. After this bout, Strickland went 14-52-2 to finish his career, while Penelton closed out by going 3-54-1.

Buck Smith

Interestingly, Reggie's point counterpart, Buck Smith, 179 (KO 120)-19 (KO 8)-2 in 224 bouts, has now retired having lost his last nine in a row, seven by way of stoppage. His early sanctuary was Oklahoma but later he became a road warrior and fought just about everywhere. When he fought one George Jackson in 1993, his record was 147-5-2 coming in! He is in Guinness for having the longest streak of bouts without a loss (105). He knocked out the then rated Kirkland Laing (who had a decision win over the great Roberto Duran) in England and fought a draw with perennial contender Harold Brazier.

In one month, Smith fought 12 times in Kansas, Kentucky, Missouri, Indiana, Tennessee and Oklahoma. He once fought twice in one night, in different states. Buck and Reggie met five times and Buck, of course, won all five.

Smith wasn't particularly exceptional, but when he landed his big hook, he was daunting. Boxing was his essence; it was what he was all about. He fought dozens of times every year and gave a real effort every time I saw him. In these days of 20 bout "veterans," Buck had over a hundred and seventy wins. This schedule can't be good for the human body, but it sure was a nice change for those who followed boxing back in the Eighties by reading one and two-line results posted in daily newspapers. Buck Smith was a steady presence when boxing offered more dilettantes than hard-nosed journeymen. (With thanks to Pete Leonitis).

But Buck didn't fight the greatest level of competition as the following discloses

Keheven Johnson 24-71-5	Six losses to Buck Smith
Reggie Strickland- 276 losses	five losses to Smith
Kenny Willis 4-31	two losses to Smith
Terry Williams 2-18	four losses to Smith
Bob Ervin 0-16	four losses to Smith
Tim Bowles 0-14	two losses to Smith
Anthony Davidson 1-13	four losses to Smith
Kenneth Kidd 25-42	five losses to Smith
Gary Brown 3-18	two losses to Smith
Verdell Smith 44-61-3	three losses to Smith
Tim Brooks 3-24	three losses to Smith
Tim Bonds 3-28	four losses to Smith
Tommy Degan 0-13	two losses to Smith
Jorge Acosta 3-13	three losses to Smith
Quintan Fox 0-12	two losses to Smith
Rico Hernandez 10-26	four losses to Smith
Bobby Thomas 0-9	three losses to Smith
Tommy Jeans 3-54	three losses to Smith
George Jackson 1-9	two losses to Smith
Richard Wilson 14-66-3	two losses to Smith

John Simmons 1-28, Reese Smith, 4-23, Ponce Ortiz 0-20, Kelly Brown , 0-10, Ira Hathaway, 0-8, Vernon Garrett 13-62, Jake Torrance, 22-79-2, and Simmie Black 35-162-4 each fought and lost once to "Tombstone.".

Verdell Smith, a worthy opponent type, and Buck Smith were once part of an unorganized group of fighters who referred to themselves as the Knucklehead Boxing Club and their claim to fame was having logged hundreds of thousands of miles on the road. Sean Gibbons was the manager, matchmaker and sometimes last-minute replacement. To save money, they drove overnight and slept in the car. Gibbons drove the Knuckleheads everywhere and reportedly logged more than 300,000 miles on his Honda hatchback. There is much more to the Knucklehead story, but I'll leave that rich vein of gold for someone else to mine.

Today, fighters (like Reggie) who take a bout on short notice knowing they have little or no chance of winning are still around but are fewer in number. New licensing regulations have tightened up and greater scrutiny is being given to ring records, medical history and whether a fighter can be competitive. A new law requires promoters to verify a fighter's record and keep doctors on hand at every fight, but most observers concede that the legislation doesn't go far enough. Still, state boxing commissions are working more closely together in an attempt to eliminate some of the alleged skullduggery of the past.[3]

It's simply more difficult for this type of fighter to get licensed today because the liability risk factor is too high.

James Holly and the Ashtabula Scene

You walk down this street today, and you'll run into four or five guys that used to fight for me.
–James Holly

I was traveling all over the world, you name it – I went there. I saved a lot of shows.
–James Holly

If it hadn't been for guys like Jim Holley, there wouldn't be a lot of these prima-donna fighters.
–Promoter Joe Furst

Boxers...aren't big into reality checks.
–Marc Gerald

Since 1996, when boxers' federal ID cards became mandatory, prize-fighters from the rust belt town of Ashtabula, Ohio have established a combined record of 25 wins and 379 losses. Of those losses, 343 were by KO or TKO, and most came within the first two rounds.

James Holly alias Virgil Holly / James Robinson, fought out of Ashtabula from 1983-2000 and was both a fighter and promoter who could provide a body (including his own) two days before a fight.

As a boxer, he had an eye-popping mark of 5-55 (KO 55) that landed him suspensions in at least six states. Yes, 55 losses coming by way of KO and 31 in the first round. Others have reported his record as having been 7-64 (KO 64). One of his few wins came against Larry Pugh, 1-7 (KO 7). Another, a major upset, was a 10th round knock out of heavily favored Sammy Scaff in 1998. The giant Scaff once fought Mike Tyson.

This heavyweight was an exemplar of those fill in last-minute vacancies on cards, the fodder that more promising fighters used to pad their records with a KO. But when you lose 55 (or 64) fights by KO, you put yourself at great risk.

As a promoter, he traveled the hillbilly circuit of West Virginia, Virginia, Tennessee, etc. and gave Ashtabula the nickname of a "Tomato-Can Capital." For over 20 years, he supplied a ready roster of lower rung fighters, some reportedly even taken off the streets with the lure of a paycheck in exchange for a world of hurt and pain. Among his more well known fighters were Mario Hereford, 0-20 (KO 17), Exum Speight, 10-38-2, and George Harris, 2-37 (KO 35). Holley was able to find members of his stable steady work and would often pile several guys into a van and drive across the country for weeks at a time. The fact that they lost just about every time out did not seem to faze him. His ability tp provide a ready supply of boxers on short notice earned him a reputation as one of the most reliable men in the business.

However, the full and complete story of James Holly is the stuff that feeds screen plays and movies. It includes a host of twist and turns that surely would whet the appetite of any shrewd writer. A few paragraphs here cannot possibly do his story justice. Suffice it to say he may have produced America's worst fighters, and he seems to be proud of it to this very day. To be continued.

Charley "Dynamite" Salas and Eddie "Another Chance" Halligan

This barnstormer deluxe fought from 1945 – 1957 and tallied an astonishing mark of 130 (KO 50) – 53 (KO 1)-13 in 197 bouts. While Phoenix was his favorite place of work, he toiled on both coasts. His one stoppage loss was to undefeated Rory Calhoun in 1955, but prior to that, he had participated in 187 outings without having been stopped. Many of Dynamite's opponents, like Ike Williams, Freddie Dawson, and Jimmy Hatcher, had impressive won-loss records.

"Another Chance," 112 (KO 14)-41 (KO 16)-41, gave many of his opponents another chance as he fought to an incredible 41 draws in 195 bouts fighting mostly in the Northwestern part of the country.

The Alabama Kid

Clarence Oland Reeves aka The Alabama Kid fought from 1928 to 1950 (1950 begins my time zone for tracking fighters) and was an older version of Buck Smith toting up an amazing record of 172 (KO 107) - 57 (KO 18) - 21 in 255 fights. A southpaw light heavyweight, he fought the best of his era and beat many of them. His bouts included two with Archie Moore, a duke with Arturo Godoy (whom he beat), one each against the great Gus Lesnevich and legendary Australian Dave Sands, 63-8-1, two with Australian Jack Johnson and five against tough Jack McNamee. As well, he KOd Ritchie Sands, Ron Richards, 93-23-9 coming in, Jack Wilson twice, Billy 'Wokko' Britt, 66-13-4, and took the measure of Gorilla Jones, 100-22-13, in a great display of boxing technique according to the Coshocton Tribune of Dover, Ohio.

He did much of his fighting in Australia, but prior to 1938, he fought in and around the Ohio - Pennsylvania region. In his third from last fight in 1939, he beat tough Buddy Walker, 79-30-5 at the time.

The following is taken from the A Knock-Out! The Arnold Thomas Boxing Collection, The National Library of Australia, Number 85 | February 2007:

"The Australian boxing scene had a very good reputation in the first half of the twentieth century and attracted fighters of many different nationalities. As it wasn't unusual for these visiting boxers to stay in Australia for several years, they often held Australian titles. Many of these international fighters are included in the Arnold Thomas collection, including Clarence Reeves, the 'Alabama Kid'. Reeves spent 10 years in Australia and fought at least 72 matches here. According to a note on the back of his photograph he even married an Australian girl, but was eventually forced to return to America by the White Australia Policy."[4]

The Kid passed away on 1970-April 22, 1970 at the young age of 58.

Tiger Jack Fox

Fox on right (Photo from the Public Domain)

Fox was an outstanding talent who fought anyone, any time, any place; He was ready, willing and able; He took 'em all on - big or small - and beat 'em...
−Tracy Callis, Boxing Historian

John Linwood Fox aka Tiger Jack Fox amassed a record of 154 (KO 97)-22 (KO 9)-12 in 191 outings during the same time period of 1928 to 1950. He too fought the best of his era and he did it in the great northwestern part of the country. Names like Freddie Beshore, Tiger Ted Lowry, Al Gainer, Melio Bettina, John Henry Lewis, Jersey Joe Walcott (whom he conquered twice) and Lou Brouillard dot his impressive resume. He also did battle with rugged Jack Trammell multiple times, went 1-1-1 with Slapsie Maxie Rosenbloom, 200-39-29, fought twice against Young Firpo, and avenged a loss to Fred Lenhart, 100-21-13, by knocking him out in the third round and ending Lenhart's long career.

According to BoxRec, Lenhart went down 37 seconds into the bout, claiming a foul, as he grabbed the back of his head. He was counted out, but his corner came in to the ring and successfully argued he had been fouled. He was given a few minutes to recover and continue. In the 3rd, Fox hit Lenhart with a body shot that finished him. He had to be helped back to his corner, as was booed as he left the ring.

Sadly, the Tiger passed away on April 4, 1954 at age 47.

Simmie Black

Black, alias Spider Black and Fred Johnson, an almost legendary loser, was both a designee and a barnstormer, albeit on the notorius southern circuit of Tennessee, Mississippi, Alabama and Arkansas with occasional forays into the Midwest during the 1970s, 80s, and 90s. Like other barnstormers, he often used aliases to hide his identity from boxing commissions and fans. Some say he even impersonated deceased boxers but that could not be corroborated. He finished his career in 1996 having won four in a row against dreadful competition.

Unfortunately and unlike the great Alabama Kid and Tiger Jack Fox, his final record was les than glorious. It was 35-162-4 in 201 bouts, and of his 162 losses, 95 came by way of stoppage. He was knocked out four times in one 33-day stretch in 1977. As might be expected, he met and lost to Buck Smith in 1987, though Buck was just 3-1 at the time. Between 1979 and 1989, he tallied a record of 2-68. When he fought Jimmy Mitchell in August 1986, he was 20-90-4 coming in but Jimmy was 0-26-0 and it appeared Simmie might just win one. But Mitchell ended his losing streak by weaving a web around "The Spider" over 4 rounds. Mitchell closed out his career with a 3-35 record with all of his fights being held in the south.

On the Circuit

Harold Brazier, 105-18-1 with 64 wins coming by way of KO, was an extremely talented light middleweight who also fought out of Indiana and was levels above the rest. The rap on Brazier is that he lost the big fight opportunities against Vince "Cool" Phillips, Livingstone Bramble, Juan Martin Coggi, Meldrick Taylor, Lloyd Honeyghan, Roger Mayweather, and Pernell Whitaker. However, in all fairness, each was a World Champion at one time or another. He did beat some very good fighters like Rockin Robin Blake and Irish Mickey Ward and split a pair with Anthony Stephens. Yes, he fought on the circuit, but unlike Buck Smith, came within a hair of capturing a world title.

Others like Marty Jakubowski, Verdell Smith, Dwayne Swift, Walter Cowans, Ray Menefee, Jim Kaczmarek, Jerry Smith, Wayne Grant, Bruce "The Mouse" Strauss, Vernon Garrett, Dave Robinson, Richard Wilson and the aforementioned Jerry Strickland (who suffered 30 first round KOs) were in or on the periphery of this Middle American troupe of boxers. Some, like Jakubowski were very good, others, like John Moore from Evansville, Indiana at 11-56-2, or Gerald "The Weasel" Shelton, 8-49-3, were not.

Rocky Berg (alias Danny Vires) was the quintessential Oklahoma fighter. With a record of 62 (KO 41)-41 (KO 26)-2 in 108 bouts, he fought many top level opponents and managed to beat some while toiling from 1986-1997. So is Craig Houk (alias Tim Bennett and Gary Meyers) who is 67-36 and fights mostly in Indiana with occasional trips outside the country. He once beat Jorge Acosta, 3-7, for the vacant USA Mid West welterweight title. Among his other victims was one Ben Tafari, 1-35. He went 2-3 against the aforementioned Berg. Terry "Buzzsaw" Rondeau was something of a "have gloves will travel" sort as he went 28-37 mostly on the East coast. But what distinguished the "Buzzsaw" was that he went 26-3 until 1971 after which he went 2-34. Kehaven Johnson, out of Tulsa, was not as good, but he was almost as active with a slate of 24-71 (KO 36) - 5.

Rob Bleakley, out of Mitchell, Indiana, tallied 77 wins against 38 losses and one draw. To his credit, he duked it out with just about anyone put in front of him including Kelly Pavlik, Raul Marquez, Jean-Marc Mormeck and Mario Veit. He seemed to have particular liking to Richard Wilson whom he defeated 16 times out of 16! He beat Reggie Strickland 5 out of 6. Walter Cowans was a prototype finishing with a mark of 26-101-1 and fighting in small towns throughout the heartland– from Prior Lake, Minnesota to LaPorte, Indiana–Grand Forks, North Dakota to Omaha and Morris, Illinois to Club Dimensions in Highland, Indiana.

Lee "The Quickster" Cargle fights throughout the Midwest with frequent trips into the south. Starting out with a 14 fight unbeaten streak, he currently has a record of 35-117-1, but has only been stopped 30 times thus fulfilling the wishes of many a promoter. Another fighter from the region, Ken "Shotgun" Manuel, retired with a slate of 3-29, but two of his wins came against "The Quickster" in Oklahoma City.

Cruiserweight David Robinson fights out of Oklahoma and is 25-55-4, He participated in 16 dukes in 1993 alone in places like North Dakota, Montana, Idaho, Nebraska,, Kansas and, of course, Indiana. He won his first fight by KO and then proceeded to lose his next 13 in a row.

In the mid-Atlantic region, middleweight Michael Grant reeled in a 2-36 record fighting in and around New York and Philadelphia as did cruiserweight Robert Thomas, 16-56-4. In fact, Thomas beat Grant in 1984. Robert "Jack of Heart" Jackson out did both finishing with a 1-30-1 record. Who did he beat? Why none other than the afore-mentioned Michael Grant in 1983.

Sandy Seabrooke who fought back in the 70's out of Southern Florida, while not on the circuit, warrants mention for his strange record of 16-37-15. He fought the "Prince of Second Avenue," Jerry Powers, seventeen times and went 2-7-8. He lost 7 out of 7 to Bobby Marie as well. As for the Prince, his final record was an active 54-85-18 with only 13 KO losses in 157 fights. Strange as it may seem, I saw him fight and lose twice at Marigold Gardens in Chicago in 1962. The Prince, if nothing else, was a survivor with an extremely low excitement factor of 11.5%.

Frankie Hines also did the Southern circuit, but his record was an abysmal 17 (KO 11)-120 (KO 78)-5 in 143 fights and being KOd in 65% of his 120 losses is an unnerving statistic. He did manage to beat one Bobby Jones whose claim to fame was closing out his career with an -0-19 record with 18 defeats coming by way of knockout, 12 in the first round.

Redtop and Tommy

Back in the day, there was one fighter who was representative of guys who had gloves and would travel. Teddy "Redtop" Davis (alias Murray "Sugar" Cain) was a staple on Friday Night Fights in the 50's and was a quintessential global barnstormer who gave as well as he received. He finished with a 70-75-6 record, but was only stopped 5 times. "Red Top" fought out of boxing crazy Stockton, California, Texas, in the Philippines, Panama, Mexico, Jamaica, Cuba, Canada, France, New York, Connecticut, Massachusetts, Rhode Island, Maryland, Louisiana, Ohio, Missouri, Pennsylvania, and West Virginia. In

1954, he beat the great Percy Bassett, 63-10-1 coming in. In fact, he split four with Bassett in all. In 1950, he beat the very tough Paddy Demarco, then 49-4-1. He also fought 3 dukes with Willie Pep and one with Sandy Saddler. Arguably, Teddy may have been the toughest fighter with a losing record.

Another was Boston lightweight Tommy Tibbs who ran up a mark of 58-77-4 but was stopped only 8 times. Fighting from 1950-1972, he did battle in such global spots as Soweto, Gauteng, South Africa, Jamaica, London, Paris, Sydney, Australia, Italy, Mexico, Puerto Rico, Canada, Cuba, Hawaii, the Philippines, Venezuela—and barnstormed up and down the Eastern seaboard and Mid Atlantic states. He split six with the great Harold Gomes. Sadly, he was shot to death in a dispute at a Roxbury bar in Boston at age 40.

Six Guys

Six representative guys who won far more than they lost deserve their due. They fought often and in a lot of different locales.

Jerry "Wimpy" Halstead, an Oklahoman, did his share of traveling, particularly at the end of his career. He closed out with an admirable 84 (KO 62)-19 (KO 12)-1 mark.

Tim "Doughboy" Tomashek chalked up a 51-12 record and won 25 of his last 27 bouts, mostly against dreadful competition. Still, wins are wins, though he did lose two to Wimpy on points. The Doughboy lost when he stepped up.

Bobby Crabtree finished with an active 56 (KO 51)-35 (KO 30)-1 and would get you if you didn't get him first. He fought extremely tough opposition and captured the WBF cruiserweight title with a SD win over undefeated Kenny Keene in 1995. Keene later avenged that loss.

Rob "All-American Prizefighter" Calloway, 70 (KO 56)- 7 (KO 3)-1, has gotten himself back into the title picture by winning his last 11 bouts and looking good in the process.

Shannon "Sandman" Landberg was that rare Indiana fighter who had a winning record of 58 (KO 26)-12 (7)-3. He did the Midwest circuit from 1989 to 2006 and rarely won when he stepped up but rarely lost when he stepped down. He beat beatable Reggie Strickland five times.

Jimmy Heair was active on both coasts from 1971- 1984 and won his first 33 in a row. He also KOd Jimmy Corkum in 1978. It came on the end of another long winning streak. He finished with a fine mark of 96 9 (KO 62) – 32 (KO 9)-1

They toiled mostly in the Midwest. Each rarely won the big one, but each was (or is) a winner.

Stacy "Goodnight" Goodson: 1995-2007

Now that I have been a manager for awhile, I've found that the money is not the greatest compared to a real job. But it's rewarding when one of your fighters does well. I feel this reward is priceless and I would not trade this job for anything...
–Stacy Goodson

A different kind of 500 hitter, this Arkansas heavyweight's chill-or-be-chilled record of 37 (KO 20)-37 (KO 26)-2 is terribly deceptive. When this barnstormer stepped up, he always got chilled; when he stepped down, he chilled– but he stepped way down (against many opponents who were 0-0 coming in). In fact, he fought 28 guys who had an "0" in their win column.

Perhaps his career highlight was a MD win over Larry Sutton, 3-37 at the time. He lost a rematch with Sutton, 3-39 coming in, 4 months later.

However, to his great credit, he has become an active and successful manager and puts on popular shows in Arkansas. Indeed, one of his recent charges, journeyman Marcus "Big Tuna" Rhode, now sports a 34 (KO 29)-34 (29)-2 slate, but, like his manager, when he steps up, the Tuna gets canned.

Mexico

Luis "Pocket Battleship" Castillo was a Mexican barnstormer extraordinaire who fought from 1940-1959 and chalked up an amazing record of 98 (KO 41)-70 (KO 13) - 12 in 181 outings. He alternated between multiple location in Mexico and Cuba with frequent stops elsewhere including Washington, California (Hollywood was a favorite venue), Oregon, Texas, Minnesota, Hawaii, Australia, the Dominican

Republic, Panama and Venezuela. He went 4-4-2 against Tony Olivera who himself finished with 81-28-14 and was only stopped twice. He was 4-2 against Otilio "Zurdo" Galvan, 104-47-5. Juan Soberanes , at 44-31-2 is another Mexican road warrior type at the highest level of competition, In fact, he was 38-1 before being KOd by rough Terrence Alli after which he went 6-30-2–an amazing career turn around.

Other Mexicans like Juan "Bombin" Padilla, 71-32-7, Humberto "Hamlet" Carrillo, 66-23 (KO 3)-7, Cesar "Chino" Saavedra, 69-42-8, and Galvan ran up hugh slates, but few ventured outside of Torreon, Coahuila de Zaragoza, Durango or Mexico City. Of course, Kid Azteca (alias Luis Villanueva Paramo), who fought from 1930-1961, occasionally would fight outside Mexico City, but only occasionally as he ran up an eye-popping slate of 155 (KO 88)-44 (KO 7) – 8 in 207 bouts. Ricardo Arredondo, 76 (KO 57) – 22 (KO3) -1, broke the mold by taking his act globally and even duked in South Korea and Denmark.

Lupe "Macho" Guerra, 24-27-2, was the quinessential midwestern fighter. Heck, he never even fought in Mexico. Go figure.

Cuba

Global barnstormer, Angel Robinson Garcia, fought from 1955 to 1978, and did his early work in Cuba, the States, Venezuela, Venezuela, Mexico, and Jamaica. He then shifted to Europe in 1961 with France and Italy being his favorite work sites with frequent jaunts into many other countries including Abidjan and Algeria. Spain soon became his new home until 1972 when he closed out his remarkable career with a series of dukes in the United States against extremely solid opposition. Angel's final record was an eye opening 133 (KO 53) - 81 (KO 3)-21 in 235 battles. Yes, only three stoppage losses in 235 fights!

Middleweight Sugar Boy Nando, from Aruba, fought throughout Europe, in the Caribbean, and in both North and South America while running up a fine mark of 64-42-7. A staple in Aruba and Jamaica, he participated in many high profile bouts against some rugged opposition.

Australia

Considering fighters activity decreases with each generation, he
[Flash Malcolm] will almost undoubtedly be the last Aussie
to punch out a 100 wins.
–Tony Pritchard-Nobbs

*The blokes I fought coming up, even in four rounders, like Wally
Carr, Brian Roberts, they were brilliant fighters, if they were around
today they'd be unbeatable here. I got a great grounding. Back then,
you had to fight who you were told. If you knocked back a fight, they
got someone else and you'd be scrapped. Fighters today are feminine;
they want to see video's, go through the opponents records, before
they accept a fight.*
–Jeff Malcolm

With a final record 100-27-11 in 138 outings, Flash was Australia's
version of Harold Brazier, but perhaps even better. This welterweight fought from 1971 to 2002 when he suffered a stoppage loss
to Fernando Sagrado in his career last. But prior to that, he had
gone 18 in a row without defeat.

In 1983, Flash knocked out Taulisi Ratu in Fiji then went into Don
King's training camp in Ohio where he was a roommate with
Azumah Nelson. He was matched with Bobby Joe Young, one of the
hardest punchers in the welterweight division. The fight was on the
Michael Dokes – Gerrie Coetzee WBA heavyweight title card, and
Malcolm was a decided underdog against Young who was coming
off a knockout win over Kronk's Darryl Chambers. Flash fooled
the experts and easily beat Young even decking him. He was then
ranked number 10 welterweight in the world by KO, which at the
time, rivaled The Ring as the world's premier fight magazine. [5]

Malcolm likely will be the last Australian pugilist to win 100 professional bouts. His uncanny footwork saw this cocky, southpaw road
warrior become an Australian, Commonwealth, WBF, PABA and
WBA Fedelatin champion in his 31 year career.

On the Circuit in the UK

The United Kingdom certainly has not been immune from this phenomenon. Whether they be designees, barnstormers or both, these
fighters definitely have something in common with their counterparts across the pond. For example, Welshman Miguel Matthews at
15-84 is almost guaranteed to go the distance. Incredibly, in 1997 at
the Alexandra Pavilion in London, he stopped Scott Harrison, 3-0
coming in, in the fourth stanza. Yes, this was the same Scott Harrison
from Glasgow who would later become the WBO featherweight
title holder. In all fairness, the fight was stopped on cuts resulting
from a head butt, but again, a win is a win.

After winning 14 of his first 17 (and losing his last 19), Rakhim Mingaleev is now 27-57-1. Though from the Ukraine, he fights out of the United Kingdom and is a global barnstormer extraordinaire in such locales as Northern Ireland, Scotland, London, Wales, Kiev, Albania, Poland, Switzerland, Gibraltar, France, Dubai, United Arab Emirates, Denmark, Georgia, Bulgaria, Kazakhstan, Moldova, Belarus, and Uzbekistan. Rakhim gets around.

The game Ojay "Me, Myself & I" Abrahams, 20-76-4, hasn't had a win since 2003. Harry Butler, 7-71-1, while useful as a survivor, also closed out his career with a long winless streak. Two of Abraham's victories came against Butler. Lance Verallo, 0-25, is striving to make his mark and is off to a "good" start.

David Hinds, a welterweight out of Birmingham, continues to fight despite a record of 7-77. A promoter's dream, he is seldom stopped with his last win coming in 2003 against Paul Rushton, 0-3-1. He has lost 29 straight since. Carl Allen, 18-72-7, has not won since 2003, but has four wins against the always beatable Peter Buckley. In 1996, he lost to one Emmanuel Clottey, then 10-0 and now a top contender.

It gets worse. David Kirk, 11-74-3, Nigel Senior, 21-70-5, Dean Bramhald, 42-106-15, Daniel Thorpe, 22-72-2, Michael Pinnock, 4-74-1, and Des Gargano, 32-87-3 are all survivors who can (or could) be counted upon to last the limit. So was Winston Burnett, 20-98 (KO 15)-3, who barnstormed in both the UK and the US and lost his last two fights in such disparate locales as Iowa (in the US) and Serbia, respectively. Delroy Spencer (10-74-3) is on a 39-fight losing streak and seems determined to reach Centurion status. Mark Phillips won his first three but is now 9-52 and seems to have found his groove. Duncan Cottier won his first duke in 2005 and then found an apparent comfort zone. He now sports a 3- 44-3 slate but has only been stopped three times. William Webster finished at a poor 3-45-1, but that diminishes when compared to Brian Coleman's eye-popping 24-141-7. Shaun "The Slasher" Walton checks in with a 4-38-3 mark that belies his nickname, Alvin "Slick" Miller, at 7-40-2, is clearly no slickster.

Like their U.S. counterparts, these blokes fought each other multiple times. But unlike Slovakian fighters with somewhat similar won-loss records, these lads know how to stay out of harm's way so they can come back to fight t again and again and again.

Karl "Plug" Taylor out of Birmingham is now 16-115 (KO 31)-6 and is always ready, willing, and able having fought just about everybody, but his record is a plug ugly 2-66-3 since 1999. Amazingly, he beat future WBA lightweight title holder, South African Dingaan "The Rose of Soweto" Thobela, in 1994. "The Rose" was 29-3-1 coming in.

Heavyweight Tony Booth also has the knack—his record is 50-105 (KO 37) - 9. Nigel "The Centurion" Rafferty closed out in 2005 with a record of 26 (KO 1)-69 (KO 27) - 9 in 104 bouts. One of his wins came against Adam Cale, 2 (KO 0)-38-1, who finished his career with a dreadful winless streak of 35. DeRoy Spencer should be included with his 10-71-3 mark.

New Centurions

Peter "Desperate" Dunn is no longer desperate. He became a Centurion of sorts when he lost his 100th fight on September 26, 2008. He currently is at a useful 12-102 (KO 11) - 4; and has done some serious barnstorming, albeit losing, across the UK. Paul Boson has reached 102 and sports an astounding record of 20-102-8; astounding because he only has been stopped three times. He is also capable of the occasional upset.

It appears these lads are in a three-way race with Tony Booth (105 losses) to see who can lose the most the quickest!

Nigel "The Centurion"Rafferty, 26-69-9, put a different spin on the term, but fell far short in the loss column.

And let's not forget centurion Seamus "West" Casey at 30 (KO 5)-129 (KO 33)-5 in 164 outings These blokes fight often and warrant continual monitoring.

Two Gypsy's

Billy "Gypsy" Smith, checks in with 12-76-1, but he too has only been stopped a handful of times and often fights twice or three times a month. Still, he has a long way to go to catch another Gypsy, this one out of Worcestershire.

Ernie "Gypsy Boy" Smith has a 13-132-5 record losing his last 42 ina row, but has been stopped oly 14 times suggesting that, like many of his compatriots, he would fit in well on the American circuits. One of his wins came against super middleweight Brian Coleman, 22-100-7 coming in (and now an astounding 24-141 (KO 21)-7). He also managed a draw with Arv Mittoo, 10-85 (KO 9)-5, and beat Marc "Too Cute" Smith (no relation), 8-42-1 at the time. Ernie has lived up to his moniker covering most of the UK since 1998.

The "Professor"

Peter Buckley has seen it all in his 257 [now 295] fight career to date and is a wily old fox when it comes to not being hurt by his youthful and exuberant opponents as he takes them through their "Initiation.
–Tom Walker

Anyone who has endured a staggering 299 professional bouts (and unbelievable 1,680 rounds) deserves special recognition, even if an equally remarkable 256 of those bouts have ended in defeat.

Peter Buckley, a welterweight from BIrmingham, has fought and lost more than any British boxer in history. He sports a slate of 31-256-12 in 299 outings, but seldom gets knocked down and has only been stopped ten times (he has gone the distance with such notables as Prince Naseem, Scott Harrison, Paul Ingle, Dave Stewart, Steffy Bull, Ruben Osvaldo Condori and Lehlohonolo Ledwaba). His excitement factor is an amazingly low 6%.

They call him "The Professor" because of his ability to engage in tutorialsfor aspirant pugilists, giving ring lessons to those new to the professional ranks was undefeated in 7 of his first 8 bouts, but after two draws, things went decidedly south. Winless in his last 85 bouts, he has not had a victory since October 2003! Amazingly, and unlike most of his compatriots, he has never fought outside the UK.

On October 10, 2008, a once again active Professor fought a draw with one Matin Mohammed breaking a 46-fight losing streak. Mohammed, 0-1, needs to consider another line of work.

While it appears the Professor seems intent on catching Reggie Strickland's less-than-glorious record, there is talk that he is finally thinking about calling it quits. Time will tell.

Argentina

Argentinean fighters in particular participate in many fights, emulating old school American boxers. Super featherweight Faustino Martires Barrios owned a righteous mark of 60-41-20 with an affinity toward draws. In fact, 6 of his first 10 ended that way. Pedro Armando Gutierrez toted up a record of 83-24-11 and was only stopped once. Ricardo Daniel Silva is at 68-27-4. The great Jorge Fernando "Locomotora" Castro's record currently stands at 130 (KO 90)-11 (KO 2)-3. One of his few defeats was to Lorenzo Luis Garcia, 79-24-18, who in turn beat Victor Federico Echegaray, 66-17-15, who drew with Oscar "Cachin" Mendez, 85-19 (KO 1)-15. Even Kid Pascualito, 85-26-20, found his way into this mix though he was from Paraguay.

Argentinean Eduardo Domingo Contreras ran up a righteous count of 33 (KO 3)-46 (KO 9) - 22 in 102 outings fighting in just about every venue in Argentina including fabled Luna Park. Yes, that's 22 draws. But for global barnstorming at the very top level, few can match the legendary "Locomotora" whose incredible record was fashioned thought the world— from South Africa and Australia to the US and Mexico and many, many places in between.

Nigeria

Abu Arrow fought during the 70's and while a prolific loser with a dismal slate of 7- 85 (KO 5)-7, he was also a survivor extraordinaire having been stopped only 5 times in 99 outings.

The Boxing Encyclopedia definition of Barnstormer seems too fit well, but only to a point. Many barnstormers made a decent living with ultra frequent activity. Most seem to do it as losers. But many, like Jorge Castro and Harold Brazier, were skilled winners and even world champions. They need to be included in the picture.

Still, it's pretty clear what this is all about. Certain fighters play a certain role. Some seemed to have found a comfortable way to lose. Said another way, they are savvy enough to survive without undue risk, but at the same time provide enough excitement to guarantee more fights. Their ability to come back time and again is their meal ticket. They are a promoter's dream; they represent reliability and virtual certainty. Indeed. It's not if; it's when.

At any rate, we may never see their like again, and I don't think that's necessarily a good thing.

[1] Boxing Encyclopedia, "Barnstormer." March 30, 2007. http://www. boxrec.com/media/index.php/Barnstormer

[2] Russ Greenspan, "Reggie Strickland: Boxing's All-Time Leading Also-Ran." July 12, 2007. www.ringsidereport.com. http://www.ring-sidereport.com:80/rsr/news.php?readmore=1583

[3] Steve Carp, "Tomato cans ripe for picking." February 8, 2008. Las Vegas Review-Journal, http://www.lvrj.com/sports/15490601.html

[4]. A Knock-Out! The Arnold Thomas Boxing Collection." Number 85. February 2007. http://www.nla.gov.au/pub/gateways/issues/85/story04.htm

[5] Tony Pritchard-Nobbs. "WBF CHAMPION JEFF "FLASH" MALCOLM – EVERGREEN ROAD Warrior." November 20, 2007. http://www.worldboxingfoundation.com/wbf/?p=465

Note: See Appendix D: Fighters with Most Career Losses and Fighters with Most Knockout Losses.

27

CAUTION: POISON

Anthony "Poison" Ivory has been called everything from a "punching bag" to a "seasoned vet." The fact is he was an ultra tough Chicagoan with a wealth of tricks in his bag and a deceptive record of 33 (KO 13)-78 (KO 5)-5. He was the classic road warrior, global barnstormer, survivor, and spoiler. Yes, all of the above.

He fought in France, Finland, England, Scotland, Wales, Germany, Denmark, Italy, Hungary, Canada, Mexico, Monaco, Andorra (where?), The Ukraine, and Puerto Rico, and was able to book-end a fight in Hamburg, Germany in 2001 with fights in North Dakota and East Saint Louis. From Muskegon to Montreal to Mexico; from Wales to Missouri to France; Italy to Chicago to Denmark, this was what "have gloves will travel" was all about, but at the highest level of competition. A fight in Brandenburg, Germany–then two weeks later one at the Fiesta Palace in Waukegan, Illinois– then on to Edmonton, Alberta, Canada. And every now and then, Poison would shock the fans by shocking one of his heavily favored opponents.

After a 23 fight winless streak, Ivory beat Cory Rader, 15-1 and Ted Muller, 15-0-1, before embarking on another negative streak. He took future champions Kelly Pavlik and Mikkel Kessler the distance and spoiled the undefeated records of Omar "Pit Bull" Pittman, Derrick Parks, Pat "The Cat" Coleman, Joe Potts, Alfredo Freddy Cuevas and Mario Iribarren with wins over all six. He iced Carl "Stuff" Griffith in 1996 in a big "upset," ending Griffith's career at 29-6-2, and shocked tough Arthur Allen with a seventh round stoppage.

The level of his opposition was absolutely at the highest, and he would go into his foe's home country for the duke. He fought Howard Eastman in London, Felix Sturm in Germany, Kessler in Denmark, Wilfredo Rivera in Puerto Rico, Yori Boy Campas in Mexico, Dave Hilton in Canada and many others in their home areas. And get this, he fought some 35 opponents who came in with no losses on their records including Chad Parker, Antwun Echols (whom he

KOd in the first round), Luis Ramon Campas, the late Randie Carver, Albert Onolunose, Sturm, Kessler, and many others.

Among his other opponents (and the location of fight) were:

Marco Antonio Rubio - Ciudad Acuna, Coahuila de Zaragoza, Mexico

Troy Rowland - Muskegon, Michigan

Andrey Tsurkan - Rosemont, Illinois

Grady Brewer - Lawton, Oklahoma

Christian Bladt - Mariehamn, Finland

Keith Holmes - Washington, District of Columbia

Skipper Kelp - Las Vegas, Nevada

Germaine Sanders - Rosemont, Illinois

Derrell Coley - Washington, District of Columbia

Viktor Fessetchko - Kiev, Ukraine (for the WBF European Middleweight Title)

Cory Rader-Mandan - North Dakota

Oscar Bravo - Stone Park, Illinois

Paolo Roberto - Budapest, Hungary

Emil Baku - LaPorte, Indiana

Vincent Pettway - Woodlawn, Maryland

Evans Ashira - Skagen, Denmark

Santos Cardona - Chicago, Illinois

Silvio Branco - Capo d'Orlando, Sicilia, Italy

Armand Krajnc - Schleswig-Holstein, Germany

Samuel Serrano - Dorado, Puerto Rico

Julio Cesar Vasquez - Essonne, France

Julio Cesar Vasquez - Monte Carlo, Monaco

Tony Badea - Edmonton, Alberta, Canada -for the IBO Inter-Continental light middleweight title

Ahmed Kotiev - Brandenburg, Germany

Ahmed Kotiev - Frankfurt, Hessen, Germany

Arthur Allen - Church Hill, Ohio

Diosbelys Hurtado - Miami, Florida

Syd Vanderpool - Toronto, Ontario, Canada

Ronald "Winky" Wright - Le Cannet, Alpes-Maritimes, France (for the NABF light middleweight title

Ronald "Winky" Wright - Hauts-de-Seine, France

Neville Brown - London, United Kingdom

Chris Pyatt - Glasgow, Scotland

Lonnie Beasley - Rosemont, Illinois

Andrew Council - Woodlawn, Maryland

Simon Brown - Las Vegas, Nevada

Laurent Boudouani - Hauts-de-Seine, France

Frederic Seillier - Canillo, Andorra

Carl Daniels - Monte Carlo, Monaco

Brett Lally - Livonia, Michigan

Anthony Ivory lost far more times than he won, but his opponents would pay if they underestimate him. In the space of 30 days in 1998, Maurice Brantley, 17-1, Alfredo Cuevas, 13-0, and Roosevelt Walker, 20-7-1 learned this the hard way.

You want tough? How about "Poison" Ivory?

28

PECK'S BAD BOY

Ricardo Mayorga (Photo Courtesy of ESB)

That's him, that's his makeup.
—Tony Gonzalez, Ricardo Mayorga's attorney and advisor

I'm the champion. You've got to recognize that. My strongest hand is my right hand. You see his eye? I'm going to detach his retina.
—Ricardo Mayorga

De La Hoya doesn't have the pants to stay in the ring with me. He is going to pay for the mistake of accepting this fight
—Ricardo Mayorga

[Mayorga] reveals himself to be nothing more than a marketing master when his check is safely in the bank and the fighting is over
—Matthew Hurley

After I knock him [Vargas] out, his wife is going to come up in the ring and have her picture taken with the real champion and that's me.
–Ricardo Mayorga

I don't like anything about Mayorga…he has a face only a mother gorilla could love. He's a stupid fighter. I'm going to be the one to finally shut him up.
–Fernando Vargas

I am going to carry a 14-pound pig named Vargas into the ring. Vargas is nothing more than a pig. That is all that he is.
–Ricardo Mayorga

I take nothing against Ricardo…He was a tough guy. I thought he would be wilder. Unfortunately, that wasn't the case. I take nothing away from him. He had a better night. It's my last fight. Thank you very much.
–Fernando Vargas

Yo gang….great interview. Mayorga and Vargas know how to sell a fight…..
–On-line poster

Peck's bad boy was a fictional star of newspaper stories and books created by George Peck in the late 1800s. Henry Peck was a mischievous lad who loved to play sneaky pranks on others for the sheer pleasure of creating mayhem. The stories were a huge hit in their era, and the name Peck's Bad Boy became a popular term for any incorrigible rule-breaker. Ricardo Mayorga, who loves to create mayhem, is a Peck's bad boy if ever there was one, but it is innocent mayhem as was Henry's.

Mayorga is known as "El Matador" for his incredible power, knockout record, and having one of the best chins in boxing. When one thinks of Ricardo Mayorga, the following expressions come to mind: raving mad man, boorish, tasteless, crass, wildman, bad ass, reckless abandon, mayhem, crazy persona, ever-dangerous, mean, street fighter, pistolero, unpredictable outlandish and –well, you get the idea.

He cultivates an uncorroborated image of a heavy cigarette smoking, beer drinking wildman outside the ring and combines that with a vicious windmill fighting style inside the square circle. Almost every fight he is in is billed as a highly anticipated grudge match, but this again is a well mastered marketing technique of one of the best marketing men in boxing—none other than El Matador. Indeed, he was featured for the first time on the cover of Ring Magazine on the December 2003 issue with a cigarette dangling from his mouth. The cover read "the craziest man in the sport: Mayorga lights up boxing."

Mayorga is a mean fighter in the ring and he throws every punch with deadly intention. He was a gang leader in Managua, Nicaragua before he was a boxer and tends to be most effective when he brawls like a street fighter. While his stamina has not always been tops, he possess immense physical strength. He has a good set of whiskers and is extremely heavy handed, but his biggest weakness is that he throws wide punches that leave him open for short counters if he misses.

He has faced five reigning world champions, three former world champs and one world-ranked fighter in his last nine fights. And get this, these opponents had a combined record of 281-13-3 going in and Mayorga went 5-3-0-1 against them.

Ricardo is married to Yesenia Vanessa Lobo and has four children: two older girls—both named Diana, one 12 and one 11—two boys, Ricardo Jr., 5, and a daughter, Mercedes, 2. He is devoted to his mother, Miriam Del Socorro Perez, as well. His favorite pastime is to spend serene time with his family in Costa Rica where he makes his home. He also enjoys romantic music like singer Ana Gabriel. He loves the typical foods of Nicaragua and misses home cooking when he's on the road.

Chronology

In 2001, he challenged the WBA's World Welterweight Champion Andrew "Six Heads" Lewis, but the fight was declared no contest after two rounds because both fighters had cuts opened by a head butt. In a rematch a year later, Mayorga won the title, the fifth Nicaraguan to do so, by knocking out Lewis in the 5th round.

Mayorga and then WBC Welterweight Champion Vernon Forrest met for a unification bout on January 25 and Ricardo shocked the boxing world by dropping Forrest in rounds one and three, winning the fight by a savage and sudden knockout in the third, and becoming the WBA and WBC's Unified World Champion. Mayorga and Forrest had a rematch, and this time Mayorga retained the title by a 12 round controversial majority decision.

During this duke, Mayorga stuck his chin out to Forrest and taunted him throughout. "I wanted him to know that he couldn't hurt me," Mayorga said with a smirk after the fight. "I know it's not a wise thing to want to get hit, and Mr. [Don] King told me after the fight that he doesn't want to see me doing that again, but it's what I wanted to do at the time. I wanted to let him know that I was the boss, I was his daddy, I was the champ."[1]

In 2003, Mayorga lost his world titles to Cory Spinks by a majority decision. This came after Mayorga had made tasteless remarks about Spinks's deceased mother. Imitating what would become a pattern, Mayorga apologized after the fight. The five-to-one underdog Spinks pulled off the boxing upset of the year by exploiting Mayorga's lack of ring discipline.

In 2004, three days after being hammered and stopped by Tito Trinidad in Madison Square Garden, he announced his retirement. Tito's return was victorious while across the ring the slumped figure of the man who trained on cigarettes needed a smoke and a strong drink. He had taken a horrific beating and it was going to be a long flight back home.

He returned to the ring, however, and in 2005, became a two division world champion by gaining the vacant WBC world Super Welterweight title with a twelve round unanimous decision over Italian Michele Piccirillo. He decked Piccirillo three times in the first four rounds on his way to the easy decision win.

The following year he lost to Oscar De La Hoya by another brutal TKO in the 6th round. De La Hoya had been very inactive, but due to the high personal disregard he had for Mayorga due in large part to Ricardo's boorish comments about his manhood and his wife, De La Hoya decided to take the fight. Ricardo's insults seemed to provide De La Hoya with the passion he was looking for after a long layoff from the ring. After the fight, Mayorga embraced Oscar and once again apologized for his tasteless and crass comments and begged Oscar's forgiveness.

Then, in 2007, in a fight billed as the Brawl, Mayorga net Fernando Vargas in a crossroads battle. The build up leading to this fight was nothing less than a masterpiece of sage marketing. Mayorga had the temerity to disrespect Vargas's wife as he did with De La Hoya's, but that's part of being boxing's ultimate marketing master.

Attesting to his marketing acumen, below are some representative comments taken off the web:

Its one thing to read about Fernando Vargas and Ricardo Mayorga taunting each other at the final press conference in Los Angeles on Monday, but it's quite different TO SEE how real the animosity between them really is. [2]

Boxing's Bad Boys, Fernando Vargas and Ricardo Mayorga, continued their vulgar, trash-talking assaults on each other during Monday's final press conference

Nicaraguans are so ashamed of Mayorga's boorish behavior (smoking and eating friend chicken at weigh-ins, arrogance, being a foul-mouthed punk and starting fights at press conferences, etc.) that they celebrated in the streets of Managua and set of rockets after he lost to Oscar de la Hoya. To repeat to hammer home the point, they were celebrating a victory by Oscar de la Hoya - no Hispanic person that I'm aware of in the US has ever done this before. [3]

If you don't like boxing, but you like to see two guys abandon all sense of professionalism and beat the living hell out of each other, here's your chance. Both Vargas and Mayorga are knuckleheads who just so happen to box for money and hate each other, there is no better mix of ingredients for an explosive fight. [4]

Fernando Vargas and Ricardo Mayorga exchange some heated words before starting an all-out brawl at a press conference in advance of their Middleweight bout.

Do you know who Vargas' best friend is? It is Jenny Craig because she helps him lose weight.

The venom that spewed between Ricardo Mayorga and Fernando Vargas leading up to their meeting in the ring was far beyond the normal pre-fight verbal sparring.

The boorish persona of Nicaraguan three-time boxing world champion is increasingly alienating his countrymen, but others are still in his corner.

I don't think he's wanted . . . by us, said a Nicaragua expatriate. [He] embarrasses us and everyone starts talking bad about us.

You see this fat girl in this photo? This is the fat girl I am going to knock out. I would like to introduce her to you today. She is Fernando Vargas.

If that plastic divider wasn't separating us, I would have definitely hit him.

As for the fight itself, it was not quite a brawl, buit it was a crowd pleasing and exciting affair though neither fighter was anywhere near his best. Vargas seemed depleted after having to lose 100 pounds and was knocked down twice during the fight. Mayorga showed uncommon patience and technical skills that surprised everyone but him. Control and a disciplined fight plan was the last thing anyone expected out of this storied street fighter, but he fooled the experts and Vargas as well. "I fought for my family," said Mayorga after the majority decision in his favor was announced. The judges voted 113-113, 114-112 and 115-111 for Mayorga. "I worked on the gym, my discipline and control and I was able to do it in this fight."

Both fighters were highly respectful towards one another after the fight, but that would only be a surprise to those who had not yet picked up on El Matador's post fight pattern of behavior. "This gentleman hits way too hard." It was a bit odd to hear Mayorga refer to Vargas as a "gentleman" considering all the names he called him leading up to the opening bell but it was nothing compared to when he walked across the dais and kissed Fernando on the cheek. Perhaps it was a mild surprise considering the feigned "hatred" between these two, but Mayorga showed post fight respect as he went from bad guy to good guy faster than you can say "cash register."

As fellow writer Mathew Hurley says: "The fighter best known for his outlandish behavior and crass remarks in pre-fight press conferences as well as his free-swinging ring style, reveals himself to be nothing more than a marketing master when his check is safely in the bank and the fighting is over..."[5]

Of course, Mayorga, 29-6-1-1, is also the man who beat the man (Forrest) who beat the man (Mosley) who beat the man (De La Hoya)—twice

Ricardo Mayorga will fight another day and leading up to the fight, he will insult his opponent unmercifully ensuring that the tickets for the predictable PPV will sell like hotcakes. Most boxing fans will be taken in by his outlandish lack of respect toward his opponent (perhaps Vernon Forrest or Corey Spinks). Ricardo Mayorga is a master of marketing the likes of which have seldom been seen in boxing. He sells tickets and that's really all that matters isn't it?

While Mayorga is complex soul, there is an unmistakable mischievous quality about him that you just cannot help but like. Even when he is bad, he is good. At the end of the fight, he will apologize to and embrace his foe. Hell, at the end of the day, he is Peck's bad boy.

Postscript: In a somewhat sloppy bout on September 27, 2008, in Carson California, former titlist "Sugar" Shane Mosley (45-5)

labored through 12 rounds against Mayorga before decking him and then taking him out in with a spectaular left hook with one second left in the 12th and last round. Before the contest, Mayorga issued his usual insults and said, among many, many other things, that after the fight, "Mosley can retire so that he can go back home with his wife and wash dishes."

[1] "RICARDO MAYORGA." HBO Boxing: Fighters. February 20, 2007. http://www.hbo.com/boxing/fighters/mayorga_ricardo/bio.html

[2] Stan Hoffman, Fightbeta.com. "Vargas vs. Mayorga- Fell the Tension (video)." http://fightbeat.com/news_details.php?NW=20801

[3] "Ricardo Mayorga is a people Person," YOUR FACE IS A SPORTS BLOG. November 20, 2007. http://www.yourfaceisasportsblog.com/2007/11/ricardo-mayorga-is-people-person.html

[4] Chuck, "Fernando Vargas vs. Ricardo Mayorga Preview." November 22, 2007. http://www.sportaphile.com/2007/11/22/fernando-vargas-vs-ricardo-mayorga-preview/

[5] Matthew Hurley, "Mayorga Weighs His Options And Will Move Down." April 19, 2008. http://www.eastsideboxing.com/boxing/Mayorga-Vargas.php

29

SHAKE, RATTLE AND ROLL

did the boogie

I did the boogie, boogie

I did the boogie

Yeah, hey hey

–John Lee Hooker

I hit him [Maskaev] with one and I him with another. Then I crack him up. My jab was good and then I him in the head and break off his head. I knew he was strong so I was careful. I feel great. I could fight again tomorrow. I'm ready for anyone.
–Sam Peter

Wladimir Klitschko took his Dave Kingman size frame and power prowess to the plate with nobody out and a man on third–and he laid down a bunt
–Jack Dunn

When Bert Cooper squared off with Michael Moorer in 1992 and George Foreman brawled with Ron Lyle in 1976, you could hear the snap of their punches and the furious shuffling of their foot movement on the mat rosin. You just knew you were witnessing something special, for they were engaging in all-out war from the get-go. These were brawls. The winner would be the last man standing. Tommy Morrison did it against Indian Joe Hipp in 1992 when he suffered a broken jaw and hand during that savage and bloody affair and Hipp had his cheekbone shattered. The last great one I remember was when Courage Tshabalala put Darroll "Doin' Damage" Wilson down twice in the first round at the Blue Horizon in 1997, before he himself was iced by Wilson in the fourth as each took turns rocking the other throughout. Golota and Bowe also did it though Andrew ended matters the wrong way; they were exciting pure and simple. More recently, Golota and Mike Mollo did it.

The thing about the above fights is that they were in the heavier weight divisions which made them all the more intriguing. No one-punch endings out of the blue in these. The outcome was in question until the very end. The winner would be the last man standing. The rumbling started from the second the bell sounded. This was boogie chillin; this was special.

Fast forward to the new millennium

A new caliber of heavyweight fighter has come from Eastern Europe with a disciplined and focused approach, one that has achieved numerous titles and has dominated the division. But when was the last time you saw one of these technical specialists engage in a full-tilt boogie? When was the last time one of the current champions fought with the fury of a Foreman-Lyle or Moorer-Cooper? Yes, Oleg Maskaev's two KOs over Rahman were sweet, and I did hear the furious shuffling of their foot movement, but Maskaev seems to stand alone as the sole Eastern European heavyweight brawler.

And maybe brawling is the key to slowing down their dominance—assuming that is a desired end. Lamon Brewster almost did it against Serguei Lyakhovich and their war took a permanent toll on both. Wlad Klitchko breaks down his opponents with jabs before he ices them with his lethal right. Sultan moves in and out and is strategic. The Giant, well, he is feather fisted and does not rumble except when he walks. I don't see the potential for an all-out war with Ruslan Chagaev, but maybe Aleksandr Povetkin can engage in one of these, though he certainly did not against a mummified Eddie Chambers. Briggs remains an immobile giant huffing and puffing in the ring. Danny Williams tries righteously but fails as much as he succeeds. Toney has eaten himself out of contention and John Ruiz ended McCline's dreams once and for all in Cancun on March 8, 2008. Tua remains a question mark, but has THAT hook. Eddie Chambers is a cutie but clearly not a brawler.

There was one fighter who tested the Russians twice and succeeded once (against Wladimir Klitchko). He let his hands fly and was very dangerous for three of four rounds. He possessed fast and heavy hands, and was willing to boogie as he did with Hasim "the Rock" Rahman in 2000. This South African name was Corrie "The Sniper"

Sanders, 42 (KO 31)-3. He had the formula, but he is no longer a factor. Is there anyone else who might have the goods?

The Russian Giant, Nikolay Valuev, beat Serguei "The White Wolf" Lyakhovich in a WBA Heavyweight Title Eliminator on February 16, 2008 in a 12-round UD victory. While the Giant was impressive, there was a distinct lack of snap in their punches and an absence of the any semblance of foot movement. It was an interesting fight, but far from a compelling one.

The manner in which Wladimir Klitschko, 50-3, beat Sultan Ibragimov on February 23, 2008 affirmed the fact that, aside from Oleg Maskaev, "shake, rattle and roll" is nowhere to be seen as the Eastern Europeans do their thing. Dr. Steel Hammer fought an overly cautious, defensive fight using his jab and a solid defense to beat Sultan in a less than exciting fight. Some of the following headlines of Eastside Boxing articles reporting on the fight tell the story:

"In Defense of Wladimir Klitschko" By Lucas White

"Photos: Klitschko Outpoints Ibragimov in Defensive Fight" By Wray Edwards:

"Klitschko vs. Ibragimov: Worst. Fight. Ever!" By Anthony Coleman

"Klitschko jabs his way to victory! Cautious, defensive-minded tactical bout doesn't win over MSG crowd." By Mike Indri

"Klitschko Wins Unanimous Decision In Dull Match" By Matthew Hurley:

Peter-Maskaev

Then on March 8, 2008, Oleg Maskaev met "The Nigerian Nightmare," Samuel Peter, in Cancun, Mexico with the WBC Heavyweight Championship at stake. After trading some rumbling thunder at a less than compelling pace, Peter hit Maskaev behind the head in the sixth and got a warning. Both landed some decent shots until Peter caught "The Big O" with a series of heavy punches forcing Maskaev backwards and covering up. Peter kept on punching and landing, and when Maskaev didn't respond, the fight was rightly halted.

While slow and ponderous, Maskaev took some risks and fought out of the mold of his compatriots who view the risk-reward equation with extreme caution. While this fight was far from the "Shake

Rattle and Roll of yesteryear, at least it somewhat mitigated the bitter taste of the Klitschko-Ibigamov affair just two week earlier.

Whether Sam Peter can force the issue remains to be seen, but at this point, he seems the only hope for one to hear the furious shuffling of feet on the ring rosin and the snap of heavy bombs being thrown with malicious intent.

Jack Dunn

Boxing writer and good friend Jack Dunn sent this email message dated March 10, 2008 which describes the situation better than just about anything else I have read:

"The HW division can't survive with guys like this... The HW division is the HITTERS LEAGUE. It isn't, nor has it ever been, the skill league. You want speed, skill, footwork and combos and pugilistic skill polished to the umpteenth degree? – go see the lightweights, the welters, the feathers. People gravitate to heavyweights for the same reason they do homerun hitters.

"I'll use a baseball analogy here to explain the HW division in relationship top boxing. Nobody will ever argue that Dave Kingman was a better baseball hitter than Rod Carew or Pete Rose was. That is understood. That being said, Kingman, who stood something like 6-6, 250 could hit a ball so damn hard, large crowds gathered around just to watch him hit during batting practice. Those same crowds vanished when Rose or Carew stepped into the cage. Nobody wants to see an opposite field, well placed hit that bounces off the grass... they want to see the ball go into orbit.

"People expect the same thing from HW champions. It's why Mike Tyson became a GOD and Chris Byrd became someone boxing fans never embraced.

"Wladimir Klitschko took his Dave Kingman size frame and power prowess to the plate with nobody out and a man on third—and he laid down a bunt. Peter got two pitches thrown past him, swinging, by the BP coach before he hit one over the wall and I'll give a pass to Maskaev. He wouldn't even be playing ball today if not for the fact that everyone else who should have come along and taken his job by now... they can't, they are inferior.

"Holyfield is there, James Toney is there...they are every bit as deserving as the rest of the lot right now.

"What do you think a virile, 28 year old Joe Frazier would do to a 45 year old Evander Holyfield today?... My best guess, a 12-15 year stint for involuntary manslaughter, eligible for parole in seven. 40 year-old and FAT (even by beer drinker's standards) James Toney in with young George Foreman?–See Death Row!

"The same James Toney and Evander Holyfield, they are serious threats today... proving not only a lack of power in the division–but a lack of talent as well.

"In short, it is like watching Rod Carew take batting practice and miss every third pitch."

30

KIRINO

When I got him, I thought I'd have to fight to get him in the gym. Instead, I had to fight to get him out.
–Trainer Felipe Delatore

Everybody saw the fight. I gave him the best beating…The Nevada commission is always corrupt.
–Kirino Garcia commenting after his fight with David Reid

I'm certainly not taking him lightly. I have to look good.
–David Reid

In an article on ESPN.com by Tim Graham, former president of The Boxing Writer's Association of America (BWAA) dated March 8, 2004 and entitled "David Reid's American Nightmare," Graham writes deftly about Olympic champion David Reid's rapid descent from the boxing heights of the pros. After pointing out Reid's losing effort against Tito Trinidad, Graham states, "His next three fights – against pugs Kirino Garcia, Urbano Gurrola and Maurice Bentley – were unimpressive victories that went the bitter distance."

What Graham did not say was that Garcia gave the onetime-sensation Reid everything he could handle before losing an unpopular 10-round unanimous decision. Reid, 14-1 at the time, was clubbed to the canvas in the eighth round following a 16-punch volley of heavy and assorted punches. Then his left eye was badly cut in the 9th and his face was a bloody mess. In the final stanza, Garcia continued to score well and Reid's legs were gone. He managed to grab and hold and did all he could to survive until the final bell.

Kirino then knocked out Frankie "The Professor" Randall, 56-8-1, a few months later–the same Randall who had previously defeated Edwin Rosario, Julio Cesar Chavez and Juan Martin Coggi twice.

Garcia was 28-20-1 at the time he fought Reid, but a review of his record discloses that he was anything but a pushover. Going into the fight with David Reid, he had already become a beloved and local legend in Juarez boxing circles and would be a four-time Mexican champion. He had just come off stoppage wins against Buck Smith, 179-14-2, tough Columbian Miguel "Memin" Julio, 32-2-1, and Alfred Ankamah, 20-5, for the WBC International light middleweight title. Previously he owned victories over former world champions Simon Brown, Meldrick Taylor and Jorge Vaca (twice by KO) as well as against ultra tough Erik Holland, Terrence Alli, and Eduardo Gutierrez. Between 1994 and 1997, he put together a 16-fight unbeaten string against very tough opposition.

Prior to launching this streak, the amply tattooed and scared Garcia lost on points to unbeaten Chad Parker, 28-0-1, in Biloxi. Three fights later, Parker would be knocked out in spectacular fashion by "Dangerous" Dana Rosenblatt and would retire with a 31-1-1 slate.

But Garcia was on a streak of his own—18 straight "defeats" right out of the professional gate (but 12 were on points and all but two outside of Mexico perhaps suggesting at first the specter of bad decisions but far more likely the result of his never having trained to be a fighter and going up against extremely skilled opposition). Three of these bouts were fought in Mississippi, three in Nevada, four in Colorado, three in Arizona, one in New Mexico and one in Michigan. Only two were fought in Mexico. Among his opponents during this streak were such future notables and top contenders as Bobby Gunn (who is still fighting), Raul Gonzalez, Paul "Ultimate" Vaden, Tim "The Doctor of Style" Littles, Billy Lewis, Lonnie "Honey Bee" Beasley, Danny "Pit Bull" Perez, Dominick 'Hurricane" Carter, and Chad Parker. Their combined won-loss record was an eye-popping 124-8-2.

Having grown up dirt poor in Ciudad Juarez, in a squatter's cardboard shanty, he engaged in running with gangs, petty crime, hustling and God knows how many street fights just to survive. The title of Pat Putnam's definitive article in The Sweet Science dated August 2, 2005 says it all: "Kirino Garcia Gutter to Great."

During this period, he fell prey to the coyotes, Mexican or Mexican-Americans from both sides of the Rio Bravo who turn young kids like the young Kirino into designated losers for anyone willing to pay them a few bucks. At Pat Putman pointed out, "There's no training. Nobody looks after them." It is reasonable to suspect that Kirino Garcia may not even have seen the inside of a gym, much less train in one, during his first eighteen fights. He was a street fighter pure and simple. Only after he hooked up with promoter Olvaldo

Kuchle did he work out in a gym and he took to it like a duck to water. Felipe Delatore was assigned as his trainer.

The fight with Parker would be the last of the 18, after which the aforementioned Kuchle would take over his career. After a few victories, he would soon assume the role of one very fearsome hombre. For those handicapping the high profile Parker-Rosenblatt fight in Las Vegas, a quick review of Parker's opponents and the trouble he had with the winless Garcia was a big clue at to how that fight would turn out.

When he fought Eric Holland, 20-19-3 coming and another tough fighter with a deceiving record, at the Gimnasio Municipal "Jose Neri Santos," in Ciudad Juarez in 1998, he earned $50,000 for successfully defending the WBC International title he first won against Terrance Alli and then regained from Rene Francisco Herrera. He was a rising IBA and WBA contender by then and making enough money to take care of his family in a fitting manner. These earnings were far from the $85 he was paid in his first fight against New Jersey junior middleweight Bobby Gunn. And his surroundings were far from the horrific background in which he grew up. By Mexican standards, Kirino is now well-off thanks to his ring earnings.

With a current record of 38 (KO 27) - 27 (KO 9) - 4 in 69 bouts, Kirino is nearing the end of his remarkable career. At 39 and after so many fights, he clearly is on the downside to being a world contender—but who knows what this best-loved hero of Juarez can do if he puts his mind to it, particularly if he does battle in the comfortable environs of Ciudad Juarez.

If you count the World Boxing Federation and the International Boxing Association, a couple of minor league members of the alphabet boxing cartels, he has twice fought for a world title. He lost by decision to the then undefeated WBF 154-pound champion Steve Roberts in London; and was a loser by decision to David Alfonso Lopez in their fight for the vacant IBF 160-pound championship. But more importantly, these fights were good paydays for the Mexican warrior.

David Reid is no longer the "American Dream." Meldrick Taylor may be something far more tragic. Simon Brown is long gone and so is Roland Rangel. Terrence Alli lost eight in a row before hanging up the gloves and now reportedly is struggling in his native Guyana. Eric Holland lost eleven of his last twelve fights before retiring. Art Serwano retired after losing to Garcia. Alfred "The Torpedo" Ankamah was never the same after being knocked out by Kirino in 2000.

Whether he continues to fight on or not, Kirino Garcia is a tough Mexican who worked his way up to No.4 in the ratings after starting his career with a 0-18 run. He has shown what boxing can do to lift one man from the bottom to a point where he can now make life choices of his own volition.

Kirino Garcia is all man.

Note: See Appendix C: Kirino Garcia's First 34 fights

31

THE TRACK OF THE CAT

I know I'm always dangerous to the 12th round.
–Carl Thompson

He was something of a deceptive destroyer, because he always had a playful little smile on his lips.
–Mike Casey

He never got the recognition he should have got.
–Brian Hughes

Carl Thompson is the modern day Matthew Saad Muhammad,
–Elliot Worsell

He may be 40, he may have poor footwork and he may look on the brink of defeat in every contest, but you can't keep a good man down and in boxing, there are few better, more deserving men than Carl Thompson.
–David Payne

"My best point is my heart," the incredibly humble Thompson admits. "I know I'm not the greatest boxer in the world, but there's not many fighters out there that can match my heart and my will to win."
–Carl Thompson

One of the most respectful, mild-mannered individuals within the game, Thompson is widely acknowledged as one of British Boxing's finest ambassadors
–Ben Carey

"The Cat" (Photo courtesy of ESB)

Exposing a chin that was less than granite, but possessing power laden fits, Carl Thompson was not unlike the American bomber of the 50's, Bob Satterfield. Like "Rapid Robert," he was a chill-or-be-chilled guy who would get you if you didn't get him first. Adding to the excitement was his habit of starting slow, falling behind, and then launching a rally for a dramatic come from behind win. He was a warrior in the mold of Danny "Little Red" Lopez, Satterfield, Matthew Saad Muhammad, and Jesse James Hughes. British writer Elliot Worsell described Muhammad as follows in a superb piece entitled, "Britain's most exciting: No. 1, Carl Thompson:" as follows:

Saad, formerly Matthew Franklin, was a big-punching buzzsaw of a fighter who terrorized the world light-heavyweight division in the late 70's, and early 80's, banking heavily on his heart, resolve and concussive, fight-ending power. He'd take brutal beatings, get put down, and rise on eight, sliced up, shaken, and catapulted to the verge of defeat - before spinning his fortunes in an instant, with that solitary right hand.[1] He might as well have been desciding Thonpson.

It was truly a pity that this rugged guy seemed to fly under the radar of American boxing writers and fans. In many ways, his exploits were just as noteworthy as those of Nigel Benn, Chris Eubank or Allen Minter. Maybe it was because he fought as a cruiserweight (a lower profile weight division) or maybe it was because he never fought outside of Europe. The answer is probably both.

The Track of the Cat

This super exciting fighter from the UK won his first eight bouts until losing to another chill-or-be chilled type, Crawford Ashley, in 1989. He then ran up a string of 9 KO wins from 1991-1994, the most notable of which were against undefeated Nicky Piper, 10-0-1, Arthur Weathers, 21-6-1 (for the WBC International Cruiserweight title), and Akim Tafer, 19-4, (for the EBU (European) cruiserweight title). Against Tafer, Thompson absorbed an early beating, but came from behind to take out the Frenchman thus establishing an extremely crowd pleasing pattern.

He was TKO'd by German Ralf Rocchigiani in a bid for the vacant WBO cruiserweight belt in 1995, but avenged the defeat by beating the German by SD in 1997 in Hannover, Germany. SD's don't come easy to visiting fighters in Germany so the closeness of this fight was somewhat misleading.

In 1998, he accomplished the remarkable feat of beating legendary Chris Eubank twice. In the second bout, (Eubank's last), Chris was stopped after the 9th round on advice of the doctor, as his left eye had closed completely. It would be the only stoppage ever suffered by "Simply the Best," who was leading on the cards at the time.

The Cat would lose his title to tough Johnny Nelson in 1999 by TKO (some thought it was a a woefully premature stoppage by referee Paul Thomas). He couldn't believe it then, and still can't believe it, but he bounced back to win the vacant BBBofC British cruiserweight title with a twelfth round knock out of Terry Dunstan, 19-1 at the time. Dunstan would never fight again.

He then won the IBO cruiserweight title with a fifth round TKO of Uriah Grant in 2001, but lost it that same year to Ezra Sellers in a cult classic in which both fighters were down multiple times. This fight was an incredible, see-saw slugfest that featured six knockdowns and a brutal ending and had to be seen to be believed. Once again, this was a wild up-and-downer for the Cat whose vulnerability provided the opportunity for such closet classics.

Never in an unexciting fight, "The Cat" captured the IBO cruiserweight title in 2004 with a spectacular one-punch icing of favored champion Sebastiaan Rothmann. Thompson unloaded a sensational right hand that almost decapitated Rothmann in round 9. Thompson was decked in the 4th while Rothmann was down in the 5th and in the fateful ninth. This was a typical ebb and flow type fight for the fan

-friendly Thompson. As for Rothman, he would never be the same and retired two years later.

David Haye

He couldn't stay there with me. I stopped him too quick considering I was 42 years old and about to retire and he was 23. He was the one who was going to set the cruiserweight limit alight and no one gave me a chance
—Carl Thompson

But The Cat wasn't finished. Later that same year, he knocked out highly touted and undefeated David Haye, then 10-0, at the Arena in Wembley. This was a classic old champion vs. hyped young prospect fight—one that could only be explosive and exciting. The fight itself was also a classic—one in which Thompson took everything but the kitchen sink and somehow withstood an early onslaught that included the young challenger's thunderous and punishing right crosses, hooks and uppercuts that had the crowd gasping. Haye, however, expended too much energy and gassed by the fourth allowing Thompson, notorious for his slow starts, to come on late to blast Haye to defeat in the 5th round.

Yes, this was the same David Haye who is now the WBA, WBC, and WBO cruiser weight titleholder with a 21 (KO 20) -1 slate. The victorious Thompson said afterwards: "I was on the receiving for the most of it. He rocked me and got me hurt. I felt David was getting tired, but I hung in there. I'm showing age is not a barrier." [2]

Carl "The Cat" Thompson, a true cult legend, last fought in 2005 and won his last six fights in a row. His record was 34 (KO 25)-6 (KO 5) reflecting his chill-or-be-chilled propensity. The Cat always gave his fans their money's worth and engaged in great battles that somehow escaped the notice of American fans.

Explosive inside the square circle, he was nice, quiet and almost a shy man outside of the ring. He was the kind of fighter who would go over to a fallen opponent to make sure he was ok. Carl "The Cat" Thompson deserves his due.

[1] Worsell. Elliot. "Britain's most exciting: No. 1, Carl Thompson." SecondsOut.com. http://romangreenberg.tv/UK/news.cfm?ccs=228&cs=17080

[2] November 9, 2004, "The CAT roars again...Carl Thompson stuns David Haye!"http://www.eastsideboxing.com:80/news.php?p=1763&more=1

32

BOOMERS AND BOXING

Guest article by Ronald "Old Yank" Schneider *

The buzzing sound that permeated the summer air was the sound of my dad's brand new electric haircutting clippers that he'd just unpacked; a mail order purchase through the Montgomery Ward Catalog. They were noisy as hell and in the humid early-evening air they must have sounded like the dinner bell for a neighborhood in the midst of an unkempt crisis. The entire neighborhood knew that the clippers had arrived and with haircuts for free, no one cared that this was "on the job training" for my dad. Mr. Schneider was taking the boys in for another adventure.

Mothers up and down the dirt road sent their sons to form a line leading to the front stoop of my house. As I counted them it was more than a baseball team; Donnie Heath, Kamal Boulos, Bobby Caiazza, Ricky, Phillip, Wayne and Rodger Gildersleeve, my cousins Richard and Tommy Bergmann and myself. Not a single one owned a pair of shoes for everyday-wear in the summer. And judging by the uniform crew-cut every one on line got, we either looked like a 1959 little league team ready for the world series or a barefoot group of underage inductees for Parris Island. This was everyday life in the rural America of my youth.

We were all poor. But not a one of us boys knew this to be the case. It was spaghetti and meat sauce until the triple batch ran out and then it was a double batch of Bonita and noodles until it was gone. Nothing went to waste. You ate what was on your plate or you went hungry; and we rarely went hungry. Small vegetable gardens on side lawns were harvested of everything edible and the local super-market coupons were harvested with equal attention. Borrowing a rinsed out Skippy peanut butter jar full of milk from a neighbor was as common as the dust that would fly off the road when a car would pass by. Next week it would be repaid with a cup of sugar. Everyone was generous.

And every boy got into fist fights.

A bloody nose was simply a right of passage from childhood into boyhood; nothing special here. There was nothing to worry about. The neighborhood pecking order was always being tested. You played tackle football without equipment and your quarterback was the guy who just gave you the bloody nose for the right to play the position. Not to worry; Ricky won't be here for every game and I'd earn my quarterback position back tomorrow.

The four Gildersleeve boys had the edge in everything that was "sport". It seemed as if they were "Irish quadruplets"; barely a year separating each of them and I was sandwiched smack dab in the middle. I could shout to them from my yard (the functional equivalent of today's cell phone) and someone would always come out of their front door to answer. Telephones were still a luxury. Gus Galluzzo's house was the closest party-line to my house and for a nickel we could make a call from their house, providing the "party-line" was not tied up by someone further up or down the road; and man, we all knew Mrs. Dyer could talk the legs off a piano stool.

You offered the nickel to Gus or Virginia Galluzzo, but it was always refused. So you left it on their kitchen counter and not another word would be spoken about the nickel until your next offer was refused like the last. But with a quick run across the street through the corner of Gus' yard and up the hill, I could be in the Gildersleeve house within two minutes. As far as I was concerned, this was the center of the boxing universe when I was a boy.

At the Gildersleeve house boxing, football and baseball were a religious experience. Richard Marvin "Dick" Gildersleeve (always "Mr. Gildersleeve" to me) was one of the young professionals who lived on my road who'd gone to work for an upstart company called International Business Machines as an electronics technician. I don't know if his gadgets contributed to the best television and radio reception in the neighborhood or if it was simply because the house was on the top of a small hill. But this house more than any other exemplified the transition that "The Greatest Generation" was going through as they pulled themselves out of poverty after returning from World War II.

It was here that my life would change from gluing an ear to the radio to an unbelievable fascination with two channels of "snowy" and "scrolling" black and white television reception; one out of New York City and the other out of Albany, NY. And it was here that names like Vince Lombardi, Y. A. Tittle, Mickey Mantle, Brooks

Robinson, Sugar Ray Robinson, Gene Fulmer and Floyd Paterson were spoken with a reverence offered to only a sacred few.

In the basement of the Gildersleeve house is where the only boxing ring within 10 miles could be found. It was set up next to the space where oscilloscopes and fine-point soldering irons blipped, crackled and smoldered in a technician's home-made shop. The ring consisted of four lolly-columns – the ring posts – and the mat consisted of two throw-away gym mats that had been sewn together with a leather cord and tightly covered with canvas. Sack cord tied old pillows to the lolly-columnsusesd as ring posts for protection. It was a small ring; probably 16 by 16 feet. But we were small so it looked big enough to us. It was here where crafting the quickest route to a bloody nose was built and modified like the gadgets in the adjoining shop; we were torn down and rebuilt in the style suited to a technician and amateur boxing trainer. It was here where the cracking of leather against flesh could be heard and the smoldering of young tempers could be sensed. Oh, this was much more then the "blips" on the oscilloscope in the shop. Inside the walls of this basement was where the foundation of a life-long love of a sport was being built.

There were boxing pads of all sorts, a heavy bag and a speed bag on an adjustable height contraption. The speed bag could be lowered so Mr. Gildersleeve could do his speed-work from his wheelchair. He'd given his legs for my freedom in the Second Great War. And it was not until I had put my draft-lottery days of the Viet Nam era behind me that I finally cried for what Mr. Gildersleeve's sacrifice had done for me.

He'd prop up his two prosthetic legs in a corner formed by a shop-made table set against the wall. On the table was a jarful of what were probably bacteria-laden, one-size-fits-all mouthpieces. And while he was working out, his "spare" wheelchair was our basement go-cart. When he was finished with his workout, it would be our turn to hone our skills. The ingenious height-adjustable contraption for the speed bag was perfect for a group of odd-sized youngsters. And Mr. Gildersleeve's agility in a wheelchair as he held those pads for us would have made any trainer of the day proud; if only Angelo Dundee had seen our workouts, he'd have been proud too.

The Gildersleeve boys were part Native American. Phil (the closest to me in age) would tell me with pride what that meant. He'd say "I've got golden skin that runs up and down my arms". And if you've ever seen in your mind's eye what a majestic Native American warrior might look like, every one of these boys had a body type that would eventually develop into that image. It was their dad's body. It was a proud body and they were my friends and no one bloodied each other's noses better than we did.

I was the Euro-born foreigner in my neighborhood and nothing seemed to bring me closer to the American Experience then having four surrogate brothers of Native American descent.

I guess I was just shy of my ninth birthday when I got my first introduction to the basement ring. And over the better part of next decade, the two older of my four surrogate brothers (Ricky and Phil) would best me the overwhelming majority of the time and I'd best the younger two (Wayne and Rodger) about as much. For all of us the basement ring provided an aura of self-confidence and self-esteem – much like the character-building that Boy Scouting did for us – that seemed like magic in holding the teen-testing, hormone-driven challengers of our youth at bay.

By the time I was eleven or twelve, the vestiges of my Euro-accent were gone and I had absolutely no need to test my basement lessons against anyone outside the neighborhood, in the halls of my school or in the road and streets of my town. To be sure, I was a gentle young man outside of the basement, but even still, I look back in amazement. How was it possible that the inner self-confidence of a pre-teen could somehow be "read" by my peers?

Through the basement ring experience, the sport of boxing became just as important to us as America's pastime and certainly as important as that fractured collection of ruffians called professional football players; whatever league they claimed was best. This was 1963 and Sonny Liston was absolutely and undeniably the best and the meanest heavyweight boxer in the world. He was unbeatable.

And then Cassius Clay came along! Even though Floyd Patterson lost to Liston a year or so earlier, Patterson had always been a local favorite due to his visits from "the city" to "apple country" in the Mid-Hudson Valley. If you loved Floyd as a heavyweight, then you loved what Floyd loved and you despised what Floyd despised. And Floyd did not like Cassius Clay. But if you felt brash and bold and something was stirring inside you over the birth of something "new" (that you could neither define nor understand), then it was the "mouth" of Cassius Clay that spoke to the "silent voices" in your head.

And in 1964, while the Gildersleeve boys and I were spinning the second bootlegged album released by the Beatles in the UK, Cassius Clay was winning the heavyweight championship of the world off of Sonny Liston. Everyone who had an interest in boxing was trying to decide if they were in Floyd's camp or if they were in a Beatles frame of discovery that seemed to tug them toward the irresistible force that would eventually become known as Mohamed Ali. Either way, if you were a boxing fan, young or old, the sport had just become a tad more important then it had been when 1963 ended. In 1964 with a brash new heavyweight champion and the first official USA album released by the Beatles (Meet the Beatles), although a little late, the '60's had arrived and so had we. The time had come to move a group of young boxers out of the basement and into the light of a new dawn.

With the arrival of the '60's also came an era of a social, cultural and generational gap that would divide Americans. Few things spoke to me about this divide better than the harsh public and private relationship that played out between Floyd Patterson and Mohamed Ali.

About a year and a half before their second meeting in the ring, Patterson had bought a beautiful home off Springtown Road in my hometown. In the years I was going to community college, he shopped at Benson's, a men's shop where I had a part-time job. And here is where his conversations with Mr. Paul Benson would help define for me a piece of the struggle we were all either witnessing or going through.

Paul had asked him why he wanted this second fight with Ali. Patterson, always gentle in his demeanor, quickly quipped back, "You mean Cassius Clay, don't you?" For Patterson, Ali would always be an "uppity Negro" (words used by Patterson in the men's shop), that was bringing too much attention to himself and to a profound struggle Patterson thought should continue down a quieter path.

In those days, even in the relatively "civil" Hudson Valley of New York, there was a nearby community that reportedly still had an active chapter of the Klan. Even though Patterson had married a white woman (their two beautiful daughters eventually going to a highly integrated school) and he owned a home in a culturally progressive college town in the Hudson Valley of New York, something was still out of place for him.

It seemed to me that he was stuck in a social and cultural divide that blinded him to the amazing positive influence Ali was having.

Patterson was a good man who appeared to me to be concerned that too much attention to civil rights might produce a backlash; he appeared to fear that the backlash could return the state of blacks to a darker period in civil rights.

Of course, the more and more I'd learn about Ali, the more I'd come to appreciate what an incredible role he had played on so many political and socio-cultural fronts. And one day Patterson would reconcile with Ali and seemingly reconcile with so much more in his life. He became involved in his community. He became involved in State politics; becoming the Boxing Commissioner for the State of New York. Patterson would become the man who came to the aid of a young friend of mine who had lost a leg to cancer. He came to the aid of anyone in need. Eventually, due to his amazing generosity, the athletic fields where I was once played high school sports would carry his name, "Floyd Patterson Field."

But in 1964 we were still climbing out of the basement; we may have thought we had arrived, but we really did not know how we got there, how many were being left behind or how we were going to get anywhere. One step at a time we made our way out of the Gildersleeve's basement; it was time to strike up a little independence. Some of us found year-round paper routes and others mowed lawns in the summer, raked leaves in the fall, shoveled driveways and sidewalks in the winter and cleaned up debris in the spring. It really did not make a difference. If you wanted to buy a new baseball glove, football, or just wanted to take a girl to the movies, you had to earn money.

"Back in the day" at the age of 12, you could work on a farm without working papers. And with our dads as our role models, we did what we had to do. We got jobs. Real jobs! It was 10 hours a day and six days a week. I rode my bike seven miles each way to and from the farm. We took in hay, thrashed grain, mixed feed, tended cows and repaired fence; mostly we took in hay. And in the summer of 1964 my wage of 90 cents an hour yielded what I thought amounted to a king's ransom – what in the world was a 12 year-old boy going to do with $54.00 per week? Well my dad knew exactly what his 12 year-old boy was going to do with $54.00 per week. He was going to put $44.00 per week in the bank to save toward college and have $10.00 of walk-around money in his pocket; so much for striking up a little independence.

Work on Brook Farm was serious physical labor. Most mornings three hay wagons and two 1946 International Harvester dump trucks lay waiting to be unloaded of the 2 1/2 ton of hay each could carry. One of those trucks, the red one, was named "Bessie" and the green one was simply called "the green truck." They each had a hi-lo range giving them a total of eight forward speeds on the standard, stick-shift transmission; double-clutching was the only way to keep them from "grinding" so hard that your sneakers would vibrate off your feet.

The wagons and trucks would be unloaded and re-loaded by noon, then unloaded by mid-afternoon and loaded again by the end of the day to be waiting for us the following morning. Five loads a day would be cycled through four rounds of unloading and loading, with my hands touching every bale at least once. That's 3,000 "reps" of 50 pounds each that was tossed, rolled or hoisted by my young hands every day during haying season. And when the day was done, I would climb on my bike and peddle the seven miles back home; somehow finding the energy to race Phil for the last half mile.

My boss was Earl Stokes and he was 76 years old the first year I worked for him. He could out-work every hand on the farm. He fancied calling me Ronnie-Boy or "Young Yank" (because of the NY Yankees hat I wore my first day of work that remained on my head for the next five years). It was he who taught me that the dirt and sweat that I wore by the end of the day was the "clean dirt" of an honest day's labor.

And when tempers flared between farm hands, he'd only come to your rescue if your usefulness as a hand on the farm was being placed in jeopardy. A couple of pairs of old horsehair-padded boxing gloves hung from rusty nails in the tool shed. Disputes were settled like gentlemen; settled in a ring without ropes on the grass behind the shed. He would actually sit back on one elbow in the grass with a sprig of hay in his mouth and he'd gesture at you with his free hand while giving us pointers on keeping our guard up or when a hook might be useful. The training advice was always delivered calmly and quietly; so softly at times that we would need to ask him, through our huffing and puffing to repeat it.

Young Butch Lawson was deceptively fast, but Phil Gildersleeve had been trained in the basement. When these two went at it Earl needed to stay close. But he needed to only whisper when enough was enough. It was best to listen because there was nothing about Earl that gave away his years except the deep wrinkles in his skin, his bald head and his out of date, horn-rimed glasses. The boys on the farm were going to develop slowly in temperament that would lead them toward becoming soft-spoken, unassuming and quietly powerful in the image of Earl.

By the time I entered High School, between the Gildersleeve's basement ring and farmhand scuffles, I'd been "boxing" for four years; enough time to lose the awkwardness of a boy and begin to look like a marginally-fluid young man. The boys in the neighborhood who had taken the "soft" jobs like a paper-route or mowing lawns had not kept pace with Phil and me. Our bodies were different and it showed. At age 13 and 14 we actually had muscles; we had muscles that had developed from doing 3,000 "weight lifts" of 50 pounds each and every day for a seven-week long haying season. We had been "sparring" on lunch hours and we had endurance from riding our bikes 14 miles every day; over 100 miles of road-work every week when added to our "recreational" cycling on evenings and Sundays.

And Earl had taught us humility and decency and pride; he'd taught us that when enough was enough you shook hands and left it alone. We were young boxers with walking money in our pockets and not a clue of what to do with our budding talent or the money.

We were also starting to notice that along with the human body changes that were going on around us the whole world seemed to be changing too. President Kennedy had been assassinated a couple of years earlier when we were still in a state of pre-teen, youthful unawareness. Cassius Clay had officially become Mohamed Ali a year earlier, and names like Elijah Mohamed and Malcolm-X and Dr. Martin Luther King were spoken in the halls of the school. It was 1965, and although the involvement of America in Viet Nam had begun a few years earlier, the escalation period was beginning and it was impossible to avoid taking sides; should we be in or should we be out.

The British invasion of the American music pop and rock culture was in full swing too. Adding to the color of the times my community was largely divided. There were the locals who were attached to the community primarily through farms, local employment and an employer called IBM that employed, by far, the largest numbers of any company in the area. On the other side of the divide were the cultural progressives associated with the explosive growth of the State University of New York campus right in the middle of town. The buzzing was no longer an idyllic scene on a rural dirt road. It was the buzzing of change coming at us like a freight train and bringing all the confusion that a divided community could deliver.

If you had a waking conscience, you were embroiled in it until you did everything you could to escape from it for a while. My dad had bought me a horn when I was about 6 or 7, and my music interest had grown and playing guitar and electric bass in a high school rock band was one of my escapes.

That next March the escape from the madness was to forever set me on the track to becoming a life-long boxing fan rather then a boxer. A few of the old neighborhood boys and a few new ones emptied their "change socks", grabbed a little "foldable stash" and snuck off to the train station in Poughkeepsie to head to New York City to catch the finals of the Golden Gloves.

What a scrubby looking crew. Richie Steffens, Bobby Lynch, Phil and Wayne Gildersleeve, David Giersch, my cousins Richard (now called "Dick" to keep the confusion to a minimum) and Tommy and myself all had hair that did its best to drive any mom crazy – we all had some version of a Beatle haircut (or un-cut) and some of us could actually afford blue suede boots. We were dressed in Levi pants, belts with large brass buckles, white turtle neck shirts under cotton broadcloth button down shirts and the warmest coats we could find. Navy crew hats were a staple and Richie Steffens definitely looked the coolest because he had a Navy Pea Coat to go with the hat and a pair of blue suede Beatle-boots to walk it all around with.

In March of 1966, the wind did not stop blowing for the entire month and it was one heck of a cold winter. But we were going to escape for a day to the cheap seats of Madison Square Garden – the Mecca of boxing – the center of the universe for the square circle.

Not a one of us had ever even been on a train before. As far as my parents were concerned, I was spending the night at Bobby's house and he at mine. All of us with an oddly noble pride shared our personal stories of how we were getting away with murder. Odder still, when reflecting on the bond of trust that each of us had with our parents and on the new-found independence they were fostering, all of us, had we simply asked, would likely have been granted permission for the adventure. But this was not a time to be thinking about parent issues, this was our time to take the basement lessons and see if they would help us "see" boxing in a different light.

Could any of us have a shot against a Golden Gloves fighter? We were anxious to assess the possibilities. Our coats were flung open in utter defiance to the bitter cold and our "steaming" voices were louder than usual. We were playing hooky from our lives in rural America and the excitement had us bumping shoulders and punching arms as we grabbed our tickets and jostled our way to the train platform.

None of us knew a single amateur fighter that was going to fight in the Golden Gloves. But we all wondered if the amateur heavyweight would bounce and jab like Cassius Clay (in rural America there was a reluctance to call him by his new name of Mohamed Ali), or if a new Willie Pastrano or Jose Torres would emerge from the ranks at light heavy. Joey Giardello had captured the middleweight championship a year and a half earlier and then lost it to Emile Griffith. We'd argue if either would ever look as good as Sugar Ray Robinson did as a middleweight. All fighters were compared to Robinson; even then he was already considered one of the best, if not the best fighter that had ever lived.

The arguments were always about which fighter was best and which one could have beaten some name from the past. And exactly like today, these fantasy bouts always had a definitive winner in one of our eyes and we could care less that nothing could ever be proven.

The notion of "alphabet soup" applying to boxing sanctioning organizations was not possible because most of the sanctioning bodies did not exist in 1966. It was the World Boxing Association (the WBA of alphabet soup sanctioning bodies), and that was about it; except for some start-up group called the World Boxing Council (WBC). Even with Congressional investigations into boxing and possible connections to organized crime, it was a simpler time and because of its simplicity, it seemed more inviting to young fans.

So the hallway controversies of our high school were left behind for some serious boxing talk; and with the boxing talk, the nearly two-hour train ride and freezing walk from Grand Central Train Station to Madison Square Garden was over before we knew it.

Our first year at the "Gloves" had us hanging from the rafters in the cheapest seats money could buy. The fights that would breakout in the cheap seats were often more entertaining then what was going on in the ring. But my attention went to the ring. I honestly cannot remember a single winner from that night. I do remember thinking that these guys were much better than I was and I'd be better off as a fan than a fighter.

What I was watching interested me greatly. Seeing great young talent "live" was an entirely different thing then cheering the neighborhood basement boys and certainly different than watching boxing on a snowy, scrolling black and white television. I found myself actually developing a knack for observing which amateur had the faster hands, the better footwork, the straighter punches and the better defense. Within three or four bouts, I was telling my buddies that if a fight lasted for one full round I'd be able to tell them who was going to win the fight.

And so it was that from the cheap seats of Madison Square Garden I began picking who would win a fight based on only what my eyes were telling me. Those cheap seats turned out to be one of the best "investments" I'd ever make in my life; picking winners would eventually make me some serious money. This time the take-home pay would be all mine because dad would never know I was ever there and gambling was illegal; both in the state and in my dad's home.

I returned to The Garden year after year to watch the Golden Gloves. And I'd get to watch amateur champions that would go on to become professional champions; they were names like Riddick Bowe, Mark Breland, Gerald "Gerry" Cooney, Chris Eubank, Zab Judah, Kevin Kelly, Eddie Gregory (better known as Eddie Mustafa Mohammed), Tracy Harris Patterson (Floyd Patterson's adolescent charge), and Kevin Rooney.

Each and every year the seats kept getting closer and closer to the ring. As the seats kept getting closer to the ring, I kept getting farther and farther away from the ring – as a boxer. The last time I would lace up a pair of boxing gloves was for a brief stint at trying my hand as an amateur while in college. By the time I'd become college age, boxing as an official collegiate sport had been banned due to a highly publicized death during a collegiate bout in 1960. So it was through a college PE course in boxing that allowed participation through instruction and an intramural program that I laced them up for the last time.

The '60's had come to a close and so had my days in the ring. The train rides with the neighborhood boys would give way to a convoy of limousines. The brown bag dinners eaten on the sidewalks of New York would give way to a steak at The Cattleman. Single would give way to married. Ali would lose to Leon Spinks. Great names like Hagler, Leonard and Duran would give way to great names like De La Hoya and Mosley and Lewis. Black hair would give way to gray hair.

As time would pass I'd come to realize that I was never meant to be a boxer; I was meant to be a fan. My years in the basement, on the farm and at The Garden had allowed me to hone my observational skills; and my years of returning to The Garden would be replaced with keeping a keen eye on amateur events and applying what I observed to the few among them who would eventually make it to the pros. I'd catch many a fine professional bout at The Garden as well. My last visit to the Mecca was in 2007 and it provided an opportunity to introduce my youngest son to his first "live" viewing of a professional championship bout; this one between Miguel Angel Cotto and Zab Judah.

For more than a moment as I shouted and laughed and shared high-fives with my son, I wondered how different my life might have been had the Gildersleeve's basement ring and sparring matches on the farm taken my life down a path toward becoming a boxer. Melodramatically, I imagined myself as much better than I ever was. Then I came to realize that having a great love of a sport had brought me much satisfaction. Everyone in my family had become a boxing fan. It brings us together. Many of the old neighborhood boys became great fans as well.

Today "fight nights" are often hosted in my home where family, friends and the old neighborhood come together over boxing. Bobby and my cousin Richard who once got "clipped" in 1959 on the front stoop of my dad's house aren't with us any more. Ricky and Kamal moved away. And the buzzing sounds of electric haircutting clippers have been replaced with the buzzing sounds of friendship over clinking glasses of wine and beer and the common love of a sport.

So in the middle of the boxing match at Madison Square Garden I told my son that I had watched a bunch of kids with names I mostly can't remember win a Golden Gloves Amateur Championship at this very place, including Zab Judah who was fighting in the ring in front of us. A basement boxing ring, a farm and a young girl that would become his mother flashed before me. Seeing the nostalgia in my eyes, my son asked me why I never stuck to trying to become a boxer. I told him I got to do the next best thing; I kept my teeth and became a fan.

* Ronald "Old Yank" Schneider is financial consultant to high net worth individuals. He is a graduate of Marist College in Poughkeepsie, NY (BS in Business Administration). He is a former national-level manager for a Fortune 500 computer firm "Old Yank" has been a boxing fan since his youth and is regarded by many as a sharp-witted handicapper. He is a contributing writer for East Side Boxing on the net.

33

THE REAL BOYOS

I was a bad guy but I wasn't evil.
–Richard Marinick

Southie's a dead end
–On line poster

*Southie, i Love it. My kinda people, Irish. Any one who
aint' Irish shouldnt be here*
–On line poster

What do you want? Tears
–H. Paul Rico

You know where I stand!
–Louise Day Hicks, political champion of the white status quo

*Paul Doyle depicts perfectly what 'living the life' is all about . . . Doyle's
dramatic account of his experiences in the drug world is . . .
serious business.*
–Joseph D. Pistone, author of Donnie Brasco:
My Undercover Life in the Mafia

*I've talked to the good good guys, the good bad guys, the bad good guys
and the bad bad guys—and the story never seems to hit bottom.*
–Dave Boeri, longtime Boston journalist

*The difference was that the bad guys in the North End left the good
people alone-even protected them. The bad guys in Southie
stole from the good people-they exploited them.*
–Anonymous

After a stroll near Castle Island with Kevin Weeks and maybe John
Connolly, you could envision Jimmy "Whitey" Bulger walking into
his safe haven, the dark Triple O's Bar in Southie–you could hear
him say to the guys in the booths drinking their shots from plastic cups, "well well lads, and how are the Boyos today?" The only

problem is they weren't Boyos; they were thugs, loan sharks, extorters and worse. They were guys who buried bodies at Tenean Beach, in the grassy areas at the edge of the beach alongside the Southeast Expressway, on Hallet Street near the Florian Hall in Dorchester, or by the Neponset River in Quincy.

Recent movies and books have chronicled South Boston, best known as Southie, in such a way that it might seem everyone from there hung out at The Triple O's and was a criminal. Sure, Boston as a whole is a unique situation. You have the Italian mob, and you've also got the Irish mafia (the Winter Hill Gang). And you can throw in street grifters, junkies and combat zone prostitutes for good measure. But that's a bad rap on both Southie and the greater Boston area of which it is a part. The blue collar towns around Boston, places like Somerville, Chelsea, East Boston, Medford, Revere and Brockton, are not all about rats, squealers, loan sharks, drugs, gangs, mean streets, codes of silence, triple deckers, Winter Hill, Triple O's, Castle Island, Brink's robbers, and massacres at the 99 in Charlestown. Admittedly, however, the crime history is compelling.

From the Great Brink's Robbery in Boston's Italian North End in 1950 to June 28, 1978, when five men were murdered in gangland-style executions in the cramped basement office of the Blackfriars Pub to November. 6, 1995, when Anthony P. Clemente Sr. and his son, Damien opened fire and killed four North End men at the 99 in Charlestown as lunchtime diners watched in horror, Boston has been more than Brahmins and a stroll down the Freedom Trail. Not unlike Chicago and New York City, Boston's crime history is the grist for the mills of many writers.

But it was in areas like Southie and Somerville (which is north of Boston alongside the town of Charlestown) where the Irish had a lock on crime and where a different kind of underworld thrived. From the Somerville neighborhood of Winter Hill, a violent and dangerous band of gangsters emerged and one James "Buddy" Mc-Clean became a leader. He later went to war with the notorious McLaughlin brothers of Charlestown, and was shot dead in 1966. Howard "Howie"'Wwinter would then emerge as a major force. Meanwhile, In Southie, Jimmy "Whitey" Bulger took over the rackets, which included shaking down loan sharks, bookies and stealing everything worth stealing and extorting everything worth extorting. This was all about Irish mobs and the mafia never was able to get a foothold.

For a superb chronological description of what transpired under Bulger's reign and his fateful hookup with FBI Agent John Connolly that what would showcase the worst federal law enforcement corruption in our nation's history, the reader is referred to "Winter Hill Gang," Organized Crime Syndicates on the Web at: http://www. geocities.com/OrganizedCrimeSyndicates/winterhill.html

George V. Higgins

The literary fascination with crime in Boston probably started in 1972 with the late George V. Higgins's "The Friends of Eddie Coyle," later made into a classic 1973 crime film starring Robert Mitchum and Peter Boyle. Full of realism, this one broke the ground for those that followed–The Digger's Game (1973), Cogan's Trade (1974), A City on a Hill (1975), and The Judgment of Deke Hunter (1976).

Dennis Lehane

Years later, Dennis Lehane raised Boston noir to another level with his "Mystic River" and "Gone Baby Gone," both made into successful films. This was gritty local fare that resonated with those who also enjoyed reading about the Irish criminals of New York's Hell's Kitchen. Lehane turbo-charged the popularity of Boston crime.

Chuck Logan

"Prince of Thieves," by the talented Logan, is about Charlestown, another blue-collar Boston-Irish neighborhood renown as the breeding ground of bank robbers and armored car thieves. Still another dark novel.

Gerald W. Clement

In his "The Cops Are Robbers," Clement writes a true story of how the Police turned on a community–Medford. The setting, characters, and accuracy of the events that took place leave you feeling as if your are there while the crime of breaking into the vault in the Former Depositors Trust bank is taking place. Back in the '70s, Medford did not have to be big to have big city crime, including an organized crime murder in a coffee shop full of witnesses.

Richard Marinick

Marinick is the latest to make his mark and his background give new meaning to the word "unique.". He was an ex-state cop from Massachusetts who became involved in the South Boston underworld. After robbing armored cars, he served over ten years for the crime. Remarkably, he earned a B.A. and an M.A. in the Boston University Prison Program. His novel "Boyos" was as authentic as it gets and a truly great piece of work. His new one, "In For a Pound," is a classic of South Boston noir, and a thinly veiled expose of that one person who was the nexus for Boston noir, James "Whitey" Bulger. Bulger – the ultimate rat, who (along with his close accomplices, Stephen "The Rifleman" Flemmi and Kevin Weeks) brought drugs into the neighborhood. In this way, he contributed to the deaths of young people resulting in untold suicides, murders, and drug overdoses. He was tough, vicious and ran the Irish mobs in Southie in a manner that would make a sociopath envious.

Speaking of sociopaths, Stephen "The Rifleman" Flemmi, a particularly vicious gangster, is currently serving a life sentence in prison for extortion, money laundering and 10 murders. It was at Flemmi's mother's house on East Third Street nestled in a quiet thoroughfare lined with trees that Flemmi's girlfriend, Debra Davis, was allegedly last seen alive in 1981. She was 26. In 2000, her body was unearthed by authorities from a grave in nearby Quincy.

Quincy another who gave special meaning to the word "sociopath" was John Martorano. A.k.a "the Basin Street Butcher," who pleaded guilty to killing 20 people in his criminal career. He later flipped and was released from prison in 2007.

Bulger remains today one of the most sought-after fugitives in the world; he and his girlfriend, Catherine Greig, may—and this is a big "may"– have been spotted in Taormina, Sicily in April 2007 by a vacationing federal Drug Enforcement Administration agent who shot a brief video of the couple before they slipped away. But hell, Bulger has been sighted so many times in so many different places, he has become something of an Elvis. The FBI recently observed the 79th birthday of Bulger by doubling the reward for leading to his capture to $ 2 million.

Ironically, disgraced ex-FBI agent Jphn Connolly remains in prison awaiting further trials. But like John Gotti, he was and is the only one to honor the mob's code of silence—at least so far. The rest were rats, flippers, and stool pigeons who jumped at the first opportunity to save their skin.

Michael Patrick MacDonald

MacDonald is the point counterpoint to all of this with his seminal best seller "All Souls: A Family Story from Southie." An activist against crime and violence, he too discusses Bulger, but in a manner that is less depressing. He writes about fierce if misplaced loyalties and how proud the residents were to be from Southie, including MacDonald himself. He also writes about the crime, drugs and violence in his neighborhood in the years following Boston's busing riots, and of his brothers and sisters, many of whom fell prey to drugs, crime, suicide and murder. As well, he laments as to how gentrification has wiped out the best elements of the neighborhood.

Paul Doyle

Doyle served as Special Agent in the Bureau of Narcotics and Dangerous Drugs and the Drug Enforcement Administration. He currently is Chairman of the New England chapter of the Association of Former Federal Narcotic Agents. He grew up in South Boston, was a solid boxer, got two college degrees, served in the Special Forces and went on to a distinguished career in Law Enforcement busting drug rings from within. He also witnessed first hand how devastating drug abuse can be – some addicts even dying in his arms. It's all chronicled in his stirring personal memoir *Hot Shots and Heavy Hits* in which he writes riveting stories about his years on the inside. As engrossing as a fiction thriller, this book provides a rare glimpse into a harsh world unknown to most of us.

Roland Merullo

If Italians are your thing, then Roland Merullo's "Revere Beach Boulevard" will resonate well. Like the Irish, this great book touches on the fiercely loyal and devoted Italian-American family of the Benedettos.

Of course, ex Bulger thugs like John "Red" Shea and Kevin Weeks have chipped in with "Rat Bastards" and "Brutal," respectively. Rather than find Jesus, they found the pen (no pun intended). But for every ex-con turned litterateur, there thankfully is a MacDonald and Merullo.

Today, many of the places portrayed by these writers that once seemed lost in time have now been transformed by inevitable gentrification and even tourism. Yuppies now reside in pricey condos and Southie is no longer the meat-and-potatoes enclave it once was. Once one of America's poorest and toughest white urban neighborhoods, it has now been discovered as a great place to live and visit; it also has been discovered by Hollywood given its storied legacy of organized crime.

Boston noir is about the smells and sounds of tough neighborhoods where the new mixes with the old, and the result is a confused mix of hope and despair. But unlike those portrayed in movies like Monument Ave., The Departed, Gone Baby Gone, and Southie, there are many lads who became true working class heroes. They are blue-collar men who overcame many obstacles and prevailed through determination and hard work to rise above an urban Irish American street culture or an Italian one in the North End that can be both suppressive and seductive.

The Real Boyos

This win [over Mike Tyson] was for the pride of Ireland.
I proved everyone wrong tonight.
–Kevin McBride

It is said that we all knew what was going on in the streets, where
the neighborhood code of silence was brilliantly maintained by the
drug lord/informant. And we did. But what matters more is that
everyone knew, at all levels of city, state, and federal government.
And kids died.
–Michael Patrick MacDonald, author of "Easter Rising:
An Irish American Coming Up from Under."

They write books and film movies about Boston Noir these days. But for every low-life thug, there is a Michael Patrick MacDonald, author of the acclaimed. "All Souls: A Family Story from Southie." For those who died of a "hot shot" – a lethal injection of heroin or coke, there were others who were able to get the hell out. For every person who held onto hardcore racism, there was someone who learned about open-mindedness. For every dead end based on misplaced loyalties, there was an exit. For every Irish mobster, there is a Jimmy Corkum (whom I saw beat Irish Beau Jaynes twice in 1977) or Chris McInerney. For every rat bastard, there is a Steve Collins or Kevin "The Clones Colossus" McBride. For every Whitey Bulger, there is a Sean Mannion or Freddie Roach. For every guy who flipped or ratted out his buddies, there is a Mike O'Han, Mike Culbert, or Kevin "Cocky" Watts. And for every guy who gave up too quickly, there is an "Irish" Micky Ward or Sean Fitzgerald.

Danny Long

A lot of guys I boxed with became wise guys…but a lot didn't.
–Danny Long

And for every bank robber or low life who dealt pot, coke or mescaline, there is a Danny Long. Danny was a slick Boston middleweight who went 31-7 while fighting from 1978-1984 against the very best including Robbie Sims, Dave "Boy" Green, Alex Ramos, Doug Dewitt and Bobby Czyz. In just his second professional outing, he fought a guy with 43 fights under his belt and beat him.

Like most Southie boxers, he started his career at McDonough's Gym and then "moved up" to Connolly's Gym, where most of the locals worked out. In fact, he trained with the aforementioned Sean Mannion and many other Irishmen.

Five years after retiring from boxing, he became a Boston police officer and now works with kids. "Among the things I teach them is how to set goals and achieve them, conflict resolution, cultural sensitivity, rules and laws, and all about crime victims and their rights as citizens. I get to talk in 45 minute increments. I hope that I reach them." [1]

"…Long has been able to teach some kids the rudiments of boxing, and has also taken many on skiing and whitewater rafting trips to show them that there is life beyond the inner city that they call home." [2]

Like Paul Doyle, Danny found another route out of Southie.

Micky Ward

Irish' Micky Ward was, in my opinion, one of the greatest champions of all time, and the biggest heart that ever stepped into the ring. I am committed to making him proud…real.
–Mark Wahlberg

Ward, well known among savvy fans as a great "club fighter" for most of his career and known for his ability to withstand punishment, achieved immortality late in his career by going to war with Arturo Gatti in a legendary trilogy in which both warriors pushed the limits and went to the very edge. But for most of his career, he was really a hero of the people. He was a humble blue collar worker from the streets of Lowell, MA who made good. Ward could be losing every second of every round, and then ice his opponent with a single devastating left hook to the body. That was his essence. This was the case in his fight with heavily favored and undefeated Alfonso Sanchez in 1997. That kind of anticipatory, albeit sudden excitement made Ward fights something special.

In a testament to Micky's appeal, Paramount Pictures has fast tracked a movie entitled The Fighter which is a biopic that co-stars Mark Wahlberg and Matt Damon in this film movie based on Ward's life and that of his half brother and trainer Dicky Eklund. There is also a terrific book "Irish Thunder: The Hard Life & Times of Micky Ward," which was written by former ESPN anchor Bob Halloran and released by The Lyons Press. From Lowell, MA to Hollywood, but Micky still lives in Lowell.

Steve Collins

I'll fight him [Roy Jones] in a phone box in front of two men and a dog.
–Steve Collins

Steve Collins, nicknamed The Celtic Warrior, hailed from Dublin but turned professional in Boston in 1986 and won 16 successive fights before losing to Mike McCallum in 1990. In 1994, he won the WBO middleweight belt and then moved up to super-middleweight where he beat the previously unbeaten Chris Eubank to win the WBO title in Ireland. In all, he beat Nigel Benn and Eubank twice each–an amazing feat. Atypically, he closed out his career with 15 wins in a row.

This warrior retired with a fine record of 36-3. He now lives in St Albans, England where one day he could likely receive a call from the International Boxing Hall of Fame. He was trained in Boston by another Irishman, albeit a Boston one, Freddie Roach.

Sean Fitzgerald

I have a love/hate relationship with boxing...It's been that way for a long time, ever since I turned pro. But in the end, I love it more than I hate it. That's what keeps me in it. That's what will always keep me in it.
–Sean Fitzgerald

Sean "The Irish Express" Fitzgerald was a lean, mean middleweight who shined in the early 1990s and fought out of Worcester, MA. He ran up a fine 29-2-2 mark in an 11-year pro career losing only to future world champion Dana Rosenblatt and the great Roberto Duran. He too closed out his career with a string of wins—eleven in all.

Sean, who fought in a fan-friendly way, now owns a boxing gym (Camp Fitzy) in Worcester, and trains fighters. "After I retired as a boxer," Sean explained, "I started training fighters. I opened a gym so I could help kids and keep them off the streets. I love training fighters and watching them grow as boxers and individuals. I encourage them to follow their dreams in boxing and life."[3]

Sean Mannion

Sean Mannion from Dorchester, Massachusetts by way of Ros Muc, County Galway, Ireland came close to winning a title in 1984, but lost a UD to Mike McCallum at Madison Square Garden. At stake was the undefeated Bodysnatcher's WBA light middleweight title. The year prior, the gritty Irishman upset the great In-Chul Baek in Atlantic City. The Korean was 26-0 coming into that fight. In 1979, Sean KOd Jimmy Corkum, then 40-2, in a high profile face off of two Boston-based Boyos. Later, in 1992, he would beat upstart Mike O'Han in Waltham, Massachusetts—far from Berlin, Hamburg where he lost to two young fighters by the names of Dariusz Michalczewski and Henry Maske. His final slate was 42-14-1.

In a memory-laden career, he never got the chance to demonstrate his skills on his native shore. However, now back in Rosmuc, Ireland, he manages unbeaten Ballinrobe cruiserweight prospect, Michael 'The Storm' Sweeney (who beat Kronk's Andy Lee as an amateur) and Castlebar's light heavyweight Keith Cresham.

Mike Culbert

Irish Mike Culbert, a super middleweight, was born in Belfast, N. Ireland almost forty years ago and closed out an eighteen-year pro boxing career in 2006 with a split decision win against a journeyman named Khalif "Panther" Shabazz in the eight-round main event at Memorial Hall in Plymouth, Massachusetts. That's right; journeymen fight eight-round main events. With his win, Culbert finished with a fine 30-4-1 record in a career that started in 1988 at the Boston Gardens when he TKO'd one Santiago Hermida. He also closes with an unbeaten streak of ten since losing in 1996 to the great Roberto Duran in six—the only time Culbert was ever stopped (in a bout he took on short notice).

Most of his fights probably didn't mean much to the average fight fan, but to the many Irish boxing fans in the greater Boston area, they provided great enjoyment. More importantly, they gave the affable and well-spoken Culbert a few days in the sun and maybe some extra money to compliment his day job as a supervisor at the Department of Youth Services in Brockton, Massachusetts.

Irish Mike really represents the blue-collar ingredient of boxing: the beer-drinking, hard-rocking, slam-banging, rugged boxing at the Roxy in Boston, the Ballroom in Baltimore, Cicero Stadium near Chicago, or some fairgrounds in Ohio or Delaware. Blue-collar stuff is all about grit and courage and even a degree of never-say-die hope. It is about a no-nonsense, lunch-pail kind of approach that Mike personified.

Freddie Roach

If you just roll over and let Parkinson's take you over,
it will, You must fight it.
–Freddie Roach

My friends who still live in the projects in Dedham, Massachusetts,
which is where I'm from, they say I'm lucky I made it out. And I tell
them, 'It's just a decision. You can make it too.
–Freddie Roach

He's a man of few words, but those words have a lot
of meaning behind the ...
–Oscar De La Hoya

Freddie Roach is a bespectacled sweetheart of a man with a Celtic cross tattoo on his left biceps. He was a respected pro, albeit a journeyman who always fought with great heart, but stayed on too long and that may have cost him in the end. He was willing to take a shot to give a shot. He went 13-12 in the last part of his career after streaking out of the gate with a 26-1 mark.

Yet he undoubtedly will be inducted into the International Boxing Hall of Fame as a trainer who works out of his Wild Card Gym in Hollywood. Freddie also has trauma induced Parkinson's. Sometimes his left arm trembles and he is easily fatigued. Sometimes, his speech is slurred, but he hasn't let it impede him from having trained such great fighters as Marlon Starling, Virgil Hill, Johnny Tapia, James Toney, Stevie Collins, Michael Moorer, Mike Tyson, Oscar De La Hoya, Lucia Rijker, and Manny Pacquiao. This soft-spoken and mild manner Irishman copes without complaint and deals with the disease like a man. "I think what I do really fights it," he said. "Hand-eye coordination, catching punches with the mitts and so forth, I think that's what keeps me from getting worse."[4]

He was voted Trainer of the Year by the Boxing Writers Association of America in 2003, 2006 and 2007. As well, he has been inducted into the Inducted into both the World Boxing Hall of Fame and the California Boxing Hall of Fame.

Freddie Roach is a sweet man in a dangerous and often dirty business. He is one of Boxing's good guys. Boxing and Freddie are synonymous.

They are the real heroes. These are the real Boyos

[1] Robert Mladinich, "The Danny Long and the short of it." March 31, 2006. http://www.thesweetscience.com:80/boxing-article/3588/danny-long-short/

[2] IBID.

[3] "Tank & The Irish Express bring pro boxing back to Worcester" HotBoxingNews.com.   http://www.hotboxingnews.com/NEWS2006/news051906.htm

[4] Elliot Spagat, "Roach fights Parkinson's while thriving as a boxing trainer." Undated. http://www.usatoday.com/sports/boxing/2008-04-04-344681383_x.htm

34

REFUSING TO ROLLOVER

It is only through a fighter's will that he makes losses impossible.
—Ted Knutson

Omar Pittman vs. Jean Pascal (2008)

Pascal's people handpicked Omar "Pit Bull" Pittman, 15-3, to show-case the highly touted Canadian's flashy form. The fight was at the Seminole Hard Rock Hotel and Casino in Hollywood, Florida and was on the same card as Edison "Pantera" Miranda vs. David Banks with the two winners ostensibly meeting each other. Pascal was the reigning NABF, NABA and WBO NABO super middleweight title holder.

Miranda did his piece by icing Banks with a malefic right hand that sent the youngster from Oregon through the ropes and into dreamland. It was a spectacular knockout.

Pascal started out fast enough and showed good hand speed and sharp combos, but then something happened around the sixth round. Pittman, from Philadelphia, started to fight back and by the eight stanza, was backing up the flashy Haitian fighter (via Montréal) with one well placed shot after another. Soon, Pascal's flash had been replaced by a cautious awareness that he was in a fight. By the end of the fight, "The Pit Bull" was more than holding his own.

As a result of their respective showings, it was clear that a fight between the Pascal and Miranda, despite Pascal's post-fight blustering, would not be in the offing. The reason was clear; a tough guy out of Philadelphia refused to roll over.

Chazz Witherspoon vs. Domonic Jenkins (2008)

On April 16 at the Hammerstein Ballroom, in New York City, ESPN Friday Night Fights televised this one and even before the fight started, Joe Tessitore and Teddy Atlas were talking about Jenkins's so-called "opponent's mentality." Apparently someone forgot to tell Jenkins that he was being served up as fodder for the up and coming, but light fisted Witherspoon.

Jenkins had been stopped by top contender Eddie Chambers and was also halted by Tye Fields over 7 rounds. Earlier, he had been TKO'd by rugged Chris Arreola. The bar had been set for Chaz to do the same, but Jenkins was having none of it, nor was he having any of Tessitore's pre-fight blather.

Jenkins started out strong and held his own for the first 3 or 4 rounds, but then Witherspoon settled down and took over the fight down the stretch with punishing work in close. Still, in the final 30 seconds, the two engaged in a all out exchange of haymakers any one of which would have ended the fight had it landed flush. Jenkins had the better of it, though he clearly had lost the fight.

Judge Robert Gilson and Tom Kaczmarek had it 91-98 and 93-97 for Witherspoon, respectively, while Julie Lederman had it a more realistic 93-96.

But more importantly, the highly touted Witherspoon could not do what Chambers, Fields and Arreola had accomplished. This tough Texan was not about to assume an "opponent's mentality" (whatever that is supposed to mean) and roll over. Teddy Atlas said "He was just doing enough to lose." Again, I don't know exactly what that is supposed to mean, but I do know that Domonic Jenkins came to fight.

Youssef Al Hamidi vs. John Murray (2008)

He may not have won the fight, but Youssef Al Hamidi certainly won a lot of fans on a primetime boxing bill that went out live to a big audience. He looks a real credit to the journeyman fraternity, but that performance left me thinking - isn't he too dangerous to be a journeyman?
—Mel Dixon

*When interviewed afterwards he [Al Hamidi] said he was on his way
to work that day when he got the call and turned around and went
home to get his kit - a true road warrior*
—Smithers

Youssef Al Hamidi is a British-based lightweight whose record consisted of four wins, eight defeats and one draw prior to his contest with unbeaten prospect John Murray, 23-0 coming in, on May 10, 2008. On extremely short notice, Al Hamidi traveled from Yorkshire to Nottingham to take the bout against the highly touted Murray at the Nottingham Ice Arena. The duke was on the under-card of the Witter-Bradley championship fight and would give Youssef some great exposure.

A close perusal of their respective records would have flashed a warning sign. Al Hamidi had fought solid opposition and only had been stopped once, and that was a TKO loss to tough Michael Gomez, 33-7 at the time. Only one of his opponents had a losing record.

As for the prospect, Murray, His competition was less than stellar and included Billy Smith twice. The firs time Billy came in at 3-39, but he improved his slate the second time to 8-43. Karl Taylor, 16-78-6, was a point's victim as was Ernie Smith, 10-68-2. So was hapless Anthony Hanna, 19-65-7 coming in. Another point's loser was Jason Nesbit, 2-32. But it's gets worse, as his debut bout was with none other than the Professor himself, Peter Buckley, 30-166-10 at the time. 13 of his opponents had losing records—and major ones at that. Let's do some math.

The combined won-loss record of Murray's foes is an astounding 259-656-42, while Al Hamidi's stands at 200-76- 10.

Indeed, Al Hamidi was introduced by Jimmy Lennon Jr. as "The Spoiler from Dewsbury" He was supposed to roll over for the Murray express. Instead, he just missed derailing it. As it turned out, "The Spoiler" was skillful in the ring and gave as well as he got utilizing sharp jabs, straight lefts and rights, and excellent lateral movement. Murray managed to finish strong as Al Hamidi tired badly on the last two stanzas. Still, he was not here to survive; he was determined to win.

Predictably, the young prospect won the 8-round fight on points as Referee Terry O'Connor scored it 77-75, but he was about the only one to see it that way, as the Syrian born fighter gave Murray almost more than he could handle. The result was soundly booed, as many thought a draw would have been the just call. Had Al Hamidi had time to prepare for this fight, many at ringside said that he likely would have stopped Murray.

Murray improved to 24-0(12), but he will not want anymore per-formances like this. Al Hamadi fell to 4-9-1(1) but despite what his poor record may say, the 30 year old is a talented fighter whose best days may be yet to come.

There was no rolling over this night in Nottingham

Dionisio Miranda vs. Sebastian De-mers (2008)

Fighting a hometown boy in Montreal is never easy, particularly if you come in from Colombia on five day's notice, but if anyone thought Dionisio "Mister Nocaut" Miranda (20-2-1) would roll over, they forgot to check out his last fight with undefeated prospect Peter "Kid Chocolate" Quillin. Miranda almost took out The Kid before losing a UD.

After 10 rounds of solid action, "Mister Nocaut" (20-2-1) beat Ca-nadian Sebastian "Double Trouble" Demers (25-2) in Demer's home town of Montreal, Canada. While Demers used his jab effectively, landed more punches and was busier throughout, Miranda landed the cleaner and more effective shots, particularly when he con-nected with his big right hand. As analyst Teddy Atlas said, it was the quality of the Colombian's punches versus the quantity of Demer's, even though Teddy gave the edge to Demers 95-94. Demer's fatal error was to engage the Colombian bomber in the final two rounds. While he showed the stuff of a true fighter, he could not land the heavier shots.

I had the fight a draw, but the judges had it 95-94, 95-94 and 94-95 giving Mr. Nocaut (his spelling) a SD and the IBF International mid-dleweight title and vacant NABA middleweight title. A knockdown of Demers in round nine counted heavily in giving Miranda the final edge in scoring.

The Judges

All in all, it was a fan friendly fight, but wait, that's not the real story here. The two judges who gave the fight to Miranda were Benoit Roussel and Pasquale Procopio, both from Canada. The judge who scored the fight 95-94 in favor of Demers was Joseph Pasquale from New Jersey. Say what?

On a night when "home cooking" seemed likely to be served (and with memories of the SD decision in the Randall Bailey vs. Herman Ngoudjo fight also in Montreal), these fine judges focused on the fight, remained objective and did their job as professionals. This one should be used as a training film on how to judge a fight, for on this steamy night at the Gare Windsor Salle des Pas Perdus in Montreal Quebec, Canada, Messrs Roussel, Procopio and Pasquale got it right.

Zuri Lawrence vs. Albert Sosnowski (2008)

The Polish crowd composed of great fight fans was poised for a party; a predictable celebration. Hell, why not? Feather-fisted Zuri Lawrence (23-14-4) was coming in on short notice against favored Albert "The Dragon" Sosnowski from Warsaw, Poland who sported a 24-fight win streak. His record coming in was a gaudy 42-1. The crowd was noisy and ready. The delicious smell of pierogis, golabki, and krokiet was in the air. The Polish flag with its two horizontal fields of white on top and red on bottom was in evidence as well.

There was only one problem to this fistic occasion; Lawrence played the role of party-pooper and then some as he beat "The Dragon" by UD. Indeed, the three judges Robin Taylor, Julie Lederman and Steve Weisfeld all saw the fight the same way—80-72.

Using his superior height and reach (of 79'), Zuri was able to out-jab Sosnowski throughout. As he gained confidence going into the later rounds, he rocked the Pole with lefts and rights. Had he been able to turn over his punches and plant his feet, he would have sent Sosnowski to Polski Dreamland. As it was, Sosnowski sported a badly swollen right eye and a cut over his left eye all of which constituted the face of a loser.

Yes, on this rainy night of August 6, 2008 at the Aviator Sports Arena in Brooklyn, the judges did themselves proud and so did Zuri Lawrence as he refused to play the role of rollover. Zuri lacks some things in the ring, but one of them is not heart.

35

THE UPSET

When World War Two ended, I can recall exactly where I was. When JFK was assasinated, I knew where I was. When 9/11 occurred, I also knew exactklly where I was. And when Mike Tyson was knocked into Japanese dreamland by Buster Douglass, I also knew where I was. It was that big of an upset.

Arguably, there is nothing more thrilling than an upset. For some, it means shocking disappointment; for others, it is sudden and pleasant surprise. Kirkland Laing shocked Roberto Duran but himself was later shocked by Buck "Tombstone" Smith. Lloyd Honeyghan did it to Donald Curry. Douglas's KO of Tyson perhaps was the greatest upset in boxing history. George Foreman's KO of Michael Moorer in 1994 was one for the ages, but then Moorer turned the tables on Vassiliy Jirov tens years later. Limited Louis Monaco stopped Kevin McBride in 1997, but McBride himself stopped Mike Tyson eight years later. More recently, Brian Vera pulled one off against a heavily favored Andy Lee. Here are some lesser known but equally interesting ones ones:

What's the Word?

In 1990, higly touted Anthony Hembrick, 14-0, fought Booker T. Word at Fort Bragg in North Carolina (where Hembrick was to perform in fron of many of his former Army buddies). At stake was the vacant USBA light heavyweight title. Hembrick was an Olympic hopeful who had missed the bus on his way to his first fight. By the time he arrived at Chamshil Students' Gymnasium, he had been disqualified and the match was being awarded to Ha Jong-Ho.

Coming into the ring, the heavily favored and over confident Hembrick did one of the most imbecilic and disgusting walk-ins ever witnessed on television. Unimpressed, Word immediately launched an all-out assault that likely ruined Hembreck's future, though he did go undefeated in his next 9 fights. If anyone deserved to be stopped in the first round, it was Hembreck.

Word never diid much after this upset, but he had the satifaction of perpatrating legal assault and battery on a heavily favored "Olympian" in the hostile environment of Fort Bragg.

Clarence's Revenge

This one was on the under card of the Jesse Feliciano-Andrey Tsurkan bout at the Utopia Paradise Theatre in the Bronx in April 2008. Home town guy Jon "The Fighting Marine" Schneider, 7-1-1, was scheduled to fight Clarence Moore, 4-3-1. The Marine had shut out Moore in a 4-rounder in 2007 and was heavily favored to do it again. Hell, what was a guy from West Virginia doing in the Bronx in the first place?

A glance at their respective level of opposition would indicate, however, that Moore had fought the better fighters and, for the most part, in their own home towns. All of Schneider's fights have been in the friendly environs of New York City. Moore was also coming in at 7 fewer pounds reflecting perhaps how determined he was to avenge his earlier loss. He also had far more quality rounds under his no longer ample belt

Still, the stage was set for a Schneider blow-out and, with a disproportionate amount of hoopla, the local fans, including many Marines, were anticipatory and excited for this televised 6-rounder to begin.

The hometown favorite won the first round impressively, but in the second, he walked into a short uppercut followed by a left hook. Stunned badly, he was stopped in his tracks and unable to tie up Moore. He then was met by a volley of wild shots until a vicious uppercut got in and positioned him for the end. Moore quickly followed up with another equally malefic uppercut which sent The Fighting Marine to Jarhead Heaven at the 2:48 mark of the second round.

The crowd was silenced and stunned at the sudden turn of events, while Moore himself seemed shocked as tears of joy welled up in his eyes. Schneider sat on his stool, dejected and wondering what had just occurred as he was consoled by trainer and former Champion Lou Del Valle.

This had been a thriller for as long as it lasted; heck, this had been an upset pure and simple, and now all the pre-fight hype didn't amount to spit. A 33 year old cruiserweight named Moore out of Charleston, West Virginia saw to that.

"Minnesota Ice" melts

On April 26, 2008, heavyweight Joey "Minnesota Ice" Abell, 20-1, met Andrew Greeley, 14-20-2 in his friendly home confines of Rochester, Minnesota. The fight was a co-feature with Raphael Butler vs. Otis Tisdale (which hometown favorite Butler Won by TKO as expected).

Abell was on an 11 fight winning streak including 10 wins by stoppage, but Nigerian heavyweight Teke "The African Prince" Oruh appeared to be the only semi-recognizable name on his schedule. Interestingly, Abell beat Oruh by a close MD in a fight televised live from Saint Lucia. Even more interesting, Abell had fought 8 times in the fabled Blue Horizon in Philadelphia and toted up a record of 7 (KO) -1 (KO). Each KO came early. He was fast becoming a Philly favorite.

As for Greeley, he had lost his last six in a row, but had fought the far better opposition and had only been stopped once in that skein. Among his conquerors were Andre Purlette (40-3), contender Kevin Johnson (19-0), Terry Smith (30-5-1), Malik Scott (30-0), Travis Walker (27-1) twice, Brit Audley Harrison (22-3), Eddie Chambers (30-1), and undefeated Chris Arreola (23-0).

Although Greeley won his first 8 professional fights, he settled in as an "opponent," albeit a tough one after losing to Tim Williamson in 2001. His last win prior to the Abell contest was against Dennis McKinney, 27-41-1 at the time.

The stage was set for Greeley to lose in spectacular style to the hometown hero. Butler had done it against Tisdale in 4 rounds. Now it was Abell's turn.

Abell won the first three rounds easily mixing his punches well. He looked particularly sharp on this night in Minnesota scoring points with a hard jab and straight lefts. Greeley was fighting cautiously seemingly waiting for an opportunity to unload though this resident of Monroe, Louisiana has never been known as a heavy puncher. Abell was dominating going into the fourth round, while Greeley was waiting to counter. At this point, the crowd started yelling for Abell to "take this guy out". But someone forgot to tell Greeley.

Abell turn up the pressure in the fourth and trapped Greeley on the ropes and let loose with two hard rights but left his hands low. Greeley answered with two hard rights to the head that sent Abell down hard over the bottom rope. Abell made it to his feet on shaky legs as the round was coming to a close. Greeley rushed Abell and landed a big over hand right to the jaw along the ropes and Abell's hands dropped to his sides where Mark Nelson shockingly waived the fight off at 2:58 of round four. The crowd was stunned and silenced.

Getting caught by this haymaker in a bout that was supposed to feature Abell in his home state and move him on to better things results in a huge road block for Joey, one from which he may not recover.

As for Greeley, he still will be considered an "opponent," but one capable of pulling off a career spoiling upset. Make that "dangerous opponent."

Sudden Lightening at the Roxy

**Trainer John Scully and Oliver
(Photo courtesy of ESB)**

Mike Oliver, 22-0, met Reynaldo Lopez, 28-5-2, at the Roxbury in Boston on April 7, 2008, and was heavily favored to remain undefeated. For all practical purposes, Oliver, out of nearby Hartford, was the home town fighter.

Lopez was coming off a one punch blow out loss to Daniel Ponce de Leon and a UD loss to talented Cristian Mijares, Fighting for 15 years, some thought he might be ring worn and made to order for the speedy Oliver.

Though he seemed overly tight and tense, Oliver won the first two rounds with his superior speed. The third started out slowly with some roughhousing and then the fighters engaged in an exchange in a neutral corner. Oliver missed with a right and Lopez threw a long left that caught Oliver flush at the 1:22 mark and sent him to the canvas face first. He barely beat the count and when the referee saw that he was helpless, the action was immediately halted.

Out of the blue, Reynaldo Lopez had pulled off a big upset derailing the Oliver Express and resurrecting his own career—and all this was done in the friendly confines of his opponent's home area.

This was the very essence of an upset in every meaning of the word and was affirmed by the silence of the stunned crowd.

Now, the challenge will be to overcome this adversity and get back on track. If anyone can do it, Mike can. As for Lopez, he gets another shot at a good pay day and deserves every penny.

The Friday Night "Mismatch"

This one was fought in Rhode Island on May 23, 2008, and was to showcase the talents of Aaron "Awsome" Williams who was coming off a sensational knockout of Andre Purlette. Many have called Williams the top prospect in boxing, though the quality of his opposition has not been all that great.

Before the fight, commentator Teddy Atlas commented on the distinct possibility of Williams ending matters early and the fact this match up might even be a mismatch based on "La Pantera" having lost 3 of his last 4 by TKO. However, these losses had come against undefeated Tavoris Cloud, the capable Lafarrell Bunting, and Jorge Fernando Castro, 129-11-3. Teddy expressed moderate surprise that the R.I. Commission had allowed it to take place, also commenting that Jose Luis had gained considerable weight for this fight thus making Williams the much bigger man in natural weight. The Columbian also had taken the fight on short notice and all the cards seems stacked against him.

What Atlas forgot to add (or maybe didn't know) was that Jose Luis Herrera stopped the great Castro back in 2006. He had also iced the admittedly limited George Blades in his last duke. "Pantera" is a KO-or-be-KOd type with one punch knockout power whose record was 15 (KO 15)-4 (KO 4) coming in. "Awesome" Aaron was 17-0-1. Between them, they participated in 17 first round blow outs.

After a fast start in round one, it looked as if Teddy Atlas would be spot on as Williams assaulted Herrera with a barrage of shots that backed him into a corner and dropped him like a sack. Inexplicitly, however, the officious doctor at ringside then took what seemed like an inordinate amount of time to examine the Columbian in effect giving him enough time to recover.

Williams fought with explosive spurts going into the fifth and completely controlled the action. All of a sudden, as he made one of his patented defensive moves to his right, he was caught with a smashing right and then another that wobbled him and slammed him into the ropes. Atlas earlier had warned about this and once again, he was on the money. Williams was given an 8 count. He was badly hurt and mugged to a corner where he went to the canvas without being punched seemingly to get himself together, but when got up, he was ready to do the Chicken Dance. At this point, Referee Sam Burgos directed him to the doctor who examined him very carefully. When "Awesome" called the doctor "Ref," the fight was halted, and rightly so since Herrera was poised to do significant damage to the defenseless prospect no more.

To Teddy Atlas's great credit, he said at the end of the telecast that "apparently the Rhode Island Commission knew what it was doing when it matched these two boxers.

2008 continued to be the Year of the Upset.

Note: See Appendix E which lists other notable and some not so notable upsets

36

THE SERENGETI

There are few things that sap the morale of an opponent more than knowing from the start that the most he can achieve is to keep the deficit respectable.
–Mike Casey

For all of the years that I'd seen him, Monzon never gasped for air, tired or opened his mouth gagging for oxygen in any round.
–George Diaz Smith

There is something primal about seek and destroy fighters that reminds me of the thrill and excitement of a cheetah chasing its prey as portrayed on the Discovery Channel. There is a beauty that goes with the danger as the predators stake out the migrating wildlife on East Africa's vast Serengeti. The images are stunning and run from majestic to wondrous to horrifying. They include the invasion of their prey's privacy and its unwanted contact, the savage execution, and brutal end. Quite simply, it is a sequence of "Stalk, Stun and Kill."

Fighters like Joe Louis, Rocky Marciano, Roberto Duran, Julio Caesar Chavez, Khaosai Galaxy, Alexis Arguello, to name a few, defined this style during their respective reigns of terror. They would start the chase as soon as the bell rang cutting off the ring and getting closer and closer until they made initial contact. Pipino Cuevas (pre-Tommy Hearns) was a classic tracker who instilled fear in his opponents and rendered them vulnerable with his jack hammer left hooks. He then dispatched them with no further adieu. The "track them down and execute style of fighting" exemplified by these men has become a part of fistic lore.

One of my favorites was Carlos "Escopeta" Monzon who seemed to push his punches and seemed stiff as he kept on coming, but "seem" is one thing and "reality" is quite another. Once he commenced the stalk, few escaped. As fellow-writer, Mike Casey puts it, "Not to put too fine a point on it, there were times when Carlos Monzon looked downright ordinary when viewed through a strictly technical eye. Perhaps that is what threw so many people in the early days and what continues to throw the new generation."

Another favorite was Galaxy. Sometimes called "The Thai Tyson," this predator possessed bricks in his fists. With a staggering KO percentage of 86%, he had one-punch knock out power. Like a spider paralyzing its prey with a sting, he could stun an opponent with a single punch, setting him up for the end. When this happened, his fists and arms would be held high ready to cut loose. As he got close, he would impose his tremendous physique as the frenzied Thai crowd would be up and roaring. He became the very essence of a stalker closing off the ring, making contact, and quickly accomplishing the kill with a variety of power shots thrown with uncanny accuracy and malefic intent.

These days, Kelly "The Ghost" Pavlick and Antonio "Tony" Margorito are premier "stalk stun and close" types offering fans a particularly thrilling kind of bout. Against a backdrop of "Puerto Rico Puerto Rico" rocking the arenas in which he did (and does) his work, Miguel "Junito" Cotto tracked and destroyed such tough fighters as Zab Judah, Carlos Quintana, Kelson Pinto, Gianluca Branco (stopped for the first time in his career), Mohamad Abdulaev, Randall Bailey and Cesar Bazan. But then he met Margarito who has refined and perhaps redefined the technique, and when two seek and destroy guys meet, it's a classic paradox of an irresistible force meeting an immovable object. Something big has to give.

Margarito

By now, all serious fans are familiar with this monster's style of starting slow but using a high punch volume and incredible incoming pressure to wear out his opponents setting them up for brutal closure.

However, with "Tony," there are three additional factors that accentuate his particular brand of seek and destroy.

1) His granite-like chin allows him to walk through his opponents and keep the Pressure on.

2) His stamina is great and he gets stronger as the fight progresses.

3) And most startling, he has a unique way of virtually jogging after his tiring foes, something guaranteed to deplete anyone's spirit. Michael Katsidis is another who does this, but he doesn't do numbers one and two above to compliment it.

Marvelous Marvin Hagler, Monzon, Arguello, Galaxy, Cuevas, Duran, Chavez, Katsidis, Cotto, Pavlik, Vic Darchinyan (who demonstrated this technique to perfection against slick Christian Mijares as recently as November 2008) and others seem to belong to this special club. But now, an incoming force out of Tijuana who continually attacks until his opponents can no longer continue has become the modern day president.

37

REELING' IN THE YEARS: PART THREE

Yesterday, everybody smoked his last cigar, took his last drink and swore his last oath. Today, we are a pious and exemplary community. Thirty days from now, we shall have cast our reformation to the winds and gone to cutting our ancient shortcomings considerably shorter than ever.
–Mark Twain

I have come to the conclusion that whether or not a person is a religious believer does not matter. Far more important is that they be a good human being.
–Dalai Lama

2001

9/11 and the sight of the second plane going into the Tower gives a new definition to horror in plain sight. Everyone will remember where they were when the second plane hits. Innocent Americans are killed. George W. Bush does the right thing and attacks the Taliban who harbor Al Qaeda terrorists. Its payback time and Americans want it badly. With carpet bombing and the Northern Alliance, revenge is achieved in Afghanistan. But Bush wants more and concludes, wrongly, that Iraq has weapons of mass destruction. Bush attacks Iraq as Iran watches the events unfold. Shock and awe makes for great theater. Body counts don't.

"Mission Accomplished" is a sign displayed on the USS Abraham Lincoln as President Bush addresses the United States on May 1, 2003. Bush miscalculates badly. We are still in Iraq in 2008 and over 4,000 U.S. soldiers have been killed. No one seems to understand Islamic culture. Secretary of State Condoleezza Rice gives stern looks to those perceived as enemies.

Chunks of ice fall out of the artic. Al Gore predicts environmental doom unless we reform. He wins big awards. Everybody becomes "green." Enviro-wakos abound. It's an express train moving fast.

Y2K Fears prove to be a sham.

Super Bowl 41 breaks ground with the first two Black Coaches. The success of football's Tony Dungy and Lovie Smith transcends sports

. . .

Boxing again reflects the changing times. It started with Russian Kostya Tszyu, but then the Klitschko brothers emerge from the Ukraine. Russians Oleg Maskiev, Nikolai Valuev, Aleksandr Povetkin, and Sultan Ibragimov make their considerable mark on the heavyweight scene and so does Ruslan Chagaev from the Republic of Uzbekistan who beats the giant Valuev. Serguei Lyakhovich from Belarus loses the title to Shannon Briggs but Ibragimov wins it back. Bottom line: these guys are the real McCoy and have changed the boxing scene as the new millennium begins. Can anyone stop them? Can anyone restore luster to the heavyweight division? Maybe Nigerian Sam Peter can do it, but this sure as hell is not the '50s, 70's or 90's.

Floyd Mayweather Jr. rules boxing and beats Oscar De La Hoya and Ricky Hatton in mega fights. De La Hoya-Mayweather II is being lined up but Mayweather "retires." Is Oscar wearing out his welcome? A kid named Pavlik excites boxing fans as he destroys opponents with a savage ferocity. But a guy named Margorito raises the bar when it comes to savage ferocity. His fight with Miguel Cotto is a classic. Paul Williams lurks And something else looms and it involves lousy Pay Per View fights that should not be Pay Per View. Is this the future?

On line boxing writers now do their thing, and boxing magazines begin to disappear. Oscar De La Hoya's Golden Boy Promotions buys Ring Magazine. Say what? Calzaghi beats Kessler in a global mega fight and then beats an aging Hopkins. A guy named Manny Pacquiao explodes onto the scene and thrills fans everywhere. He is the new Mr Charisma."

Mike Quarry dies of pugilistic dementia; he is only 55. Incredibly, Tommy Morrison is still fighting, and Saoul Mamby and Iran Barkley almost fought on some Indian Reservation in Idaho in February 2008. Mamby later fights off shore at age 60. The more thing change the more they stay the same.

I want to say to Tommy and I hope he's listening. Give it up. You
were former heavyweight champion of the world. You beat George
Foreman. You should put that on your chest and wear it. No matter
what people say, you were the heavyweight champ of the world
so why continue to go out there and stress yourself out.
–Larry Holmes

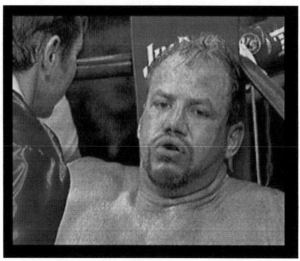

An older Tommy Morrison (Photo courtesy of ESB)

•   •   •

Elsewhere in sports, steroids are the rage in more ways than one as wrestlers do horrible things and baseball players are named in a growing scandal. Asterisks loom.

In 2004, a monster earthquake generates a monster Indian Ocean tsunami that ends up killing more than 225,000 people in many different countries.

Hurricane Katrina hits in 2005 and is the costliest and one of the deadliest in US history. Katrina is Bush's Hurricane Andrew but far worse. In New Orleans, the flood protection system designed and built by the US Army Corps of Engineers failed in 53 different places. FEMA director Michael Brown resigns in spite of having received praise from Bush with the phrase, "Brownie, you're doing a heck of a job," as hundreds die and thousands become homeless. Huh?

Geraldo Rivera of Fox News "tearfully" pleads for authorities to either send help or evacuate the thousands of evacuees. An exhausted and frustrated Shep Smith of Fox tells Bill O'Reilly "now you just wait a minute, O'Reilly" and immediately becomes a righteous dude, something Geraldo will never become, but Anderson Cooper will. *Mississippi Gov. Haley Barbour rocks; Gov. Kathleen Blanco of Louisiana does not. Mayor Ray Nagin is hard to read.*

"We just learned of the convention center – we being the federal government – today." –FEMA Director Michael Brown, to ABC's Ted

Koppel, Sept. 1, 2005, to which Koppel responded: "Don't you guys watch television? Don't you guys listen to the radio? Our reporters have been reporting on it for more than just today."

Bush's popularity sinks to new lows. The Beltway Snipers don't help. Virginia Tech becomes Bush's Oklahoma City.

Movies like Mystic River, The Departed and Gone Baby Gone vibe Boston noir and are well received. So are the American Gangster and Frank Lucas. Daniel Day Lewis once again shows how talented he is. New Country for Old Men features a new type of monster.

Here comes the credit crunch and foreclosures. "Prime evil" fear permeates. The stock market goes down 360 points on October 19, 2007, exactly twenty years from Black Monday. Monster write-offs are taken at Wachovia, Citicorp, Merrill Lynch and other financial institutions and are scary as hell. The market begins the painful process of self-correction. Bear Stearns wobbles and is bought before a panic ensues. Freddie Mac and Fannie Mae need a rescue. Greenspan says "wipe out their shareholders." Huh! It's more bad news for Bush. Self correction won't work in this crisis. He seems oblivious. What me worry? Paulson fills the breech.

Monday, september, 15, 2008 signals another Black Monday as the Dow loses over 500 points sparked by Lehaman Brother's bankruptcy filing. Other institutions are on the precipice. This is scary and ugly; people are plainly worried about their life savings as Corporados leave with hefty severance packages. The giant insurance company AIG, is bailed out. Finally, Paulson comes up with a plan to stem the tide and get the toxic stuff off the table, but at what cost? Will it work? A trillion is no longer an unusual number. For the first time. Some even refer to a quadrillion. This is a paradigm shift of historic proportions. Could this be the end of capitalism as we have known it?

Wild fires rage in California but victims receive more attention than those who suffered in New Orleans. Chalk it up to "lessons learned" or is it something else?

The former Pakistan Prime Minister Benazir Bhutto is assassinated on December 26, 2007 at a political rally in Rawalpindi. The world grieves.

People are openly challenging the religious right and blaming them for the chaos and turmoil that abounds under Bush.

Here come Hillary, she is female, hear her roar. Romney looks like the GOP'S man but falters. A guy named Huckabee is making some noise, but McCain comes on strong and rules the GOP. Obama is making the most noise. He seeks change; he is change. But his reverend is a millstone around his neck. After North Carolina, Obama, Obama, OBAMA. Hillary hangs on as the 10th begins, but she needs a knockout to win. She doesn't get it. Obama, Obama, OBAMA.

It's McCaine vs. Obama. The debates begin. The signs go up. The inuendos fly.

Iraq continues……. Iran looms.

An earthquake in 2008 kills over 60,000 in China. The death toll in a cyclone in Myanmar exceeds exceedes 100,000.

The price of gas hits $ 4.00 a gallon in 2008. Oil hits $ 147 a barrel but then drops below 100. The price of Escalades drops. It's time for the hybrid; maybe it's time for a recession.

Obama selects Biden; McCaine picks Palin. Where's the Beef? Will Bush's legacy be the Dot Com fiasco, Iraq, corporate accounting scandals, Katrina, and the unwinding of our financial system? History will be the judge.

Obama wins! History is made. Hope springs eternal…..

APPENDIX A

Career record of Joey LaMotta

Date	Opponent	Location	Result
1946-11-05	Freddie Flores	Park Arena, Bronx, NY,	L PTS 10
1946-10-21	Freddie Flores	Laurel Garden, Newark, NJ	L KO 4
1946-09-12	Anton Raadik	Wrigley Field, Chicago	L PTS 10
1946-08-07	Gene Boland	U. of Detroit Stadium	W PTS 10
1946-05-10	Joe Blackwood	Boston Garden	L PTS 10
1946-04-12	Joe Blackwood	Boston Garden	D PTS 10
1946-03-29	Johnny Johnson	Boston Garden	W TKO 4
1946-03-18	Tony Riccio	Laurel Garden, Newark, NJ	W PTS 8
1946-03-12	Bobby Berger	Park Arena, Bronx, NY	W PTS 8
1946-02-05	Bobby Berger	Park Arena, Bronx, NY	W PTS 8
1945-12-07	Art Brown	Chicago Stadium	W PTS 10
1945-11-23	Johnny Jones	Boston Garden	W KO 5
1945-10-23	"Indian" Gomez	Park Arena, Bronx, NY	W KO 2
1945-10-15	Larney Moore	Stanley Arena, New Britain	W KO 5
1945-10-09	Dan Aldrich	Park Arena, Bronx, NY	W KO 1
1945-09-26	Martin Doyle	Comiskey Park, Chicago	W TKO 2
1945-09-15	Ballesandro Carubia	Brooklyn	W TKO 4

Date	Opponent	Venue	Result
1945-09-04	Jimmy Mills	Sterling Oval, Bronx, NY	W KO 48
1945-08-13	Lew Perez	Stamford, CT,	W KO 2
1945-08-10	Billy Johnson	Madison Square Garden, NY	W PTS 6
1945-06-29	Jack Garrity	Carney Auditorium, Erie, PA	W KO 2
1945-06-25	Charlie Finley	Stamford, Ct	W KO 1
1945-06-19	Jimmy Davis	White Plains, NY	W KO 4
1945-06-11	Tom Collins	Queensboro Arena, LI City	W PTS 6
1945-05-16	Jimmy Mills	Paterson, NJ	L PTS 7
1945-05-02	Jimmy Mills	Paterson, NJ	D PTS 6
1945-04-28	Lee Black	Ridgewood Grove, Brooklyn	W TKO 3
1945-04-27	Dave Carver	Boston Garden	W KO 2
1945-04-20	Fernand	Demers St. Nicholas Arena, NYC	W TKO 1
1945-04-10	Baudelio Valencia County	Center, White Plain	W KO 3
1945-03-26	Al Jackson	Chicago	W KO 1
1945-03-19	Jimmy	Campbell Norfolk, Virginia	W KO 1
1945-03-13	Lee Black	County Center, White Plains	W KO 2
1945-03-06	Baudelio	Valencia Jersey Gardens Jersey City	W PTS 6
1945-02-27	Ernest Barnwell	County Center, White Plains,	W PTS 6
1945-02-24	Jerry McGee	Ridgewood Grove, Brooklyn	W KO 2
1945-02-20	Buddy Jackson	Jersey Gardens, Jersey City	W KO 1
1945-02-13	Lew Perez	County Center, White Plains	W PTS 4
1945-02-06	Charley Howard	Westchester Cty. Center	W TKO 1

Career Record: 32 (KO 22) - 5- 2 (39 fights)

APPENDIX B

Career Record of Willie Pep

© Cyber Boxing Zone

Record Courtesy of Tracy Callis, Historian, International Boxing Research Organization

Date	Opponent	Location	Result
1940-07-03	James McGovern	Hartford, CT.	W PTS 4
1940-07-25	Joey Marcus	Hartford	W PTS 4
1940-08-08	Joey Wasnick	Hartford	W KO 3
1940-08-29	Tommy Burns	Hartford	W KO 1
1940-09-05	Joey Marcus	New Britain, CT	W PTS 6
1940-09-19	Jack Moore	Hartford	W PTS 6
1940-10-03	Jimmy Riche	Waterbury, CT	W KO 3
1940-10-24	Jimmy McAllister	New Haven,	W PTS 4
1940-11-22	Carlo Daponde	New Britain	W KO 6
1940-11-29	Frank Topazio	New Britain	W KO 5
1940-12-06	Jim Mutane	New Britain	W KO 2
1941-01-28	Augie Almeda	New Haven	W KO 6
1941-02-03	Joe Echevarria	Holyoke, MA	W PTS 6
1941-02-10	Don Lyons	Holyoke	W KO 2
1941-02-17	Ruby Garcia	Holyoke	W PTS 6

1941-03-03 Ruby Garcia	Holyoke	W PTS 6
1941-03-25 Marty Shapiro	Hartford	W PTS 6
1941-03-31 Joey Gatto	Holyoke	W KO 2
1941-04-14 Henry Vasquez	Holyoke	W PTS 6
1941-04-22 Joey Silva	Hartford	W PTS 6
1941-05-06 Lou Pugliese	Hartford	W KO 2
1941-05-12 Johnny Cockfield	Holyoke	W PTS 6
1941-06-24 Eddie DeAngelis	Hartford	W KO 3
1941-07-15 Jimmy Gilligan	Hartford	W PTS 8
1941-08-01 Harry Hintlian	Manchester, CT	W PTS 6
1941-08-05 Blond Tiger	Hartford	W KO 3
1941-08-12 Eddie Flores	Thompsonville, CT	W KO 1
1941-09-26 Jackie Harris	New Haven	W KO 1
1941-10-10 Carlos Manzano	New Haven	W PTS 8
1941-10-22 Connie Savoie	Hartford	W KO 2
1941-11-07 Buddy Spencer	Hollywood, CA	W PTS 4
1941-11-24 Davey Crawford	Holyoke	W PTS 8
1941-12-12 Ruby Garcia	New York City	W PTS 4
1942-01-08 Mexican Joe	Fall River, MA	W KO 4
1942-01-16 Sammy Parrota	New York City	W PTS 4
1942-01-27 Abie Kaufman	Hartford	W PTS 8
1942-02-10 Angelo Callura	Hartford	W PTS 8
1942-02-24 Willie Roache	Hartford	W PTS 8
1942-03-18 Johnny Compo	New Haven	W PTS 8
1942-04-14 Spider Armstrong	Hartford	W KO 4
1942-05-04 Curley Nichols	New Haven	W PTS 8

1942-05-12 Aaron Seltzer	Hartford	W PTS 8
1942-05-26 Joey Iannotti	Hartford	W PTS 8
1942-06-23 Joey Archibald	Hartford	W PTS 10
1942-07-21 Abe Denner	Hartford	W PTS 12
1942-08-01 Joey Silva	Waterbury, CT	TKO 7
1942-08-10 Pedro Hernandez	Hartford	W PTS 10
1942-08-20 Nat Litfin	West Haven, CT	W PTS 10
1942-09-01 Bobby Ivy	Hartford	W TKO 10
1942-09-10 Frank Franconeri	NYC	W TKO 1
1942-09-22 Vince Dell'Orto	Hartford	W PTS 10
1942-10-05 Bobby McIntire	Holyoke	W PTS 10
1942-10-16 Joey Archibald	Providence, RI	W UD 10
1942-10-27 George Zengaras	Hartford	W PTS 10
1942-11-20 Chalky Wright	NYC	W UD 15

NYSAC World Featherweight Title

1942-12-14 Jose Aponte Torres	Washington, DC	W KO 7
1942-12-21 Joey Silva	Jacksonville, FL	W TKO 9
1943-01-04 Vince Dell'Orto	New Orleans	W PTS 10
1943-01-19 Bill Speary	Hartford	W PTS 10
1943-01-29 Allie Stolz	NYC	W PTS 10
1943-02-11 Davey Crawford	Boston	W PTS 10
1943-02-15 Bill Speary	Baltimore	W PTS 10
1943-03-02 Lou Transparenti	Hartford	W KO 6
1943-03-19 Sammy Angott	NYC	L PTS 10
1943-03-29 Bobby McIntire	Detroit	W UD 10
1943-04-09 Sal Bartolo	Boston	W SD 10

1943-04-19 Angel Aviles	Tampa, FL	W PTS 10
1943-04-26 Jackie Wilson	Pittsburgh	W PTS 12
1943-06-08 Sal Bartolo	Boston	W UD 15

NYSAC World Featherweight Title

1944-04-04 Leo Francis	Hartford	W PTS 10
1944-04-20 Snooks Lacey	New Haven	W PTS 10
1944-05-01 Jackie Leamus	Philadelphia	W PTS 10
1944-05-19 Frankie Rubino	Chicago	W PTS 10
1944-05-23 Joey Bagnato	Buffalo, NY	W KO 2
1944-06-06 Julie Kogon `	Hartford	W PTS 10
1944-07-07 Willie Joyce	Chicago	W PTS 10
1944-07-17 Manuel Ortiz	Boston	W PTS 10
1944-08-04 Lulu Costantino	Waterbury, CT	W PTS 10
1944-08-28 Joey Peralta	West Springfield, MA	W PTS 10
1944-09-19 Charley Cabey Lewis	Hartford	W TKO 8
1944-09-29 Chalky Wright	NYC	W UD 15

NYSAC World Featherweight Title

1944-10-25 Jackie Leamus	Montreal QC	W UD 10
1944-11-14 Charley Cabey Lewis	Hartford	W PTS 10
1944-11-27 Pedro Hernandez	Washington, DC	W PTS 10
1944-12-05 Chalky Wright	Cleveland	W UD 10
1945-01-23 Ralph Walton	Hartford	W PTS 10
1945-02-05 Willie Roache	New Haven	W UD 10
1945-02-19 Phil Terranova	NYC	W UD 15

NYSAC World Featherweight Title

1945-10-30 Paulie Jackson	Hartford	W PTS 8

1945-11-05 Mike Martyk	Buffalo	W TKO 5
1945-11-26 Eddie Giosa	Boston	W PTS 10
1945-12-05 Harold Gibson	Lewiston ME	W PTS 10
1945-12-13 Jimmy McAllister	Baltimore	D PTS 10
1946-01-15 Johnny Virgo	Buffalo	W KO 2
1946-02-13 Jimmy Joyce	Buffalo	W PTS 10
1946-03-01 Jimmy McAllister	NYC	W KO 2
1946-03-26 Jackie Wilson	Kansas City, MO	W UD 10
1946-04-08 Georgie Knox	Providence	W KO 3
1946-05-06 Ernie Petrone	New Haven	W PTS 10
1946-05-13 Joey Angelo	Providence	W PTS 10
1946-05-22 Jose Aponte Torres	St. Louis, MO	W UD 10
1946-05-27 Jimmy Joyce	Minneapolis, MN	W PTS 8
1946-06-07 Sal Bartolo	NYC	W KO 12
1946-07-10 Harold Gibson	Buffalo	W TKO 7
1946-07-25 Jackie Graves	Minneapolis	W TKO 8
1946-08-26 Doll Rafferty	Milwaukee, WI	W KO 6
1946-09-04 Walter Kolby	Buffalo	W KO 5
1946-09-17 Lefty LaChance	Hartford	W TKO 3
1946-11-01 Paulie Jackson	Minneapolis	W PTS 10
1946-11-15 Tomas Beato	Waterbury, CT	W KO 2
1946-11-27 Chalky Wright	Milwaukee	W KO 3
1947-06-17 Victor Flores	Hartford	W PTS 10
1947-07-01 Joey Fortuna	Albany, NY	W KO 5
1947-07-08 Leo LeBrun	Norwalk, CT	W PTS 8
1947-07-11 Jean Barriere	North Adams, MA	W KO 4

1947-07-15 Paulie Jackson	New Bedford, MA	W PTS 10
1947-07-23 Humberto Sierra	Hartford	W PTS 10
1947-08-22 Jock Leslie	Flint, MI	W KO 12
1947-10-21 Jean Barriere	Portland, ME	W KO 1
1947-10-27 Archie Wilmer	Philadelphia	W MD 10
1947-12-22 Alvaro Estrada	Lewiston, ME	W UD 10
1947-12-30 Lefty LaChance	Manchester, NH	W TKO 8
1948-01-06 Pedro Biesca	Hartford	W PTS 10
1948-01-12 Jimmy McAllister	St. Louis	W PTS 10
1948-01-19 Joey Angelo	Boston	W UD 10
1948-02-24 Humberto Sierra	Miami, FL	W TKO 10
1948-05-07 Leroy Willis	Detroit	W PTS 10
1948-05-19 Charley Cabey	Lewis Milwaukee	W PTS 10
1948-06-17 Miguel Acevedo	Minneapolis	W PTS 10
1948-06-25 Luther Burgess	Flint, MI	W PTS 10
1948-07-28 Young Junior	Utica	W KO 1
1948-08-03 Teddy 'Redtop'	Davis Hartford	W PTS 10
1948-08-17 Teddy 'Redtop'	Davis Hartford	W PTS 10
1948-09-02 Johnny Dell	Waterbury	W TKO 8
1948-09-10 Paddy DeMarco	NYC	W UD 10
1948-10-12 Chuck Burton	Jersey City	W PTS 8
1948-10-19 Johnny LaRusso	Hartford	W PTS 10
1948-10-29 Sandy Saddler	New York	L KO 4
1948-12-20 Hermie Freeman	Boston	W UD 10
1949-01-17 Teddy 'Redtop'	Davis St. Louis	W PTS 10
1949-02-11 Sandy Saddler	NYC	W UD 15
1949-06-06 Luis Ramos	New Haven	W PTS 10

1949-06-14 Al Pennino	Pittsfield, MA	W UD 10
1949-06-20 Johnny LaRusso	West Springfield, MA	W PTS 10
1949-07-12 Jean Mougin	Syracuse, NY	W UD 10
1949-09-20 Eddie Compo	Waterbury, CT	W TKO 7
1949-12-12 Harold Dade	St. Louis	W PTS 10
1950-01-16 Charley Riley	St. Louis	W KO 5
1950-02-06 Roy Andrews	Boston	W PTS 10
1950-02-22 Jimmy Warren	Miami	W UD 10
1950-03-17 Ray Famechon	New York	W UD 15
1950-05-15 Art Llanos	Hartford	W KO 2
1950-06-01 Terry Young	Milwaukee	W UD 10
1950-06-26 Bobby Timpson	Hartford	W PTS 10
1950-07-25 Bobby Bell	Washington, DC	W UD 10
1950-08-02 Proctor Heinold	Scranton, PA	W PTS 10
1950-09-08 Sandy Saddler	Bronx	L RTD 8
1951-01-30 Tommy Baker	Hartford	W TKO 4
1951-02-26 Billy Hogan	Sarasota	W KO 2
1951-03-05 Carlos Chavez	New Orleans	W UD 10
1951-03-26 Pat Iacobucci	Miami Beach	W UD 10
1951-04-17 Baby Neff Ortiz	St. Louis	W TKO 5
1951-04-27 Eddie Chavez	San Francisco	W PTS 10
1951-06-04 Jesus Compos	Baltimore	W PTS 10
1951-09-04 Corky Gonzales	New Orleans	W UD 10
1951-09-26 Sandy Saddler	NYC	L RTD 9
1952-04-29 Santiago Gonzalez	Tampa	W UD 10
1952-05-05 Kenny Leach	Columbus, GA	W PTS 10
1952-05-10 James Buddy	Baggett Aiken, SC	W KO 5

1952-05-21 Claude Hammond	Miami Beach	W UD 10
1952-06-30 Tommy Collins	Boston	L TKO 6
1952-09-03 Billy Lima	Pensacola, FL	W PTS 10
1952-09-11 Bobby Woods	Vancouver, BC	W PTS 10
1952-10-01 Armand Savoie	Chicago	W UD 10
1952-10-20 Billy Lima	Jacksonville	W UD 10
1952-11-05 Manny Castro	Miami Beach	W TKO 5
1952-11-19 Fabela Chavez	St. Louis	W UD 10
1952-12-05 Jorge Sanchez	West Palm Beach, FL	W PTS 10
1953-01-19 Billy Lauderdale	Nassau, Bahamas	W UD 10
1953-01-27 Dave Mitchell	Miami Beach	W UD 10
1953-02-10 Jose Alvarez	San Antonio, TX	W PTS 10
1953-03-31 Joey Gambino	Tampa	W UD 10
1953-04-07 Noel Paquette	Miami Beach	W PTS 10
1953-05-13 Jackie Blair	Fort Worth, TX	W UD 10
1953-06-05 Pat Marcune	NYC	W TKO 10
1953-11-21 Sonny Luciano	Charlotte, NC	W UD 10
1953-12-04 Davey Allen	West Palm Beach	W PTS 10
1953-12-08 Billy Lima	Houston	W KO 2
1953-12-15 Tony Longo	Miami Beach	W UD 10
1954-01-19 Dave Seabrooke	Jacksonville	W PTS 10
1954-02-26 Lulu Perez	NYC	L TKO 2
1954-07-24 Mike Tourcotte	Mobile, AL	W UD 10
1954-08-18 Til LeBlanc	Moncton, NB, Canada	W UD 10
1954-11-01 Mario 'Eladio' Colon	Daytona Beach, FL,	W PTS 10
1955-03-11 Merrill Olmstead	Bennington, VT	W PTS 10
1955-03-22 Charley Titone	Holyoke	W PTS 10

1955-03-30 Gil Cadilli	Parks AF Base, CA,	L SD 10
1955-05-18 Gil Cadilli	Detroit	W UD 10
1955-06-01 Joey Cam	Boston	W TKO 4
1955-06-14 Mickey Mars	Miami Beach	W TKO 7
1955-07-12 Hector Rodriguez	Bridgeport, CT	W PTS 10
1955-09-13 Jimmy Ithia	Hartford	W TKO 6
1955-09-27 Henry 'Pappy' Gault	Holyoke	W UD 10
1955-10-10 Charley Titone	Brockton, MA	W UD 10
1955-11-29 Henry 'Pappy' Gault	Tampa	W UD 10
1955-12-13 Lee Carter	Houston	W TKO 4
1955-12-28 Andy Arel	Miami Beach	W UD 10
1956-03-13 Kid Campeche	Tampa	W UD 10
1956-03-27 James Buddy Baggett	Beaumont, TX	W PTS 10
1956-04-17 Jackie Blair	Hartford	W PTS 10
1956-05-22 Manuel Armenteros	San Antonio	W TKO 7
1956-06-19 Russell Tague	Miami Beach	W UD 10
1956-07-04 Hector Bacquettes	Lawton, OK	W KO 4
1957-04-23 Cesar Morales	Ft. Lauderdale	W PTS 10
1957-05-10 Manny Castro	Florence, SC	W UD 10
1957-07-16 Manny Castro	El Paso, TX	W PTS 10
1957-07-23 Russell Tague	Houston	W UD 10
1957-12-17 Jimmy Connors	Boston	W UD 10
1958-01-14 Tommy Tibbs	Boston	L SD 10
1958-03-31 Prince Johnson	Holyoke	W UD 10

Date	Opponent	Location	Result
1958-04-08	George Stephany	Bristol, CT	W PTS 10
1958-04-14	Cleo Ortiz	Providence	W UD 10
1958-04-29	Jimmy Kelly	Boston	W PTS 10
1958-05-20	Bobby Singleton	Boston	W UD 10
1958-06-23	Pat McCoy	New Bedford, MA,	W UD 10
1958-07-01	Bobby Soares	Athol, MA	W UD 10
1958-07-17	Bobby Bell	Norwood, MA	W PTS 10
1958-08-04	Louis Carmona	Presque Isle, ME	W PTS 10
1958-08-09	Jesse Rodrigues	Painesville, OH	W UD 10
1958-08-26	Al Duarte	North Adams, MA	W UD 10
1958-09-20	Hogan 'Kid' Bassey	Boston	L TKO 9
1959-01-26	Victor Sonny	LeonCaracas, Venezuela	L UD 10
1965-03-12	Harold McKeever	Miami	W PTS 8
1965-04-26	Jackie Lennon	Philadelphia	W UD 6
1965-05-21	Johnny Gilmore	Norwalk, CT	W PTS 6
1965-07-26	Benny (Red) Randall	Quebec City, Canada	W UD 10
1965-09-28	Johnny Gilmore	Philadelphia	W PTS 6
1965-10-01	Willie Little	Johnstown, PA	W KO 3
1965-10-04	Tommy Haden	Providence	W TKO 3
1965-10-14	Sergio Musquiz	Phoenix	W KO 5
1965-10-25	Ray Coleman	Tucson	W KO 5
1966-03-16	Calvin Woodland	Richmond, VA	L PTS 6

Record: 230 (KOs 65)-11-1 Total: 242

APPENDIX C

Kirino Garcia's First 34 fights

© boxrec.com

1997-07-04 Terrence Alli 52-13-2	Ciudad Juarez, Chihuahua	W UD 12
1997-04-25 Armando Campas 2-15-4	Ciudad Juarez	W TKO 4
	~ Mexican light middleweight title ~	
1997-02-21 Martin Quiroz19-37-4	Ciudad Juarez	W TKO 8
	~ Mexican light middleweight title ~	
1996-11-30 Jorge Vaca 57-15-1	Ciudad Juarez	W KO 10
	~ Mexican light middleweight title ~	
1996-09-13 Eduardo Gutierrez 20-3-2	Ciudad Juarez	W TKO 12
1996-07-05 Erwin Villaver 12-6-1	Ciudad Juarez	W TKO 3
	WBB Light Middleweight Title	
1996-04-26 20-8-1 Art Serwano	Ciudad Juarez	W KO 2
1996-02-23 27-9-0 Luis Vazquez	Ciudad Juarez	W PTS 12
	Mexican middleweight title	

Date	Record	Location	Result
1995-12-22 Jorge Vaca	55-14-1	Ciudad Juarez	W KO 3
1995-11-17 Rene Herrera	22-4-0	Ciudad Juarez	W TKO 8
1995-10-06 Eduardo Gutierrez	19-3-1	Ciudad Juarez	D PTS 12

Mexican middleweight title ~

Date	Record	Location	Result
1995-08-18 Salomon Olvera	0-1-0	Ciudad Juarez	W KO 1
1995-06-30 Pedro De La Cruz	5-7-1	Ciudad Juarez	W TKO 1
1995-04-01 Antonio Mora	4-10-0	Ciudad Juarez	W TKO 6
1994-11-05 Mario Maciel	11-5-0	Arena Coliseo, Mexico City	W TKO 3
1994-09-10 Norberto Bueno	18-12-0	Nezahualcoyotl, México	W TKO 6
1994-01-29 Chad Parker	28-0-1	Biloxi, Mississippi	L PTS 10
1993-09-23 Dominick Carter	16-2-0	Biloxi	L PTS 10
1993-08-26 Brian Shaw	4-0-0	Biloxi	L PTS 6
1993-04-24 Chris Johnson	1-0-0	Las Vegas	L PTS 4
1993-03-20 Mario Munoz	8-0-0	Denver	L KO 1
1992-09-03 Danny Perez	9-2-0	Albuquerque	L TKO 1
1992-04-11 Lonnie Beasley	11-1-0	Las Vegas	L PTS 6

1992-04-02 Billy Lewis	14-0-0	Reno	L PTS 6
1992-02-15 Anthony Brown	0-0-0	Thornton, Co	L PTS 4
1991-11-22 Mario Munoz	1-0-0	Denver	L PTS 6
1991-11-06 Augustine Renteria	0-0-0	Phoenix	L PTS 4
1991-09-27 Mario Munoz	0-0-0	Denver	L PTS 6
1991-04-09 Tim Littles	11-0-0	Auburn Hills, Mi	L KO 3
1991-04-05 Paul Vaden	0-0-0	Albuquerque	L PTS 4
1990-10-26 Raul Gonzalez	11-1-1	Juarez, Mexico	L KO 2
1990-09-28 Arturo Garcia	0-1-0	Tucson	L PTS 4
1990-06-01 Raul Gonzalez	9-1-1	Juarez	L TKO 4
1990-04-27 Bobby Gunn	2-0-0	Tucson	L TKO

APPENDIX D

Fighters with Most Career Losses

Losses	Boxer
276	Reggie Strickland
256	Peter Buckley (Still active)
164	Donnie Penelton
162	Simmie Black
157	Arnold "Kid" Sheppard
152	"Tiger" Bert Ison
141	Brian Coleman
132	Ernie Smith (Still active)
129	Seamus Casey
122	Jerry Strickland
120	Frankie Hines
117	Lee Cargle
116	Karl Taylor (Still active)
115	Joe Grim
108	Lew Perez
107	Benji Singleton
106	Dean Bramhald
105	Tony Booth (Still active)
102	Peter Dunn (Still active)
102	Paul Bonson (Still active)
102	Danny Wofford

101	Walter Cowans
101	Jozef Kubovsky (Still active)
98	Winston Burnett
95	Kenneth Bentley
94	George Marsden
93	Jose Pagan Rivera
91	Keith Jones
91	"Wild" Bill McDowell
87	Des Gargano
86	Brian Yates
86	Graham McGrath
85	Arv Mittoo
85	Giuseppe Agate
85	Arrow Abu
85	Len Wickwar
85	Jerry Powers
84	Miguel Matthews
84	Johnny Cockfield
84	Jerry Fiorello
83	Jim Kaczmarek
82	Billy Marsh
82	Young Farrell
81	Manuel Baptista
80	Dick Loadman
80	Angel Robinson Garcia
80	Paul Murray

Fighters with Most Knockout Losses

KO losses	Name	Active
95	Simmie Black	1971-1996
78	Jerry Strickland	1974-2000
78	Frankie Hines	1980-2002
64	James Holly	1983-2000
50	Stefan Stanko	1996-2008 (still active)
43	Marvin Ladson	1977-2000
43	Roy Bedwell	1986-2003
42	Robert Woods	1986-1995
42	Marris Virgil	1985-2004
41	Lorenzo Boyd	1983-2003
39	Anton Glofak	1996-2005
39	James Mullins	1987-2003
38	Jose Pagan Rivera	1970-1985
38	Tony Booth	1990-2008 (still active)
37	Robert Zsemberi	1992-2008
37	Caseny Truesdale	1990-2004
37	Len Wickwar	1928-1947
37	Stan Johnson	1981-2002
36	Wayne Grant	1980-1992
35	Patsy Zoccano	1946-unknown
35	George Harris	1991-1999
35	Billy Marsh	1961-1973
35	Nelson Hernandez	1992-2004

APPENDIX E

A sampling of notable upsets © boxrec.com

Winner on left

Randy Turpin	PTS 15	Sugar Ray Robinson (1951)
Dan Bucceroni	L UD	Roland LaStarza (1951)
Ernie Cab	PTS 6	Mike De John (1954)
Johnny Cousins	TKO 5	Mike De John (1954)
Charles Powell	TKO 8	Nino Valdez (1959)
Paul Pender	SD 15	Sugar Ray Robinson: twice (1960)
Eloy Sanchez	KO8	Jose Becerra (1960)
Terry Downes	KO10	Paul Pender (1961)
Pete Rademacher	L UD	Bobo Olson (1962)
Rubin Carter	KO1	Emile Griffith (1963)
Cassius Clay	KO7	Sonny Liston (1964)
Don Fullmer	UD 10	Emille Griffith (1965)
Manuel Gonzalez	SD 10	Emille Griffith (1965)
Fighting Harada	UD 15	Eder Jofre (1965)
Fighting Harada	SD 15	Eder Jofre (1966)
Ki Soo Kim	W 15	Nino Benvenuti (1966)
Del Kid Rosario	W PTS	Yoshiaki Numata (1966)
L.C. Morgan	TKO 4	Jose Napoles (1967)
Oscar Bonavena	W12	Karl Mildenberger (1967)
Jose Luis Lopez	W PTS	Ricardo Arredondo (1968)

Lionel Rose	W15	Fighting Harada (1968)
Alton Colter	SD 10	Fighting Harrada (1969)
Leotis Martin	KO9	Sonny Liston (1969)
Isao Ichihara	W PTS	Flash Elorde (1970
Billy Backus	KO4	Jose Napoles (1970)
Terry Rondeau	PTS 10	Bobby Richard (1970)
Alfredo Marcano	KO10	Hiroshi Kobayashi (1971)
Ron Stander	PTS 10	Thad Spencer (1971)
Abu Arrow	TKO 6	Pedro Pinto (1972)
Roger Philipps	PTS 8	Al Romano (1972)
Esteban DeJesus	W10	Roberto Duran (1972)
Lino Cordero	PTS 10	Bernardo Caraballo (1973)
Terry Rondeau	KO 3	Leo DiFiore (1973)
Ken Norton	W12	Muhummad Ali (1973)
Abu Arrow	D 8	Jose Bisbal (1973)
Muhummad Ali	KO8	George Foreman (1974)
Rudy Barro	PTS 10	Jimmy Heair (1974)
Henry Clark	KO 1	Jeff Merritt (1974)
Memphis Al Jones	KO 3	Boone Kirkman (1974)
John H. Stracey	KO6	Jose Napoles (1975)
Stan Ward	TKO 3	Jeff Merritt (1976)
Jimmy Young	UD 12	Ron Lyle (1976)
Wilfred Benitez	W15	Antonio Cervantes (1976)
Jimmy Young	UD 12	George Foreman (1977)
Freddie Harris	PTS 10	Jimmy Heair (1977)
Arturo Leon	PTS 10	Jimmy Heair (1977)

Jorge Lujan	KO 10	Alfonso Zamora (1977)
Leon Spinks	W 15	Muhummad Ali (1978)
Chan-Hee Park	UD 15	Miguel Cantos (1979)
Vito Antuofermo	D 15	Marvin Hagler (1979)
Lynn Ball	KO 2	Ron Lyle (1979)
Joergen Hansen	TKO 3	Dave Boy Green (1979)
Ramon Ranquello	TKO 7	Mike Rossman (1979)
Yasutsune Uehara	KO 6	Sammy Serrano (1980)
Roger Stafford	UD 10	Pipino Cuevas (1981)
Everett Martin	SD 10	Tim Witherspoon (1982)
Charles Atlas	PTS 10	Sonny Barch (1982)
Gerrie Coetzee	KO 10	Michael Dokes (1983)
Mustafa Hamsho	UD 12	Wilfred Benitez (1983)
Eric Winbush	TKO 3	Matthew Saad Muhammad (1983)
Oscar Muniz	SD 10	Jeff Chandler (1983)
Gene Hatcher	TKO 11	Johnny Bumphus (1984)
Sammy Floyd	W PTS	Clint Jackson (1984)
Dee Collier	KO 1	Randall Cobb (1985)
Clarence Osby	PTS 8	Fulgencio Obelmejias (1985)
Dave Jaco	TKO 8	Donovan Ruddock (1985)
Adam George	PTS 8	Reggie Johnson (1985)
Michael Spinks	UD 15	Larry Holmes (1985)
Alfredo Layne	TKO 9	Wilfredo Gomez (1986)
Michael Spinks	SD 15	Larry Holmes (1986)
Mark Wills	TKO 9	Greg Page (1986)
Robbie Sims	SD 10	Roberto Duran (1986)

James Smith	TKO 1	Tim Witherspoon (1986)
Sugar Ray Leonard	SD 12	Marvin Hagler (1987)
Michael Simuwelu	KO 7	Proud Kilimanjaro (1987)
Angel Sindo	TKO 5	Dennis Milton (1987)
Souleymane Sadik	KO 1	Drake Thadzi (1987)
Tim Anderson	W SD	Jimmy Young (1988)
Iran Barkley	TKO 3	Thomas Hearns (1988)
Rene Jacquot	UD 12	Donald Curry (1989)
Dennis Milton	PTS 6	Gerald McClellan (1989)
Ralph Ward	UD 8	Gerald McClellan (1989)
Brinatty Maquilon	TKO 8	Buster Drayton (1989)
Mark Wills	TKO 6	Greg Page (1990)
Pedro Ruben Decima	TKO 4	Paul Banke (1990)
Booby Czyz	KO 7	Andrew Maynard
James Toney	KO 12	Michael Nunn (1991)
Pat Lawlor	TKO 6	Roberto Duran (1991)
Jerry Jones	PTS 10	Carl Williams (1992)
Lionel Butler	KO 1	Tony Tubbs (1992)
Iran Barkley	SD 10	Thomas Hearns (1992)
Azumah Nelson	TKO 8	Jeff Fenech (1992)
Jerry Jones	PTS 10	Carl Williams (1992)
Lawrence Carter	TKO 7	Pinklon Thomas (1993)
Garing Lane	TKO 10	Alex Garcia (1993)
Simon Brown	KO 4	Terry Norris (1993)
Mike Dixon	TKO 2	Alex Garcia (1993)
John Michael Johnson	TKO 11	Junior Jones (1994)

Stanley Wright	TKO8	Peter McNeeley (1994)
John Carlo	TKO 1	Leon Spinks (1994)
Bobby Crabtree	TKO 1	King Ipitan (1994)
Herbie Hide	KO 7	Michael Bentt (1994)
Luis Santana	W DQ 5	Terry Norris (1994)
Steve Littles	SD 12	Michael Nunn (1994)
Tony LaRosa	KO 3	Lenny LaPaglia (1994)
Nate Tubbs	KO 2	Corrie Sanders (1994)
Corrie Sanders	TKO 1	Carlos De Leon (1994)
Exum Speight	TKO 7	Jade Scott (1994)
Oliver McCall	TKO 2	Lennox Lewis (1994)
Willy Salazar	KO 7	Danny Romero (1995)
Brian Yates	KO 2	Earnie Shavers (1995)
Luis Santana	W DQ 3	Terry Norris (1995)
Marion Wilson	Ws 10	Mike Hunter (1995)
Mitch Rose	TKO 2	Eric Esch (1995)
Lou Monaco	TKO 5	Peter McNeeley (1996)
Brian Scott	TKO 2	Courage Tshabalala (1996)
Maurice Harris	Wu 8	David Izon (1996)
Junior Jones	UD 12	Marco Antonio Barrera (1996)
Evander Holyfield	TKO 11	Mike Tyson (1996)
Darroll Wilson	KO 3	Shannon Briggs (1996)
Manny Melchor	PTS 10	Masamori Tokuyama (1996)
Marcos Gonzalez	UD 10	Everett Martin (1996)
Marcos Gonzalez	KO 2	Peter Smith (1996)
Michael Pinnock	TKO 5	Darren Sweeney (1996)
Junior Jones	DQ 5	Marco Antonio Barrera (1997)

Levi Billups	KO 6	Terrence Lewis (1997)
Jorge Fernando Castro	UD 10	Roberto Duran (1997)
Anthony Green	TKO 7	Carl Williams (1997)
Vince Phillips	TKO 10	Kostya Tszyu (1997)
Carlos Palomino	KO 1	Rene Arredondo (1997)
Micky Ward	KO 7	Alfonso Sanchez (1997)
Darroll Wilson	TKO 4	Courage Tshabalala (1997)
Miguel Matthews	TKO 4	Scott Harrison (1997)
Keith Mullins	TKO 9	Terry Norris (1997)
Marion Wilson	MD 6	Paea Wolfgramm (1998)
Drake Thadzi	MD 12	James Toney (1997)
Exum Speight	TKO 2	Lyle McDowell (1997)
Ivan Robinson	SD 10	Arturo Gatti (1998)
Tony LaRosa	UD 8	Dwight Muhammad Qawi (1998)
Ross Purrity	TKO 11	Wladimir Klitschko (1998)
Joe Bugner	TKO 1	James Smith (1998)
Tony LaRosa	UD 10	Iran Barkley (1998)
Cesar Bazan	SD 12	Stevie Johnson (1998)
Terry Verners	TKO 3	Alonzo Highsmith (1998)
Dickie Ryan	TKO 10	Brian Nielsen (1999)
Willy Wise	UD 10	Julio César Chávez (1999)
Tony LaRosa	SD 8	Trevor Berbick (1999)
Julio Alvarez	KO 10	Israel Cardona (2000)
José Luis Castillo	MD 12	Stevie Johnston (2000)
John Kiser	TKO 1	Andrew Maynard (2000)
Virgil Hill	TKO 1	Fabrice Tiozzo (2000)

Chris Byrd	TKO 10	Vitali Klitchko (2000)
Uriah Grant	TKO 2	Thomas Hearns (2000)
Willie Chapman	TKO 4	DaVarryl Williamson (2000)
Humberto Herrera	D	Freddie Pendleton (2001)
Billy Schwer	UD 10	Newton Villarreal (2001)
Sam Hill	TKO 9	David Reid (2001)
Wes Taylor	TKO 1	Michael Bennett (2001)
Hasim Rahman	KO 2	Lennox Lewis (2001)
Jeff Ford	KO 1	Tye Fields (2001)
Terrance Lewis	KO 9	Ed Mahone. (2001)
Carlos Bojorquez	TKO 4	Pernell Whitaker (2001)
Vernon Forrest	UD 12	Shane Mosley (2002)
Corey Sanders	TKO 8	Oleg Maskaev (2002)
Juan Carlos Rubio	UD 10	Francisco Bojado (2002)
Chris Walsh	W TD 7	Hector Camacho (2003)
Corrie Sanders	TKO 2	Wladimir Klitschko (2003)
Ricardo Mayorga	TKO 3	Vernon Forrest (2003)
Willie Chapman	SD 4	Malcolm Tann (2003)
Mindaugas Kulikauskas	TKO 3	Herbie Hide (2004)
Danny Williams	KO 4	Mike Tyson (2004)
Glen Johnson	KO 9	Roy Jones Jr. (2004)
DaVarryl Williamson	UD 10	Oliver McCall (2004)
Antonio Tarver	TKO 2	Roy Jones Jr. (2005)
Ed Mahone	TKO 10	China Smith (2005)
Zahir Raheem	UD 12	Erik Morales (2005)

Armando Cordoba	TKO 7	Daniel Maldonado (2005)
Kevin McBride	TKO 6	Mike Tyson (2005)
Virgil Hill	W UD	Valery Brudov (2006)
Jose Luis Herrera	TKO 4	Jorge Fernando Castro (2006)
Grady Brewer	WD 10	Steve Forbes (2006)
Broco McKart	W SD	Enrique Omelas (2007)
Johnathon Banks	KO 4	Eliseo Castillo (2007)
Nonito Donaire	KO 5	Vic Darchinyan (2007)
Andres Ledesma	KO 5	Gray Stark Jr. (2007)
Alex Bunema	KO 5	Roman Karmazin (2008)
Raul Marquez	D 10	Bronco McKart (2008)
Paul Bonson	D 4	Neil Simpson (2008)
Osborne Machimana	KO 1	Corrie Sanders (2008)
Carlos Quintana	UD 12	Paul Williams (2008)
Brian Vera	TKO7	Andy Lee (2008)
Cornelius Bundrage	UD 10	Kassim Ouma (2008)
Verno Phillips	SD 12	Cory Spinks (2008)
Rendall Munroe	MD 12	Kiko Marinez (2008)
Reynaldo Lopez	TKO 3	Mile Oliver (2008)
Choi Tseveenpurev	KO 5	Derry Matthews (2008)
Wes Taylor	KO 3	Mike Dietrich (2008)
Gabriel Rosado	UD 8	James Moore (2008)
Shawn Hammack	TKO 8	Zach Walters (2008)
Allfred "Ice" Cole	SD 6	Joey Abell (2008)
Malcome Klassen	TKO 2	Manuel Medina (2008)
Bernard Hopkins	UD 12	Kelly Pavlik

BIBLIOGRAPHY

Books

Doyle, Paul E. Hot Shots and Heavy Hits Tales of an Undercover Drug AgentNortheastern University Press, University Press of New England 2005 240 pp.

Hauser, Thomas. The Black Lights: Inside the World of Professional Boxing. New York: McGraw-Hill. 1986.

Hauser, Thomas and Stephen Brunt, The Italian Stallions. Sport Classic Books. Toronto, Ontario, Canada. 2003.

Mailer, Norman. The Fight. Vintage International, New York City. 1997. 240 pages.

Marinick, Richard. Boyos. Justin, Charles & Co. (October 25, 2004). 336 pages.

Sares, Theodore, Boxing is my Sanctuary. Lincoln, Nebraska. IUniverse 2007. 379 pages.

Shea, John "Red," Rat Bastards: The Life and Times of South Boston's Most Honorable Irish Mobster. Publisher: New York, London, Toronto, Sydney. Harper Collins. Date: March 2006. 282pp.

Weeks, Kevin and Phyllis Karas. Brutal. Publisher: New York, London, Toronto, Sydney. Harper Collins. Date: March 2006. 283 pages.

Book Reviews

Charles C. Euchner. Review of - "All Souls: A Family Story from Southie." Michael Patrick MacDonald. Center for Urban and Regional Policy at Northeastern University, Boston. 27 April, 2000; available from http://www.curp.neu.edu:80/sitearchive/staffpicks. asp?id=1125 (accessed April 9, 2008).

Magazine Articles

AARP The Magazine. 1968 "THE YEAR THAT ROCKED OUR WORLD," May/June 2008.

Acevedo, Carlos. Boxing Digest, "NO EXIT: THE SHORT LIFE AND STRANGE CAREER OF EDDIE MACHEN." May/June 2008.

Boeri, David. Bosto, "The Martyrdom of John Connolly," September 2008.

Ecksel, Robert. Boxing Digest, "Ten Count for Norman Mailer," February 2008.

Nichols, Joseph. IBRO Journal. "Cerdan Knocks Out Roach." Issue 97, March 12, 2008.

Prospero, Angelo. Boxing World. "Around the Boxing Scene-Holman Williams." Feb-2008.

Newspaper Articles

Kanigher, Steve. "Can boxing be made safer?" Las Vegas Sun. 23 October, 2005.

Price, Terry. "HE'S A GOOD SON...EVERYBODY SHOULD BE SO LUCKY" TOUGH GUY, DEVOTED CARETAKER." The Hartford Courant. Mothers Day, 1966.

Puleo, Tom. "The Great Willie Pep Is Laid To Rest." The Hartford Courant. 28 November, 2006.

Online and electronic sources

Amato, Jim. "Doug DeWitt: True Grit." EastSideBoxing.com. 3 September, 2006; available from http://www.eastsideboxing.com:80/news.php?p=8133&more=1 (accessed January 22, 2008).

Amato, Jim. "EDDIE MACHEN: He Met The Best (More..." StraightJab.com. 5 January, 2006; available from http://www.straightjab.com/modules.php?name=News&file=article&sid=1257 (accessed September 10, 2007).

Amato, Jim. "When Dick Tiger Tamed The 60's." WWW.TRUFAN-BOXING.COM. Undated; available from http://www.trufanbox-ing.com/fighters_of_the_twentieth_centur.htm (accessed May 1, 2008).

Associated Press "Boxer injured in 2000 fight sues Gatti. Gamache sustained brain damage, says opponent weighed too much in ring,". MSNBC.COM. 2 March, 2006. http://www.msnbc.msn.com/id/11643791/ (accessed November 12, 2007).

Bad Lefty Hook:: A Boxing Blog. Posted on Mon Sep 24, 2007 at 09:13:56 AM EDT by SC. 24 September, 2007; available from http://www.badlefthook.com/story/2007/9/24/91356/4639 (accessed November 1, 2007).

Bailey, Michael J. "Willie Pep, 84; featherweight reached boxing world's pinnacle," boston.com news, 25 November, 2006; available from http://www.boston.com:80/news/globe/obituaries/articles/2006/11/25/willie_pep_84_featherweight_reached_boxing_worlds_pinnacle/ (accessed January 11, 2007).

Baynes, Ciaran. "Cat tips Enzo to beat Haye." 27 February, 2008; available from http://83.245.38.233/en/Sport/News/Other-sports/2008/02/25/Boxing-Cat-tips-Enzo-to-beat-Haye/ (accessed May 10, 2008).

Baxter, Kevin. "National divide for Mayorga," From the Los Angeles Times, latimes.com, 20 November, 2007; available from http://www.latimes.com/wireless/avantgo/la-sp-mayorga20nov20,0,5858254.story (accessed November 25, 2007).

BBC SPORT, "Golota cops a load of trouble," 6 February, 2002; available from http://news.bbc.co.uk/sport1/hi/funny_old_game/1805338.stm (accessed November 25, 2007).

Berkwitt, Brad. "Interview w/ Former Contender Mustafa Hamsho." Boxing Insider. Bodog.com. 5 January, 2003; available from http://www.boxinginsider.net/news/stories/53779391.php (accessed March 8, 2008).

Bernath, Clive. "Buckley approaches history making 200 fight mark." SecondsOut.com. Undated; available from http://www.secondsout.com:80/uk/colbernath.cfm?ccs=216&cs=12149 (accessed March 16, 2008).

"Better than ever?" Cnnsi.com. 25 November, 2000; available from http://sportsillustrated.cnn.com/more/news/2000/11/25/Reid_boxing_ap/ (accessed May 1, 2008).

The Boston Globe. "FBI posts pictures of possible Whitey Bulger sighting in Italy." Boston.com. 14 September, 2007; available from http://www.boston.com/news/globe/city_region/breaking_news/2007/09/fbi_posts_pictu.html (accessed May 1, 2008).

Boxing Encyclopedia, "Muhammad Alfaridzi," 24, September, 2007; available from http://www.boxrec.com/media/index.php?title=Human:38416 (accessed January 18, 2007).

Boxing Encyclopedia, "Barnstormer." March 30, 2007, http://www.boxrec.com/media/index.php/Barnstormer (accessed February 5, 2008).

Boxing Insider, "A look at Ricardo Mayorga." bodog.com, 7 November, 2007; available from http://www.boxinginsider.com:80/columns/stories/186209300.php (accessed November 26, 2007).

BOXING NEWS - YOUR BOXING BIBLE, "Billy Schwer." boxingnewsonline.net, 21 March, 2008'; available from http://www.boxingnewsonline.net/billyschwer.asp (accessed March 25, 2008).

Campbell, Bob. "One-time boxer fights streets of Odessa, 13 years removed from the ring, 'Rockin' Robin' enjoys his life as Odessan and a police officer." The Cyber Boxing Zone Message Board. 8 august, 2005; available from http://www.cyberboxingzone.com/cbzforum/showthread.php?t=1490 (accessed November 12, 2007).

Carey, Ben. "Interview: Carl "The Cat" Thompson." EastSideBoxing.com. 23 February, 2004; available from http://www.eastsideboxing.com:80/news.php?p=693&more=1 (accessed April 10, 2008).

Carey, Ben. "Carl Thompson banned for 6 months!" EastSideBoxing.com. 28 April, 2004; available from http://www.eastsideboxing.com/news.php?p=1046&more=1 (accessed April 2, 2008).

Carp, Steve. "Tomato cans ripe for picking." ReviewJournal.com Las Vegas Review-Journal. 10 February, 2008: available from http://www.lvrj.com/sports/15490601.html (accessed March 14, 2008).

Casey, Mike. "Ezzard Charles Feature." EastSideBoxing. 30 December, 2005; available from http://www.eastsideboxing.com/news.php?p=5679&more=1 (accessed December 1, 2007).

Casey, Mike. "Helter Skelter: The brutal rock 'n' roll ride of Bobby Chacon." EastSideBoxing.com. 29 January, 2006; available from http://www.eastsideboxing.com/news.php?p=5906&more=1 (Accessed January 10, 2007).

"Cavalcade of Sports (1944) Friday Night Fights Are On The Air." 4 July 2006 Author: krorie from Van Buren, Arkansas the Internet Movie Database, http://www.imdb.com/title/tt0268788/ (Accessed January 10, 2008).

Chandler, John. "Tommy Morrison." KOCORNER.COM. 14 June, 2007; available from http://www.kocorner.com/boxing/category/ Tommy-Morrison/ (Accessed March 5, 2008).

Chuck, "Fernando Vargas vs. Ricardo Mayorga Preview." Sportaphile. 22 November, 2007; available from http://www.sportaphile. com/2007/11/22/fernando-vargas-vs-ricardo-mayorga-preview/ (accessed December 27, 2007).

Colgan, Don. "Emile Griffith? The Champ?" eSports. 14 April, 2005; available from http://www.e-sports.com:80/articles/469/1/Emile-Griffith-The-Champ/Page1.html (accessed Novemebr12, 2007).

COMBAT-HOOLIGANS.COM. "Final Press Conference Quotes: Vargas, Mayorga Let It Rip." 19 November, 2007; available from http:// combat-hooligans.com/2007/11/20/final-press-conference-quotes-vargas-mayorga-let-it-rip/ (accessed February 2, 2008).

Cooper, Bryn. "Schwer is sent home after scan." The Independent. 17 July, 2001; available from http://www.independent.co.uk/sport/ general/schwer-is-sent-home-after-scan-678019.html (accessed March 25, 2008).

Cyber Boxing Zone. Ezzard Charles. Record courtesy of Tracey Callis, International Boxing Research Organization. 28 August, 2006; available from http://www.google.com/search?hl=en&rls=com.microsoft:en-us:IE-SearchBox&rlz=117WZPA&sa=X&oi=spell&resnum=0&ct=result&cd=1&q=EZZARD+CHARLES+BOXING+RECORD&spell=1 (accessed August 2, 2007).

Cyber Boxing Zone Message Board, "Re: Most Times Knocked Out (List)." 25 May, 2006; available from http://cyberboxingzone.com:80/ cbzforum/showthread.php?t=1456 (accessed March 12, 2008).

Cyber Boxing Zone Message Board, "R.I.P. Willie Pep," 24 November, 2006: available from http://cyberboxingzone.com/cbzforum/ showthread.php?t=3985 (accessed January 16, 2007).

Cyber Boxing Zone Message Board, "The 1950's." 8 October, 2007; available from http://www.cyberboxingzone.com/cbzforum/ showthread.php?t=6452 (accessed November 1, 2007).

Cyber Boxing Zone –Willie Pep. 25 August, 2006; available from http://www.cyberboxingzone.com/boxing/wilpep.htm   (accessed January 2, 2008).

DiMichele, Ron. "Iceman' John Scully: 'No Picnic." EastSideBoxIng. com. 3 February, 2004; available from http://www.eastsideboxing. com/news.php?p=556&more=1 (accessed November 1, 2007).

Dickinson, Matt. "Bringing the nation together with tales of the unexpected." Timesonline. 11 March, 2008; available from http://www.timesonline.co.uk/tol/sport/columnists/matt_dickinson/article3525596.ece (accessed March 15, 2008).

Dixon, Mel. "The Spoiler who came to fight." EastSideBoxing.com. 12 May, 2008; available from http://www.eastsideboxing.com:80/news.php?p=15634&more=1 (accessed May 13, 2008).

Duffy, Joe. "WILLIE "PEPPED UP" OUR FRIDAY NIGHTS" Reminisce. 22 January, 1997; Available from http://www.skypoint.com/members/schutz19/willie.htm (accessed March 1, 2008).

Dunn, Jack. "Chillin'With "The Ice Man," Max Boxing.15 February, 2001; available from http://www.maxboxing.com/ (accessed January 15, 2008).

Ecksel, Robert. "Boxing, Boston and Tony DeMarco." TheSweetScience.com. Undated; available from http://www.thesweetscience.com/boxing-article/2286/boxing-boston-tony-demarco/?article_id=2286#comments (accessed January 1, 2008).

Fattah, Geoffrey. "Justices hear boxing-death case." Desert News (Salt Lake City). LookSmart Ltd, 4 May, 2007: available from http://findarticles.com/p/articles/mi_qn4188/is_20070504/ai_n19066495 (accessed September 10, 2007).

Gerald, Marc. ""The Opponent – losers in boxing." Men's Fitness. November 1998; available from http://findarticles.com/p/articles/mi_m1608/is_n11_v14?pnum=6&opg=21240305 (accessed May 1, 2008).

Graham, Tim. "David Reid's American Nightmare." Special to ESPN. com. 8 March, 2004; available from http://sports.espn.go.com/sports/boxing/columns/story?columnist=graham_tim&id=1750780 (accessed February 26, 2008).

Gray, Geoffrey. "BOXING; Boxers Who Are Losers; Promoters Who Love Them."The New York Times. 10 May, 2004; available from http://query.nytimes.com/gst/fullpage.html?res=9801E0DB123CF93 3A25756C0A9629C8B63&sec=&spon=&pagewanted=all (accessed March 15, 2008).

Gray, Geoffrey. "While Panel Digs Deeper, Journeymen Put Up Fight." The New York Times. 14 May, 2006; available from http://www.ny-times.com/2006/05/14/sports/othersports/14boxing.html (accessed May 1, 2008).

Greenspan, Russ. "Reggie Strickland: Boxing's All-Time Leading Also-Ran." www.ringsidereport.com, 12 July, 2007; available from http://www.ringsidereport.com:80/rsr/news.php?readmore=1583 (accessed February 6, 2008).

Greg, John. –Reid Scores Lucky Win over Garcia–. www.boxing-times.com The Boxing Times. 26 November, 2000; available from http://www.sweetscience.com/analyses/2000/001126reid_garcia.html (accessed February 27, 2008).

Grollmus, Denise. "The Tomato-Can Man-He produced America's worst fighters, and he's proud of it." 8 August, 2007; available from http://www.clevescene.com/2007-08-08/news/the-tomato-can-man/full (accessed April 20, 2008).

Groves, Lee. "Closet Classic - Lee Roy Murphy vs. Chisanda Mutti." MAXBOXING.COM. 25 March, 2008; available from http://hwww.maxboxing.com:80/Groves/Groves032508.asp (accessed April 20, 2008).

Groves, Lee. "Closet Classic: Pernell Whitaker vs. Diosbelys Hurtado." Max Boxing Available from http://cyberboxingzone.com/cbzforum/showthread.php?t=3974 (accessed February 6, 2008).

Groves, Lee. "Boxing's Might Have Been Men - Part III." maxBOX-ING.com. 6 February, 2007; available from http://www.maxboxing.com/Groves/Groves0206a07.asp (accessed March 30, 2008).

Hampton, Rick. "Lattes, lofts invade mean streets of Southie." USA-TODAY. 27 November, 2006; available from http://www.usatoday.com/news/nation/2006-11-26-south-boston_x.htm (Accessed April 2, 2008).

HBO Boxing: Fighters. "RICARDO MAYORGA." 20 February, 2007; available from http://www.hbo.com/boxing/fighters/mayorga_ricardo/bio.html (accessed March 26, 2008).

Highfill, Bob. "A Champion Without A Belt." Recordnet.com. 1 September, 2005; available from http://www.recordnet.com/apps/pbcs. dll/article?AID=/20050901/SPECIALREPORTS03/509010315/-1/A_ SPECIAL26 (accessed January 31, 2008).

Stan Hoffman, Stan. "Vargas vs. Mayorga- Fell the Tension (video)." Fightbeat.com. Undated; available from http://fightbeat.com/news_ details.php?NW=20801(accessed March 1, 2008).

Hulse, Richard. "The Tiger" of the Fens: RSR Looks Back at the Career of Dave 'Boy' Green." Ringside Report.com 9 August, 2007; available from http://www.cyberboxingzone.com/cbzforum/showthread. php?t=6096 (accessed September 10, 2007).

Hurley, Matthew. "Mayorga, Vargas Fight On Fumes And Pride." EastSideBoxing. 21 November, 2007; available from http://www.east-sideboxing.com/news.php?p=13377&more=1 (accessed March 26, 2008).

Hurley, Matthew. "Mayorga Weighs His Options And Will Move Down." EastSideBoxing. 19 April, 2008; available from http://www. eastsideboxing.com/boxing/Mayorga-Vargas.php (accessed March 26, 2008).

Hurley, Matthew. "Yo Sam Choi: Diary of Stricken Boxer Reveals Troubled Young Man," Eastsideboxing.com. 29 December, 2007; available from HTtp://www.eastsideboxing.com/news.php?p=13839&more=1 (accessed March 1, 2008).

Kanigher, Steve. A brutal, vicious sport, 'Sweet science' of the boxing ring results in many brain injuries. Las Vegas Sun. 23 October, 2005; available from http://www.lasvegassun.com/sunbin/stories/ lv-other/2005/oct/23/519549567.html (accessed November 10, 2007).

Katz, Michael. The Tragedy of a Middleweight Loser." The New York Times. 7 September, 1981; available from Http://query.nytimes.com/ gst/fullpage.html?sec=health&res=9F04EFDE103BF934A3575AC0 A967948260 (accessed March 8, 2008).

Lewis, Mike. "Boxing: Schwer still feels cheated over world title." Telegraph.co.uk. 11 July, 2000; available from http://www.telegraph. co.uk/sport/main.jhtml?xml=/sport/2000/10/08/sobox08.xml (accessed March 25, 2008).

"London's dream goes up in flames." Mail Online. 22 February, 2008: available from http://www.dailymail.co.uk/sport/article-517642/Londons-dream-goes-flames.html (accessed May 1, 2008).

MacDonald, Michael Patrick. "Revisiting Southie's culture of death." Boston.com News. 11 October, 2006; available from http://www.boston.com/news/globe/editorial_opinion/oped/articles/2006/10/11/revisiting_southies_culture_of_death/?page=1 (accessed May 4, 2008).

Malinowski, Scoop. "Andrew Golota's New York City Adventure." The Biofile. 5 October, 2007; available from http://www.thebiofile.com:80/news/articles/1191605989.php (accessed November 10, 2007).

Mark Wahlberg Talking About Micky Ward On Conan. Ken Savage Making IT in Massachusetts Undated; available from http://www.kensavage.com:80/index.php/archives/mark-wahlberg-and-micky-ward/ (accessed April 10, 2008).

Merron, Jeff. "Reel Life:'Raging Bull: Special to Page 2." ESPN.com Page 2, undated; available from http://espn.go.com/page2/s/closer/020703.html (accessed November 1, 2006).

Mladinich, Robert "The Danny Long and the short of it." The Sweet Science. 31, March, 2006; available from http://www.thesweetscience.com:80/boxing-article/3588/danny-long-short/ (accessed April 3, 2008).

Mladinich, Robert. "Yaqui" Lopez Finally Gets His Due." The Sweet Science. Undated; available from http://www.thesweetscience.com/boxing-article/5425/yaqui-lopez-finally-gets-his-due/ (accessed April 25, 2008).

National Library of Australia. "A Knock-Out! The Arnold Thomas Boxing Collection" Number 85. February 2007; available from http://www.nla.gov.au/pub/gateways/issues/85/story04.html (accessed March 3, 2008).

"Origin of the 'win or die' name." Dils. 14 November, 2007); available from http://dilsmusings.blogspot.com/2007/11/origin-of-win-or-die-name.html (accessed January 5, 2008).

Otty, Harry. "Holman Williams Belongs in the Hall of Fame." WAIL! THE CBZ JOURNAL. July 2006; available from http://www.cyberboxingzone.com/boxing/0001-otty.html (accessed December 12, 2007).

Payne, David."Old-man Carl Thompson Stops Unbeaten Haye In 5." BOXINGWRITER.CO.UK. 3 May, 2007; available from http://boxingwriter.co.uk:80/2007/05/03/archive-old-man-thompson-stops-unbeaten-haye-in-5/ (accessed April 10, 2008).

Pennington, Bill. "BOXING; Tyson and Golota: Protect Yourself at All Times." The New York Times, nytimes.com. 18 October, 2000; available from http://query.nytimes.com/gst/fullpage.html?res=9D07 EFDC173EF93BA25753C1A9669C8B63&sec=&spon=&pagewante d=print (accessed October 15, 2007).

Pollitt, Ken 'KSTAT,' "MASAO OHBA." The 13th Round Forum Index >> Old School Fighters. 21 January, 2007; available from http://www.the13thround.com/phpBB2/viewtopic.php?t=6781&sid=787a467d1 ce2f5b763d2d5f1d9b9a993 (accessed 1 December, 2007).

Pritchard-Nobbs, Tony. "WBF CHAMPION JEFF "FLASH" MALCOLM – EVERGREEN ROAD WARRIOR." www.worldboxingfoundation.com. 20 November, 2007; available from http://www.worldboxingfoundation.com/wbf/?p=465 (accessed February 7, 2008).

Putman, Pat."Kirino Garcia Gutter to Great."The Sweet Science. 2 August, 2005; available from http://www.thesweetscience.com/boxing-article/2456/kirino-garcia-gutter-great/?article_id=2456#comments (accessed February 26, 2008).

Quello, Joe. "Classic bout: Masao Ohba vs. Orlando Amores." SecondsOut.com. Undated; available from http://www.secondsout.com:80/Legends/classic.cfm?ccs=236&cs=8498 (accessed 1 December, 2007).

"Ricardo Mayorga." Wikipedia, the free encyclopedia. 13 May, 2008; available from http://en.wikipedia.org/wiki/Ricardo_Mayorga (accessed May 15, 2008).

"Ricardo Mayorga is a People Person," Posted by The Duke of Kickball on Your Face is a Sports Blog, 20 November, 2007; available from http://yourfaceisasportsblog.blogspot.com/2007/11/ricardo-mayorga-is-people-person.html (accessed November 24, 2007).

Rice, Xan. "When the Music Stops-Part 2, Billy Schwer." The Observer, 9 May, 2004; available from http://observer.guardian.co.uk:80/osm/story/0,,1210207,00.html (accessed March 25, 2006).

Rosenthal, Michael."CURTO'S LIFE STORY PACKS SOME PUNCH." THE FREE LIBRARY BY FARLEX. Undated; available from http://

www.thefreelibrary.com/CURTO'S+LIFE+STORY+PACKS+SOME+ PUNCH-a083942601 (accessed April 2, 2008).

Saraceno, Jon. "Roach now a trainer, but always a fighter." USA TODAY. Undated; available from http://www.usatoday.com:80/sports/columnist/saraceno/2007-05-02-roach_N.htm (accessed April 3, 2008).

Slater, James. "Dennis Andries, The Only Brit To Face 'The Hitman.'" EastSideBoxing.com. 25 February, 2006: available from http://www. eastsideboxing.com/news.php?p=6119&more=1 (accessed May 2, 2007).

Slater, James. "Exclusive Interview with Joe Hipp - "The Morrison Fight? That Was A Great War!" EastSideBoxing.com. 22 April, 2008; available from http://www.eastsideboxing.com/news. php?p=15350&more=1 (accessed April 22, 2008).

Slater, James. "John Murray Keeps Perfect Record With Close Points Win Over Youseff Al Hamadi." EastSideBoxing.com. May 2008; available from http://www.eastsideboxing.com/news. php?p=15608&more=1 (accessed May 14, 2008).

Slater, James. "Somsak Sithchatchawal Vs. Mahyar Monshipour - Could It Be The Greatest Prize Fight Ever Captured on Film?" EsatSideBoxing. 21 March, 2008; available from http://www.eastsideboxing.com/news.php?p=14923&more=1 (accessed March 21, 2008).

Spagat, Elliot. "Roach fights Parkinson's while thriving as a boxing trainer." USA TODAY. Undated; available from http://www.usatoday. com:80/sports/boxing/2008-04-04-344681383_x.htm   (accessed April 7, 2008).

Sweeney, Emily. "The Mob Guide to Boston." boston.com. Undated; available from http://www.boston.com:80/travel/boston/mob/the_ tour/ (accessed August 20, 2008).

"Tank & The Irish Express bring pro boxing back to Worcester." HottBoxingNews.com. Undated; available from http://www.hotboxingnews.com/NEWS2006/news051906.htm (accessed April 8, 2008).

Ten & Out. 6 March, 1950; available from Http://www.time.com/ time/magazine/article/0,9171,858660,00.html?iid=chix-sphere (accessed November 3, 2007).

"The World's Best Quotes in 1-10 Words." Nothing gold can stay. —Robert Frost. Undated; available from http://www.careerlab.com/comments.htm (accessed January 3, 2008).

"10,365 FANS ON THEIR FEET ROOTING FOR FELICIANO AT STAPLES CENTER!" EastSideBoxing.com. 27 November, 2007; available from http://www.eastsideboxing.com/news.php?p=13423&more=1 (accessed November 27, 2007).

UPNE – Hot Shots and Heavy Hits: Paul Doyle, undated; available from http://www.upne.com/1-55553-603-4.html (accessed August 19, 2008).

Walker, Clarence. "FBI Dark Secrets." Rick Porrello's Amerciacn Mafia.com, December 2003; available from http://www.americanmafia.com/Feature_Articles_257.html (accessed April 1, 2008).

Walker, Tom. "Boxing with the Bard." BritishBoxing.net. 24 January, 2006; available from http://www.britishboxing.net/news_1201-Boxing-with-the-Bard.html (accessed March 18, 2008).

WikiAnswers. "What was life like in the trenches during World War 1?" Undated; available from http://wiki.answers.com/Q/What_was_life_like_in_the_trenches_during_World_War_1 (accessed May 1, 2008).

Worsell. Elliot. "Britain's most exciting: No. 1, Carl Thompson." SecondsOut.com. UK Boxing News. Undated; Available From http://romangreenberg.tv/UK/news.cfm?ccs=228&cs=17080 (accessed May 1, 2008).

ACKNOWLEDGMENTS

I wish to thank the EastSide Boxing on-line boxing site for allowing me to use many of its photos. As well, sincere thanks are extended to my editor Emmy Eoff and image consultant Mark Graffam, and to Mitchell DeFer, Pete Leonitis, Mike Casey, Brian Hughes Jack Dunn, Lee Groves and the staff at the Staples Copy Center (North Conway, NH), whose valuable contributions made completion of this project possible.

I also wish to thank Ron Lipton and Ronald Schneider for their guest articles.

ABOUT THE AUTHOR

Theodore R. (Ted) Sares is a private investor who lives in the White Mountains area of New Hampshire with his wife, Holly, and dogs Kater and JackDog.

He holds graduate degrees in economics and business administration, and has lived in many different countries. Upon retiring from the corporate world, he became a boxing historian and advocate for boxing reform.

1578349